A Past of Possibilities

A Past of Possibilities

A HISTORY OF WHAT COULD HAVE BEEN

Quentin Deluermoz and
Pierre Singaravélou

Translation by Stephen W. Sawyer

Yale UNIVERSITY PRESS

New Haven & London

Published with help from the Institut Universitaire de France.

Yale University Press books may be purchased in quantity for educational, business, or promotional use. For information, please e-mail sales.press@yale.edu (U.S. office) or sales@yaleup.co.uk (U.K. office).

Set in Adobe Garamond type by
Printed in the United States of America.
Library of Congress Control Number: 2020952104
ISBN 978-0-300-22754-3 (hardcover : alk. paper)

A catalogue record for this book is available from the British Library.

This paper meets the requirements of ANSI/NISO Z39.48-1992 (Permanence of Paper).

10 9 8 7 6 5 4 3 2 1

Contents

PART THREE: EXPERIMENTS

Preface

THE DARK ENERGY OF HISTORY

Unrealized possibilities and counterfactuals are the dark energy of history. Though it fills the universe, dark energy, as its name suggests, remains invisible to astrophysicists. It is of little surprise, then, that the concept met with a certain skepticism before being taken seriously. Once it was accepted, however, there remained the vast enterprise of its analysis and its potential for explaining some of the most fundamental workings of the universe. As the dark mass in the shadow of actually realized history, past possibilities may well experience the same fate. Touching on some of the most essential elements of historical analysis, counterfactual reasoning may prove equally indispensable for developing a more profound understanding of our past and present. As a thought experiment, it invites us to revisit some of the most important questions of history and social science: causality, historicity, the place of imagination and experimentation, structure and individual agency, as well as civic and political engagement. Above all, it allows us to render history less reified and deterministic, uncovering a more complex an unpredictable past.

So what is at stake in the following pages? In short, our ambition is to engage with what Nietzsche described as the "cardinal question": What if such and such had happened? We seek to explore the shape, potentialities, and ramifications of this common form of reasoning. We are certainly not alone in this endeavor. Counterfactual reasoning and past possibilities have found fertile soil in the decades surrounding this turn of the millennium, a world marked by the end of ideologies, a shift in the relationship between reality and fiction, and a radically heightened sense of uncertainty in a globalized world. It is our conviction that amid this increasing relevance, researchers ignore this question at their own peril.

This volume is the translation of an essay that originally appeared in French. There is no doubt a certain irony in bringing counterfactual history from France, where it has been decidedly less widespread, into English, especially considering that this approach has been the most successful and has solicited the most interest and debates in the British and American contexts. Nonetheless, beyond the obvious fact that works in the English language reach far beyond the Anglophone world, we have at least three motivations for translating our perspective into English. First, though one of the earliest and most common terms for referring to this form of reasoning, uchronia—*uchronie* in French—was invented in France by the philosopher Charles Renouvier in the nineteenth century and was followed by a relatively abundant interest in the issues explored in this book, since the mid-twentieth century historians in France have remained decidedly more skeptical of this approach. The paradox that one of the national traditions that did the most to initiate counterfactualism has since almost entirely turned its back on it was part of our motivation for writing this book in the first place. Perhaps more importantly, it had the positive effect of forcing us to provide a very thorough and extensive argumentation for why and how past possibilities may be useful for historical understanding. It is our conviction that these analyses may provide an original set of perspectives and arguments for debates in other national contexts outside France, especially in the Anglophone world. Second, alongside a certain reticence to counterfactualism, the field of history in France has developed—like all national historical traditions—within a particular institutional and cultural landscape. One key feature of this French context is that history has evolved in an acutely close-knit exchange with other social sciences, in particular sociology, anthropology, psychology, and economics. Though this has obviously been the case in other parts of the world as well, the pervasive tendency toward these interdisciplinary dialogues in France pushed us to develop what we think to be a unique approach to past possibilities that has not received sufficient attention in previous works. Third, by participating in a historiographical debate that had previously largely taken place elsewhere, we also developed greater attention to the development of counterfactualism in other parts of the world, which may or may not be as well-known as historical debates among Anglophone scholars. We therefore elaborate a more global historical perspective. The book provides a self-conscious reflection on the plethora of national "traditions," which are being constantly renewed, not only in North America and Britain but also across the European continent as well as India and Latin America.

Within this surfeit of methodologies, the terms used to describe counterfactual reasoning have taken on different meanings. In France, the notion "uchronia" (*uchronie*) has come to signify the more literary style of this practice, while "alternate history" has come to designate a more credible method.[1] Both, however, are based on the principle of drawing out a given history beyond a specific turning point or bifurcation, when something did or did not happen. As such, they do not necessarily provide insight into our understanding of the past per se. So, in spite of their ludic virtues and even moral character, we have turned away from these different, more "literary" versions of counterfactualism. This preference captures a key difference between our work and the "virtual history" of Niall Ferguson. While he has no doubt fostered the most elaborate version of this style and heightened the visibility of a counterfactual history in the Anglophone world, it is our view that the very popularity of "virtual history" has posed serious challenges for a rigorous and scientific approach to counterfactual history. *A Past of Possibilities* thus looks in a different direction. We propose a path that explores the major social-scientific and political consequences inherent in this line of reasoning in order to grasp the practices and discourses of the actors—including their future hopes and fears—through the archives and invent a new way of collectively writing and sharing history.

At the same time, we have attempted to render the diversity of possible modes of this type of reasoning in different disciplines, including parafactual, counterfactual, virtual, alternative, hypothetical, and potential histories, as well as a variety of forms from the most humorous to the most scientific, from the human sciences to astrophysics. Our ambition has been both to introduce this variety to the reader while also highlighting its relevance for the social sciences. As many examples developed in this book show, when this approach is accompanied with an analysis of sources and a knowledge of specific contexts, it can provide crucial insights into our understanding of a given historical event, process, or phenomenon. We have sought to explore how it can be employed in fields that seek today to break free from some of the "grand narratives," that have emerged within global history or the history of science, at the same time that we have been attentive to more traditional areas of historical investigation, such as military, political, social, or cultural history. We have also sought to provide insight into specific elements of historical methodology by showing how employing counterfactual reasoning and past possibilities shapes the role of the imagination in the writing of history, sheds new light on the tension between determinism and contingency or between modeling and narrative, revisits the balance between fun and precision, and finally reconfigures the indispensable necessity of escaping the constant temptation of teleology.

We have had the good fortune since this book appeared in French to present our approach in seminars and conferences with students, wider publics, and colleagues in France, Geneva, Lausanne, Santiago, Mexico City, Rio de Janeiro, Buenos Aires, Boston, New York, Shanghai, Tokyo, and elsewhere. These exchanges have reinforced our conviction that the counterfactual, in all of its forms, is not only a widespread mode of thinking but also of pervasive interest among scholars and the broader audiences. Through these interactions, we have deepened our understanding of the issues at play and engaged with an even greater variety of historiographies, methods, and disciplinary approaches, notably in those countries or regions where the discipline of history is, for historical reasons, more open to such reflections than in France.

Among our many discoveries, we have learned that readers are drawn to the reflexive dimension of this approach. Asking why the world is as it is and not otherwise sits at the heart of all critical thought. We engage in such exercises on an almost daily basis, whether it be to give meaning to our personal lives ("If I had not missed that bus, I never would have met my husband") as well as the great events of history ("What if COVID-19 had not spread around the world?"). The study of past possibilities and counterfactual analysis may open one's eyes and provide new opportunities for acting in the present, thus opening possible futures in a moment when fatalism and determinism seem to reign supreme. An instrument of emancipation, counterfactual analysis also holds a particularly strong capacity for interaction and transmission, since it enables an original form of exchange between academics and the larger public that breaks with a traditional vertical diffusion of knowledge. We are encouraged by the development of "workshops for a shared history" (*ateliers d'histoire partagée*) in France since the publication of this book. In these sessions, the participants develop their curiosity, often with great dynamism, in a unique space of discussion and interpretation of what took place and what might have come. This technique, which establishes a more horizontal relationship between the historian and his or her public, seeks out interactions with nonacademic knowledge (family history, historical platitudes, collective imagination, and so on). Out of these interactions, a more reflexive definition of history emerges as both open and co-constructed between the participant and the professional historian. Little surprise then that beyond universities, teachers in French secondary education have recently developed a growing interest in the pedagogical potential of this approach and have implemented it in their classrooms. Once the logic and the stakes have been discussed, the study of past possibilities indeed allows us to blur the boundary between the one who knows and the one who supposedly does not. As such, this book argues for a history that is demanding, critical, inventive, and shared with the greatest number.

Introduction

ON THE EDGE OF HISTORY

> The question: "What would have been the consequence if such and such had not happened?" is almost unanimously thrust aside, and yet it is the cardinal question.
>
> —Friedrich Nietzsche[1]

"What would have been the consequence if such and such had not happened?" Who hasn't posed this question? And yet, as common as it may be, today it would seem to have become, once again, a novelty. In recent years, every summer seems to bring with it a budding new crop of uchronias: books, graphic novels, films, "special summer editions" of our favorite newspapers, national magazines, and video games. What if Cleopatra's nose had been smaller? What if Napoleon had been victorious at Waterloo? What if Hitler had won the war? Variations on such questions are converted into eye-catching titles, filling bookstores and newspaper stands: *100 Great Errors of History, The Day That Changed History, The Great Turning Points of History,* and the list goes on. Paradoxically, this vast phenomenon has been largely ignored by researchers who have brushed it aside as mere entertainment.

Truth be told, the invitation to wander into the universe of past possibilities is hardly new. Nonetheless, historians' views on the question would seem to have been settled. French historian of the nineteenth century Guillaume de Bertier de Sauvigny recounted in an essay published in 1980 on the historiography of the 1830 Revolution that he had "given a talk in a setting that required a half-serious, half-lighthearted tone. Having chosen an unusual title, he offered an exploration of the perilous domain of conjectural history. The examination of different possible scenarios revealed that at any moment events might have gone in a different direction."[2] "The perilous domain of conjectural history," wrote Bertier de Sauvigny. The expression captures the misgivings of specialists when faced with counterfactual questions. And no doubt for good reason. These explorations leave the domain of history, the realm of past facts. They do not require the use of sources, which provide the sole resource for constructing knowledge of past societies. So the verdict would seem clear: such pleasant fictions may be entertaining, but they are ultimately of little or no utility.

But is the issue really so straightforward? Starting in the late 1990s, the appearance of studies, largely written in English, calling for a counterfactual or virtual history, most notably the well-known forays by the historian Niall Ferguson,[3] troubled such an apparent consensus. These books attracted media attention and some achieved a certain success—even as French researchers have remained largely indifferent. The success of the edited volumes that revisited this question and responded to contemporary concerns necessarily raised a new set of questions. Do we not regularly use counterfactual reasoning in our daily lives, either to evaluate a situation or to express regret? One sees it on the Internet, on television or radio, as well as during important investigations following an accident, where it can be a question of establishing the real unfolding of events and the responsibility of those involved.[4] It provides scenarios for films. Just as the social sciences have on occasion taken an interest—though not without some debate—whether it be economists attempting to interpret our planetary "crisis" or sociologists studying the effects of public policy.[5] Even historians have occasionally ventured into this domain. One may stumble upon works on "moments" that changed history,[6] or military, economic, political, social, or cultural histories, when such reasoning appears discretely, though often accompanied by an almost shameful apology.

So what problem do counterfactual approaches pose exactly? While it is a common form of reasoning, it continues to provoke the ire of historians. In spite of regular recourse to counterfactualism, we pretend it is not worthy of further investigation. But is it somehow not only helpful, but necessary? For the moment, this question remains unanswered. Ever prudent, historians have developed the habit of warning their readers with a ritual phrase—"without falling into the trap of a counterfactual history"—that precedes analyses of this type, in order to symbolically mark the boundary between the serious and futile, the limit between the domains of truth and the merely hypothetical. Why do we take so much care in constructing such barriers? Exploring such interrogations may allow us to approach history obliquely, exploring the territory of what has not taken place, what could have taken place, and all forms of past possibilities. In many ways, counterfactual analysis envelops the social sciences, what is otherwise a realm of facts: from its effervescence to its foundations, counterfactualism gnaws at them, filling the cracks and threatening their apparent solidity. It is a perilous exercise in which the most subjective feelings mix with the most absurd speculations, and the most serious hypotheses encounter some of the deepest questions. One begins to suspect that the very boundary between fact and "what could have been" is not as absolute as one might have hoped, and that behind this reasoning, which at first seems so trivial, some important questions may be hidden: the exigencies of honesty and the pleasure of reading, the relationship between history and fiction, the problem of determinism and contingency, the question of causality or the history of political uses of the past. Amid such interrogations, the essential problem is no doubt that of historical truth. As we know, history is knowledge of the past, produced through traces that have been preserved and questions posed in the present. It is not a search for absolute truth, but rather situated truths. This singular investigative enterprise mobilizes a researcher with sources, an approach, a narrative, and the ambition of truth, brought together into an ensemble in which historians consistently recognize its power and fragility as well as its political and social necessity. As Pierre Laborie explains, "The discourse of history is, more often than not, an overlapping mixture of affirmations of truth, of questions about truth, and tests of plausibility."[7] From this perspective, the counterfactual approach, which looks to invent a "counterfeit" history, seems contrary to the very principles of the historical discipline. Nonetheless, if the past does not lead ineluctably to our present, or in other words, if the actions of the men and women who preceded us had meaning, what is the status of the pasts that could have been? Should they be placed among those truths that concern the historian? If not, and if they are set aside, how can we be sure they will not resurface, implicitly or explicitly, in some way or another? One quickly understands why the subject has been so controversial among historians. It forces us to ask if the approach were not a pleasant but vain exercise, to be pushed forever outside the historical discipline because it blurs the conceptual and emotional? Or rather, on the contrary, whether it should be a "cardinal" question, as Nietzsche argues in the epigraph to this introduction. In the latter case, could it serve to raise questions that shift the very frameworks used for the production of historical knowledge? Without going to either of these extremes, it may be possible to ask what the counterfactual means as well as to inquire into the significance of the historical discipline's hesitations on the matter. Is there not in the counterfactual approach something that requires careful consideration? Something that may be useful to the historian, to the approach's modes of construction, expression, and transmission of knowledge? Such is the aim of this book.

Initially, this book emerged out of an attempt to respond to the variety of uchronic invitations in our present by understanding the underlying issues and elaborating a response. We were convinced that historians should neither confront this question with blind enthusiasm nor reject it outright. But the problematic and the field of investigation rapidly expanded as we considered the epistemological, methodological, and pedagogical problems to be identified and treated as a part of this circuitous method. It thus appeared to us that in order to effectively pursue this investigation, it was necessary to let ourselves wander freely into this unexpected and obscure world and then return: walking along the edge of history, from its ostensible margins, in hopes of pushing toward new horizons.

So how might one to advance into this realm of the unknown? The territories have been attributed different names, each corresponding to a given intention: fictional history, uchronic history, alternative history, and so forth. Researchers themselves have employed other names with a more "scientific" ring: counterfactual history, speculative history, conjectural, hypothetical, parafactual, possibilistic, and so on. There is an opposition between those for whom counterfactual reasoning serves to establish causes and formulate hypotheses, and those for whom, on the contrary, it is an original tool for narrative and historical fictionalization. Are such interpretations contradictory? This study took all of these approaches into account. Counterfactual reasoning, properly speaking (the "what ifs" of the past), was subject to multiple definitions and subtle distinctions, varying according to each author and his or her discipline. It quickly became apparent in reading these works that these different interpretations were connected. Once again, to appreciate all of the ramifications and issues at hand, it was necessary to grasp counterfactual reasoning in its indeterminacy and explore the plurality of its uses. We also decided to explore all of the processes in play: counterfactual reasoning (the observation that in the absence of a given historical fact, things could have happened differently, without going any further); the chain of possible outcomes (either in the form of a more or less fictional narrative or through analytical reasoning); and finally the question of the futures of the past or possible futures, which necessarily draw upon, in one way or another, counterfactual reasoning (tipping points or turning points that could be, as we will see, very simple or multiple, sudden or gradual, and so on). In order to investigate the different facets of this approach, we have taken as our point of departure counterfactual reasoning and uchronia, which recount outcomes of historical alternatives in a fictional mode. We have used the term "counterfactual" because it is the most commonly employed expression across disciplinary fields and cultural domains and thus constitutes the lowest common denominator in attempts to write unrealized histories. At the same time, we will make reference in the following pages to "counterfactual analysis and possible futures" to designate the entire chain of reasoning that may be mobilized by the researcher.

In pursuing this research, we have progressively moved away from the sole domain of works that self-identified as counterfactual. We were also pushed far beyond our precise fields of competence. In these pages, we navigate from prehistory to the present, from the realm of emotions to quantum physics. We have attempted to explore with caution, recognizing that at times we did not master all the epistemological issues at hand in these varied areas of expertise. We therefore regularly consulted specialists. This was the only way to grasp the singularity and value of such approaches, which are ultimately less exotic than they often appear to historians. There are no doubt counterfactual endeavors and experiments that we have not uncovered; we have visually navigated this ocean, using social scientific tools of data sampling and processing. But we consider our discoveries sufficiently fecund to respond to our initial line of questioning. The structure of the book therefore retraces our path of inquiry. Part I attempts to grasp the diversity of uses of counterfactual reasoning and their extensions or applications from the soberest to the most fantastic. Following is part II, a phase of deciphering, or decoding, focused on methodological issues, in which we attempt to come to terms with the specific problems they pose and their pertinence for historical study. Such relevance was then determined through experimentation, which is the focus of the last section, part III. Here we test the questions and tools that have been forged, in the fields of research as well as with a wider public. The reader is invited to either follow the logical order of the demonstration or wander through the chapters as he or she wishes according to his or her interests and desires.

So, while you will discover in the following pages the extraterrestrials who landed in Paris in 1900, elaborate time machines, or Hitler's reign over the world in 1960, this book mainly addresses historiographical questions, methodological issues, the problem of sources, and the writing of history. These extravagant cases may serve to remind us, however, that laughter, play, the superficial, and even the absurd can and undoubtedly should have a place in the production of history and its teaching. With that, let's set off on our journey, equipped with map and compass.

PART ONE

Inquiry

In the rivers north of the future
I cast the net

—Paul Celan[1]

For those drawn toward counterfactual reasoning and possible futures, a particularly rugged landscape awaits. Such reasoning seems commonplace in our daily lives. In the realm of culture, it seems at once a relic of an antiquarian nineteenth century and yet startlingly contemporary in graphic novels, films, or even video games. It is reminiscent of those strange "multiverses" studied by astrophysicists and is frequently used by historians, just as it often raises suspicions. It is therefore necessary to shed light on the subject by conducting an inquiry, with the help of a spyglass, as it were. It is impossible at this stage to provide an exhaustive account of all the uses of counterfactual reasoning or possible futures. The skein is too entangled. However, it is possible to follow leads, set milestones, map out intersections, and make distinctions. Four clusters emerge out of such an inquiry: ancient historical practice, the international dissemination of "what-if" history, uchronic and literary approaches, and modes of reasoning in the social and natural sciences. The patient observer thus begins to clear a path, which opens toward a first perspective.

CHAPTER I

In Thucydides' Wake

AN ANCIENT AND UNKNOWN GENEALOGY

Seed, in its original sense: as an index of possibility.

—Cornelius Castoriadis[1]

"What-if" history did not originate in the provocative minds of a few Anglo-American historians at the beginning of our millennium, nor from the pen of some nineteenth-century novelist. The approach was adopted early on by historians and then by researchers in other social sciences who defended very different, even contradictory interpretations of counterfactual analysis. It is necessary first to probe these historical depths, by quickly presenting some of the most famous cases. The Enlightenment and the French Revolution seem to mark a decisive turning point in this itinerary. It is only at the end of the eighteenth century that there emerged a form of writing that was specifically dedicated to this kind of investigation. From this point on, one may follow, more slowly, the paths and connections that have led to the most striking and coherent or original proposals. Our point of departure will be enriched by unexpected knots and branches. This will allow us to more fully appreciate the sort of familiar strangeness that characterizes what we call today counterfactual, or "what-if," history.

AN ANCIENT FORM OF HISTORICAL ARGUMENTATION: COUNTERFACTUAL DIGRESSIONS

Counterfactual argumentation was employed early on as a kind of digression. One finds one of the oldest occurrences of this type of historical reasoning in *The History of the Peloponnesian War* by the Athenian historian

Thucydides, in the fifth century BCE. Historians have pointed out the extensive use of this type of reasoning in his work, including twelve that were explicitly formulated by the author:[2]

> This, with a little more courage, he might easily have done, in which case he would either have increased the dissensions of the city by his presence, or, if he had stayed to besiege it, have compelled the fleet from Ionia, although the enemy of the oligarchy, to come to the rescue of their country and of their relatives.[3]

These counterfactuals are part of a debate that follows the fall of Athens's maritime empire in 404 BCE. The question is whether the Athenians have lost the war because of internal disagreement or because of their military defeat in the face of the Peloponnesian league.[4] Thucydides opposes this argument with the idea that the situation could have been worse, in order to weaken the imperialist ardors that are still strong among his compatriots.

In the first century CE, the Roman historian Livy (Titus Livius) also envisaged an unprecedented scenario. According to him, Alexander the Great wanted to extend his power to the west and was tempted to conquer Rome instead of focusing on the Orient. This digression gives him the opportunity to compare the merits of Alexander and the great Roman generals as well as the Macedonian armies and the Roman legions. Livy's stimulating comparative method is grounded in an anachronism, since it compares piece by piece the Macedonians of the fourth century BCE and the Romans of the first century CE. One easily surmises the conclusion of his argument, which ably shows the superiority of Rome. What is of particular interest, however, is how Livy introduces the counterfactual digression by proposing a pact with the reader:

> Nothing can be found farther from my intention, since the commencement of this history, than to digress, more than necessity required, from the course of narration; and, by embellishing my work with variety, to seek pleasing resting places, as it were, for my readers, and relaxation for my own mind: nevertheless, the mention for so great a king and commander, now calls forth to public view those silent reflections, with which it has oftentimes occupied my mind; and disposes me to inquire, what would have been the consequence, respecting the affairs of the Romans, if they had happened to have been engaged in a war with Alexander.[5]

According to Livy, counterfactual reasoning came to him by association of ideas, almost instinctively or naturally. He pretends it were unworthy of explanation while brazenly inserting it into his argument. The author's deliberate staging and reflexivity appear to be the sine qua non of any counterfactual reasoning. In the first century CE, we find the same type of digression and the same obsession with Alexander the Great in the work of Tacitus. The author of *The Annals of Imperial Rome* criticizes the Macedonian emperor in order to celebrate Germanicus, who would have surpassed Alexander the Great in all areas had he become emperor.[6]

Let's take a giant leap forward. Alongside these comparisons that aim to evaluate the importance of an action or to flatter a historical figure, there is another use of the counterfactual approach, also based on highly improbable hypotheses. In this case, it is a question of radically reversing the reader's perspective. Thus, Philippe Duplessis-Mornay, Protestant theologian and political advisor to the king of Navarre, wrote in 1581 for the future Henry IV of France, "In short, it is as if the Indians of the West conquered us as we did them, first landing in Ireland or in France or Greenland where they could have said of us what we have said of them."[7] By inverting the process of the conquest of the New World, the author succeeded in relativizing the notion of the savage. The counterfactual argument thus made it possible to decenter the historian's gaze in order to read events and grasp the world in a new light.[8]

A century later, Blaise Pascal became one of the first to explicitly use this mode of reasoning to identify and question the causes of historical evolution. The philosopher formulated two plausible hypotheses that have since become famous:

> Cromwell was about to ravage all Christendom; the royal family was undone, and his own for ever established, save for a little grain of sand which formed in his ureter. Rome herself was trembling under him; but this small piece of gravel having formed there, he is dead, his family case down, all is peaceful, and the king is restored. . . . He who will know fully the vanity of man has only to consider the causes and effects of love. The cause is a *je ne sais quoi* (Corneille), and the effects are dreadful. This *je ne sais quoi,* so small an object that we cannot recognize it, agitates a whole country, princes, armies, the entire world. Cleopatra's nose: had it been shorter, the whole aspect of the world have been altered.[9]

Pascal highlights two factors that are beyond human control: feelings, in this case love, and illness, which may be the expression of divine power.

Without the beauty of Cleopatra and Cromwell's urinary stone, Rome and England would have remained republics. Pascal's famous *Pensées* have enjoyed an exceptional posterity, to such a degree that so-called popular wisdom has adopted it with the synecdoche of "Cleopatra's nose," which in some cases stands in for counterfactual reasoning itself.

The *Pensées* subsequently provoked a recurrent debate on historical causation. Outside Mark Antony's love for Cleopatra, other more pragmatic and political motives may explain their union, and thus the war against Octavian. "Cleopatra's nose," however, still fascinates historians who have not found commentary on her physical appearance among the Latin chroniclers and have attempted to reconstruct the queen of Egypt's facial features. Archaeologists at the University of Newcastle, England, exhumed in 2009 a silver coin from 32 BCE, representing a sovereign with an elongated forehead, a sharp chin, an angular nose, and very fine lips that did not correspond to the canons of beauty of the time. Shakespeare supposedly invented the myth of the queen's beauty in his *Antony and Cleopatra,* published in 1623, which later inspired Pascal. This thesis could be validated or confirmed through current archaeological research off the coast of Alexandria, where Cleopatra's mausoleum has been discovered. Of course, the debate on Cleopatra's physical attributes seems inextricable and rather vain to the extent that beauty and charm remain subjective. The same may be said for the origins of Cromwell's death: the Pascalian theory of bladder stones was widely accepted until a book published in 1999 attempted to show that Cromwell had in fact been assassinated.[10] The question remains undecided, but this most recent interpretation suggests a human act was responsible whereas Pascal had attributed it to fate and divine will.

In their own way, Pascal's *Pensées* also raise the question of the relevance of this approach when it is not based on historical sources. This has been the case, for example, in recurring counterfactual analyses devoted to the victory of the Arabs of Abd al-Rahman against the Franks of Charles Martel at Poitiers in 732. The historian and politician Edward Gibbon offered the prototype of such analyses in his *The Decline and Fall of the Roman Empire,* published in the eighteenth century:

> A victorious line of march had been prolonged above a thousand miles from the rock of Gibraltar to the banks of the Loire; the repetition of an equal space would have carried the Saracens to the confines of Poland and the Highlands of Scotland; the Rhine is not more impassable than the Nile or Euphrates, and the Arabian fleet might have sailed

> without a naval combat into the mouth of the Thames. Perhaps the interpretation of the Koran would now be taught in the schools of Oxford, and her pulpits might demonstrate to a circumcised people the sanctity and truth of the revelation of Mahomet.[11]

Here, Gibbon invents a playful, even ironic approach to the counterfactual. Unlike his epigones, he does not highlight the role of Charles Martel and the extent of the Muslim threat. Quite to the contrary, this approach allows the author to mock the Christian religion (entirely interchangeable with Islam), especially the conservative Anglicanism of Oxford, where he was so uncomfortable. This example has been cited for more than two centuries by historians. Nonetheless, the point of contention, namely the Battle of Poitiers, has been examined: historians of medieval Western Islam have shown that this famous alternative history was impossible because the Muslim troops were not pursuing a war of conquest but were set on a simple, hastily organized raid exaggerated by Christian chroniclers.[12]

More seriously, Chateaubriand offered another hypothesis during the same period on the flight of the king on June 21, 1791, which has become a classic of counterfactual history.[13] If Louis XVI had not left Paris, he would have saved his head, since it was the sovereign's flight that desecrated the power of divine right and opened the way to the separation between the executive and the national body. The French Crown would therefore not have been condemned on June 20, and the flight to Varennes would not have marked the true turning point of the French Revolution. This revolutionary moment undoubtedly had a strong capacity to inspire counterfactual scenarios. As early as 1791, Jean-Baptiste-Claude Delisle de Sales published *My Republic,* which suggested that a stronger king would have altered the history of the French Revolution. Similarly, there was an early "revolutionary" use of the counterfactual approach. Karl Marx himself did not hesitate to mobilize this type of reasoning in his *Eighteenth Brumaire of Louis Bonaparte* published in 1852 when he asked the question:

> Why did the Paris proletariat not rise in revolt after December 2? The overthrow of the bourgeoisie had as yet been only decreed; the decree was not carried out. Any serious insurrection of the proletariat would at once have put new life into the bourgeoisie, reconciled it with the army, and insured a second June defeat for the workers.[14]

Unlike Chateaubriand, Marx was not interested in the particular event or contingency in general, but used the counterfactual approach to uncover structural phenomena as well as power and class relations. Marx also opened another useful approach with his analysis: he assumed that the revolutionary proletariat carried out counterfactual operations in order to guide its decisions. We will consider later the influence such thought experiments have had on revolutionary practice.[15]

These few examples of counterfactual digressions reveal the distant roots of this mode of reasoning and reveal some of its possible uses for comparing, criticizing, praising, or relativizing the importance of an event or a historical figure. Most of them confirm a vision of the world based on the actions of great people, and all too often great men, in history.

Each of these uses deserves to be placed in a more elaborate context. Studies have shown, for example, that among historians of Greek or Roman antiquity, the use of this type of reasoning was based on the small difference between factual and fictional narratives, as well as Aristotle's reflections that distinguished a history "that was" as opposed to a *poiesis,* "that could be." According to the philosopher, only the latter provided the generality necessary for the construction of a plausible narrative when documentation and sources were lacking. The distinction also had a moral and political dimension: in this case it was a matter of imagining possible past actions that could have served humankind.[16] Inserted into the frameworks of enunciation and reception, this mode of reasoning becomes richer than it may appear at first sight. However, from Tacitus to Marx, it would seem that counterfactual reasoning was never fully deployed. It remained limited to parenthetical interrogations or a simple question. It was only at the beginning of the nineteenth century that a real practice, almost a genre, of writing emerged, based entirely on the counterfactual approach.

BIRTH OF AN UNUSUAL GENRE BETWEEN FICTION AND HISTORY: NINETEENTH-CENTURY UCHRONIAS

With the rise of the novel and a growing interest in history, counterfactual scenarios proliferated from the beginning of the nineteenth century. The search for the "origins" of the first alternative history, or uchronia, is a risky venture. In fact, alternative narratives gained in consistency across the eighteenth century, as revealed by the famous *Memoirs of the Year Two Thousand Five Hundred* by Louis-Sébastien Mercier, which appeared in 1771,[17] then after the American and French Revolutions in the aforementioned chapter of *My Republic* by Jean-Baptiste Isoard, known as Delisle de Sales.[18] The first work entirely devoted to an alternative history, written by Louis Geoffroy, the pseudonym of Louis-Napoléon Geoffroy-Château, was published in 1836, entitled *Napoleon and the Conquest of the World, 1812–1832: History of the Universal Monarchy* and republished under the title *Napoléon Apocryphe* in 1841. In this work, written after Waterloo by the son of an officer who died at Austerlitz, Napoleon defeats Russia in 1812, invades Great Britain in 1814, remarries Josephine, resumes the conquest of Egypt where Bonaparte had left it, and attacks India, China, and Japan. The emperor then explores the Australian outback after conquering Africa and returns to Europe in 1827. The American Congress acquiesces to Napoleon of its own accord the same year, and Napoleon then becomes emperor of the known world before dying in 1832. His prestige, Geoffroy explains, is such that the day of his second consecration, two stars of Orion "die out forever" and give way to the constellation of Napoleon.[19] By transforming the Napoleonic military defeats into victories, Geoffroy constructed an unprecedented world that anticipated the end of the century: the emperor imposed the French language on all continents, organized an expedition to the North Pole, dug the Suez and Panama Canals, and promoted the development of filtering seawater and of electric airplanes. Nevertheless, amid this panegyrical disguise, one discovers a satire that depicts a world desolated by Napoleonic tyranny and standardization brought on by a universal monarchy.

The counterfactual method was also used for political purposes by the famous philosopher Charles Renouvier. A graduate of the prestigious École Polytechnique and a disciple of neo-Kantianism, Renouvier was also a politician committed to the socialist-republican cause. He is, however, better known for his *Republican Manual of Man and Citizen,* published in 1848, and for the foundation of "critical philosophy" in 1872 than for his uchronia. The text was first published anonymously under the title "Uchronia," in 1857, in *La Revue philosophique et religieuse,*[20] before being reedited in 1876 with a new more provocative title that became the eponymous founder of a new literary genre: *Uchronia (Utopia in History): An Apocryphal Historical Sketch of the Development of European Civilization* (*Uchronie [L'Utopie dans l'histoire]. Esquisse historique apocryphe du développement de la civilisation européenne*). Thanks to this book, the term "uchronia," defined as "a utopia in history," found its place in the dictionary.[21]

The text is presented as the translation of a manuscript written by a religious figure and burned by the Inquisition in Rome in 1601. But Renouvier reveals the deception in the postface, in which he presents himself as the author and explains the difficulties of writing this alternative historical narrative. In this version of the story, it was not Commodus who succeeded Marcus Aurelius in 180, but Avidius Cassius, presented as a Stoic philosopher, who had for a time usurped this power and was in fact assassinated.[22] Instead of sinking into debauchery as Commodus did, he allegedly, according to Renouvier, promulgated a series of important laws in the fields of legislation, technology, and public freedom. In this account, the enlightened West thus repelled the barbarian assaults; Christianity did not develop, or would have emerged in a purified form; the Renaissance would have taken place a century earlier, and so on. The work shows remarkable inventiveness, taking the form of a treatise on imaginary legal and technical knowledge. Furthermore, the adoption of the counterfactual approach allows the anticlerical Renouvier to write an ode to philosophy and freedom in the face of Christianity, determinism, and the role of Providence.[23]

At the moment when the writings of Geoffroy and Renouvier were published, uchronia was developing widely across Europe: during this period it emerged as a mode of writing for historians, philosophers, politicians, and novelists who proposed new reflections on temporality or were playing with history. "Uchronic" texts were written in Italian, Spanish, and especially English.[24] In 1819, Archbishop Richard Whately, inspired by Hume's skeptical philosophy, published *Historical Doubts Respecting Napoléon Buonaparte,* which argued that Napoleon had never existed.[25] During the same period, the father of Benjamin Disraeli, Isaac D'Israeli, published his "A History of Events Which Have Not Happened."[26] He focused more on turning points than possible consequences (Charles Martel, Charles VIII, Cromwell, and so on). In 1845, the writer Nathaniel Hawthorne published in the United States alternative biographies of illustrious personages (Lord Byron, Walter Scott, John Keats, Napoleon Bonaparte), while Auguste Blanqui published *Eternity by the Stars* in 1872.[27] In this astonishing work, the aging revolutionary applied Laplace's scientific principles to history and concluded that there were a number of possible worlds. Furthermore, he proposed that what will take place on this earth had already taken place in another world. The misfortune is that one cannot draw lessons for our world from the histories that have taken place in others. In the English-speaking world, Edward Hale's tale *Hands Off* was published in 1881, and in 1895 there appeared what was probably the first uchronic novel in the English language, *Aristopia: A Romance-History of the New World* by Castello N. Holford.[28]

This emergence of counterfactualism in novels was part of several trends during the period. The divide between knowledge about society and the literary remained fluid during the first two-thirds of the century (as revealed at the beginning of the century by the role of Walter Scott's novels in structuring historical discourse).[29] The nineteenth century, which was the first to be thought of as a century by its contemporaries, also experimented with a new relationship to time. Often described as the historical century, it was the period when the "historical sciences" took form and played a growing role in society. The major chronological milestones were increasingly established during this period, in particular the great events and great people staged by such uchronias. This was also part of the slow emergence of a "modern regime of historicity," to quote the German historian Reinhart Koselleck, that began in the eighteenth century. With the revolutionary rupture, there emerged the idea of a breach in the unfolding of time, which generated an uncertain future, bringing with it both the idea of "progress" as well as numerous uncertainties and ruptures. It also marked a break between the past and the future. This perception, consisting of overlaps and contradictions, was accentuated at the end of the eighteenth century and manifested itself little by little in the modes for understanding historical development in many areas of social life.[30] Uchronia, which consists in imagining another course of history, proved well adapted to this period and became a means of reasserting through thought the control over time that seemed to have escaped them. It is precisely such an observation that establishes the distinction between uchronia and utopia. Uchronia is a product of the nineteenth century, while utopia has a longer history. Its origins lie in the publication of Thomas More's famous *Utopia,* which gave birth to a tradition that developed in the seventeenth and eighteenth centuries.[31] Utopia invents another place, out of time. It constitutes an *out-of-place* where a philosophical and political fable can develop that proposes an alternative model and undermines the social and political organization of its time.[32] By elaborating another place, it produces another time. For this reason, some authors suggest that utopia is often a uchronia.[33] But while they share certain functions, uchronia as such tends to escape time in an effort to imagine another historical becoming and another temporal dynamic.[34] In this sense, it would appear to have been one of the narrative devices used to respond to the new impression of the passage of time that marked the nineteenth century.

THE TURN OF THE TWENTIETH CENTURY: THE QUEST FOR HISTORICAL OBJECTIVITY AND ENTERTAINMENT

Changes took place as early as the turn of the century, especially among historians. They echoed in part what in France was known as the "methodical school" and, more generally, the interest in objectivity that characterized the historical discipline at the beginning of the twentieth century. Its advocates claimed to provide history with firmer scientific foundations, excluding the use of fiction or any similar mode of writing.[35] Professional historians became increasingly wary of this approach, even though some exploited this uchronic vein in a ludic and moralizing manner. Historical devotees thus practiced a counterfactual history of events that was difficult to distinguish from literary uchronia. In 1907, Joseph Edgar Chamberlin published *The Ifs of History,* which was a repertory of the greatest "what-if" questions, including the victory of the Arabs in Poitiers in 732, the success of the Invincible Armada in 1588, or the victory of the Southerners during The Civil War.[36] The American historian Chamberlin put alternative history at the service of his political nationalism. His chapter entitled "If Columbus Had Kept His Straight Course Westward" offered the opportunity to celebrate the Genoese explorer's change of course, which spared the future United States from the Spanish yoke. In the same year, the *Westminster Gazette* organized a literary contest on the themes "What if Napoleon had won the Battle of Waterloo?" George M. Trevelyan described Great Britain under Napoleonic control, which, in spite of an attempted revolution by Lord Byron, sank into deep obscurantism. The Whig historian thus made Waterloo appear as a key moment in the history of British liberal democracy.

In the interwar period, the counterfactual approach posed little problem for these, notably English, academics.[37] So much so that such a respected authority within the discipline as Arnold Joseph Toynbee turned to it, writing six "what-if" essays between 1934 and 1961. He took up the theme of the defeat of Charles Martel in describing Muslim France,[38] explored the conquest of the medieval world by Vikings,[39] imagined the expansion of Christianity to East Asia,[40] and in two texts on Macedonian history considered what would have happened if Philip and Alexander had survived.[41] At the end of his life, Toynbee attempted to popularize this approach by publishing a little compilation of alternative histories in *The New York Times Magazine.*[42]

The volume edited by the historian John Squire subsequently conferred a certain nobility upon this approach. Entitled *If It Had Happened Otherwise: Lapses into Imaginary History* and published in 1931, this book gathered the finest among the British intellectual elite. Philip Guedalla described a Spain where the Moors triumphed and the Marrano Benjamin Disraeli serves as grand vizier in the nineteenth century. G. K. Chesterton considered the consequences of a marriage between Don Juan of Austria and Mary Stuart, queen of Scotland. André Maurois conjectured on the evolution of France if Louis XVI had "an ounce of firmness." Hilaire Belloc wondered how the carriage of Jean-Baptiste Drouet could have impacted the flight of Louis XVI and thus shaped the course of the French Revolution. The most innovative essay in methodological terms was signed by Winston Churchill, entitled "If General Lee Had Won the Battle of Gettysburg." He describes an alternative world where the Confederacy won the Civil War and then a historian tries to imagine what would have happened if the North had been victorious. This was an unprecedented version of counterfactual history: the alternative vision of a real world that actually did happen. This approach is at the origin of a subgenre of counterfactual history: *alternate-alternative history* or *double blind "what if."* Thanks to the brief and humorous texts on such popular subjects, this collective volume exerted a real influence on English-speaking historians and inspired several experiments in other countries some decades later.

In France, a series of twelve articles was published in 1956–1957, which have since been forgotten, in the journal *Les Annales: Revue mensuelle des lettres françaises.* The articles were written by French historians and writers, including ancient historian Jerome Carcopino ("If Brutus had not dared . . .") and scholars dealing with subjects of "national" history, such as Paul Guth ("If the great men had died at twenty . . .") or Adrien Dansette ("If the bomb of Orsoni had killed Napoleon III . . ."). This literary and humorous tradition was renewed once again in the English-speaking world, notably with the collective volume edited by Daniel Snowman, *If I Had Been,* in which ten historians put themselves in the shoes of great statesmen and imagined, for example, how Thiers avoided war with Prussia in 1870 and how Gladstone solved the Irish question.[43] In 1985, the collective volume entitled *For Want of a Horse: Choice and Chance in History,* edited by the historian John M. Merriman, proposed a new interpretation of alternative history.[44] If Fidel Castro had enjoyed a successful career with the Giants baseball team, what would have come of the Cuban Revolution? If Voltaire had emigrated to Pennsylvania, would the American Constitution have been a different document? The originality and limitations of this venture lie in the importance attached to the role of chance and "bad luck" in history, illustrated by the unluckiness of Richard III who, in 1485, desperately sought a horse on the battlefield of Bosworth to save his kingdom. John Merriman thus reproaches classical counterfactual history for underestimating the importance of contingency: the taking into account of "chance" must relieve the historian of the dangerous temptation to explain everything down to the finest detail.[45]

Until World War II, uchronia remained the prerogative of historians. Novelists who had begun working with the idea had been largely on the margins. Authors focused on a few popular themes both for their readership and the historical community: the Roman Empire, the first Napoleonic Empire, the Civil War. These essays took the form of collective works, which made it possible to juxtapose different objects and augment a sense of experimentation. Such uchronias, which were based on a rather simple model, were systematically based on the invention of a specific point of divergence out of which an alternative story developed. As for most of the digressions studied before, the point of divergence in the majority of these uchronias was rooted in the action of a "great man" who was the motor of history. It was precisely against this literary tradition of uchronia that a more exacting version of counterfactual analysis developed, highlighting the "scientific" dimension and progressively analyzing the counterfactual approach itself. It was the social sciences that mobilized counterfactual analysis to renew their own vision of history.

THE COUNTERFACTUAL BETWEEN SCIENCE AND REFLEXIVITY (SECOND HALF OF THE TWENTIETH CENTURY)

The first theorization of the counterfactual approach in history dates back to the beginning of the twentieth century. In his *Collected Methodological Writings,* published in 1906, Max Weber argued that only counterfactual analysis could confer upon history the status of a true science. In his view, historians needed to accept all the implications of this form of reasoning to which they constantly resorted, consciously or unconsciously. Indeed, this imaginary experience made it possible to establish and hierarchize historical causation.[46] This Weberian counterfactual model, which clearly broke with the more imaginative uchronic practices, has influenced most of the counterfactual experiments in economics, sociology, and international relations that have developed since World War II. This form of causal analysis inspired the founding of cliometrics, a branch of economics and other fields based in part on the counterfactual method. Beginning in the late 1950s, this new approach developed in the United States, initially seeking to question the interpretations commonly accepted by economists and historians. In order to do this, practitioners of cliometrics broke with traditional economic history of literary inspiration by paying more attention to economic theory, statistical analysis, and econometric analysis in order to promote mathematical economics.

In 1958, two Harvard researchers, Alfred H. Conrad and John R. Meyer, posed the question: Would the South have abolished slavery without the Civil War? The two economists demonstrated with a barrage of statistics the dynamism and efficiency of the slave economy that would no doubt have continued in the absence of a Union victory: "In sum, it seems doubtful that the South was forced by bad statesmanship into an unnecessary war to protect a system which must soon have disappeared because it was economically unsound. This is a romantic hypothesis which will not stand against the facts."[47] In 1964, economist Robert Fogel explained the use of counterfactual analysis in history with his work *Railroads and American Economic Growth,* wherein he tackled an everyday assumption of science economics and history that he referred to as the "axiom of indispensability" of the railway in the growth of the United States in the nineteenth century.[48] Fogel tested the relevance of this axiom, which implicitly rested on the absence of an efficient alternative to the railways, by substituting another type of transport to the train—canals, in this case—to evaluate the economic and social impact of the development of the railway during the nineteenth century. He concludes that without the railway, the level of growth would have been comparable in 1890. More broadly, the counterfactual analysis allows cliometric economists to demonstrate the scientific character of economic history by proving that it is possible to test historical phenomena: it is sufficient to construct fictitious situations and then to measure the discrepancy between what has actually been observed and what would have occurred under different circumstances.[49] Only the measurement of this discrepancy allows the historian and the economist to evaluate the influence of a given factor on an observed evolution. The specialists of this "new economic history" focus on the study of one or two more variables and are not interested in alternative history nor its plausibility.[50] In the face of numerous criticisms of cliometrics, Robert Fogel took a cue from Max Weber arguing for the banality of counterfactual reasoning, which the historian has difficulty doing without:

> Like it or not, counterfactual conditional statements are too integral a feature of their discourse to be banished. Should we advocate that historians give up the practice of making judgments about mistakes?

> Do we mean to exclude from history such statements as: "Woodrow Wilson miscalculated the consequences of his failure to appoint a prominent Republican to the delegation that represented America at the Paris peace conference" or "Andrew Johnson played into the hands of his enemies by suspending Stanton and making Grant ad interim Secretary of War"? There are few historians who would accept a ban on such judgments. To do so would transform history into mere chronology.
>
> But historians who write that Wilson or Johnson made mistakes are implicitly asserting that the particular course of action that each man followed was inferior to an alternative that was available to him. In branding actual behavior as an error, one presumes knowledge of the course of events in situations that never occurred.[51]

Like economists, philosophers have adopted a reflexive approach and begun to take up the counterfactual approach—the intellectual operation itself—as an object of their analysis. Thus, gradually, reflection on the conditions of possibility have become of greater interest to researchers than the narrative of alternative events in the uchronic mode. This involves questioning the notion of causality along the lines of Patrick Gardiner:

> "Were shots on the boulevards the cause of the 1848 Revolution in France?" Does this mean: "Would the Revolution have broken out at the precise time at which it did break out if they had not occurred?" Or does it mean: "Would the Revolution have broken out sooner or later even if there had been no shots?" And if, after receiving an affirmative answer to the latter question, we ask: "What then was the real cause of the Revolution?" further specification is again required. For there are a number of possible answers. . . . And there are no absolute Real Causes waiting to be discovered by historians.[52]

Counterfactual theories of causality are inspired by the "second definition" of causality proposed by David Hume, who asserted that "we may define a cause to be an Object follow'd by another, and where all the Objects, similar to the first, are follow'd by Objects, similar to the second."[53] These theories were profoundly renewed in the 1970s in the works of David Lewis, to whom we shall return. The considerable development of philosophical research in this field has concentrated on problems of logic by distancing history itself. This reflection on the counterfactual or the question of possibilities in history has also continued outside the field of philosophy. This is evidenced by one of the first openly reflexive works on counterfactual history, *Plausible Worlds,* written in 1991 by Geoffrey Hawthorn, professor of sociology at Cambridge.[54] Amid multiple inquiries, the British sociologist also focused on the nature of explanation and historical interpretation through counterfactual definition: if A is the cause of B, this means that all things being equal, without A there would be no B. By explaining ties of causality, the historical inquiry thus assumes that other worlds have been possible but not realized; paradoxically, historical investigation increases our knowledge while at the same time reducing total certainty.[55]

"WHAT IF . . .": THE INSTITUTIONALIZATION OF A NEW HISTORY?

In the late 1990s, these multiple interpretations of counterfactual analysis in history—both recurrent and relatively discrete—became an object of indictment by the historian Niall Ferguson, who attempted to stigmatize his predecessors' efforts. The economic historian wrote the history of the failure of traditional counterfactual methods in order to highlight the relevance and singularity of his project. In his account, his predecessors—Squire, Merriman, Snowman, and so on—had focused on "reductive inference" and on a single point of divergence, an event or the character trait of great men, and therefore produced a teleological narrative instead of restoring the field of possibilities of a given moment and taking into account the knowledge and constraints of contemporary actors. Unable to ask credible questions and provide plausible answers, these pioneers and their "pleasant" stories discredited the counterfactual approach, in his view. Ferguson thus attempted to scientifically establish his "virtual history" against this literary tradition.

He claimed to be inspired by approaches in the so-called "hard" sciences: probability theory, quantum mechanics, fractal theory, or even paleontology offered him a few possible analogies, but chaos theory provided the foundation for his historiographical project which he named *chaostory.* Chaos theory, defined as a set of stochastic behaviors within the framework of a deterministic system, made it possible to reconcile the notions of causality and contingency. In other words, "Chaos . . . means unpredictable outcomes even when successive events are causally linked."[56] Thus, Ferguson had the intention of elaborating a methodology that went beyond the alternative between the deterministic conception of a single past and the relativistic view of an endless number of possible pasts. Given the infinite number of possible alternative histories from the same point of divergence, the counterfactualist historian must exclusively consider plausible alternatives. These "plausible" alternatives correspond to the possibilities envisaged by the contemporaries themselves: it is therefore necessary to focus on the knowledge and information available to the contemporaries just before the point of divergence. The historical event often provokes the surprise of the actors because it is the realization of an alternative that had not been envisaged by the majority of contemporaries. Thus, at the critical moment, just before the event occurs, the counterfactual scenarios are more "real" than the events about to happen.[57] In addition, Ferguson invites researchers to randomly substitute probability calculations. Under these conditions, counterfactual scenarios become "simulations based on calculations about the relative probability of plausible outcomes in a chaotic world."[58] However, the author does not really delineate what "historical probability" may be, but rather admits that it cannot be reduced to a mathematical calculation.

Published following the collapse of the Berlin Wall, the book appeared at the right time: it corresponded to historiographical transformations of the time—the "return" to agents, event, and narrative.[59] It was also part of a set of more widespread social transformations, which are now well-known: a discourse on the "end of ideologies," the supposed difficulty of projecting into the future, a fascination with the connections between reality and fiction, and so on. The book also distinguished itself by bringing together widely recognized historians such as J. C. D. Clark, Mark Almond, Diane Kunz, and Andrew Roberts, giving it a strong institutional foundation. Finally, the personal success of Niall Ferguson, who quickly became a renowned historian, professor of political and financial history at Oxford in 2000, and the professor of history and business administration at Harvard from 2004 onward, certainly also helps explain the visibility of this project.

The approach then enjoyed a new excitement, and "what-if" history embarked on worldwide success. In 1999, *Virtual History* was reedited in the United States, while military history specialist Robert Cowley edited three volumes of this kind in 1999, 2000, and 2001, which also went through several reprints.[60] Among historians, the echo was essentially captured by the debate, both scientific and political, that accompanied the publication of the works of Geoffrey Hawthorn and especially Niall Ferguson. Critics took up the same body of arguments, to which we shall return: historical reality is sufficiently broad, so there is no point in adding alternative realities; the historian must concentrate on the study of what happened from work grounded in sources; or the proposed alternative realities are necessarily tainted by value judgments or political presuppositions. The latter risk seemed all the more real because Niall Ferguson had expressed his neoconservative sympathies elsewhere. In his book *Empire: The Rise and Demise of the British World Order,*[61] he proposed a counterfactual suggesting that without the British Empire, the world would be worse off than it is today. The prestigious journals *Social History* and *History and Theory* proposed critical and well-argued book reviews.[62] The growing interest in the question for historians could also be measured by the shear inflation of studies: there were more than fifty books and articles in English between 1997 and 2010, accelerating in the 2000s.[63] These reproaches have gradually led to methodological revisions. As early as 2000, most "what-if" history books, whether theoretical or practical, emphasized the difference between the "wrong"—naïve or awkward—way to do counterfactual history, and the "right"—reflexive and effective—way. The authors also tended to support their approaches within a scientific foundation in order to ensure a certain degree of seriousness: chaos theory, cosmological analyses inspired by Stephen Hawking, cognitive psychology, modal logic, and so on. And there has been a multiplication of warnings and user's guides, disseminated and commented upon on the Internet.[64] Such a trajectory explains the peculiar tone of the Anglo-Saxon approach: this version cannot be associated with postmodernism, the linguistic turn, or the blurring of the relations between reality and the imaginary. To the contrary, it seeks to present itself as a characteristic of a certain nondeterminist social history, articulated around facts and reasoning presented as rigorously as possible.

Thus, a certain normalization may be observed in recent years, even if debates on the relevance or flaws of the approach have not come to an end. In 2004, historian Richard Evans, a Germanist and holder of the chair of modern history at the University of Cambridge, firmly formulated the criticisms noted above,[65] later writing in 2014 a work entitled *Altered Pasts: Counterfactuals in History.*[66] However, as early as 1997, Eric Hobsbawm, though a traditional opponent, was engaged in a skillful counterfactual exercise in *On History,*[67] about the Russian Revolution of 1917, all the while reiterating his mistrust of such techniques. Little by little, the approach seems to have gained some legitimacy. Counterfactual history has slowly shed its openly "neoconservative" dimension and has been reappropriated by openly progressive, or "left," historians and philosophers, as well as researchers who appreciate the neutrality that such a process may offer. Symposiums, conferences, and academic seminars on "what if" have also multiplied. The approach has become more consensual, to the point of being integrated into conferences for generalists or appearing as a field of research on the personal web pages of some historians.[68] Nonetheless, one cannot speak of a process of institutionalization. The approach, often mobilized playfully, is rarely considered a field of "specialization" of its own within history departments.

We now understand more clearly the plurality of uses of so-called counterfactual history, the trajectories they have followed, and the selective memory that has classified them. It is apparent at the end of this broad panorama that while the approach has become increasingly associated with Anglophone studies, its past and the debates surrounding it are rooted in a much deeper history and have been subject to an extremely varied set of uses and critiques. But now we must expand the depth of field to propose a more accurate state of the art.

CHAPTER 2

From Delhi to Vienna

COUNTERFACTUAL HISTORY ACROSS THE WORLD

If you are in a hurry, take a detour.

—Japanese Proverb

As deeply as this initial survey may have plunged, the explorations of the previous chapter were too narrowly focused geographically. As if the waters of history only washed over the shores of the Western world—a problematic assessment to say the least. Nonetheless, the impossibility of studying the great varieties in this approach on a global scale over a long period have pushed us toward a more modest ambition: the development of counterfactual reasoning with "scientific" pretentions, as it has developed since the 1960s and especially the 1990s. In spite of this limitation, original elements come forward: while the Anglo-American origins remain preponderant, new variations have appeared in the modes of circulation, which in turn have resulted in appropriations and redefinitions of the counterfactual approach.[1]

THE "ANGLO-AMERICAN IMPETUS"

Considering their importance in the circulation and reception of counterfactual practices, it may be useful to revisit the debates within the English-language approach, as well as those to which it has given rise. Two "sources" have fostered this diffusion. The first is Robert Fogel's cliometry, which has become an entire subfield within the discipline of economics and has now been institutionalized in the form of chairs, specific journals, and teaching positions. Fogel's arrival at Harvard University in 1975, followed by his Nobel

Prize in Economic Sciences in 1993 brought wide legitimacy to his work and its diverse ramifications. Although the counterfactual approach has not been institutionalized in history departments, it has established a coherent set of propositions, techniques, and analytical schemes that spread far beyond the sole field of economic history.

The other approach has been less widely accepted even if it has enjoyed tremendous visibility: that is, the "what-if" history properly speaking, associated with Niall Ferguson. It took shape within the context of Cambridge and Oxford Universities and has also provoked bitter debates.

Coming from a variety of angles, the first strong critiques were brought together into a coherent whole by counterfactualist researchers themselves. The book by Geoffrey Hawthorn was the first to point out the main criticisms of Edward Hallet Carr, Eric Hobsbawm, and Edward Palmer Thompson.[2]

In 1960, E. H. Carr, a former diplomat and professor of international politics, historian at the University of Birmingham, editorialist at *The Times,* and world-renowned specialist on the Soviet Union, presented a series of lectures at the University of Cambridge.[3] The one devoted to "causality in history" was a specific reaction to the organization of a seminar the previous year within the same university, which proposed to engage in "what-if" history exercises. It was inspired in particular by the analyses of the liberal, anti-Marxist philosopher Isaiah Berlin.[4] Carr's lecture was aimed at him, among others, and his ideas and theories on the role of freedom and contingency in history. As a Marxist historian, Carr was dubious of "what ifs," the approach of the it-could-have-been school of history, something more akin to a "Carrollian" relation to the past (in reference to Lewis Carroll) than a true historical method.[5] On the contrary, he presented himself as a determinist, attached to the search for historical causes.[6] In light of the extremely rich historical material that had already come to pass, exploring alternative issues appeared sterile.

Moreover, such questions as Was the Russian Revolution inevitable? was politically motivated.[7] Such "parlor games" betrayed, above all, the dreams of the present. Theories of the accidental would thus be generally characteristic of groups or nations "in the hollow of the wave. . . . The view that examination results are all a lottery will always be popular among those who have been placed in the third class."[8] Such considerations were not worthy of historians, in his view. Moreover, the problem was redoubled in the search for causation. Cleopatra's famous nose may have had historical significance, like thousands of other causes, but these are not the elements that research should consider relevant. The entire problem is one of creating a hierarchy of causes, those that are significant and those that are not, and then organizing them rationally. This operation necessarily implies a value judgment, based on the idea that the role of history is to better understand the past through the light of the present and vice versa. The rest is vain, in Carr's account. His argument, written according to the modes of history writing of the 1950s, was radical and yet more subtle than the summaries presented by some counterfactualists since. The British historian's discussion is tightly knit, and the demonstration is convincing. Moreover, he does not deny the existence of other options, nor their impact on the choice of actors. He simply considers the game of hypotheses to be "theoretically conceivable" but otiose. Faced with the infinite past, with a certain humility, it is better, in his view, to make a choice: apply a clearly defined analytic framework of the past in a rational way.

Later critiques, formulated in the 1970s, were even less generous. In *The Poverty of Theory*, E. P. Thompson leveled his since-famous formula:

> [T]he self-extrapolating programmed developmental series; the mildly disequilibrated equilibrium models, in which dissensus strays unhappily down strange corridors, searching for a reconciliation with consensus; the systems-analyses and structuralisms, with their torques and their combinatories; the counter-factual fictions; the econometric and cleometric groovers—all of these theories hobble along programmed routes from one static category to the next. And all of them are *Geschichtenscheissenschlopff*, unhistorical shit."[9]

This critique was targeting Robert Fogel's cliometry. It is part of the book's general framework, which stigmatizes the tendency toward theorization of the conception of history, and in particular Marxist abstraction as developed by Althusser, whose audience was gaining steam across Europe. Thompson reproaches Althusser for dehistoricizing the notion of class. In his view, the historian must carry out a more dialectical and comprehensive approach to the past on the basis of an intimate knowledge of the archives in order to find conflicts, contradictions, and the experience of actors and their agency instead of inventing reassuring ex post facto reconstructions. In this perspective, the mathematical reduction imposed by cliometrics and the schematic vision of the mechanisms underlying it threaten to be a counterproductive illusion.

Eric Hobsbawm's critique during roughly the same period shared a similar perspective, though it was aimed toward a different purpose. Counterfactual reasoning, he argued, is often centered on the actor, and in particular the "great man." As a result, it tends to set aside the dramatic or happy consequences of a crucial decision. In an article from 1974, the British historian noted that it risked promoting a flat and relatively useless "heroic history." Hobsbawm preferred to put value on a *longue durée* analysis of socioeconomic processes.[10] "History is what happened, not what might have happened," he argues, before recognizing: "Now sometimes the probabilities are so high that we can speculate with some realism, normally about what couldn't have happened rather than what could." This comment bares resemblance to another famous critique by Marc Bloch, which is less common in the Anglophone debate, on historical inquiry into the famous shots fired on the Boulevard des Capucines in February 1848: Would the Revolution of 1848 have taken place without them? This question, notes the father of the Annales school, is vain to the extent that it risks missing the essential issue of the *longue durée.* This oversight is problematic, since "what is most profound in history is also what is the most certain."[11]

The gathering of these three authors into Hawthorn's text, designed to serve as a breviary of anti-counterfactual criticism, is not without merit: all three are giants of British historiography, situated on the left of the political spectrum with a focus on economic and social history. At the same time, however, it is also possible to reexamine this trio, if only because the dates, the authors, and the critiques they focused on and the importance they accorded to counterfactualism itself varied. Above all, Hawthorn was looking to reveal the originality of his approach. Building on a British academic tradition, with its experiments and rejections, he hoped to offer a true scientific analysis of the possibilities of counterfactual reasoning. Three years later, Niall Ferguson offered a similar collection in his *Virtual History.* He revisited the critical tradition of Carr, Thompson, and Hobsbawm, but this time in opposition to what he referred to as the "determinisms" of religion, materialism, and linguistics.[12] He more explicitly attacked Marxist-inspired social and economic history in favor of a relational approach that refused simple models of causation, highlighting his anti-communism.

These elements of discord benefited from a favorable context and are still discussed today. They have also contributed to the internationalization of this form of history. They provide a partial model of the attractions and critiques, the definitions and the propositions, as well as the problems that are associated with them and then taken up in different countries and their disciplinary fields.

"IMPERIAL" RELAYS

The first areas of dissemination included regions under British and the US influence, either for historical, economic, or political reasons. Thus, for example, works of counterfactual history have been produced in the former

British dominions or colonies, where their influence remains strong, at least on an intellectual level. The most remarkable case is no doubt India, where Robert Fogel inspired works in this vein long before the appearance of Ferguson's work. As Sanjay Subrahmanyam reminds us in his article on the question, it is one of the only countries where counterfactual history constitutes a separate genre of its own, nourished by debates around how colonization struck down a great Indian power.[13] The classic work of reference is the much discussed *Private Investment in India, 1900–1939* by Amiya Kumar Bagchi, which was originally defended as a thesis at Cambridge.[14] The book argues that Indian entrepreneurs did not have the means to develop because of the omnipotence of European capitalists and large colonial firms. The development of the subcontinent would have been more precocious, even if it quickly caught up after independence. Counterfactual history was early on integrated into the university pedagogy, most notably at the University of New Delhi in courses on economic history in the 1960s and 1970s. It taught a version of nationalist historiography that attempted to respond to a recurrent question: What would India have become in the absence of the British colonial state? To which the student was supposed to respond, using the material from the course, that it would have been more developed, more powerful, dominated south Asia, and so on. This is probably one of the most deeply anchored and most solid, but also most political, traditions within the counterfactual approach.[15]

Though less institutionalized, it has also been prevalent in Australia, as attested by the thesis of Paul Burns, which was published in 1998 under the title *The Brisbane Line Controversy*.[16] In this analysis of military strategy, the author imagined a Japanese invasion of Australia during the Second World War, which was one of the country's great fears in 1942. The simulation calls into question the existence of a plan that sought to abandon the northern portion of the island above the Brisbane Line, to Japanese forces, in order to facilitate the defense of the rest of the territory. The "Brisbane Line controversy," revealed in 1942, was at the origin of the Labour Party's victory in 1943. The author suggests that the myth was used to hide the government's insufficiencies in matters of defense and electoral issues. Closer to the current modes of counterfactual history is the work *What If? Counterfactual Essays in Australian History* edited by Stuart Macintyre and Sean Scalmer, which appeared in 2006.[17] The former, a graduate of Cambridge University, most notably edited *The Oxford History of Australia,* while the latter worked on political and social movements in Australia. The work explicitly takes up the historiographical proposals of Niall Ferguson. Following this model, the book includes articles by researchers who study the bifurcating moments deemed significant in Australian history: the possible French colonization of Tasmania in the eighteenth century, the Gallipoli Campaign during World War I, a less assimilationist politics for the Wiradjuri populations, and so on. As opposed to its Indian version, this Australian counterfactual history appears quite similar to the British tradition. It focuses on the two great wars, the role of different governments or heads of state, but has rarely (only on one occasion) evoked the moment of British colonization as a turning point. In some sense, the essays propose another form of history written by the descendants of immigrants from Old Europe.

Other attempts have been pursued in Oceania. In 2005, a conference on "what-if" history dedicated to the history of New Zealand brought together political scientists and historians from the universities of Victoria, Auckland, and Otago. It was held at the University of Victoria and organized by a professor of political science, Stephen Levine. The introduction to the book drawn from the conference evokes a number of references, including the works of Geoffrey Hawthorn, but does not mention Ferguson.[18] The work's ambition is similar to its predecessors': "to combat the deeply rooted human propensity to see the future as more contingent than the past." And to transform "our world from a static and predictable place, filled with inevitabilities, into a dynamic environment, one in which at every moment there are unfulfilled possibilities, each possessing unknowable consequences." The turning points that they pursue are equally interesting: next to case studies from the country's history (the Treaty of Waitangi in 1840,[19] the founding of the Commonwealth of New Zealand in 1907, the two world wars, or the threat of Japanese invasion in 1942), they also envisage more original situations, such as the perception of the first great strikes on the perspective of social classes, or the role of the Save Manapouri[20] movement in the emergence of environmental awareness.

The same influence can be found in Latin American countries, probably more marked by the proximity of their US neighbor, even if the circulation of ideas obviously obeys more circuitous routes than mere proximity. There is no single work in this case that explicitly claims to champion such an approach. There are, however, a few traces indicating that a discussion took place. In 2005, for example, the economic historian John H. Coatsworth from Harvard University wrote a short article, "Counterfactual Mexicos," which spans Mexican history—especially Spanish colonization—through the lens of "what if."[21] The references here are certainly not solely to US researchers. In 2003 and 2007, the professor of political economy and Brazilian diplomat Paulo Roberto de Almeida published two articles, "História virtual: Limites e possibilidades" and "História virtual do Brasil."[22] The former made explicit reference to Fogel and Ferguson as it asked what would have happened to Brazil if the lineage of the Tordesillas had remained where Pope Alexandre VI had placed it, that is in the middle of the ocean. The very idea of "Brazil," he notes, would probably not have existed. More abstractly, the question allows the author to emphasize the importance of "historical contingency." In Colombia, Victor Hugo Palacios Cruz, a philosopher from the University of Bogota, also engaged in a reflection on this approach in a conference at the University of La Sabana in 2003.[23] In Mexico, the literary journal of reference *Letras Libres* proposed in 2008 a special issue dedicated to exercises in counterfactual history.[24] Presented by Humberto Beck, these essays were written by Mexican or American writers and historians.[25] One can find John Coatsworth, Federico Navarrete, the historian of "indigenous" peoples at the National Autonomous University of Mexico City, or even the novelist and poet José Emilio Pacheco. The issue placed itself overtly under the sign of a dual inspiration: literature and social science. Vladimir Nabokov, José Saramago, and Philip K. Dick are referenced, as are Edward H. Carr, Niall Ferguson, and Hugh Trevor-Roper. As for the turning points staged by these political analyses and literary exercises, they are always adapted to the place of production: they treat the French conquest, the expulsion of the Jesuits, or the guerrilla war of 1847.[26] That this well-known journal of the Hispanic world devoted an entire issue to the approach is indicative of a certain curiosity, at the very least.

Counterfactual history has thus spread to different regions, through historians, but also politicians, philosophers, literary scholars, and many others. The influence of the Anglophone "what if" has not only marked the former colonies but has also been exported to Europe.

EUROPEAN OFFSHOOTS

The country that most directly borrowed from the Anglophone approach to counterfactual history is undoubtedly Spain, where the translation of Ferguson appeared as early as 1998.[27] In 2004, the collective volume *Historia virtual de España* (1870–2004) was published by Nigel Townson. This book presents features already employed by others who have promoted the approach. After having attended Cambridge and defending his doctoral thesis in London, Townson became a lecturer in the history of political thought and social movements at Complutense University of Madrid. The volume gathered reputed Spanish researchers, most of them from Complutense (Javier Tusell, José Álvarez Junco, Pablo Martin Aceña), as well as some foreign historians (Edward Malefakis, Charles Powell[28]). The introduction evokes Anglophone work and offers an analysis similar to that of Ferguson: the book is not a political exercise or a historical fantasy, but rather a tool of analysis mobilized against a whole set of determinisms. The subjects differ somewhat from those targeted by Niall Ferguson, since Nigel Townson seeks to contradict Charles Darwin, Karl Marx, George Trevelyan, as well as the total history of Fernand Braudel. Various turning points in Spanish history are envisaged, such as the vacancy of the throne in 1870 (which culminated in the Franco-Prussian War), the loss of the colonial empire following the war against the United States in 1898, the Civil War of 1936, and the rise of Franco and even the Aznar government.

As for other European countries, there are works of counterfactual history by Ukrainians, Norwegians, and Poles, though the language barrier has limited our exploration of these regions.[29] In Italy, the approach remained of little interest to historians for many years.[30] A cycle of meetings was devoted to the question in Rimini in 2005, without any Italian historians present. The following year, the historian Emilio Gentile proposed a counterfactual reflection on fascism: "What if Mussolini had not entered the war in 1940?"[31] Then the 150th anniversary of Italian unification gave the journalist and historian Pasquale Chessa an opportunity to publish a short book of counterfactual essays, with the participation of well-known politicians and historians (Giuseppe Berta of Bocconi University, Mario Isnenghi of the University of Venice, and Gentile from the University of Rome).[32] In his introduction, Pasquale Chessa invokes François Rabelais, Niall Ferguson, Robert Cowley, John Squire, Philip K. Dick, and Philip Roth, to whom he adds some Italian references: the reticence of Benedetto Croce (*La Storia come pensiero e come azione,* 1938) or recent articles by Italian journalists and historians such as Gian Enrico Rusconi and Sergio Romano.[33] The introduction recalls the relative lack of interest for this kind of approach in Italy, whether in the public debate or in the broader scientific discussion, for various reasons: counterfactual history, associated with intellectual acrobatics, is considered an Anglophone practice, which further suffered from Ferguson's anti-determinism and anti-Marxism. Chessa, however, insisted on its relevance for understanding Italian history, and in particular the period of unification, with its projections, points of bifurcation, and retrospective readings.[34]

This form of historical reasoning developed in other directions as well, for example, in German-speaking countries, where the "*kontrafaktische Geschichte*" or "*virtuelle Geschichte*" has followed a unique path. The first text to claim the approach, *Ungeschehene Geschichte* (*History That Never Happened*), appeared in 1986 and participated specifically in ancient historiography. Its editor, Alexander Demandt, was a professor of ancient history at the Free University of Berlin. The book was drawn from a seminar on methodology organized by the modern historian Hagen Schulze at the Free University in the winter semester of 1983–1984, which seems to have been subject to heavy controversy.[35] The references mobilized by Alexander Demandt were part of a specific intellectual universe with respect to those discussed thus far. No doubt the epigraph is taken from Pascal on Cleopatra's nose, and opens with a quotation of Nietzsche pondering the question: "What would have happened if this or that had not happened?" as "the cardinal question."[36] Presented as both an epistemological and an empirical contribution, the work was written in four parts: a first part evokes the obstacles to the approach; a second explains its objectives; the third proposes exercises in which one can find well-known events and figures (the Battle of Marathon, Alexander the Great, and Brutus all the way to Hitler); the last introduces questions that remain unanswered. It also sketches another intellectual tradition. Over the course of the analysis, Alexander Demandt signals individuals who could be considered opponents to this approach and others who could be considered to be inspired by it. Johann Gottfried von Herder (1744–1803), Leopold von Ranke (1795–1886, the "father" of objective German history starting in 1824), the medievalist Karl Hampe (1869–1936), and the historian and philosopher Golo Mann (1909–1994) all belonged to this first group. The second group included Martin Luther (1482–1546), Max Weber (1864–1920), the physicist Carl Friedrich von Weizsäcker (1979), the philosopher Ludwig Wittgenstein (1889–1951), and the historian Thomas Nipperdey, author of one of the classic references of German history. Eluding British works, the volume traces a purely German philosophical and historical genealogy.

The works that followed reinforced this approach in German historiography. Between 1990 and 2010, at least six works of counterfactual, alternative, or virtual history were published. The books of Geoffrey Hawthorn, Niall Ferguson, and even Robert Cowley were translated very early in 1994, 1999, and 2006, while that of Alexander Demandt was translated into English in 1993.[37] The latter was republished in Germany in 2005, followed by another book in 2010, entitled *Es hätte auch anders kommen können: Wendepunkte deutscher Geschichte* (It could have been different: Turning points in German history).[38] In the meantime, the approach has generated particular interest among historians of antiquity as witnessed by the book *Virtuelle Antike* by historian Kai Brodersen.[39] Another movement took place around the University of Kiel, with the volume edited by the professor of modern history Michael Salewski, *Was Wäre Wenn, Alternativ- und Parallelgeschichte: Brücken zwischen Phantasie und Wirklichkeit.*[40] Bringing together historians of different periods from the Universities of Kiel, Jena, Griefswald, Berlin, and Wisconsin—Madison (United States), the work was also divided into a theoretical section and a series of counterfactual narratives ("Facts and Counterfacts"). Some *Wendepunkte* were classics (the sacking of Rome, Hitler), and others were more specific to German history (the defeat at Auerstaedt in 1806, the Battle of Verdun in 1916). In the introduction, Michael Salewski evokes the work of Robert Fogel and Geoffrey Hawthorn, without mentioning the work of Ferguson, and he lists several other German language precedents, including the publications of Demandt.[41] The reflection here again intends to fit into another lineage, including Plato, Immanuel Kant, George Berkeley, Karl Jaspers, or Jon Elster.[42] In this collective work, the authors also mobilize other stimulating references, which the Anglophone works previously mentioned make little mention of: Peter Burke, Reinhart Koselleck, or Hayden White.

In other words, there is a tradition between history and philosophy in the German universities wherein the two disciplines are often studied simultaneously. The approach can therefore be one of the theoretical tools that is usable in the context of university research. Joachim Losehand, historian of antiquity in Vienna, for example, dedicated an entire portion of his thesis to counterfactual reasoning applied to the "last days of Pompeii."[43] The work revisits the biography of Julius Caesar's rival, who was killed by Ptolemy XIII during his flight to Egypt. After studying the life of Pompey and his last days, Losehand pursues a controlled counterfactual exercise, inspired by the work of Robert Fogel, Niall Ferguson, and Kai Brodersen, entitled "Not the last days of Pompey" (Nicht die letzten Tage des Pompeius). We will return to this project later.

Though it is subject to critique, as elsewhere, the counterfactual approach seems to have stimulated interest more easily. It has found its way into pedagogical practices: the University of Cologne proposed in 2004 courses on "counterfactual history" in the context of the themes of "history and philosophy, history and dialectics."[44] Exchanges with the Anglophone tradition exist, as demonstrated by the Centre for British Studies at the Humboldt University of Berlin, where German and American researchers came to discuss the strengths and weaknesses of the approach.[45] The papers were published in the special issue of the *Historical Social Review (Historische Sozialforschung)* in 2009: "Counterfactual thinking as a scientific method" (Kontrafaktisches Denken als wissenschaftliche Method").[46] Finally, in 2012 another pluridisciplinary research team was created that brought together the universities of Konstanz, Geneva, Bochum, and Humboldt University of Berlin around the program with a suggestive title: What If? On the Meaning, Epistemology, and Scientific Relevance of Counterfactual Claims and Thought Experiments. The project was more specifically epistemological: it sought to reflect on the status and functions of conditional reasoning in general, and counterfactual reasoning in particular, in literature, physical sciences, biology, psychology, and neurosciences, but also in the human sciences. It contained a historical aspect, which was reflexive, dedicated to the study of uses of counterfactual reason in history and philosophy at the turn of the twentieth century.[47]

Thus, since the 2000s, the counterfactual approach in history has been spreading unevenly on a global scale, adapting each time to the geopolitical, academic, historical, and intellectual configurations in place. The numerous and varied circulations of counterfactual reasoning eventually blur or enrich the initial questionnaire, proposing a more open set of problems. In this global context, the singularity of the France case offers an important perspective.

A THWARTED PRESENCE IN FRANCE?

Restricting the focus on the case of France makes it possible to grasp the logics of reception in greater detail and at the same time to better understand the conditions of production of research in this field. The absence of a frank, even critical, discussion about the capacity of the counterfactual approach as a tool of analysis is patent. And yet it was French historians who took an early interest in this approach in the nineteenth century, mobilizing more or less implicit counterfactual modes in their writing practices. Fernand Braudel employed this type of reasoning a dozen times in his famous study of the Mediterranean.[48] He explains, for example, in the second volume: "What had failed to occur was by no means an impossibility. It is not entirely fanciful to imagine a French Empire supported by Florence in the same way that the Spanish Empire (though not at first, it is true) was supported by Genoa."[49] In other places, he used the method more directly:

> One has only to think of what Philip II might have been—ruler over both England and the German empire—to appreciate the immense significance of these events. The title of emperor, even stripped of all substance, would have avoided the irritating disputes about precedence: it would have reinforced Spanish authority in Italy and conferred upon the war against the Turks, both on the plains of Hungary and in the Mediterranean, a single command. Moreover, with the support or neutrality of England, the war of the Netherlands would have gone very differently, and the struggle for control of the Atlantic, which dominated the second part of the century, would not have ended in disaster. But above all, who could fail to see that the center of gravity of Philip II's empire was being shifted from the North to the South by force of circumstances? The Peace of Cateau-Cambrésis, by confirming the Spanish presence in Italy, helped to make southern Europe the focus of the foreign policy of the Catholic King at the expense of other more urgent and possibly more fruitful endeavours.[50]

Such digressions are inscribed into a Braudelian logic: they allow him to play with events, the "foam" (*écume*) of history in his words, so that he may insist on the more stable structures of the *longue durée.* But, more generally, the use of "if" is commonplace in the historian's texts, even if it has not been consciously practiced or declared to be a method as such.

There have been other more direct invitations to pursue this method, but they have remained discreet. They appeared with reference to Fogel in works of historical demography. Hervé Le Bras, for example, developed "realistic fictions" to analyze the trajectory of the French population.[51] The approach is mentioned more cautiously in certain works of economic history, wherein statistics play an important role.[52] Suggestions have also been made by historians who have been attentive to narrative and imagination. Jacques Revel, citing the excesses of Robert Fogel's attempts, proposed such narrative possibilities.[53] More recently, in his reflections on the relationship between theater and history, Gérard Noiriel expressed interest in a footnote for "this new area of research"—that is, Ferguson's virtual history—as a means of mobilizing the historical imagination to enrich our analyses of the past.[54] Moreover, it is interesting to note that such suggestions for reflection on the specific resources for narration and imagination in this reasoning appear more specific to France, even if researchers remain cautious.

More revealing, no doubt, have been the failings of some of the more overt attempts. This was most notably the case with the experiment of alter-history proposed in the 1990s by Daniel Milo and Alain Boureau.[55] It was a question of submitting the narrative and the historical modes of reasoning to radical forms of experimentation aimed at destabilizing the mental habitus of historians. "Historical possibilism" or "counterfactualism" was part of the panoply of methods that were envisaged, alongside new approaches to sources, as well as comparativism and anachronism. Daniel Milo pointed out the value of this approach in an article published in the *Annales.*[56] Drawing in part its inspiration from Robert Musil's *The Man Without Qualities,*[57] he wrote:

> If the field of possibilities in a given historical moment is infinite, it is never unlimited. It is incumbent upon the historian to push back the limits, that is to say, to define the impossible of that particular moment; to reconstruct the passage from the possible to the realized; to retrace the process of rewriting the possibilities in deterministic terms, which is a universal tendency: the possible aspires to become necessary in order to escape randomness (or arbitrariness). He also responds to the rolling of the Aristotelian dice, according to which history treats only what really took place, leaving poetry and philosophy to reflect upon the possible and the necessary.[58]

Milo proposed the stimulating idea of shifting the starting dates of our era. Had it not been Jesus's circumcision that had been chosen, but the Passion, all of our dates would be shifted by thirty-three years. This simple displacement would alter our representation of historical periods: the eighteenth century would become the "Age of Enlightenment and Romanticism," while the October Revolution, World War I, and Einstein would be part of the nineteenth century. The experiment reveals the arbitrariness of certain conventions of historical thought: this exercise, Milo writes, invites us to "de-autonomize [the] notion of the century." The proposal was made, among many others, in the mode of an experiment and provocation. Overall the program was poorly received or ignored by historians. "We were extraordinarily naïve,"[59] Alain Boureau explained later. And thus one of the rare attempts to elaborate the possibilities of counterfactual history in France was brought to a close.

Other stimulating propositions were also promised and then forgotten. This was the case for a subsection of Antoine Prost's historiographical work

Twelve Lessons on History, clearly entitled "Writing History with Ifs."[60] The theme provides a transition between the role of imagination in history and the question of causality. The reflection is based on the experiments of Robert Fogel, but the chapter develops a more original argument. In turn, Antoine Prost reconstructs a French genealogy of the process. While recalling the role of Max Weber, he also invokes the works of Paul Lacombe and Raymond Aron, to which we shall return.[61] He then proposes an example of social history from the work of Jay Winter, who was teaching at Cambridge. This was part of the debate on the disastrous demographic effects of the 1914–1918 war on civil society. Numerous studies have shown that the war interrupted a steady, or even slightly upward growth curve leading to "higher civilian mortality," that is, a greater number of civilian deaths than in times of peace. This last claim, Antoine Prost notes, is already in itself an implicit counterfactual: it presupposes a comparison with what would have happened without the war. The author proposes to make it explicit in order to clarify the analysis: if we take into account female deaths (women who were not on the front lines) and statistical projections, it would seem that from 1915 to 1917 there were "fewer female deaths than there should have been, if everything else had been normal," whether in France or in England.[62] These societies thus succeeded in preserving the living conditions of their civilian population during the war, unlike Germany, for example. In his view, it is "an irrefutable example" of an approach that he deems "perfectly legitimate."[63] The author then turns to a more in-depth argumentation about the "past, present and future of the past," closer to what we will treat in our discussion of past futures, which have been explicitly nourished by the reflections of Paul Ricoeur and Reinhart Koselleck. The chapter thus distinguishes between original uses, that is, between a hierarchy of causes and an emphasis on the unpredictability of the past, which in his view go hand in hand. Although he still relies on Fogel, Antoine Prost emphasizes the value of counterfactual analyses of causality and draws ambitious consequences. "Anchored in reality and armed with social knowledge, the imaginary experience leads the historian to identify past possibilities which were objective but which were not realized and which were therefore not necessary, but merely probable. The difficulty . . . is to assign to each objective possibility an adequate degree of probability."

This difficulty no doubt explains why he formulates a specific proposal. The chapter concludes with a discussion of the fragility of history at this stage and the crucial problem of the search for truth, which is the subject of the following chapter. "French historians," writes Antoine Prost, "have generally remained reluctant to pursue this approach." Indeed, in spite of the fact that this suggestive text was taken from a historiography course at the University of Paris Panthéon-Sorbonne and therefore is well-known to students, it has enjoyed few acolytes.

It would seem that in France, in spite of these reflections, the counterfactual approach is not, indeed cannot, be considered relevant or taken seriously by historians. This is what, in their own way, Fabrice d'Almeida and Anthony Rowley suggest in their volume *Et si on refaisait l'histoire?*[64] The book, published as articles in the "summer series" in 2008 in the weekly leftist magazine *Marianne,* was written for a general audience with playful, short texts without references. As a result, the book attracted public attention without having any real impact on the academic world. The situation seems to have taken a turn in recent years, however, especially since our project began in 2009. The publication in 2010 of a book devoted to the possible alternative scenarios of May–June 1940, entitled *1940: What If France Had Continued Fighting the War? An Essay in Alternative History,* based on an Internet forum discussion, enjoyed enough success in bookstores that a sequel was published.[65] And yet it has been the object of no book review in academic circles. It is noteworthy that the first substantive discussions were proposed by reviews like *Labyrinthe* and *Tracés,* or in research seminars, which tend to be more interested in epistemological questions, or so-called "undisciplined" approaches, including social sciences interested in history.[66]

In France, concern for this approach is relatively recent and has taken a winding path. French historians have resisted and not taken it seriously enough to debate it within a university context. The question, however, is not whether the approach is known or not, but rather why it has not, for the moment, been openly considered worthy of interest.

THE HISTORY OF AN ABSENCE

Answering that question is no easy task, especially if one hopes to avoid base generalities about "French" approaches as opposed to so-called "American" or "British" approaches to history—perceived as respectively "profound" as opposed to "ample"[67]—and thereby to reify national intellects.[68] The story of a failure may, however, provide the opportunity to question "national traditions within the social sciences."[69] While it is well-trodden, this realm of reflection is still new enough within the discipline of history that we can do little more than venture a few conjectures.[70] First, does not this lack of interest simply reflect the relatively weak international openness of French research? According to Gisèle Sapiro and Ioana Popa, the rate of translation into French in the social sciences is indeed particularly low.[71] The choice of translated authors also usually corresponds to those who have already been recognized in the field or have a place in the French academic world. This explanation remains insufficient, however, in itself. On the one hand, there are resources available in French, which, though old, could have generated reflection in this direction. On the other hand, as Christophe Charle suggests, foreign references in France tend to be sporadic, coming in fits and starts, and are used to pose questions within the national historiographical field.[72]

It is therefore necessary to suggest other, more historical explanations. At the end of the nineteenth century, the imperative of objectivity and the emergence of new more scientific demands, often inspired by the natural sciences, impacted western Europe and the United States differently. In France, the historical method of Gabriel Monod was characterized by the importation of German erudition and a rejection of Romantic history. Moreover, it needed to respond to the vigorous criticisms of Durkheim's sociology, before the Annales school appropriated part of its heritage.[73] However, French sociology, based on the journal *L'Année sociologique* and a coherent research program, was structured in ways that were not dissimilar to that of Germany or England. This situation may have led historians to focus on certain specific methodological traits. For example, the socioeconomic history of Ernest Labrousse and then French structuralism took on a more specifically "scientific" color than they did elsewhere. In England, while building on a similar intellectual foundation, that is Marxism, historical approaches proved to be less quantitative and more concerned with the notion of "experience," as demonstrated by Edward P. Thompson's studies and those who followed. In the opposite direction, the more theoretical and radical proposals by US historians, particularly those associated with "postmodernism,"[74] cultural studies, postcolonial studies, or the "linguistic turn," never took root as such.

Second, from an academic perspective, the institutionalization of the disciplines within the university system at the end of the nineteenth century (the creation of chairs and professorships, new recruitment methods, the construction of a professional identity) took place on a European scale, characterized by the transnational circulation of knowledge and practices. But like its neighbors, France retained certain characteristics because of its long academic history. This was the case, for example, with the recruitment by examination and the competition between the universities and the *grandes écoles* (elite institutions with entrance based on competitive examination). Similarly, the state in the French Republic conferred a particular importance on the discipline of history in the project of defining the nation and in republican pedagogy. In spite of the profound changes that marked the academic world in the years to come, the singularities of the French university system remain: the variety of institutional forms (universities, the National Centre for Scientific Research/CNRS, *grandes écoles, grands établissements*), the strength of a professional identity, which is particularly closed off from amateur historians, the lifetime tenure of research professors, and so on.

These scientific and academic aspects complement one another.[75] A third explanation, of a social order, is equally important. That is, the place of the national narrative within French society. An object of considerable tensions within French debates,[76] it may be more difficult to play with. To this may be added the relationship between university research and the primary and secondary school system in France. Even if all knowledge does not systematically circulate from postsecondary education down to the secondary and primary levels, they contribute to the constitution of a specific "school culture" within French society. According to Pierre Bourdieu, this "school culture" is characterized by the "possibilities of invention and closures of improvisation" peculiar to France and its longer history.[77] In this sense, reluctance to the counterfactual approach and the difficulty of taking it seriously has spread beyond the field of the university. And yet, as we have seen, it is in France that the question of fiction and narration within counterfactual narratives was posed in the clearest terms. In this sense, the singularity of the French case, precisely because of its resistance to the "what if," may paradoxically be an effective starting point for shifting the terms of the debate and making room for new propositions.

This geography of the uses of counterfactual reasoning in history confirms its great diversity. It has generated debate everywhere. And in each case it would seem that it must be tested against the national narrative to reach an audience of specialists or amateurs. Thus, paradoxically, these circulations of counterfactual practices underline the resistance to this conception of history and the "methodological nationalism" of our current phase of globalization.

CHAPTER 3

From Pterodactyls to Piccadilly Circus

UCHRONIAS OF THE NINETEENTH AND TWENTIETH CENTURIES

> As Kim moves back in time he leaves a wake of disasters behind him, which is only logical since he is retracing his space in time, leaving a time vacuum behind him. . . . Traveling back in time is like being at the controls of an intricate ship that requires the most delicate and precise touch to steer through shallows and reefs and enemy fire.
>
> —William S. Burroughs[1]

We cannot fully grasp the current state of counterfactual history without examining uchronia in its more explicitly "literary" sense. Mentions of "what-if" history and revisions of the past spontaneously bring to mind H. G. Wells's famous time machine.[2] And the epigraph quoted above from William S. Burroughs's *The Place of Dead Roads* indicates how widely accepted this type of fictional voyage has become. No doubt it is even more common, or in any case solicits less reluctance in literary genres than within historical writing. But at the same time, Burroughs also raises an interesting problem. Through Kim's (the ambiguous lead character's) tribulations, the novel explores the very limits of literature, working on the literary material itself through the so-called practice of "cut-up." Alongside the deconstruction of supposedly "popular" forms, such as westerns, gangster narratives, and fantasy stories, or the search for a "primal scream," Burroughs's voyage into the past and its consequences come to be one of those rich and dangerous "places of dead roads." If uchronia is defined by its playful nature—a point that actually must be taken quite seriously—it must also be noted that it is a literary form with its own set of techniques, which cannot be ignored, precisely because they draw us toward such "places." Such explorations are not without their dangers, however. Though the definition of uchronia seems simple enough—"a work of fiction based on the principle of the divergence of a historical event that has actually existed in our chronology, usually at what is considered a critical moment in history"[3]—it can take various forms and operate in different registers. So we must guard against overly rigid definitions and boundaries between genres as we approach a literary world full of surprising contrasts.

THE NINETEENTH CENTURY: PLAYING WITH TEMPORAL ORDERS

We have already explored how the fictional reinvention of the past developed its own set of writing practices in Europe and the United States since the end of the eighteenth century. We now turn then to its more specifically literary manifestations.

Thomas Pavel recalls that the nineteenth century, for reasons suggested earlier, was also a moment when the novel increasingly focused on geographical and historical contextualization, as seen notably in the works of Balzac and Flaubert. Authors abandoned idealism and the search for absolutes that had occupied previous writers and returned to the "real." In so doing, these works harbored a specific ambition: bringing forward a new order and organization.[4] This approach participated in the previously discussed intention to master a new "modern" regime of historicity through novelistic writing. Of course, such explicitly literary uses were also motivated by creative intentions as well as, in some cases, a simple desire to entertain.

Joseph Mery's (1797–1866) novel *A History That Did Not Happen* published in 1854 illustrates this tendency. Mery was a polygraph who ran in the Romantic literary circles of the first half of the nineteenth century and also wrote texts on ruins, the Moon, and possible futures (*The Ruins of Paris, Future Paris, The Lunarians*).[5] Mery exploited anew the well-worn path of Napoleonic possibilities, with an original take on the Egypt campaign and the failure of the Bonapartist expedition in Saint-Jean-d'Acre at the foot of an old tower significantly called "the Cursed": "the fate of the world resides in that tower," Bonaparte supposedly claimed. Referring to Athenians, Romans, Alexander the Great, and Hernán Cortés, Joseph Mery imagined the consequences of such a victory: it would have modified our understanding of the opposition between East and West and created a likeness between Napoleon and Alexander the Great, since he would have become the emperor of India.

The story describes the arrival of Napoleon on the subcontinent as the result of a peace, which awakened the Indians "after a long sleep." The meeting of the two worlds opened the door to a fecund partnership:

> The West let out a scream of enthusiasm heard across the two neighboring seas; the East responded with a religious hymn, in this harmonious language, made of golden notes, the sound of pearls, the sweet melody of the waves, the murmurings of palm trees, and the rays of sunshine. All ranks joined together: people and soldiers, conquerors and conquered, joining hands, laying down their weapons, the banners, the flags; there was neither victory nor vanquished. Everyone entered the capital city at nightfall and the day was immediately lit by the thousand lights of Bengal, that allowed all people to contemplate the young French hero, framed in an aureole of apotheosis, on the horizon of the Indian sky.[6]

In his preface, Mery emphasizes the oneiric quality of his text. The idea supposedly came from a rather meaningless discussion in front of an omnibus stop, the symbol of an increasingly mechanized Paris. At once romantic and disenchanted, imbued with dreams of writing a great history and the grayness of everyday life, the tone of the text was characteristic of a disillusionment that fell upon French authors and intellectuals after the Revolutions of 1848.[7] "We console ourselves with dreams, as our nightly fabrications often compensate the truths of daylight," he concludes. The political intent is obvious but would seem to be based more on the moral comfort produced through the exercise of the imagination than on the search for a critical reflection on the meaning of history. The text thus bears witness once again to the many possible gradations within nineteenth-century counterfactual narratives.

1914–1980: *FICTIONALIZING UCHRONIA*

A slow change occurred at the beginning of the twentieth century, at variable intervals depending on the location: this narrative form slowly took on a more literary register, and its achievements were increasingly defined and associated with the world of fiction. There were still many overlaps, particularly in England where political leaders and historians cultivated such narratives on the margins of their work. Nonetheless, there was a gradual tendency toward literary forms. Jacques Rigaut, who was close to the surrealists, amused himself in 1921 by imagining a time traveler who provoked ridiculous historical changes in *A Brilliant Subject.* Cleopatra underwent cosmetic surgery that mistreated her nose, and Jesus poisoned a child. In England, Guy Dent published *The Emperor of Ifs* in 1926, which drew its originality from the period it covered: prehistory followed a different course, England avoided glaciation, and humanity lived a very different history in which pterodactyls flew above Piccadilly Circus.[8] A new mutation started in the 1930s through the reappropriation of cheap and popular American pulp magazines. The temporality of these studies was less rigorous. There were also fewer attempts at any real coherence, because the focus was on the creation of new universes. For example, in "Sidewise in Time," published in 1934 in the science fiction flagship journal *Astounding,* Murray Leinster described a world in which several historical periods existed simultaneously as a result of a spatiotemporal rupture. The man who predicted the cataclysm, Professor Minott, discovers an America where the sequoia forests have sprung up, where a Roman legion appears around St. Louis, Missouri, and Chinese villages occupy the shores of the Potomac. Uchronia moved into a new register, gradually becoming a branch of science fiction and a genre in its own right.[9]

This fictionalization resulted in part from a methodological transformation and the search for objectivity that characterized the historical discipline at the beginning of the twentieth century. It was also part of a series of changes specific to the genre of the novel. After the concern with contextualization that marked the previous century, there emerged novels of "detachment" (Thomas Pavel), which were more concerned with the formal dimensions of writing. In the face of these new demands, uchronias and their distorted universes no doubt seemed more trivial and "popular." In addition, there was the literary event marked by the publication of H. G. Wells's *The Time Machine* in 1895. Considered by some to signal the birth of science fiction,[10] the work provided a narrative motor for time travel. From this moment on, its usage within literature grew steadily.

Uchronias became more popular after 1945 as a result of both the trauma of World War II and the expansion of mass culture through new medias. As early as 1941, Douglas Brown and Christopher Serpell imagined the world after Hitler's victory over the Allied powers (*If Hitler Comes*). Such anxieties flamed up after the end of the conflict. The most famous of the novels in this new wave was no doubt *The Sound of His Horn* by Sarban, published in 1952. An immediate best seller, it recounted the adventures of Alan Querdillon, an escaped German prisoner who was transported into an alternative future where the Reich had been victorious. The action took place in "the year 102 of the first German millennium, as fixed by our First Fuhrer and Immortal Spirit of Germanism, Adolf Hitler." And in a world where "the surgical excision from a perfect body of the element that lights it with in a human soul was not a nightmare fancy to her but a commonplace practice."[11] The practice of uchronia thrived in the 1960s. During this period some works became references. The most important among them, since it reached far beyond the limited circle of readers of science fiction, was no doubt *The Man in the High Castle* by Philip K. Dick, which once again tells a story of Nazi victory. In this case, however, its narrative virtuosity gave it a new dimension as it plunged the reader into a world wherein, after the victory of the Axis powers, the United States lived partially as a Japanese protectorate and underwent a wave of terror. In his chateau, a man writes a uchronia, "The Grasshopper Lies Heavy," that describes the world after the Allied victory (that is, the "real" history), which circulates clandestinely. In *The Alteration,* which appeared in 1976 and is also considered a reference, Kingsley Amis describes a Catholic England (the Reformation never took place), where science is shunned and the country stays on the margins of "modernity." The text is also marked by a series of implicit references, since in this universe, the authors of science fiction invent technological "dreams," such as electric lighting and the airplane. Among the rapidly growing number of titles during this period, it is also worth mentioning *The Iron Dream* by Norman Spinrad from 1973, which recounts a world in which Hitler emigrates to the United States. The story brings together pieces of a novel that Hitler supposedly wrote, which appeared in 1954 under the title *Lord of the Swastika.* The literary scholar Richard Saint-Gelais has spoken of it as a "uchronic artefact," since one discovers that it is a uchronia through the fragments the novel brings the reader to decipher.[12] Even more eccentric plots can also be found: in his 1978 *And Having Writ . . . ,* Donald Bensen[13] describes extraterrestrials arriving in San Francisco in 1908 and provoking a decisive technological transformation. They are then captured by Thomas Edison, who uses them to become what he had always dreamed of: president of the United States.

The transformation of uchronia since the nineteenth century is patent. Within science fiction, it lost in probability what it gained in narrative efficacy. This fictionalization was also characterized by other traits. Its literary nature and playful design became more pronounced; the characters were more imagined (as opposed to the "serious" speculation borrowed from history); and the novelist's attention focused less on the moment of bifurcation than on the universe that emerged as a result. The latter took on different forms: the new world could be better, nightmarish, or simply offer a lesson. As for the bifurcations, they could be simple or plural, limited or complete; or, in some cases, the narrative evoked parallel worlds. It is therefore difficult to classify uchronia as a simple "subgenre" of science fiction. A more precise appraisal might suggest that it occupies a unique place: whereas in sci-fi, it alters science and tends toward a future world, in a uchronia, fiction alters history and tends toward the past.

Such narratives obviously appear fanciful, not only to historians, but they must be carefully considered nonetheless. Precisely because of their popularity, they offer insight into the anxieties and apprehensions of a given period. Moreover, they develop formal properties and specific fictional universes: heeding Jean-Claude Vareille's warning, it is important not to take for granted the "false naïveté" that these "popular" narratives play upon and that deceive a critic who is too sure of him or herself.[14]

The world that didn't come to pass, into which uchronia offers a path, maintains a certain coherence, at the same time that it plays with the reader.[15] Such a nod to the reader is an essential aspect of this fundamentally interactive narrative. It makes a strong appearance at the beginning of the nineteenth century in Louis Geoffroy's *Napoleon and the Conquest of the World.* When he leaves to conquer the rest of the non-European world, Napoleon crosses on his route toward the Americas an island in the middle of the South Atlantic Ocean. Suddenly, "the Emperor grew pale, a cold sweat appeared and gleamed on his forehead; one might have spoken of an unknown danger, of a frightening apparition that had frozen his heart and soul. 'Saint Helena,' he said in a somber voice, and he let his head fall to his chest, as if struck by an acute pain."[16] The emperor finally bombards the island before going on his way. A similar act can be found in the work of Philip K. Dick. In *The Man in the High Castle,* the text that circulates among the people, a uchronia within a uchronia, contains significant disparities: in the supposed "true" version for the reader, Germany and Japan did indeed lose the war, but not until 1947, and Churchill still governs Great Britain in 1960. These subtle games remind us that these texts are by definition ironic and establish a knowing distance with the reader. *The Alteration* by Kingsley Amis goes further yet. It establishes three levels of reading, each reflecting one another: that of the uchronic narrative, the reader, and the uchronia within the uchronia, which, written by a mysterious author named "K. Dick," plays with the genre itself. The interlacing of the referents disorients the reader, giving the test a vertiginous effect.

The uchronic narrative is further distinguished by a very particular relationship to the "real." Though it is, by definition, excluded from the narrative, the real remains a hidden referent: the "other" history that is told only takes on meaning in relation to the "truth" that actually took place. This approach requires a comparative reading and the active participation of the reader: the reader must constantly fill in this separation him- or herself and thus maintain the gap necessary for interpretation. The effects of the uchronic novel go deeper still. By definition—since it depicts a bifurcation that actually took place in history—the text generates a split between the "real" and the "fictional." This effect can be expressed in several ways. For Thomas Pavel, all literary texts are heteronymous: they produce fiction based on elements taken from what is "real." This fact can be illustrated from the first pages of the novel *The Pickwick Papers* by Charles Dickens (1836–1837), in which Mr. Pickwick notices the pleasant weather: the sun and the umbrellas are elements that are borrowed from the real, while Mr. Pickwick is a literary invention. Novels depend on such crossings,[17] which uchronic writing attempts to undermine. Other specialists consider each text to be a performative "language game" whose aim and nature (fiction or nonfiction, for example) depends upon usage.[18] But there again, the uchronic text reduces any implicit literary foundation and provokes a breach in the ordinary status of the text. It becomes an open text, "in crisis," where the effect of the real is impossible. This dimension transforms it into an extremely rich literary technique, permitting the wildest extrapolations within a clearly defined framework and producing a sense of discomfort, but also power, which is no doubt reinforced by the fact that it has the ability to control time while simultaneously evoking its fragility. This makes it an original context for creation and partially explains the success of these works.

This advantage also has a consequence however: to work, the technique must rely on a bifurcation that is well-known to its readers. Otherwise, the author is forced to reveal the "thing," along the lines of Charles Renouvier in his postface. This explains why these texts draw upon a relatively elementary scholarly knowledge of "major events" and "great men." Hence, the poverty in the choice of referents because the characters or the moments of predilection are in fact relatively limited.[19] While they reflect the interests of their respective countries and build upon the supposed results of scientific discoveries, one may easily draft a short list of these bifurcations along the lines proposed by Éric Henriet: the Yucatan meteorite (that supposedly provoked the extinction of the dinosaurs sixty-five million years ago), the Roman Empire, Jesus, Charles Martel, Genghis Khan, Joan of Arc, the Reformation and/or Calvin, the discovery of the New World, Louis XIV, the American War of Independence, Napoleon, the American Civil War, World War I, the Russian Revolution, World War II, and so on. Echoes of the contemporary world can easily be found: "The Histronaut" by Paul Seabury, which appeared in 1963 in *The Magazine of Fantasy and Science Fiction,* for example, sits squarely within the context of the Cold War.[20] The author recounts the history of an American anti-communist who uses a time machine to travel back in time to explode the train that brought Lenin to Russia in 1917. The operation is a success. But he returns to his present day only to discover in horror that his country is under the control of the Nazis! May 1968 also inspired uchronic narratives in France. One of the most imaginative is Jorge Semprun's *L'Algarabie,* published in 1981. He imagines the death of General de Gaulle returning from Baden-Baden, in a helicopter accident. The event leads to a civil war that requires, among other plot twists, the intervention of the French actress Mireille Darc to free Orleans from the Gallic menace! Elsewhere, a novelist imagines a story in which de Gaulle was not killed in the accident, while discussions multiply in the "Zone of Popular Utopia" on the Left Bank of Paris.[21] These cases aside, the stories are more often inspired by the model of a Western universal history discussed earlier, structured by key dates, heroic figures, and great discoveries.[22]

1980–2010: *THE EXPANSION OF UCHRONIC GENRES (ALTERNATE HISTORY, STEAMPUNK, AND "ACADEMIC" LITERATURE)*

Uchronia, or alternate history,[23] has undergone an impressive period of growth since the 1980s. France has been no exception to this trend, as witnessed by the publication in 1983 of an anthology of uchronic writings assembled by Gérard Klein, entitled *Histoires de la quatrième dimension* (Histories of the Fourth Dimension).[24] Publishing houses, like Les Moutons électriques, created in 2004 by the writer André-François Ruaud, have been established with the ambition of publishing alternative histories in French.[25] Websites like La Portes des Mondes and Uchronies were created in 2009, providing the latest contributions on the subject.[26] Various works have described the state of the art, such as the previously cited Éric Henriet or the volume edited by André-François Ruaud, *Passés recomposés, anthologie uchronique,* which was published in 2003.[27] A French current has emerged in the context of these alternative projects, with new authors who engage in these "practices of the imaginary." Their approaches vary (they are writers, critics, academics, and so on), but they are brought together by the world of science fiction. One may cite P. J. G. Mergey, Johan Heliot, Ugo Bellagamba, among others. In 2009, Bellagamba published *Tancrède: Une uchronie,*[28] which traces the story of the young Tancredi, who left on a crusade to the Holy Land in 1096 before changing sides, disillusioned by the battles of the Crusaders. In search of his identity, he contributes to changing the course of history, which leads to the construction of the unification of the Orient under a system of faith and justice. These French experiments are admittedly timid compared to those in the United States, where alternate histories have become a widely accepted popular genre. Novels and novellas have been published with increasing frequency to the point that one now finds numerous anthologies. In 2010, the American website Uchronia counted sixty-three, the first dating from the middle of the 1970s.[29] One of the most complete anthologies, at least in terms of its bibliography, is likely *Alternative Histories: Eleven Histories of the World as It Might Have Been,* edited by Martin Greenberg and Charles S. Waugh in 1986.[30]

Multivolume uchronic series have been published following common practice within science fiction. One of the most famous is perhaps *The Domination* by Stephen M. Stirling, written between 1988 and 1999. The narrative follows the annexation of the Dutch colony of the Cape by Great Britain at the end of the eighteenth century. The colony takes on the name Draka, chosen in honor of Francis Drake, and becomes the destination of Tory refugees after the American War of Independence, then of French royalists after the Napoleonic victories, Southerners after the American Civil War, and finally all the racists of Europe. The Domination of Draka thus became "a giant forge, serf-manned factories pouring out tanks and dirigibles and steam cars as the Janissary legions gather for the final triumph and the ultimate revenge."[31] Draka becomes an independent empire with a totalitarian, industrial, slave society that spreads its dominance across the world.

Harry Turtledove is a recognized master of the genre. Born in 1949, he began by studying history and completed a thesis on the Byzantine Empire in 1977. He then worked for the Los Angeles County Office of Education before he set out on a literary career in 1991. To date, he has published seven series focusing on different periods (the Byzantine Empire, the Civil War, the year 1941, and so on). One of his first books, *Flesh,* appeared in 1988, and imagined a world where the Bering Strait was never crossed. When the portion of the continent that was to become the United States was discovered, the conquerors did not find Native Americans but a *Homo erectus* named Sim, who was even less well treated than blacks or Native Americans: this uchronic detour offers an allegory of the Indian massacre perpetrated by the colonial settlers. In another famous work, *The Two Georges,*[32] the two Georges—George Washington and George III—strike a deal in 1760. As a result, there is no American Revolution and it is only in the twentieth century that the "British colonies of America" form a "North American Union." Turtledove has won more than eleven literary prizes since 1991, his works have been translated into five languages, and his oeuvre has been the subject of multiple academic studies.

As an indicator of this broader trend, a prize for uchronias in English was created in 1996, the Sidewise Awards for Alternate History. The first laureate was Paul James McAuley, for *Pasquale's Angel,* a uchronia in which the Industrial Revolution took place in Florence thanks to Leonardo de Vinci.[33] Éric Henriet has argued that alternate history seems to have developed at the expense of science fiction. Faced with a more tenuous relationship to the future, he argues, science fiction has difficulty imagining distant futures modified by technology, while uchronias, looking toward the past, can potentially respond more directly to contemporary concerns.

At the same time, the practice of uchronia has spread through other media (cinema, television, graphic novels, and so on). The most well-known examples are the trilogy *Back to the Future* by Robert Zemeckis (1985, 1989, 1990), one of the most famous uses in film of a time machine. With the help of the savant Emmett Brown, the young Marty McFly discovers the 1950s, when his parents were young, and confronts the challenge of making sure they meet. On television, one of the most popular series was probably *Quantum Leap* (1989–1993), which mixed scientific innovation and quasi-divine intervention to recount the tribulations of the doctor Sam Beckett, who was pushed into the past in order to save people and do good by taking over their lives in crucial moments. The diversity of the situations (the hero is sometimes a man, a woman, a child, an elderly adult, white, black, rich, poor, or so on) and the constant allusions to the American past (in one episode, the hero takes the place of Elvis Presley) no doubt contributed to its success.

It is certainly not possible to retrace all the uses of this form of reasoning, which have become so common across the planet (we will discuss role-playing and video games elsewhere). It is sufficient to note, however, that there has been a tremendous expansion since the 1980s as alternate history benefits from a new legitimacy, at the crossroads of a narrative that is at once "popular" and has strong creative potential. The film *Inglourious Basterds* by Quentin Tarantino (2009), which imagines a successful Jewish plot against Hitler, effectively illustrates the latter tendency. In keeping with the filmmaker's previous works, the film proposes a mélange of various pulp and cinematic references, temporal disorder, and homage to the cathartic power of cinema and formal inventiveness. The last season of the well-known television series *Lost* also proposed a sophisticated uchronic exercise that initiated a new narrative strategy: the flash-sideways.[34] The phenomenon is similar to a graphic novel. In 1977, the famous editor of Marvel Comics launched a "what-if" series that imagined alternative outcomes building on the same plots in the collection: the first opus asked "*What if Spider-Man Joined the Fantastic Four?*"[35] A more ambitious usage was found in the series *Watchmen* by Alan Moore and Dave Gibbons (1986–1987). The action took place in an alternative world in which the United States of the 1980s won the Vietnam War thanks to a superhero, Dr. Manhattan, and was governed since 1968 by Richard Nixon. This alternative universe became the context for a reflection on the destiny of superheroes in the world of comics, but also in our contemporary mythologies. Series specifically dedicated to this narrative technique have also been created in France, such as *Uchronie(s)* (2008), or in the form of a history that actually "happened," *Jour J* (2010), the first volume of which is titled *Les Russes sur la Lune!* This multiplication of sites of production have no doubt contributed to making uchronias a familiar aspect of the media and cultural landscape.

Two recent phenomena illustrate, each in their own way, this latent affirmation of uchronia in contemporary narratives. First, there has been the development of the steampunk trend, born in the 1990s. This veritable science-fiction subgenre was originally a response to cyberpunk, which appeared in the 1980s and described near, dystopian futures marked by the dominance of computers, artificial intelligence, and multinational conglomerates (as in William Gibson's novel *Neuromancer*). "Steampunk," coined by the science-fiction writer Kevin Wayne Jeter, describes uchronias that are anchored in the Industrial Revolution of the nineteenth century, modified by marvelous or anachronistic elements (computers, genetic manipulation, and so on). Suggestive references as well as tributes to the "founding fathers" of the genre, such as Jules Verne or Albert Robida, play an important role.

For lovers of the genre, the most important works are *Morlock Night* by Kevin Wayne Jeter (1979), *The Anubis Gates* by Tim Powers (1983), and *Homunculus* by James P. Blaylock (1986).[36] The most famous is no doubt *The*

Difference Engine by two authors who came out of the cyberpunk movement, William Gibson and Bruce Sterling. The story takes place in 1855 in Victorian England, where Lord Byron is in power. The scientist Charles Babbage succeeds in crafting a "difference engine," a steam computer, made with connecting rods and levers,[37] that generates an unprecedented innovation in science and technology, to the point that Great Britain becomes entirely disinterested in earthly exploration. Considered a masterpiece by specialists of science fiction, the novel has enjoyed tremendous success. Nominated for multiple prizes, it has been the object of academic studies in literature as well as gender studies,[38] and even a dictionary, *The Difference Dictionary,* available on the Internet.[39]

The field has also expanded in France, through translations and publication. Éditions Mnémos, founded in 1999, has published *Confessions d'un automate mangeur d'opium* by Fabric Colin and Mathieu Gaborit, *Bouvard, Pécuchet et les savants fous* by René Reouven, and *La Lune seule le sait* by Johan Heliot.[40] In the last novel, Napoleon III wins at Sedan against the Prussians in 1870. With the help of Ishkiss extraterrestrials, who come to Earth at the time of the closing of the Universal Exposition in Paris in 1889, he spreads his domination across the world. But one man rises up to stop him: Jules Verne. Though it is difficult to measure the interest and diffusion of this particular genre, it would appear that it is gaining recognition,[41] as witnessed by the first retrospectives and exhibitions in academic and cultural circles. Thus, in the History of Science Museum at the University of Oxford, which was inaugurated between 2009 and February 2010, an exhibition dedicated to the aesthetic of steampunk attracted seventy thousand visitors while another entitled Rétrofuturisme/Steampunk/Archéomodernisme was organized in Paris in 2012 at the Galerie du Jour agnès b.[42]

Another phenomenon concerns more traditionally "legitimate" literature—by which we mean, inspired by Pierre Bourdieu, a literature that does not self-identify with a popular or critical subculture, but that is produced by writers who foreground stylistic qualities in works that are distributed within consecrated and widely recognized editorial networks. The use of this technique is not new, as suggested by Roger Caillois's *Pontius Pilate,* which appeared in 1961.[43] The process seems to have been increasingly used by writers. In France, *Les Trois Rimbaud* (The three rimbauds) by Dominique Noguez (1986), imagines the next phase of Rimbaud's life; he doesn't die in 1891, but in 1937. In *La Part de l'autre* by Éric Emmanuel Schmitt (2003), Hitler is not refused entry into the Academy of Fine Arts in Vienna and becomes an artist. In the United

States, Philip Roth wrote *The Plot Against America* (2004), a uchronia in which Charles Lindbergh wins the election against Roosevelt in 1940, makes peace with Germany, and leads a fascist America for two years. One of Paul Auster's later works, *Man in the Dark* (2008), also proposes a uchronia: the narrator, August Brill, imagines a parallel universe in which September 11 doesn't take place, but a civil war rages between the states. In the widely read trilogy by the Japanese Haruki Murakami, *1Q84* (2009–2010), the two heroes are thrown into a parallel world, another present with no possibility of return called 1Q84 (1984's "other") where the Earth has two moons.

This increasing (though still moderate) development of alternate history is not just the result of chance. In the case of the United States, the shock of September 11 and the sense of radical shifts in our contemporary world no doubt offer a partial explanation: there would seem to be a link between collective traumatic experiences and the development of the genre, in which one either imagines a world "as it should have been" or one attempts to grasp the full scope of changes that have taken place. Certain authors also offer a critical "political turn." At the same time, "crisis texts" bring forward the idea of new possibilities, which these books reveal to their audiences. In 1Q84, uchronia serves a largely creative function: in continuity with Murakami's other novels, it offers the possibility of generating a shift that disturbs the real and the characters, which had been well defined. From there, a gradual insertion into an increasingly imaginary world—attested by the intrusion of characters called "Little People"—where the literary elements are fully deployed and create an indeterminate and gripping narrative space.[44] Auster's *Man in the Dark* operates differently: the novel tries to establish a difference between the registers of dreams and of uchronia, the latter serving as a means through which the narrator resolves his own anxieties. The alternate history comes to an end when the hero, the clown Owen Brick, is killed by the US federal army in the middle of the work. This opens the path toward another form of more direct narration when the narrator confronts his demons. In the novel's organizational structure, uchronia is an external fable that contains both collective and individual anxieties and allows for a rediscovery of the self through a fictional detour.[45]

The Plot Against America adheres more tightly to the rules of the genre. Through novelistic narration, Philip Roth recounts the emergence of a fascist America by limiting suggestive nods and insisting on the effect of the real: his uchronia stages radio programs, newspapers, events, and historical figures, imagining their words and acts. The extent of the simulation is such that the author proposes, at the end of the work, a list of "real" biographies for the characters. The novel takes full advantage of a literary method that remains inaccessible to the historian: immersion. And the reader is plunged into a uchronic universe that confounds all realism. Warned by the title that it is also a literary "plot," he or she is invited through the constant questioning and the association of ideas to rediscover in the novel real aspects of American life at the time.

In this way, the evocation strongly criticizes American nationalism and racism. No longer in a state of latency, they reveal their full potential in the novel, expressing their severity to the reader. This use of fiction and the play between registers are some of the more powerful modes in the deployment of uchronia.

In sum, this expansion of the uchronic genre fits in well with the vast contemporary changes mentioned above, which it echoes in a variety of ways: modification of the relationship to science, the "end of the great ideologies," meaning in an uncertain world, the difficulty of projecting into the future, mutation of forms of hope, and fantastic or anxiety-ridden playfulness that shifts between the real and the virtual. In so doing, the phenomenon is not unrelated to the historical practice of the counterfactual and the discomfort generated by its reception.

THE TURBULENT "PLACE OF DEAD ROADS"

This combination of uchronia and historical practice of the counterfactual is hardly banal. Connections obviously exist between the two: while this may not pose a problem for literary authors, it has for researchers. And yet, there is no doubt that the current success of "what-if" history rests on a mode of alternate history, as suggested by the anthologies that mix freely (uchronia, steampunk, conjectural history, and so on), or the fact that the two tend to mobilize the same turning points (no doubt for the same reasons of narrative efficacy). It may also be the fuzziness of such boundaries that provoke legitimate mistrust on the part of some historians.

This panorama also reminds us of the creative, entertaining, and imaginative dimensions of uchronia, which establishes a recognizable pact with the reader. The narrative and fictional technique appears rich and unique. The "fractured" text provokes a distinction between the real (or a history that really occurred) and fiction (an alternative history), inviting the reader to take part through his or her imagination and reflection. In this way, it also constitutes an original way of reminding us that "factual formulations and fictional formulations are discernable" and push the author to play with these different registers.[46] If the audacity and scale of temporal shifts presented by these novels may provoke surprise, they also attest to a form of "literary knowledge" that can provide precious insights.

The path remains challenging, as the *Place of Dead Roads* that opened this chapter suggests. After crossing vastly diverse worlds, Kim's quest inevitably comes to its tragic end: he dies in a trite dual between two gun-slinging cowboys. Uchronia is undeniably a singular path. It is filled with peril, but it opens at the same time other paths that underscore our relationship to the world and the narrative schemas that we rely on to tell our stories.

CHAPTER 4

The Test of the Social (and Natural) Sciences

> In my opinion, in order to pursue "interesting" sociology the sociologist must cultivate something like a distance from the world he or she is describing through an experience of thought. What does it mean to cultivate distance in this case? It means treating the world that one describes as if it could be something other than what it is. This consists of removing that part of necessity and nature that politicians and especially the politicians in power seek to give it. At the same time, it generates a critical perspective because the foundation of the critical regard is an act of denaturalizing the ordinary meaning of "that's natural." To consider that the state of the social world could be other than it is becomes a methodological requirement.
>
> —Luc Boltanski[1]

The fields of history and literature are vast enough already, but we must push further. In the previous discussions, we have already touched upon the question of the relationship between counterfactual reasoning and the full range of social and human sciences. What connection might there be between relative deprivation theory in psychology, strategic deterrence theory, the economic theory of opportunity costs, and of the juridical theory of legal fiction? All are based either explicitly or implicitly on counterfactual analysis. In what follows, we describe the variety of uses of counterfactual reasoning in its broadest sense, whether they be discrete or, on the contrary, clearly demonstrated within the framework of these subdisciplines. Embracing a vast body of work in the social sciences should help to measure their intensity and apprehend possible transfers of knowledge across disciplines. In the end, when these human sciences confront these questions, they often hide behind other forms of knowledge: analytic philosophy, metaphysics, literary theory, or natural sciences. The realm of the counterfactual and possible futures poses in its own way the problem of disciplinary boundaries and especially the role of history within the milieu of the other human sciences.

A PRIVILEGED OBJECT FOR SOCIAL PSYCHOLOGY AND THE COGNITIVE SCIENCES

Psychologists have been grappling with this question for some time. Each individual performs a number of counterfactual operations on a daily basis, including comparing what he or she has or is, with what he or she could have or be. Psychologists and cognitive scientists study what they term "counterfactual thinking," which they say is one form of reasoning among others (conditional, deductive, probabilistic, and so on). Thus, psychology seems to be one of the only disciplines to take this mode of reasoning as an actual object of study instead of using it, like other social sciences, as a method. This area of research has spawned innumerable studies of decision-making in all areas of social life, from the world of finance to sexual behaviors, including card-playing strategies.[2] Over the last fifteen years, many dozens of articles have been published, notably in two scientific journals, the *Journal of Experimental Social Psychology* and the *Journal of Personality and Social Psychology.* The specialists of psychology and cognitive sciences have identified multiple types of counterfactual reasoning (upward/downward, additive/subtractive, self/other counterfactuals) that condition one's behavior as well as emotions such as regret, a sense of injustice, or relief and satisfaction.

In their pioneering work on "simulation heuristics" from the 1980s, Amos Tversky and the psychologist Daniel Kahneman (2002 Nobel Prize winner in Economic Sciences), demonstrated multiple characteristics of counterfactual thought. Emotional reactions are stronger when a situation results from an error rather than the absence of an action, because it is easier to invalidate or modify an action mentally about which we have information than it is to do so in the absence of an action that does not provide us with any factual information. They noted that in general we regret far more having said something inappropriate than having not said something relevant. Likewise, individuals have a greater tendency to apply this type of reasoning to exceptional rather than ordinary events. And it would appear that the more tragic the situation seems, the easier it is to imagine an alternative course of events. Thus, counterfactual reasoning is often triggered by sudden traumatic events, perceived by some to be harmful, such as revolutions and criminal and terrorist attacks.[3] Depression, sadness, lack of satisfaction also favor the creation of counterfactual simulations.[4] Thus, counterfactual reasoning may be misleading to the extent that it overestimates the probability of certain events and underestimates other phenomena. It may also induce "emotional amplification."[5] Bronze-medal winners at the Olympic Games are thus much happier than silver medalists, who think only of the gold medal they could have won, while the holders of a bronze medal consider they could reasonably have won nothing at all. Finally, we more easily modify the last event in a series than an earlier event: from this derives our propensity to bluntly criticize a sportsman who misses his chance at the last minute of the match, while we tolerate missed opportunities at the beginning.[6]

In the 1990s, researchers defined multiple types of "counterfactual thinking" by conducting numerous surveys and tests. According to these works, there are two ways of producing a counterfactual: subtracting (subtractive counterfactual) or adding an element (additive counterfactual). Subtraction, which underlines the causal links,[7] increases analytical capacities, while addition opens new possibilities and favors creativity and imagination.[8] The first operation may be mobilized toward prevention in order to reduce possible losses, while the second, which is more offensive, looks to maximize gains.[9] Thus, economic actors have different "cognitive styles": entrepreneurs tend to be more concerned with increasing their profits, while managers of large firms attempt to prevent losses and risks.[10] One can distinguish between two types of reasoning based on the positive or negative nature of the modification at hand.[11] For example, "upward counterfactual," which imagines a more favorable alternative than the events that happened, and "downward counterfactual," which simulates the unfolding of less desirable events. Positive simulation allows one to improve one's knowledge of a situation and one's future performance by becoming aware of one's errors[12] and generating a sense of regret.[13] Negative simulation has an immediately positive impact on the humor of the individual, who congratulates him- or herself for having avoided a situation that could have been worse, or less positive.[14] In each case, the counterfactual operation generates a change in behavior.[15] Moreover, it allows one to take contradictory information into consideration and thus to protect oneself against the tendency of individuals to neglect information that contradicts their decisions.[16] Counterfactual thinking has a tendency to give meaning to events and more generally to one's life. In a recent collective experiment, individuals who were questioned identified an important event in their lives and then measured how significant it was by imagining alternatives.[17]

This "simulation heuristic" allows one to explain the origin of a sense of regret, injustice, dissatisfaction, or even guilt that result from cognitive simulations. As early as World War II, Samuel Andrew Stouffer and his colleagues forged one of the founding concepts of social psychology: the theory of relative deprivation. This team of researchers studied the behaviors of soldiers in the United States and observed that even though US Air Force officers benefited from greater possibilities of advancement and promotion than foot soldiers, they were less satisfied and experienced a greater sense of unfairness. This paradox could be explained by the fact that these highly qualified officers had a higher level of aspiration than the foot soldiers. Deception and frustration result from a simple mode of counterfactual reasoning, which consists in comparing what one obtained with what one should be able to expect. While many psychologists argue that counterfactual rewards are in principle higher than actual rewards, one can imagine counterfactual thinking that would lead to lesser rewards, which could lead not to frustration but to satisfaction or humility. Moreover, proponents of the theory of justifications of a decision tend to demonstrate that a well-justified decision, which is at the origin of negative outcomes, is regretted less than a decision that is poorly justified that leads to the same consequences. The higher the quality of the justification, the less easy it is to pursue a counterfactual simulation.[18] The authors of Referent Cognitions Theory (RCT) have thus situated counterfactual thinking at the origin of a sense of injustice, notably in the context of work relations. For example, Robert Folger and Russell Cropanzano argue that when faced with potentially prejudicial managerial decisions, individuals evaluate who was responsible for the harm by performing "cognitive simulations."[19] The first counterfactual operation consists of asking to what extent a more favorable alternative would have been possible (a "would counterfactual"). The second operation is based on a plausibility calculation of the alternatives considered (a "could counterfactual"): the employee questions the ability and willingness of the manager to proceed otherwise. Finally, the individual evaluates the degree of morality of a decision by measuring the gap between what the individual did and what he should have done (a "should counterfactual"). Moreover, the counterfactual alternatives that we formulate can have an impact on our judgment. G. L. Wells and I. Gavinsky presented Karen's case to a group of individuals. Karen died following a food allergy to wine after a dinner with Mr. Carlson.[20] The researchers proposed two versions of the same story with slight differences. In the first version, Carlson hesitated between the mussels with white wine sauce and another dish that did not contain any alcohol. He ultimately ordered the seafood, and Karen, who was unaware of the contents of the recipe, died a few minutes later at the hospital. In the second version, Carlson also ordered the mussels marinière, but after having hesitated to order fish that also had a wine sauce. The majority of the people drew different conclusions concerning the responsibility of Mr. Carlson in Karen's death based on the version they were told. Even though Carlson made the same choice in each version of the story, those who were questioned judged his responsibility was greater in the first version when he was presented with a plausible alternative that would have saved Karen. The authors of the study deduced that individuals take into consideration counterfactual evidence to make sense of an event and ultimately to establish responsibility.

According to these works, the counterfactual approach is therefore not only a method but also a mode of reasoning, which is at once banal and indispensable with its own constraints, dispositions, and reflexes. Against the so-called Western intellectual tradition, which has systematically opposed deductive thinking based on truth and imaginative thought grounded in the possible or the plausible, psychologists have tried to show that counterfactuals partly determine the factual, since an individual evaluates what he or she has relative to what they could have had. Ruth M. J. Byrne, a specialist in cognitive sciences, has attempted to demonstrate that "imaginative thought is more rational than scientists imagined,"[21] and that human thought depends on the mental representation of possibilities. Counterfactual reasoning is therefore omnipresent, with only a few exceptions: individuals suffering from schizophrenia cannot consider possible alternatives and thus cannot engage in counterfactual reasoning.[22] Some researchers credit this deficit to a dysfunction within the orbitofrontal cortex, which is the location for "counterfactual thinking," as suggested by an MRI study.[23]

Social psychology and cognitive sciences—to which could be added the economy of anticipation, which is connected to them—occupy a place of their own: they do not use the counterfactual method, but rather take it directly as an object of study. On the other hand, the other social sciences have, to different degrees, adopted the counterfactual approach, beginning with law, which often draws on this form of reasoning in its juridical techniques and practices.

THE SOURCES OF LAW: "LEGAL FICTIONS" AND THE BUT-FOR RULE

Jurists perform thought experiments:[24] fiction seems to constitute one of the most widely used juridical techniques. Indeed, contrary to popular belief, the law is not exclusively tied to established facts but depends on the imagination both in legal theory and in judicial practice, as evidenced by "legal fictions" on the one hand and but-for causation on the other, that is, counterfactual reasoning in the determination of causes.

In the tradition of Roman law, jurisconsults demonstrated the need to develop fictions.[25] Thus, the Roman praetor who was not able to modify a law could order the magistrate to rule as if such or such a condition was fulfilled. This procedure, called *fictio,* allowed for an extension of the application of the law.[26] Yan Thomas has demonstrated that "legal fictions," such as the legacy of ancient Rome or the juridical person rooted in the Middle Ages, fostered a detachment from juridical formalism;[27] these legal fictions often acted like metaphors. It would be impossible to try to gather an exhaustive list of the fictions on which Western law was founded: for example, the expression *terra nullius* (nobody's land) in colonial law or the "civil death" of an individual who may be physically alive but who no longer exists in civil law, abolished in France in 1854, or the famous adage *Nemo jus ignorare censetur,* which is one of the pillars of the juridical edifice. Indeed, "Ignorance of law excuses no one" cannot be taken as real in any meaningful sense, since no individual can know all the laws that govern him or her.[28] Recently, certain authors have extended the concept of "legal fiction" to the regime of slavery.[29] This expanded definition, which ultimately is a kind of moral judgment, does not possess any heuristic value and may even complicate the legal dimension of the slave regime.

A legal fiction is thus a technical juridical process "consisting of imagining a fact or a situation that differs from reality in order to produce a legal effect."[30] The use of fiction allows law to expand its hold over social worlds.[31] These false statements allow lawyers to solve new legal issues through the use of analogical reasoning. By filling in a gap in the law, they help to optimize legal systems. In addition, they shift the debate from the substance to the evidence and the causes. Legal issues can be likened to counterfactual histories in that they are based on a convention (they take for granted what we know to be false). In addition, they have a creative dimension in that they explore "possibilities of reality" while bending to the constraints of plausibility.[32] In so doing, they contribute to the development of legal and historical science,[33] while also having real social impact. This is why counterfactual history, like legal fictions, are considered by Jean-Marie Schaeffer to be "instrumental fictions."[34] Some Anglo-American theoreticians even define these legal fiction as "counterfactual laws."[35] And yet, when examined more carefully, legal fictions are less a mode of counterfactual reasoning ("what if") than assumptive analysis ("as if . . .").[36] Moreover, juridical fictions open an "imaginary mental space" in the legal universe that is itself "artificial" to the extent that it is not indexed on the real world: "the juridical fiction is not an unreal exception in the real world. It reveals the unreality of the juridical world."[37] This is a difference with counterfactuals that is founded on the comparison with the factual. Juridical norms, like literature—and as opposed to history—are defined across truth and falsehood.

While the counterfactual nature of legal claims is uncertain, this mode of reasoning has nonetheless strongly influenced the practice of law, especially in the United States. It is clear that jurists are as concerned with the causes of past events as historians. On the other hand, more so than historians, jurists must take into consideration what could have happened if the course of events had been different.

Indeed, judges and jurors must strike a balance and measure the importance of all factors in order to identify the determining cause.[38] In civil liability, a causal link exists between a particular action and a damage if one can prove that the damage would not have occurred without the action. This is what is called "but-for" causation, a principle that was laid down in 1989 by the US Supreme Court:

> But-for causation is a hypothetical construct. In determining whether a particular factor was a but-for cause of a given event, we begin by assuming that this factor was present at the time of the event, and then ask whether, even if that factor had been absent, the event nevertheless would have transpired in the same way.[39]

Jurists now refer to this principle as the sine qua non rule.[40] Counterfactual reasoning allows one to determine the causes of harm and to identify the necessary cause—the determining cause—among the *causa proxima* (the closest chronologically) and the *causa remota,* which is situated at the beginning of the causal chain. Counterfactual analysis is used to assess the mitigating or aggravating circumstances of a crime.[41] Thus, the lawyers of the victims who died in the crash of the Rio–Paris Air France flight in 2009 based their argument on a counterfactual analysis: whereas the report of the Bureau of Investigation and

Analysis (BEA in French) of civil aviation brought forward a series of mistakes made by the pilots, Olivier Morice told Reuters on July 29, 2011, "If there had not been a defect with the Pitot tubes [which measure velocity], the pilots would not have been faced with such a complex situation. So, as far as I am concerned, it was the Pitot tubes that were the primary cause of the crash."[42] The first cause, technical dysfunction of the Airbus A330 predominated over the *causa proxima,* the incapacity of the pilots to resolve the problems that took place following the mechanical flaw. Nonetheless, the BEA demonstrated that, without the pilot's maneuvers, who pitched up instead of down, the plane would not have crashed, even if the Pitot tubes were defective: the trial served to establish a hierarchy between the causes and to determine the necessary cause.

The counterfactual approach has become so important in the judicial practice of US judges that the development of but-for questioning is taught in the courses and textbooks of future judges. Magistrates must evaluate damages and analyze behaviors. Then they must create a counterfactual by imagining what would have happened, for example, if a driver involved in an accident had complied with the law—and they must take into consideration any "alternative causes." There are other legal procedures that use counterfactual reasoning, such as the harmless error: in case of error committed by the magistrate in the conduct of a trial, this procedure requires one to imagine a different course in order to determine whether the error committed impacted the trial's outcome. If the error is considered harmless, the party who has lost cannot appeal to change the judgment.

Finally, beyond the use of counterfactual reasoning for judicial practice, jurists, like historians, have begun to apply it to legal history,[43] while their colleagues in economics have been developing counterfactual analysis in history for more than half a century.

THOUGHT EXPERIMENTS AND COUNTERFACTUALS IN ECONOMICS: MEASURING FACTORIAL EFFECTS AND "CLIOMETRICS"

As in law, thought experiments have helped create several rules and theories in economics. For example, one can ask, like the philosopher of science Marc Lange, what is the counterfactual dimension of the Latin phrase *ceteris paribus,* that is, "all other things being equal." This principle makes it possible in theoretical economic models to analyze the influence of a variable by excluding all other factors. It is a fiction that allows an economic law to be valid at any time and in any place: "*Ceteris-paribus* generalizations of an 'inexact science' qualify as *laws* of that science in virtue of their distinctive relation to counterfactuals: they form a set that is *stable* for the purposes of that field."[44] There is another constraint as well for economics, which has attempted to pattern itself on the natural sciences: economic laws are verifiable if and only if actors possess a perfect knowledge of the situation and behave in a perfectly rational manner. Viewed from this angle, the laws of economics seem counterfactual by definition: a given set of conditional propositions allows, for better or for worse, to understand reality.

Other modes of economic reasoning mobilize this type of operation, like the economic theory of "opportunity costs," which makes it possible to consider alternatives abandoned by economic actors. The value of the best unrealized option is called the opportunity cost. This notion makes it possible to determine the hidden costs of choices. Through this operation, investors make trade-offs between different financial investments, while individuals at work evaluate the cost of one hour of leisure in light of the income earned in one hour of work. This leads to a paradox: the more money one earns through work, the more leisure time costs the individual. This paradox partly explains "overwork" among senior executives.

Alongside analyses of opportunity cost, economists have developed a counterfactual methodology to identify the factors of economic evolution. Starting at the end of the 1950s, this new interest contributed to the development of cliometrics, a new discipline also referred to as the "new economic history." Developed in the United States by economists and management scholars, this approach was originally intended to challenge the interpretations commonly accepted by US economists and historians. As a part of this effort, cliometricians Alfred Conrad, John Meyer, and especially Robert Fogel proposed to break with a traditional narrative-based approach to economic history and promoted a more mathematical approach. Cliometrics meant conferring the status of experimental science onto the discipline of history. This new economic history seduced only a handful of historians, like Jean Heffer, a French specialist of the United States, who in the mid-1970s emphasized the method's ability to emancipate the researcher from "narrative history" while at the same time pointing out some potential dangers. "These simulations must be used when they are helpful and not to impress amateurs."[45] This method is also shaped by the creativity of the economic historian and his or her ability to ask pertinent questions.[46] Counterfactual analysis does not apply to all economic phenomena: it corresponds to the theoretical framework of microeconomics based on a cost-benefit paradigm, which studies the effects of innovation and the role of institutions on economic growth. At the same time, the philosopher Jon Elster revealed an epistemological limit within the development of this "new economic history." The methodology proposed by Robert Fogel relies on proven trends and an alternative evolution based on a succession of states of equilibrium. But the economy never reaches such a level of stability. So we must pay attention to the micromechanisms that ensure the passage from one state to the other. While articulating these micromechanisms with conceivable regularities makes it possible to imagine a bifurcation toward one innovation or another, they make it difficult to imagine the succession of alternatives that would follow. In addition to the economic, one must also take into consideration relational innovation. For example, railways not only generated a reduction in costs, they also increased speeds and, therefore, facilitated the linking of sectors and economic actors, increasing both the flexibility and the predictability of operations. In this sense, an economy founded on canals, which would have been more susceptible to fluctuations due to the slowness of communications between actors, would nonetheless have been different.[47]

Cliometrics was renewed in the 1980s in response to these critiques.[48] During this period, it was still defined as a combination of economic theory, quantitative methods, and economic history, but it took on different forms. First, it was further institutionalized with the creation in 1983 of the Cliometric Society.[49] It also developed in American universities and to a lesser extent in Great Britain, Canada, and then Germany and France.[50] The objects of study changed as well. Alongside the "major questions" of American and world history (the role of railways in the development of the American economy or slavery in the South, the causes of economic decline in this region after the Civil War, the causes of the crash in 1929, and so on[51]) there were also new objects of study designed to help understand "the present through the past," through studies on the origins of social progress, the effects of female employment, racial inequality, or the effectiveness of macroeconomic policies, and so on. Finally, the methods also became more diverse. Without always succeeding in getting rid of the presuppositions of neoclassical economic theory—though this was discussed early on[52]—the "new economic history" more thoroughly examined institutional questions, analyses in terms of path dependency and its "qualitative dimensions."[53] The counterfactual approach itself, which was only ever one tool among many—though no doubt the most visible—continued to be practiced, though it became less obviously apparent: it was both the object of tough critiques and at the same time regular and confident usage, illustrating different styles within the current itself.[54]

Drawing inspiration from cliometrics, economists are now using counterfactual analysis to evaluate and increase the effectiveness of economic policies. The causal impact of an economic measure can be assessed by measuring the gap between two groups of people: the first benefits from the new economic policy, and the second—real or imaginary—is deprived of the same measure. So when politicians claim that the reform of the thirty-five-hour work week (2000) or the active solidarity income (*revenue de solidarité active*) (2007) increased the employment rate by *x* percent in France, counterfactual reasoning invites us to analyze what would have happened had these measures not been passed. If, in this case, employment would have been augmented $x + 3$ percent, one could consider that the policy had a negative impact on employment. The method can also be used to measure the impact of legislation, such as article 55 of a recent law on urban renewal (SRU) in France, for the creation of social housing. Article 55 focused on developing mixed urban neighborhoods by forcing towns of more that thirty-five hundred inhabitants to have at least 20 percent social housing. Under these conditions, it is impossible to compare towns that are subject to this obligation to towns of equivalent size that are not subject to the law. Researchers at Aix-Marseille University have attempted to get around this problem by deciding to study past information on towns to develop counterfactual values, as if they had not been subject to article 55. The method also allows them to bring to light natural tendencies toward the construction of social housing—and to relativize the impact of article 55.[55]

POLITICAL SCIENCE, OR THE NEW FRONTIER IN COUNTERFACTUAL EXPERIMENTATION

Following the economists, political scientists—most notably specialists of international relations—have become the principal promoters of the counterfactual approach in history. Today, political science constitutes a key area for the development of a variety of forms of counterfactual analysis, from narrative interpretations to more positivist experiments.

Though not always referred to as such, counterfactual reasoning is omnipresent in international relations.[56] This is the case for one of the canonical examples in the discipline: Imanuel Geiss's analysis of the causes of World

War I, which affirmed that the conflict was "inevitable" due to the German *Weltpolitik* and the politics of entrenchment of the Triple Entente by France, Great Britain, and Russia.[57] It would appear that the adjective "inevitable" implies an implicitly counterfactual proposition: if Archduke Franz Ferdinand had not been assassinated, the war would still have broken out. Philip Tetlock and Richard Lebow also attempted to alleviate some the peculiarities of counterfactual analysis by demonstrating that the differences between counterfactual and factual reasoning are often exaggerated: it is a difference of degree rather than of nature. Indeed, this difference shows itself to be quite small when the sources are scarce, such as the case of the Peloponnesian War or certain decision-making processes behind closed doors.[58]

At the same time, alongside these many implicit or unintentional uses, counterfactual analysis was used explicitly in international relations theory after World War II. This approach informed the design of deterrence strategy. Researchers most notably studied international relations in the 1930s and the policy of appeasement of liberal democracies against military dictators. They proposed a counterfactual hypothesis that pondered whether Hitler's ambitions would have been restricted by a show of force on the part of Great Britain and France. It was a question of determining the point of no return for deterrence, that is, how long this strategy could have contained Hitler.[59] In the same way, the military "crisis," defined as a decisive event that clearly delimited a before and after, was attractive to counterfactualists. Internationalists and geopoliticians saw the crisis as a rare moment when "history hesitated," where it seems to have escaped the will of the actors. The international crises of the so-called "Cold War" period have led to numerous counterfactual studies. Some studies on the Cuban Missile Crisis have therefore shown how great the risk of confrontation was and have highlighted the role of contingency in the crisis's resolution. As a result, historians have profoundly revisited this period, wrongly referred to as the "Cold War."[60]

Today the renewal of the counterfactual approach in the field of international relations is illustrated by Philip Tetlock, Aaron Belkin, and Richard Lebow, who have proposed a constructivist multidisciplinary model combining history, psychology, and political science, in order to develop "plausible" counterfactual proposals and deconstruct positivist theories in international relations.[61] These US researchers have identified several criteria to circumvent the pitfalls of historical speculation. The conditions that make counterfactual analysis possible must be clearly defined, since the main counterfactual assumption is often based on antecedent counterfactual propositions that may invalidate the original hypothesis.[62] There should be as few historical changes as possible in the formulation of a counterfactual alternative, so that behaviors remain predictable. The causes, the consequences, and the type of causal connections that they maintain must be explained in order to guarantee the logical coherence of the proposals made. Counterfactualists must also make explicit reference to the theoretical model used, especially the one relative to causation. Respecting such a procedure, does not guarantee the validity of a counterfactual proposal, but it does make it possible to exclude certain anachronistic or incoherent proposals, or "miracle-world counterfactuals."[63]

Alongside this constructivist interpretation of counterfactual analysis, a "hard" scientific version has been developed through the "what-if" software of Gary King and Langche Zeng, which promotes a mathematical vision of international relations and political science.[64] They collected multiple data sets on the processes of democratization in the world in order to determine the "causal effects of democracy."[65] The counterfactual test is essential to answering this question: what would happen if more countries in the world were democratic? According to sophisticated calculations, Haiti, for example, had a greater chance of becoming a full-fledged democracy in 1990 than in 1996. Overall, 28 percent of autocracies would have a chance of becoming democracies while 53 percent could move in the opposite direction. This ultrapositivist counterfactual analysis seduced experts in the US Army, who developed new models and strategies as a result.[66] At the same time, the pertinence of the categories, the type of causal relation, and the mathematical reduction of such vastly different situations challenge some of these arguments' conclusions.

This overview of the social sciences shows the widespread use of the counterfactual method; in some cases it has taken the form of everyday intellectual operations such as but-for causation for jurists or opportunity-cost for economists. It has been applied in multiple ways, covering a vast spectrum, from the humanistic interpretations of certain historians to the mathematical versions of a variety of political scientists. We will discuss the sociological and anthropological approaches farther on in the book. Beyond psychology, history, economics, and politics, counterfactual analysis is now of interest to some Anglophone geographers, who have set out to explore "what-if" geographies.[67] In 2010, David Gilbert and David Lambert published a stimulating research program in historical geography in the *Journal of Historical Geography*.[68] They questioned the type of spatial representations induced by counterfactual analysis in order to restore contingency. Space, too, they argued, may be apprehended through a world of possibilities, not to mention that counterfactual analysis can make it possible to rethink fundamental notions of geographical thought, such as "underdevelopment," mesological determinism, or spatial forms. In the journal issue devoted to "counterfactual geographies," Colin G. Pooley, for example, attempts to denaturalize the supposedly obvious rise of the automobile in the twentieth century by imagining the impact of a severe restriction on the number of private cars at the beginning of the century on infrastructures and modes of transportation.[69] This geographer of social change demonstrated that in the absence of the car, other types of transport would have allowed the development of similar possibilities for daily mobility. He reminds us that the extremely dense British railway network at the beginning of the twentieth century has been gradually reduced to a skeleton linking only large cities. A car-free world would also have dramatically changed the face of cities and the daily lives of urban dwellers by limiting the level of air pollution and maintaining services close to home. The absence of a car would, however, have disadvantaged the most remote rural areas, and limits on car traffic would not necessarily have led to a significant change in everyday mobility. Here, counterfactual analysis reveals the complex and profound nature of the social transformations induced by the development of the automobile.

Paradoxically, the counterfactual method therefore seems more explicitly used in social sciences outside history. We mentioned the reluctance of historians—and particularly those in France—to employ this experimental approach. The attraction it exerts on the other social sciences is undoubtedly partially related to their own epistemological foundations, which places comparison at the heart of their methodology. Counterfactual analysis in this sense is ultimately an exercise in comparing what is and what could have been. This thought experiment allows the researcher to create a certain distance and to denaturalize the object at hand. It therefore emerges as a methodological requirement that is particularly useful in the social sciences.[70]

ON THE EDGES OF THE SOCIAL SCIENCES: POSSIBLE WORLDS IN PHILOSOPHY, LITERATURE, AND ASTROPHYSICS

These uses of counterfactual reasoning invite us to push beyond the boundaries of the social sciences. Researchers who use counterfactual analysis reference the supposed "hard" sciences, alongside philosophy and literary theory to justify this type of reasoning. It is helpful then to explore other theories or experiments, especially to the extent that they open up more possibilities for uses of counterfactualism.

Counterfactualists frequently mobilize the work of philosophers who have, since Aristotle's *Metaphysics* and *Poetics,* reflected on past events that could have happened otherwise and on parallel universes that would have emerged from them. Inspired by the Stagirite (Aristotle), theologians and philosophers of the thirteenth and fourteenth centuries, such as Thomas Aquinas and Duns Scotus, developed an interest in possible outcomes: it was a question of exploring the extent of divine power, determining if it was omnipotent or if its power could only be expressed within the realm of the "createable."[71] In the seventeenth century, in his *Theodicy,* Leibniz investigated the dream of Theodore, priest of Delphi: an infinite pyramid would have contained a library with all the possible versions of the life of Sextus Tarquinius had he listened to Jupiter's advice and renounced his throne. At the top of the pyramid was the best of all worlds, the world as it is. The description makes it possible to imagine a world that could have been different, to varying degrees, but also to ask the question of the relationship between necessity and freedom, as well as the evaluation of these different worlds, which were distinctly isolated from one another in this case.

The area of philosophy that has been most commonly drawn upon by the social sciences, however, is the philosophy of science and the modal logic of Saul Kripke and David Lewis.[72] In *Counterfactuals* (1973) and *On the Plurality of Worlds* (1986),[73] Lewis seeks to clarify the theories of causality and proposes a tool that makes it possible to distinguish between true and false by resorting to modal logic. To do this, he proposes to establish possible worlds that respond to elaborate logical criteria and a combination of coherent sequences, and then compare them to the current world by considering various "accessibility relations." In the semantics of possible worlds, a phenomenon is possible when it is true in at least one possible world, and necessary when it is in all possible worlds. It is therefore less a question of establishing causes, with some mysterious power, than determining laws according to logical—as opposed to chronological—relations between phenomena. Moreover, unlike Kripke, who focuses on abstractions, these worlds of possibilities possess a concrete reality for Lewis.

This reinforced positivism has been abundantly commented upon, adapted, and applied in recent years.[74] It has also been much criticized because of the logical restrictions it imposes on reality. Other propositions have been developed as well. Among them are the theories referred to as "fictionalist": they consider unrealized possibilities, those that have been tested by time, to be a detour for more effectively apprehending the real—with the risk, according to these logicians, that they may neglect some of the true possibilities hidden within the real.[75] Jacques Bouveresse has proposed another interpretation based on his readings of Robert Musil and Antoine Cournot. Counterfactual reasoning offers a hold on the "accidental residue" of history. Far from grand theories of history, they give the observer access to historical worlds in which we must distinguish between the diversity of the past and the past that remains in our memories. It also allows us to consider the fabric of historical causation through a perspective in which the plurality of determinations opens up space and leaves room for chance: chance is thus not in contradiction to a given history.[76] In another register, the philosophers Pierre Livet and Frédéric Nef, one close to economics and the other to metaphysics, have proposed an approach founded on what they call the "virtual"—"states of things the existence of which is avoided or that have not yet succeeded in having an existence"—and the "substitutable," or the capacity to mobilize something virtual in relation to an actual situation. They then deduce a "social ontology" founded on interactive dynamics and processes, which integrates an analysis of possibilities and counterfactuals in order to refine their understanding of social reality.[77] Some young researchers have further pursued this philosophical mode of inquiry.[78]

Although less common than in the social sciences, literary theory has also taken up the question of possible outcomes and the counterfactual, particularly in the context of the analysis of fictional universes. Modal logic has influenced literary analysis, without there being direct translation from one model to the other. Possible fictional worlds, as opposed to those of modal logic, is by definition incomplete because it is bound to the text that produces it. The works of Thomas Pavel clearly demonstrate this intersection. This specialist of French literature has adapted Kripke's theory of possible worlds, as well as Lewis's more "realistic" version, for literary analysis.[79] He explains in *Univers de la fiction* that this allows for the study of fictional universes in themselves, in addition to the uses of fiction or the context of its production. This approach allows us to reflect on its content, and the fact that its worlds can be perceived by some as really possible, as well as the porosities between fiction, nonfiction, and the possible. He specifies in an interview, "The realm of counterfactuals provides a natural habitat for fictional works. The works that I have recently discovered clearly demonstrate a certain relationship between literature, religion and freedom."[80]

But he goes on to say later that "for the literary theorist, the theory of possible worlds is only a source of inspiration" and that one must also consider the way in which these works of art impact the reader and thus make him or her participate in their universe.

The theoretician and literary critic Marie-Laure Ryan proposed another usage of these possible worlds. She also grounds her study in modal analyses that allow one to define the conditions of truth for counterfactual assertions (she uses the example: if a few hundred voters in Florida had chosen Al Gore, there would not have been a war in Iraq) and the proximity of sentences by modal operators that express necessity and possibility.[81] She considers possible worlds to be real, but nonetheless different from the "actual world." This allows her to distinguish between our actual world (AW), the "textual actual world" (TAW, constructed by the author) and the "textual referential world" (TRW, or the world described by the text). This analytic framework provides a more secure examination of the degrees of reference between the real world, the reader's mind, and the textual world. The boundaries between "reality" and "fiction" still exist but are less clear than they seem. Other more cautious uses have also emerged. Françoise Lavocat, professor of comparative literature, has recently proposed an example: refusing to confound real and virtual worlds, she uses the tool of possible worlds to distinguish between different kinds of fiction. She can thereby analyze how texts generate worlds and then define the "counterfactual" as one form among others of "alternative action": the relationship to the actual world is of a comparative order, as opposed to the allegorical or hermeneutic.[82] On another register, Marc Escola has proposed in recent years to enrich literary criticism through a "theory of possible texts." It is a question of tracing and then developing scenarios that have been abandoned or lives that remain to be written, which are present in the works themselves. By rewriting Racine, for example, it becomes possible for the critic to rediscover the impulse of the text itself in its most creative dimensions, before it was completed and hardened. More than a word-for-word adherence to the text, what becomes essential is the "priority of possibilities over the real": the "theory of possible texts . . . therefore invites one to appreciate within the great literary texts not only the past they contain but the futures that are emergent."[83] Within the context of these more measured uses, counterfactual literary analysis can be used to clarify the boundary between fiction and nonfiction, in opposition to a postmodern argument that there is no border between them, particularly in history.[84] The narratologist Lubomír Doležel, another theoretician of possible worlds,[85] has questioned the distinction between counterfactual historical fiction (uchronias) and counterfactual fiction, which is more "appropriate for history." Both are fictions and cannot be conflated with history as it actually took place (expressed for example in the proposition "Germany won the war in 1945"). However, drawing on the work of Niall Ferguson and Alexander Demandt, Doležel recalls that counterfactual "scholarly" narratives in history impose constraints (plausibility, insertion into social contexts, support for documentation), which is not the case for uchronias. Contrary to the assumptions of some postmodernists, the counterfactual historical account shows that there is no confusion between history and religion: the counterfactual statement is only a source of knowledge to the extent that it restores these boundaries and submits them to the epistemology of the historical discipline.[86]

Both varied and stimulating,[87] these literary analyses make it possible to confront questions as complex as the line between reality and fiction, the degree to which they interpenetrate, and the problem of the nature of fictional universes and their projective force.

Alongside literary theory, physical and life sciences have also developed an interest in the question of possible worlds. There is a clear relationship to the areas discussed above: the most commonly cited text in popular works is no doubt that of Jorge Luis Borges, "The Garden of Forking Paths," which evokes "This web of time—the strands of which approach one another, bifurcate, intersect or ignore each other through the centuries—embraces every possibility."[88]

This interest for possible worlds is the result of transformations within these sciences, which moved from an "absolute rationality" to a "limited rationality" across the twentieth century.[89] Today, the theorem referred to as Godel's incompleteness theorems (1932), according to which all theoretical systems contain some necessarily indemonstrable element, as well as Heisenberg's uncertainty principle (1927), which considers that since the position of a particle in the quantum world can only be established on a probabilistic model, it is impossible to have a 100 percent grasp of reality (it is the observer's intervention that reduces this uncertainty). Without losing any of their rigor or experimental ambition, researchers have generally abandoned Laplace's dream of knowing all, once the laws of nature are discovered, even the future. The notions of unpredictability and irreversibility have become essential.

Chaos theory is one of the best examples of taking into consideration situations of chemical or physical uncertainty and instability. Identified by

Henri Poincaré, who had already evoked the idea of the "sensitive dependence on initial conditions," it was refined by the work of Otto Rössler, and then Edward Lorenz, author in 1972 of a famous paper on the "butterfly effect."[90] This theory describes dynamic systems determined by laws but marked by instability. This renders them unpredictable, a characteristic that is as concerned with present futures as those of the past. In biology and chemistry, theories of self-organization have been nourished by this approach and shown themselves to be just as sensitive to situations of instability and bifurcations. Against the entropy thesis, which established that a system—living or not—is exhausted over time, it describes systems that, beyond a certain degree of complexity, self-perpetuate and allow for a process of unexpected and irreversible emergence. Such is the case for the famous "dissipative structure" of the physicist and chemist Ilya Prigogine, who described how the dissipation of energy and matter does not constitute a loss but becomes a source of order far from the initial equilibrium. These sciences have a variety of relationships to a more probabilistic, fluctuating, and anchored conception over time than previous models,[91] a notion that inspired Niall Ferguson and his proposal for "chaostory."[92] As Ilya Prigogine noted, one can find in this conception the emergence of the irreversibility of time in the area of life sciences: "Today there is then a distinction between two types of situations. This distinction is between stability on the one hand and instability and chaos on the other."[93] But unstable systems turn out to be the most common.

And "for [them] the laws of nature express what is possible and not what is 'certain.' This is particularly striking for the early moments of the universe. In these moments, one may compare the universe to a newborn baby who may become an architect, musician, or a bank employee, but who cannot become all three at once."[94]

The question of other possible worlds and counterfactuals has been more clearly posed in the realm of quantum physics and astrophysics—from the infinitely small to the infinitely vast. In 2001, in an article in the *Physical Review D,* Jaume Garriga and Alexander Vilenkin noted in an intentionally polemical tone: "Some readers will be pleased to know that there are infinitely many-regions where Al Gore is President and—yes—Elvis is still alive. . . . Whenever a thought crosses your mind that some terrible calamity might have happened, you can be assured that it *has* happened in some of the-regions."[95]

This other expression of alternate worlds, sometimes referred to as "multiverses" or "plural worlds," has been clearly posed in quantum mechanics. It is grounded in the idea of the impossibility of establishing with certainty the position of elementary particles such as protons, electrons and neutrinos which, during their experiments, appear in two places at once depending on how they are measured. Rather than understanding them as points, it is therefore necessary to conceive of them at once as particles and as waves; from this perspective, reality is divided continually into multiple possibilities. The phenomenon is known through famous thought experiments such as Schrödinger's cat (1935): a cat is enclosed in a box with a device that kills the animal as soon as it detects the disintegration of a radioactive atom. According to quantum mechanics, as long as the observation has not been made, the atom is simultaneously in two states (intact and disintegrated). In the mechanism imagined by Erwin Schrödinger, the cat would be simultaneously in two states (dead and alive), until one opened the box and set off the choice between the two states. So we cannot tell if the cat is dead or not after a minute has passed. Only the observer ensures the passage from a world of potentialities to a world of existing realized outcomes. Mach Zehnder's interferometer associates the movement of a photon and the potential explosion of a bomb and arrives at the same result: in quantum mechanics, an event that could have occurred and has not yet happened has observable physical consequences. In other words, according to this marvelous quantum world, while the counterfactual may have proven impossible in the context of classical physics, it is compatible with quantum physics.[96] In 1957, the American mathematician and physicist Hugh Everett theorized the possibility of "many worlds": instead of only reaching the state of one in particular, the one that is measured, the superposition of the states of quantum waves can be explained by the fact that the universe splits in two on each occasion. From there, multiple universes are born, in some of which we would not be born, in others Napoleon would not have lost at Waterloo. While it has a humorous dimension, this potential mathematical counterfactual has not elicited much attention.

Other proposals have been formulated as well. For example, there are those within the context of research on unitary theory, which attempts to establish a connection between the results of quantum physics and those of cosmology founded on general relativity. The most famous is string theory. It is based on the idea that elementary particles are vibrations at the end of infinitely small strings (10^{33}) that extend into nine dimensions. This allows for extremely sophisticated calculations that allow one to integrate gravitation into quantum mechanics. It helped describe the behavior of black holes in

1997 and may even provide access to the pre–big bang. Nonetheless, its critics suggest that the theory leaves too much room for error (to the extent that it proceeds only through logical extensions). The theory does, in any case, leave open the possibility of a plurality of universes. One of the most clearly demonstrable principles that allows for such possibilities is the following: since the big bang produced far more space and energy than we can actually observe, it may have created in different spaces other possible universes, even some that we cannot imagine, simply by changing the values of the fundamental constants of physics from place to place. Earth is therefore a place where the conditions were united such that humanity could appear, roughly 13.8 billion years after the big bang. This reading excludes the fact that these different space-time areas can be reconnected, or connected to our current history. They are simply connected by what happened in the 1^{38} first seconds, at a moment when matter did not yet exist.

This point has been mentioned several times and was developed in the 1990s, under the term "multiverse," coined by Alexander Vilenkin and Leonard Susskind.[97] The hypothesis gave rise to numerous versions and discussions: some physicists have accepted it, others, such as the Nobel Prize–winning "stringer" David Gross, has refused it. This is not to mention the other unitary theories, such as those proposed by Lee Smolin and Carlo Rovelli's loop theory, based on the idea of nodes of space-time.[98] Nevertheless, the multiverse has found a place within contemporary scientific debate, and its powerful suggestive force is demonstrated by the echo it has received in the media.

These different worlds of possibility should not be confused with one another: the possible worlds of Lewis rely on a construction based on common sense, while those in physics require data analysis, lawmaking, and probabilities, as well as experimental verification. However, these physical theories are based on the resources of fiction as evidenced by the frequent use of metaphors to account for phenomena that are observed or deduced. Moreover, when they extend beyond the field of the observable, they become metaphysical, posing problems or provoking a certain conceptual audacity. These worlds of possibility constitute an undefinable space of knowledge on the world and the cosmos.

This first overview allows us to better understand the variety of forms, layers, trajectories, and temporalities covered by the uses of counterfactual reasoning and paths not taken. They belong to disparate domains of exploration, knowledge, and everyday life. This diversity gives rise to many confusions, uncertainties, rejections and enthusiastic supporters. It is therefore necessary to offer two points of clarification.

First of all, we have identified the multiple connections that link these different practices. Some of them can be put aside, especially those that link a historical approach to the field of pure fiction to the most abstract philosophy and fundamental physics. Not that their uses are irrelevant, but rather they combine fields that are too distant and that would require more rigorous and systematic connections.

There is also the risk of ceding to a certain fashion, which runs the risk of blurring such divergent registers. This helps explain why this approach has raised some concerns and circumspection during this moment of heightened reflexivity within the social sciences. Such a critique remains insufficient on its own, however, since counterfactualism is also used by individuals as an everyday mode of reasoning. Moreover, this mode of thinking has existed for a long time in history, giving rise to various expectations and definitions and carrying with it a set of problems that have not yet been solved (notably imagination, causality, temporality, political uses, and so on).

How then can we proceed in the specific field of history? The question is not whether or not one should mobilize this mode of reasoning, which is often simply unavoidable, but rather of asking whether or not it is necessary to explain why one has recourse to it and assume its effects. What underlying questions does it contain? What gains, and what losses, can one expect when one employs it?

PART TWO

Decoding

> The consequences that must have resulted, had this scheme succeeded, are so incalculable, that it is not too much to say they would have completely changed the political history of Europe. The power of Bavaria would have outweighed that of Austria in both German and Slavonian countries, and Zapolya, thus supported, would have been able to maintain his station; the Ligue, and with its high ultra-montane opinions, would have held the ascendency in eastern Europe. Never was there a project more pregnant with danger to the growing power of the house of Austria.
>
> —Leopold von Ranke[1]

A surfeit of delicate questions remains, hidden within this common though often-unacknowledged form of reasoning. So let's leave the spyglass behind and pick up the magnifying glass to better understand the problems that a counterfactual approach poses for historians, and to specify the conditions under which it may be useful. This focus comes with a cost: in the pages that follow, there shall be no butterflies flapping their wings to create tornadoes, nor shall there be time machines. We will now limit ourselves to the examination of counterfactual reasoning with a certain plausibility, more clearly zeroing in on specific spatiotemporal situations with their own documentary bases. We turn then to a study of the relationship between different modes of counterfactual reasoning and methods in history and the social sciences. We will address some of the main areas of inquiry that appeared earlier: the role of the imagination, the question of causality, the forms of historicity, and the political and social problems involved in the work of historians. It will then be possible to identify the risks and determine the relevant uses of this process.

CHAPTER 5

The Historical Imagination and Counterfactual Approaches

> Imagining possibilities and changing them through thought . . . is at once the source of scientific knowledge and the imaginary worlds of myths and the arts.
>
> —Maurice Godelier[1]

> Jesus is ninety-seven years old, and very frail. He can barely see now: he who once healed the blind. Cataracts. He can barely walk: he who once made the lame dance. His hearing is still fine, though. The Word incarnate, as John calls him, can hear just fine. He suffers from arthritis, and his mind is somewhere else most of the time. . . . it is then that he suffers a massive stroke, alone in his room, alone with his Father, and the Spirit he is always talking about too, the Spirit he so desperately wants to see take over the world. "My God, My God, why have you forsaken me?" Jesus dies within two minutes, his blood spilled, finally, inside his own head.
>
> —Carlos M. N. Eire[2]

This is how Carlos M. N. Eire, professor of history and religious studies at Yale University, describes, in his 2001 counterfactual history, the death of Jesus after escaping crucifixion. Wondering what would have happened had Pontius Pilate spared him provides important insights. After showing the probability of the hypothesis, Eire describes a more muffled diffusion of Jesus's ideas, though he no doubt would have been well recognized, over the years, as a prophet in his own right. Jesus would quickly have come to be protected by the Roman emperors who would have been favorable to this religion, which taught docility and submission. Upon his death, they would have organized a new religion in keeping with their own needs, reinforcing an empire that could have more effectively resisted external attacks. The highpoint of Eire's demonstration comes with the death of Jesus, sixty-four years after he didn't die on the cross.

This example reveals the important links between counterfactual history and imagination. Generally opened by "Imagine that . . . ," the technique is often explicit. But isn't this precisely where the difficulty lies? While the counterfactual detour allows one, as this historian suggests, to disentangle the interrelationship between a nascent belief, a dogma, events, a religious institution and a geopolitical situation, do the last words of Jesus at ninety-seven years old not suffice to disqualify what would, for many researchers, be judged simply a poor use of imagination? The process may, above all, produce extravagances or useless fantasies, which may even be prejudicial to historical understanding. But let us not forget that the imagination is not an enemy of the examination of the past. It is, to the contrary, a key element of historical analysis. The problem is rather the type of imagination proposed by counterfactual history: What difficulties does it pose, and under what conditions might it be useful?

IMAGINATION IN HISTORICAL REASONING

Let's begin with a few obvious points of reference on the difficult question of the role of the imagination in historical reasoning.

The Status of the Imagination

The relationship between history and imagination has long been established: history is knowledge through traces of the past, insofar as access to the past is conditioned by the existence of archives. It is a knowledge that is also said to be "filled with holes" or "incomplete." This explains its status of uncertainty on the one hand, and the need to use imagination, alongside data compilation methods and documentary analysis, on the other. As Krzysztof Pomian recalls in a synthetic work on the writing of history,[3] all knowledge draws upon imagination. But this does not mean that all forms of knowledge are entirely interchangeable: imagination, he argues, is never autonomous. It remains unique, bound to its author. Knowledge on the other hand may be understood to be stable, independent of its own production and objective. The relationship between history and fiction is of the same order: historical narration, by definition, requires the contribution of fiction, though it is far from being a mere invention. It attempts to "escape its own textuality" and examine the past according to this objective.

Such a presentation brings new life to a classic debate. When we look at the moment when history emerged as a discipline and as an autonomous field of investigation in the nineteenth century, we see that most historians recognized the enduring link between imagination and historical practice. It is, of course, a controlled, as opposed to entirely unrestricted, imagination. The question that drives the debates is thus not so much that of choosing between science and literature as knowing where to put the cursor between the two poles.

A few brief incursions into the classic texts of French historiography make it possible to further appreciate this debate. Jules Michelet, who defined himself as a son of history ("in the lightning flash of the July Revolution," he wrote about the political upheavals of 1830, "I have seized France"[4]), incarnates a specific moment of Romantic history, even as he occupies a singular position within it. According to his famous 1869 preface to the *History of France,* the dispassionate historian, "who aims to disappear while writing" is not a historian: he is at best a chronicler. Recourse to imagination, emotion, and the capacity to paint life are essential for coming into physical contact with the lives of past people and for producing a history with the ambition to perform an "entire resurrection of the past." But this required "so many days of hard work and study in the depths of the Archives!" He insists in this text on the importance of the patient work of immersion in the sources, for "to rediscover historical life, one must follow it patiently along all of its paths." As essential as they are, creative imagination and the depth of the historian's very self only gain meaning in the context of an intimate knowledge of the archives.[5]

Gabriel Monod recognized this fact in another classic text in 1876, his introduction to the new *Revue historique.* Here he attempted to make a clear break with his predecessors:[6] in a country stricken by the defeat of 1870 against Prussia, confident in the superiority of German education, he believed that France had fallen behind in historical studies because "the national genius was subject to the seduction of the imagination and art." The reference to Michelet is obvious. It was necessary then, on the contrary, to apply a rigorous method that allowed one to set the historical narrative aside, to make it objective, and "though one is never sure that one can discover the complete truth, at least distinguish in each case between what is certain or most likely and doubtful or false." The historian defines his or her scientific capacity less through the ability to tell the truth than to reveal falsehoods. This approach marked a radical break. And yet Monod expressed in this text his respect for Michelet, who looked for "man instead of facts," and accepted the contributions of Romantic historiography.[7] In a small aside, he recalls that the historian "cannot forget his own feelings, nor his own ideas" in order to "put himself in the place of the men of old." Since historians cannot be entirely absent from the narrative, they must try to distance themselves as far as possible.

The paradox is even more evident in the work of Charles-Victor Langlois and Charles Seignobos. Their *Introduction to the Study of History* (1898) offered a methodological reconsideration of facts through an internal and an external critique.[8] Once again, there was an explicit ambition to make history a scientific discipline, regulated by the methods of rigorous validation. They quickly posed the problem "How then is it possible to imagine facts without their being wholly imaginary?" History, they recognized, is necessarily subjective, without being unreal. The historian "is obliged to picture the facts in his imagination, and he should make it his constant endeavor to construct his mental images out of only exact elements." Thus, even the most positivistic historians did not evacuate the use of imagination, since it appeared to be a necessary evil. Fustel de Coulanges was no doubt an exception when he asserted in 1888 that "History is a science; one does not use the imagination."[9]

The tension was expressed in the postwar period, when the debate with Durkheimian sociology was coming to fruition, generating a renewal of historical investigations. Lucien Febvre, one of the "fathers" of the historical journal the *Annales,* founded in 1929, disagreed early on with Gabriel Monod and a type of history that he considered too narrow—more concerned with establishing a chronicle of events than solving historical problems. On multiple occasions, he highlighted the role of emotion, invention, and creative thought, or what he referred to as the "life" of historical work.[10] There were regular calls for "efforts of imagination," to such an extent that he later insisted in his *Combats pour l'histoire* that "the first quality for the historian is imagination."[11] It is not entirely certain that Lucien Febvre was giving the same meaning to this term as previous historians, since he also meant the capacity to invent historical questions. But even so, there is a call for erudition and to rigorous and renewed documentary evidence. Only such proof may ensure that one avoids the sin of all sins, psychological anachronism.[12] His article, which invites us to "reconstitute the affective life of the past," since it treats a difficult object that is subject to misinterpretation, is indicative of this double requirement.[13] The heart of the demonstration is dedicated to the examination of available sources (literature, diaries, and so on) and the traps that they contain. He examines at length the manner in which they are used, based on the question that is posed, revealing how difficult the problem is to solve. "Does the historian not have the right to abandon ship?"[14] Once again, imagination depends on establishing a rigorous and enlightened proximity with the documentation.

The quantitative history that emerged in the 1950s under the dual inspiration of Ernest Labrousse and Fernand Braudel also explored this tension as they sought to impose a more rigorous approach that was more objective and less literary. In the introduction to his famous *La Crise de l'économie française* (1944), Ernest Labrousse rallied for an exacting statistical analysis of prices based on objective data. In so doing, he evacuated, even down to the writing itself, the role of the historian. At the same time, he did not ignore the fact that these curves, once they were established, could be "lived and perceived differently by men of their time." They therefore necessitated an effort of historical interpretation that supposed a capacity to produce images in order to feel a closer connection to people of the past.[15]

Such a back-and-forth on the question of imagination could go on indefinitely. It has been addressed through the different problematics and perspectives of Fernand Braudel, Henri-Irénée Marrou, Jacques Le Goff, Paul Veyne, Roger Chartier, and Alain Corbin, who, in the conclusion of a book of interviews with Gilles Heuré, takes up Lucien Febvre's claim: "the first quality of the historian is imagination."[16] Outside the historical field, the philosopher Paul Ricoeur also showed interest in the historical imagination, revealing how Braudel's *The Mediterranean* provided an alternative to narrative history, with a plot, characters, and key passages. According to Paul Ricoeur, the singularity of the historical investigation was tied to its recourse to documentary evidence as well as methods of explanation and understanding, but also a historical imagination and a reconstruction of the past, all of which are driven by a desire for truth.[17]

This brief account shows that the return to questions of imagination today should not be distinct from historical methods. These explorations also make it possible to define more precisely what we now understand by the term "imagination." It may be defined as the capacity to produce images, in its creative dimension. In this sense, it is related to fiction (understood as something that is "not real" and that it produces), empathy (the capacity to put oneself in the place of another), subjectivity (linked to emotion and the individual), visibility (through the power of images), and narration (through the creation of a plot structure). All of these elements are linked without ever entirely overlapping.

The Role of the Imagination

Let us further examine the role of the imagination defined in these terms within historical reasoning. Most of the historians mentioned above agree on one point: imagination runs the risk of adding to the past something that does not belong there or that is simply false. This is a common critique of imagination, perceived as the "mistress of error and falsehood," "the superb enemy of reason," in the words of Pascal.[18] This conception is based on an old notion that defines imagination as the lowest level of knowledge, since it is turned toward the self and is nourished by sensations from the outside world. It is true that projecting one's own images onto the past, be it representations of one's own time, political opinions, or personal expectations, is a serious mistake in history. This is the famous "sin of anachronism," which holds an important place in the repertory of historical criticism. Lucien Febvre levels precisely this critique, in his book on Rabelais, against Abel Lefranc, author of the preface to a new edition of *Pantagruel,* where it was suggested that Rabelais had been a nonbeliever. The proposition sparked Febvre's ire: "Is it possible that he was a nonbeliever?" he asks in his introduction.[19] The historical inquiry that follows seeks to demonstrate precisely the opposite: the study of the "mental tools" of this period reveal that he could not possibly have been a nonbeliever.[20] One finds a similar approach in Jean-Pierre Vernant's famous *Mythe et pensée chez les Grecs.* The introduction is similarly based on a critique of Zevedei Barbu's *The Emergence of Personality in the Greek World.* "Because he has not taken all the different kinds of evidence into account, and particularly because he has not studied them closely enough [Zevedei Barbu] sometimes imposes too modern an interpretation on them and projects onto the Greek personality certain features that, in my opinion, did not emerge until more recently."[21] Beyond these famous clashes, it is common to reproach a work of history for expressing the expectations and reflections of its author instead of the modes of conceptualization and thought of the society under study. When presented in these terms, imagination is the enemy of historical research.

It can also, however, play a more positive role. Imagination allows, for example, to fill in the blanks of information. Krzysztof Pomian and Charles-Victor Langlois both recalled its importance within the context of historical research: since knowledge of the past is full of holes, it is necessary to fill the gaps, more or less explicitly through the fruits of the imagination.

Georges Duby's *William Marshal* offers a good example of explicitly employing this resource.[22] He wrote a biography of the "best knight in the world" of the thirteenth century, William Marshal, Earl of Pembroke, who was a great tournament competitor, Crusader to the Holy Land, and then victorious over the French in 1217. Duby relies on a vast *chanson de geste* from the period, of just under twenty thousand verses, but presents his story as a novel. The narration constantly crosses the examination of sources, historical analysis, and quasi-fictional embellishments. The text alternates between different well-identified registers, sometimes through a simple game of styles and scripts, while following the course of the hero's life. The style jumps out at the reader from the opening lines:

> The Earl can bear no more. The burden is too great for him now. Three years ago, when he was urged to assume the regency, when he reluctantly agreed, becoming "master and guardian" of the boy king and of the whole realm of England, he had said and said again, "I am too old, too weak, too out of joint." Over eighty, he had claimed, exaggerating a little, not really knowing how old he was. Who knew such things in those days?

The question then leads to historical commentary. One frequently finds this approach in works of history, although it can be more discreet. It is most common in the "effects of reality" created by researchers: the psychology of the characters, invented scenes, the addition of living details, setting the stage at the beginning of a chapter, and the choice of isolated examples that are designed to give more flesh to statistical analysis. Beyond the artifice of writing, recourse to such techniques is also employed for the pleasure of the reader.

Imagination does more than just fill gaps, however. Through its capacity to create images, it is also necessary for contextualization, that is, for the reconstitution of the situations historians study. In order to "move outside the documents" and build out of them to develop an analysis, one must stop looking at the archive and ask oneself what was happening, what took place on this site, and so on, if only to search for other archives. This work can be based on erudition, but recreating the "*décor*" and immersing oneself in the past in general require further effort of imagination.

The approach is common within ancient history: from a few fragments and the information that can be drawn from them, researchers strive to reconstruct social organization, politics, and even the landscape, especially in order to confront these proposals with other elements or historiographical debates and refine our understanding. This can clearly be seen in Egyptology, where researchers manage to reconstitute whole areas of society and its material universe from archaeological excavations. This is obviously also the case for prehistory. The discovery in South Tyrol, in 1991, of the frozen body of a man who lived in about 3300 BCE, quickly named Ötzi, gave rise to work of this type, based on data collection, from pollens to his clothes, the results were presented in various fiction-documentaries.[23]

It is, of course, used in other fields as well. The series collection La Vie quotidienne (Everyday Life) published by Hachette, for example, proposed a series of books that highlighted a choice of topics for which there were insufficient sources. The book by Philippe Vigier on everyday life in Paris and the provinces in 1848,[24] one of the first to propose an analysis of the revolutions of February–June 1848 and of the Second Republic outside the Parisian context, was exemplary in this regard. The author passes from one village or city to the next. In each new place, the narrative stops and the author describes the environment, the social relations, and then the events and their effects. The staging partially seeks to reproduce the historian's approach: based on an archive (oftentimes a personal diary), the vision spreads out to the surroundings to propose other questions and pursue more research. These attempts to reconstruct the context, through documentation and imagination, give more substance to the narrative, but also provide for greater historical intelligibility.

This approach has provided an opportunity for some historians to pursue experiments on the edges of history. This was the case for Patrick Boucheron who, in *Léonard et Machiavel,* imagined a meeting between Leonardo da Vinci and Machiavelli based on his knowledge of the period and these individuals. It is known from various documents that the meeting took place, but no trace of it exists. In an original style, he explores the possible situations, the various facets and implications of this encounter about which we only know one thing: that it happened.[25] Alain Corbin's *Le Monde retrouvé de Louis-François Pinagot* also sparked debate on this subject.[26] The project embraced a historiographical challenge: reconstitute the life of an unknown individual chosen at random within the archives. The author attempted to paint a portrait through careful archival work, restoring the material and mental universe of Louis-François Pinagot, a cobbler living in the Orne department in

France. Faced with the difficulty of reconstructing the thoughts, perceptions, and environment of Pinagot's daily life, the book frequently has recourse to imagination, presenting it as a means of mobilizing the reader. "At the very least, we can attempt to hear, through our imagination, the conversations and exchanges that took place around him," he suggests with regard to the type of language and conversation used in the region of the Perche at the time.[27] The work sparked discussions, interest, and criticism, nourished by the revelation of sources that might have allowed greater precision on certain key aspects of the biography. These clarifications ran the risk of undermining the stakes of this singular experience that highlighted the historian's position, the problem of traces of the past and the individual in history. It also raises the question of the means available to the researcher for gaining access to those places where archives are silent—a condition that characterizes a large majority of the population at any given moment.[28] Imagination becomes the default technique, which remains indispensable for meeting the demands even of social history.

Thus, it seems to challenge the idea discussed above that the imagination is bound to the author and therefore does not allow one to escape the fictional text as he or she turns to investigate the real. In this case, it seems to be a necessary condition for understanding the real. According to Thomas Pavel, only imagination, and what it produces, that is, fiction, made up of proximity and distance, allows for comparison and the ability to step outside oneself. Historians must also consider this elusive, and perhaps even excessive, understanding. It may be noted that to the contrary, retreating to a posture that is purely "scientific," meaning in this case objective and bereft of all imagination, is no guarantee of complete distantiation on the part of the researcher. Recourse to neutral scientific practices and technical decisions, destined to ensure that research (the isolation of individual elements, the establishment of facts, and so on), can be, as Norbert Elias has shown, a part of "engagement." Such an approach can be motivated by a tremendous confidence in a historically situated conception of the science in which collective imagination plays a role: hence the model of intelligibility borrowed by the social sciences from the physical sciences "in many cases, creates a façade of distantiation behind which one hides a clearly engaged position."[29] Established as an absolute principle, this posture reassures the researcher without necessarily contributing to establishing a real social scientific "distance," which implies more openness of mind and a careful consideration of interrelations. Truth be told, the German sociologist did not offer a precise method for achieving such distance. But his remarks invite us to temper the accusations of the frivolity of imagination on the one hand and the seriousness of a more scientific approach on the other. This reflection on imagination is not only a question for history. It has also been treated in sociology,[30] as seen in Howard Becker's sociology of deviance and the "worlds of art." In his view, "telling stories," either in the form of case studies or in the construction of an object of study, constitute veritable "tricks of the trade": they allow one to refine hypotheses and familiarize oneself with the context of a given subject of study.[31]

Imagination can be mobilized even more dynamically, especially when researchers are trying to understand the ways of seeing and thinking within the societies they study. This was established by the first authors to explore the question of historical psychology and the social imaginary,[32] who were often also specialists of antiquity: Paul Veyne, Jean-Pierre Vernant, Pierre Vidal-Naquet, as well as Georges Duby for the Middle Ages.[33]

This imagination remains constrained: it "puts itself in the place" through extended work in the archives.[34] Michel de Certeau retraced more precisely the steps of this creative process: a first phase of objectification through the patient reading of sources; followed by a phase of listening, a moment of being open to the other; and finally there is the process of formalization through writing. Openness here is not passive, to the extent that it also implies active listening and an effort toward mental reconstruction.

This work is not detached from the more scientific aspects of history: the historian proceeds with an inquiry, works based on sources that are treated with a specific method, which allows one to bring forward facts and certain phenomena. Then comes a leap of the imagination to "see with one's own eyes" the people of the period[35] and apprehend the ways of feeling or thinking of a society or a group under study. This approach is also very useful for grasping modes of social divisions, categories of perception, or political forms that have become foreign to us.

In this sense, it is possible to say that history also has a poetic dimension, in the fundamental sense of creation, which makes it possible to describe the "other" and to make it comprehensible to readers.[36]

Finally, this perspective requires reflection on the writing of history: understood in this way, it must neither be too dry in its attempt to imitate pure objectivity, nor eloquent by relying on the artifice of style. On the other hand, historical writing can reproduce the different phases of reasoning, render its approach explicit, and join in the effort of reconstituting the past by mobilizing literary possibilities.[37]

There remains one last essential point: narration—that is to say, the conception of a plot and the articulation of facts and elements of the analysis according to a particular setup—is clearly linked to imagination (it is a matter of producing or inventing the connections). However, this is not the same as fiction, since it can be based on precise empirical data. One of the issues consists of using the cognitive resources of narrative to produce a new intelligibility, which the usual modes of history cannot provide.[38] One of the most well-known examples is perhaps Carlo Ginzburg's *The Cheese and the Worms.* The author studies a Friulian miller from the sixteenth century, Menocchio, who was condemned by the Inquisition for heresy. Imitating the style of police investigation, he uses the trial documents to reconstruct Menocchio's mental landscape.[39] The narrative, which is at once dynamic and adapted to an investigative analysis, is opposed to a reading of overly collective or coherent mentalities. It shows instead how the miller reconstructs his own universe based on elements belonging to different registers and assembled in a very original way. This method has found a wide audience: it proposes a distinct use of the historian's imagination as well as a particular mobilization of literary techniques, from which the research borrows a more daring organizational form to enrich the repertoire of descriptions, connections, and analysis.[40]

These ways of doing history are increasingly widespread among historians, and all of them depend on the functions and definitions that one accords the discipline. It would appear, nonetheless, that imagination, once it is constrained, is clearly a part of the modes of historical inquiry.

IS COUNTERFACTUAL IMAGINATION OPPOSED TO THE HISTORIAN'S IMAGINATION?

The distinctiveness of counterfactual history is clear from the outset. Contrary to the examples mentioned earlier, it is necessary to trace possible futures and dynamics that have not actually happened in the past. This approach is also accompanied by a specific narrative device: a "fractured" text that conventionally separates the story that really happened, that is the "truth," from an imaginary history, or one that is "false." In this proposition there is a particular use of the historical imagination, which is also presented as a "constrained imagination," a status that is made explicit in its pact with the reader. But does this suffice to make it an interesting tool?

In fact, quite to the contrary, such a device can pose serious problems, or even be counterproductive. We may take the canonical example: if Napoleon had won at Waterloo . . . he would have conquered Europe, established a foothold for his empire over the long term, and modified the geopolitical equilibrium. Spain, Italy, and Germany would not exist in their current forms, and so on. What is the interest in describing such alternatives? Do they not risk drying up, rather than stimulating the imagination?

So let us return to the mechanisms involved in these fictional projections, considering the three points of the triangle implied by the bifurcation. First, the turning point is often relatively impoverished: Waterloo, Charles Martel in 732, the US Civil War, the world wars, and so on. All of these points of bifurcation fit into an apprehension that is dated by historical periods and a relatively conventional reading of "the event." By definition, counterfactual history is "factual," sometimes in the narrowest sense of the term, in that the fact itself is not called into question, and its causes and consequences are assumed. This approach may also imply a kind of historiographical regression: what emerges—in particular in the alternative histories written for a large audience—is a linear history of great men and important dates. Such a definition of the turning point risks indirectly to reestablish a conception of the event, the actor, and the cause that is inherent in a positivist history associated with the nineteenth century.

The second point is even more problematic. In this narrative framework, the normal historical narrative, understood as that part of history "as it really happened," is also affected. The exaggerated division on either side of the turning point tends to mask the complexity of historical work, most notably the recourse to imagination that was just signaled. It tends to accredit "truth" to a text that is itself full of tensions, while it should in fact be the foundation for a critical examination. In addition, it has a tendency to artificially separate the real from the imaginary, whereas the imaginary is part of social reality and thereby proposes a very staid historical vision.

The most troubling, however, is the counterfactual narrative itself. It is supposed to represent a possible reality. The imagination is therefore employed to provide a mimesis of reality and must function "as if" it described a reality. Such an objective appears in the method defined by counterfactual researchers, which is similar to the imperatives necessary for tracing such a fictional path (logical, historical, theoretical coherence that takes into consideration the series of facts and consequences).[41] But while they are necessary for satisfying the approach's scientific ambitions, they carry the risk of imposing stereotypical historical sequences that supposedly form the fabric of a new "real," according to some impoverished definition. Paradoxically, such a fictional narrative undermines the very interest that recourse to imagination brings to history. Instead of exploring realities that grow ever richer, they become stifled.

On top of the risk of mobilizing a noncreative imagination and proposing an essentialized "real," there is also the danger that imagination, in this "outerfactual" realm, threatens to feed only on itself or on the expectations and perceptions of its author. The critique offered by E. H. Carr in 1961, when he denounced a practice of "losers in history" (we only rewrite the history that we wish had ended differently) or "vain speculation," remains sound in this respect. The alternative narrative can be composed either of a chain of reasoning that is ultimately empty, or the author's imagination, or both. The problem is in part tied to the question of the historical traces left behind. The archive, as we have said, is at the heart of the historian's work. Not as a passive reflection of former societies, but as a flash of reality that has actually taken place, a "distorted mirror" upon which the historian explores an estranged past.[42] The use of imagination has meaning only in conjunction with this documentation, out of which the examination and interpretation of the past is constructed. The risk is that we do not live up to this exigency.

The difficulty has only increased with the recent debate on the relationship between history and fiction. Analyses inspired by Hayden White's work and the linguistic turn have tended to throw doubt on historians' capacity to establish a true narrative of the past, which extends beyond literature, even if it is oriented toward the "real." Many historians have responded by insisting upon the real, which history must strive to describe. They have also recalled the boundary between history and fiction and explained, once again, the manner in which the former may be nourished by the latter.[43] The counterfactual narrative, which is at once false and possible, risks in this context to increase the confusion between the genres, especially since its success depends on this very incertitude.[44] In this case, the threat appears just that much more serious.

Finally, it should be noted that the full range of the proposed alternative remains limited. Nikolay Koposov, in a reflection on "historical imagination," has shown how, beyond language and argumentation, mental images provide an underlying structure to historical reasoning.[45] One type of structure, which appeared in the eighteenth and nineteenth centuries is what he calls the spatial imagination. The spatial metaphor is indeed one of the implicit foundations of historical reflection, as illustrated by the vocabulary of history books when they evoke the "course," or the "winding path" of history, or the "strata" and "layers" of past societies. This metaphor is in itself neither good nor bad. One must keep in mind however that it offers opportunities while constraining historical understanding. Nevertheless, counterfactual reasoning clearly does attempt to imagine another "path" of historical development, which is often coherent and well-founded. And in this way, it can reinforce a rather straightforward and simple conception of historical change. The imagined alternative in this case remains caught within a limited and profoundly unoriginal framework. All these elements may help to explain the reticence on the part of a certain number of historians.

UNREALIZED OUTCOMES AS A MODE OF INTERPRETATION

As common as they may be, these pitfalls are escapable. Reflective use of the imagination can prove interesting. Beyond playfulness (to which we will return), it can also serve an analytical function. First of all, counterfactual narratives do not necessarily depart from their sources. They can be based on documentation that was not questioned from the angle initially envisaged, or they can even be mobilized to enrich the interpretation of traces of the past, by exploring the contours that the historian must carefully follow.[46] The significance of a given document is not always one-dimensional: it can carry within it imagined futures or possible interpretations that have not yet taken place at the moment of their production. "Truth is a point of arrival, not a point of departure."[47]

This usage can be broadened in several ways, for example by participating in a process of contextualization: evoking possible futures, based on a turning point, allows one to take into consideration a broader range of situations and suggest the importance of phenomena that are judged insignificant a posteriori. This, in turn, invites one to reinterpret sources or return to the archives.[48] Thus, John Keegan, in a chapter entitled "How Hitler Could Have Won the War," imagines that Hitler abandons his pursuit of Operation Barbarossa to concentrate on conquering the Middle East, where German troops had made easy advances after supporting Italy at the beginning of 1941.[49] Following a plausible military reasoning, the Führer could have appropriated the region's oil, which was increasingly in demand for the German army, and then attacked the Soviet Union a year later, on two fronts and with the necessary fuel. The outcome could have been different. This detour allows Keegan to emphasize the irrational character of Hitler's war, but also invites researchers to use other sources and recall the diversity of operational possibilities at the time. The Middle Eastern theater is indeed often overshadowed by the importance of Operation Barbarossa (because of its failed outcome, which caused the beginning of the Axis defeat) and perhaps also due to the implicit idea that what happened in the Middle East was necessarily peripheral. This recourse to imagination makes it possible to fight the retrospective illusion of the decisive character of this or that event. Counterfactual history fights against the counterfactual operation that historians follow anyway by unduly associating two phenomena, omitting elements or discarding aspects that do not fit into their analytical framework.

More original uses may also be envisaged. Faced with a partial or biased corpus, the projection of a counterfactual allows one to establish a reflexive distance that may be difficult to implement without it. This approach was adopted by the Austrian historian Joachim Losehand, discussed in chapter 2. The death of Pompey, madly and desperately fleeing toward Egypt, gave rise, he explains, to many stories that have sedimented over the centuries into an authoritative reading. Given the documentary constraints, imagining and explaining Pompey's successful escape gives credence to the idea that the departure for Egypt was not necessarily the result of a "great man's" despair, but may also have been part of a coherent strategy, even if it was ultimately ineffective. The episode may therefore be seen from another angle to offer a renewed analysis of geopolitics and the nature of power in antiquity. The use of fictional history here authorizes the researcher to deconstruct the fictions underlying the available documents and the historian's work.[50] Conversely, the approach can also be used to overcome a lack of documentation. This is what the medievalist Jacques Dalarun suggests in his study of the *First and Second Lives of St. Francis*. Available sources suggest that another *Life* was written between the two *Lives* that were currently known, those of 1228 and 1248, by the same author, Thomas de Celano. The missing text was suggested by "three carved words, that are difficult to read and of uncertain attribution." To advance his research after the careful study of the texts, the historian went from "the reconstruction via hypotheses to hypothetical reconstitutions, which overstep the line of over-interpretation and speculation more than once."[51] He offered three plausible scenarios, based on an intimate knowledge of the period, which explained how and in what context the "Umbrian legend" could have been produced, if it existed at all. A comparison of the scenarios allowed the historian to retain the most plausible of the three. This marked the limit of this type of reasoning, even if they were simply "narrative projections of a very classical historical conjecture," two of which were incorrect. And yet, seven years later, in September 2014, a manuscript of the *Life* in question was discovered during an auction in the United States and was purchased by the French National Library (Bibliothèque nationale de France). This document confirms the medieval historian's initial hypothesis.[52] The case clearly demonstrates the possibility of a connection between fictional explorations and the quest for sources.

It is also conceivable to more effectively use the approach's capacity of projection. This requires increasing our ability to interpret the ways of seeing contemporaries by analyzing future fears, hopes, and possibilities of a given moment in the past. The idea is to take seriously several aspects of Reinhart Koselleck's earlier proposals. The first concerns the examination of future fears and hopes. It is a question of extending the imagination, giving these futures that were envisaged but not realized more depth. This is the least problematic use, since, when it is backed by widely available documentation (literature, diaries, speeches and political achievements, official reports, and so on), the historian's imagination is fed just as it reveals the imagination and sensibilities of the groups and societies under investigation. This explains why this path has been explored within cultural history and other areas. The study of "imagined" wars of the twentieth century provides examples for the first half of the twentieth century.[53] A recent conference on the subject even suggested that "reconstituting the multiple senses of a future war, or wars, which existed before 1914 would thus contribute . . . to an interpretative triptych of the Great War as a fundamental rupture in modern history."[54] The proposition may seem close to a more classical analysis of social representations. But it also allows for an interpretive leap: instead of constraining oneself to exploring a representation that we know implicitly has failed, taking these elements into consideration and adding fiction gives it more flesh and a greater capacity to project into the future. This fictional extension could cover a wider array of objects, such as social utopias of the nineteenth and twentieth centuries. It can also take into consideration the schemas or tools of anticipation produced by a given society—calculations, probabilities, scientific and financial discourses, and descriptions of the "real" world.[55] These past futures were inscribed in the projective capacities and the possibilities allowed by a given technical environment. The historian David Carr has remarked that to the extent that individual actions are partially determined by these horizons, the latter belong fully to past realities, even if they did not take place or appear strange within our understanding of the world.[56]

These suggestions bring us toward another dimension of counterfactual analysis: a more direct confrontation with "fields of experience." Based on an increased knowledge of issues, of the social, political, and cultural conditions and the institutions and groups, informal as well as formal, we are able to examine more possible and unrealized futures, which we may refer to as "past possibilities," whose scientific status remains uncertain. Eric Hobsbawm proposed an analysis of this type when he agreed to "welcome excursions into imaginary or fictional history known as 'counterfactual'" with regard to the Russian Revolution. He proposed a typology that distinguished between the fascinating but ultimately useless hypothesis, the hypothesis inscribed in the hopes of a moment but which remain impossible, and finally the hypothesis that is hoped for and really possible.[57] In this case, it is about using imagination to give relief to these virtual elements, and thus modify our perception of the social, political, or cultural landscapes under study. Sociology and historical sociology have shown themselves to be more open to this approach, on a variety of objects (collective mobilizations, social and political groups, public policies, and so on). It has also been used in the field of sociology of art: the counterfactual scenario serves to explore the work of creation, to highlight the hesitations, the unfinished stages, the choices made between financial, institutional, and artistic constraints. In this way, counterfactual imagination makes it possible to pose clearly the question of the "state" of achievement of a work of art.[58] It also makes it possible to study other phenomena, such as the social order, in order to show how "the dead seize the living" as Pierre Bourdieu put it.[59] In this article, Bourdieu reveals a tension between the analysis of dispositions and possibilities. In his view, it is necessary to denaturalize the social order and the way in which the latter, by the weight of the objective positions and the habitus of the individuals, tends to reduce the field of the virtual. Housing policies in France in the 1970s provide an example. The laws that opened the market led almost immediately to a situation brought on by the interplay of competing economic and political interests. This new situation became a "reality" to such an extent that it was impossible to imagine an alternative. The sociologist then proposes an interesting distinction: he suggests that it is easier to describe "probable" outcomes, to the extent that they reproduce an existing order that has some familiar mechanisms, than "possibilities" that invite us to (re)think what didn't happen and thus struggle against the illusion of necessity.[60] This exercise strikes him as useful despite the risks involved. The more recently published courses on the state further developed this discussion. The approach is described in this case as one research strategy among others, specific to "genetic critique" (*la pensée génétique*). "To de-banalize and overcome the amnesia of beginnings that is inherent to institutionalization, it is important to return to the initial debates, which show us that where only one possible outcome remained for us, there were in fact several, with camps supporting each of these." It is a question of rediscovering them in order to continue the struggle against the linearity of history and the "coup d'état" that makes all alternatives unthinkable: "at every moment history contains a spectrum of possibilities. We might have not developed nuclear power, but we did develop nuclear power; we might have not had a housing policy based on individual investment and support for individuals. . . . There are possibilities that are abolished once and for all, more seriously than if they were simply forbidden, as they are made unthinkable."[61]

There even broader areas of application for such a historical sociology. This is the case for Christophe Charle's analysis of "imperial societies" on the scale of Europe. With this notion, Charle explores comparisons that avoid the determinism of structural analysis and the contingencies of traditional political history. Sensitivity to the plurality of interactions requires one to take counterfactual hypotheses seriously: "We shall see how, even in Germany which appears to be the most hopeless of cases, other paths were possible outside those taken which led to the 'German catastrophe,' . . . the French collapse and British decline."[62] The book then devotes its final pages to exploring these unrealized possibilities. Without constituting the heart of the analysis, recourse to the counterfactual makes it possible to insist on the discontinuity of the fields of power whose reconfiguration is socially constrained and varies according to the circumstances and the actions of the individuals. The counterfactual is hardly mentioned here, and the author does not adopt it explicitly, but it is worth noting that it stimulates the reader's imagination, leading him or her discreetly to pursue such reflection in order to grasp the importance of the analysis.

The counterfactual approach corresponds to a certain way of thinking about change, as a constant updating of dynamic configurations. A quick review suggests that any thought in terms of constraints and possibilities implicitly accepts this type of analysis, whether pursued or simply sketched out. One can then question the status of these probable outcomes. Are they pure scientific hypotheses? Past possibilities produced by the contemporaries of the time, or, more straightforwardly, fictions created by historians who make it possible to increase our understanding of a given situation?[63]

In a similar register, counterfactual analysis also makes it possible to escape a reductionist vision of historical events. A classic criticism of the approach is that it contains an impoverished definition of the event and thus focuses exclusively on the mere "surface of history." This critique can be found in Marc

Bloch's arguments on the shots fired on the boulevard that set off the Revolution of 1848.[64] But like actors and narrators, the event has also been reevaluated in the social sciences since 1990s without effecting some simple return to the "three idols" of yore.[65] Today, researchers insist less on the event as a singular fact or given once and for all, than on the way the event happens. They study the articulation of dynamics with shorter or longer temporalities, social and mental reconstructions across a longer time frame, power relations that operate within it, the fleeting moments when possibilities open up and are closed off, and then the reorganization of situations, later reappraisals and the official readings that are imposed gradually. A detour by way of the counterfactual may therefore nourish novel readings of key moments that make up a given event or borrow from possible outcomes that were never realized. A well-known example is Mona Ozouf's revisiting of the "flight to Varennes."[66] She interrupts her story and imagines what would have happened if Louis XVI had escaped his pursuers: troops were waiting for him at the border, he could have mobilized them against the young Constituent Assembly that, disorganized as it was, would have been unable to respond. The minutes lost along the way were "fatal moments." These reflections allow her to combat the idea that the escape was banal and the fruit of a misunderstanding of the situation on the part of Louis XVI. She allows for a different interpretation of the king's behavior and his context: while the sovereign may not have understood what was coming, the fate of the Revolution was not yet decided and his decision was situated between the two. This presentation therefore does not permit an infinity of other possible paths (even if it can suggest some impossible options). To the contrary, it reveals the realm of constraints and possibilities by revealing their constant actualizations. The sociologist Pierre-Michel Menger, one of the rare French researchers to have explicitly reflected on this question, describes this practice as "a realistic version of the work of the imagination."[67] The field of observation is extended through a "heuristic of situations," or the disciplined usage of the imagination through knowledge of the available information. Using this technique becomes a kind of mental disposition, understood as a "cognitive and creative performance" that increases the researcher's ability to simulate and grasp alternatives.

In the end, this reasoning allows for a less linear perception of historical development. This is both its most simple and most effective usage. Imagining multiple, unrealized futures allows one to identify the clashes, potentialities, and limits that affect what seems a homogeneous process and simultaneously to understand the complexity of past realities. The fields of application are varied: long-term linear developments (histories of the senses, global, imperial, environmental history, gender history, history of science and technology[68]); great dates (revolutions, battles, wars, scientific theories, technological inventions, and so on); ways of seeing contemporaries and sequences within a given process (artistic creation, structuration or disaggregation of social groups, power relations, the creation of disciplines, modification of an economic or political field, the progressive limitation of the frameworks available for any given individual's development). Obviously, historians who are the most concerned with avoiding teleology agree with these requirements. But it is clear that we still must keep in mind the idea that, after all, we do know what happened next, and the weight of the progressive imaginary of what will come, inherited from the nineteenth century, remains palpable. So the bifurcations are generally rather respectful, eroded by our knowledge of the events to come, subsequent appreciations and the rigor imposed by the historical discipline. Various techniques have been put forward to counter this propensity. Among others, the counterfactual approach invites us to subvert the unshakable imaginary of continuity, which is nonetheless always present in the historian's practice. Taking the time to reconstitute alternative outcomes is one of the ways of breaking the implicit principle of linearity. Moreover, by multiplying the turning points, the approach can open toward other ways of experiencing temporalities, deconstructing spatial metaphors that traditionally order historical understanding, and suggest unexpected intersections. It is then also possible to question the resonance of the configurations that did not happen: failed events, avoided incidents, dashed hopes, and the effects after the fact. This is the case for the nineteenth century, which, according to Alain Corbin, established "expectations for a new epoch whose configuration—even though it had not happened—continues to weigh on the hopes of our twentieth century."[69]

While these proposals aren't entirely original, they can help to augment our capacities of historical interpretation.

PLOTTING POSSIBILITIES? NARRATIVE AND LITERARY EXPERIMENTATIONS

One could imagine other experimental applications, which might exploit more effectively its narrative dimension, that is to say take into account the original mode of organizing information. In one sense, many of the suggestions presented in the previous section suggest that the counterfactual is above all an outline of possibilities. Whether the "other" outcome is evoked or actually pursued, it is a means of clearly posing the question, often underlying, historical possibilities.

From this perspective, it is possible to take advantage of the subjective dimension of this reasoning. Thus, the American historian Benjamin Wurgaft revisits intellectual history by examining the different biographies of Walter Benjamin and the commentaries on his work that the writers imagined would have become of the philosopher if he had not committed suicide in 1940. Through these excursions outside his "real" biography, these authors reveal much about themselves and their implicit expectations: the counterfactuals appear, Wurgaft writes, to be "the most explicit illustration of an affective and selective relation to the past that suffuses all historical writing."[70] It is therefore conceivable to use it to make explicit, and thus put at a distance, one's own investment in the research process, which is usually masked in the final process of writing. In other words, it is a specific and original exercise in reflexivity.

Other uses, designed to reveal tacit elements of historical narratives, are conceivable. For example, the status of the counterfactual narrative, as a "fragmented text," can be put to use by developing, alongside a more classical historical analysis, a coherent counterfactual narrative that exactly reproduces narrative structures, presuppositions within the demonstration, and modes of causal development. By comparison, this "false real narrative" makes it possible to highlight the underlying logic of the original historical narrative and call it into question. On the other hand, it reminds us that the historian's text is indeed riddled with holes, that it is not a homogeneous text, and that there is a complex historical reality toward which it is directed. In this sense, the counterfactual reminds us that the historical narrative is not reducible to literature. To employ Roger Chartier's metaphor, recourse to the counterfactual, in this case, consists of dangling a foot over the edge of the cliff into the void, in order to prove through contrast that terra firma actually exists.[71]

These games can be very elaborate. We must remember that, since such a narrative is an explicit space of distinction between what happened and what didn't, one cannot entirely accuse it of confusing the true and the false or fiction and reality. But elaborating counterfactual narratives adapted to the types of questions that are posed, one can appreciate the pertinence of the uses of fiction: from useless or dangerous fictions to those mobilized in comparison or in favor of the search for empathy. This tool can allow us to more wisely apprehend the boundaries between representation, virtual realities, and the realities of past societies.[72]

Finally, there is the possibility of clearly assuming a more frank recourse to imagination in this portion of the narrative: the risk is reduced if the approach is made explicit at its outset. This can involve a deliberate fictional development within the gaps of the historical narrative, further exploiting the literary capacities of immersion. Thus, in a text, which unfortunately remains unpublished, a historian of architecture, Gérard Monnier, takes seriously an old rumor in which a portion of Cezanne's great works were actually completed by American students. What if Cezanne did not paint some of his most famous paintings? This fiction plunges us into a fictitious world that is informed by a great knowledge of the artistic milieu of the time, and helps us understand the organization of the field of production and its institutions at the end of the nineteenth century. It also forces us to reconsider our notion of genius, the creation of an oeuvre, and the recognition of the artist in history. In this case the fiction does not alter the real story, since, after having tried to assert their rights, the students sank back into oblivion.[73] The counterfactual landscape, a space outside the real but which remains within the historical narrative, may then constitute a laboratory for "literary knowledge," but in a very specific sense: it is not a question of researching more elaborate forms of narrative arrangements or temporalities, but of using its content. Specialists in literature have on occasion defined it as a "pre-theory," characterized by its suggestive power and its multidimensionality, which should not be confused with knowledge in the social sciences.[74] In addition to its playfulness, the counterfactual text can therefore offer the reader a particular form of knowledge and perspective on the world. From the strict point of view of the social sciences, we are certainly in less certain territory. And yet we cannot afford to ignore it.

While the uses and functions of the imagination within the counterfactual approach are determined by an initial contract with the reader, this does not mean that they are a given. In many ways, they appear vain, even counterproductive. However, when mobilized rigorously, they can prolong the historian's use of imagination and even offer original resources, whether they echo a traditional set of questions around linearity and discontinuity, or open up a singular space of experimentation of the narrative's cognitive resources. It does not then require a call for revolution, but rather of well-regulated uses within a historical analysis that combines multiple resources. A little imagination is indeed necessary when it comes to using our imaginations.

CHAPTER 6

Causal Inference and Counterfactual Reasoning

> The causal chain is a warp on a loom; the moment a woof is put in, the causes disappear into a woven texture."
>
> —Robert Musil[1]

> In order to have a good understanding, it is necessary to focus only on what is fundamental and categorical within the notion of chance, that is the idea of the independence or the absence of solidarity between diverse series of facts and causes.
>
> —Antoine Augustin Cournot[2]

> I call this experiment "replaying life's tape." You press the rewind button and, making sure you thoroughly erase everything that actually happened, go back to any time and place in the past. . . . Then let the tape run again and see if the repetition looks at all like the original. . . . Then each replay of the tape will yield a different set of survivors.
>
> —Stephen Jay Gould[3]

We have discovered that the counterfactual approach seems to be as linked to the imagination as it is to the dimension that we generally considered to be historically "scientific." By this we mean the establishment of facts, the formulation of hypotheses, the use of a theoretical apparatus or mathematical tools, and the search for objective as well as causal relationships between phenomena. And yet the paradox may not be as obvious as it appears. And here we must challenge a dichotomy that we have already encountered on multiple occasions. The radical opposition between the use of the imagination and a so-called "scientific" approach centered on a strictly "objective" reality. In short, it does not seem to hold. The dividing lines are subtler. Imagination, as we have seen, clearly fits within the realm of scientific investigation.[4] Many researchers have tried to overcome these apparent contradictions by showing how these conceptions of science, these modes of relation, or these divisions of the world (for example into real and fictional) were the products of history or were substantiated and inspired by "primary" imaginations, which testify to human creativity.[5] Nonetheless, the opposition remains common, particularly with regard to the counterfactual, and the positions, methods, and styles in the social sciences remain extremely diverse. So we are confronted with another realm of interrogations: the question of causality or causal argumentation in history.

This vast problem has occupied philosophers of history as well epistemologists. Few historians have focused on this question, however, even if "reconstituting causalities" is one of the most common ways of reading the past, either implicitly or explicitly, consciously or unconsciously. It is one of the most common, everyday practices for a historian to identify and hierarchize "causes." On occasion, researchers have been dissatisfied with a reasoning referred to as *post hoc* and *cum hoc,* sophisms that establish a causal relationship between two phenomenon, when in fact it is a mere question of precedence or correlation.[6] Today, historians are even more mistrustful of this form of linear causality and have abandoned the idea of mono-causal explanation (A leads to B) in favor of an analysis of the plurality of causes of a historical phenomenon. Moreover, since the beginning of the twentieth century the positivist definition, according to which scientific analysis can entirely grasp the emergence of historical facts,[7] has slowly given ground to a constructivist position, which understands causality as the construction of a connection between two elements, in this case between two historical facts.

Counterfactual questioning is thus omnipresent in theories of causality: it has proven essential for thinking about the relationships between elements over time (facts, gestures, thoughts, phenomena, dynamics, and so on). At the same time, it remains undefined as a principle and, as a result, finds itself at the heart of reflections on the crisis of causality.

CAUSALITY IN HISTORY: A FEW MARKERS

It is once again worth mentioning a few points regarding this delicate problem that has sparked numerous studies, even if it has often been ignored by historians in their daily practice. All researchers face a similar problem. They analyze a given fact, which, in the words of Raymond Aron, "always has multiple antecedents."[8] In most cases, the historian is forced to pose the question of how to determine the true cause. In 1952, for example, Patrick Gardiner questioned the connection between the assassination of Archduke Franz Ferdinand and World War I, between World War I and the rise of communism, as well as the connection between the rise of Protestantism and the development of capitalism and between the writings of Rousseau and Robespierre's government.[9] These different examples raise a question of terminology: What do we consider a historical fact, event, effect, or the like? Furthermore, is there a real causal link between these different elements?

This is an old problem. The discipline of history was defined early on as the study of causes of past events. Thus, Polybius, in the second century BCE, pursued a search for causes in connection to the Punic Wars and deduced a theory of particular and general causes. According to him, the real cause lies in the moral dispositions and the intentions of the actors themselves.[10] But he also took into consideration the structural cause that led to the confrontation between the Romans and the Carthaginians: the Roman constitution.[11] Following the model proposed by Aristotle[12] and Polybius, historians have had a tendency to distinguish between different types of causality: conjunctural and structural, particular and general. These different types of causality map onto different temporalities. Historians consider the identification of so-called deep causes to be the most perilous, even if they are necessary, since these structural causes are often considered the most important. The search for causality produces a hierarchy of causes, which is specific to historical work.

Nonetheless, a series of tensions remain within the idea of causal plurality. One of these tensions opposes determinism and contingency or, more precisely, raises the question of the continuum from one to the other. Of course, historians prior the nineteenth century based their narratives on laws of history. But in many cases these laws provided a practical framework into which less deterministic forms of causal logic fit. This was the case with Polybius, who, within the historical law of the birth, life, and death of constitutions, pondered the psychology of political leaders. Philosophers and historians of the Renaissance and the Enlightenment also participated in this deterministic system of the laws of history, finding inspiration for their model in the sciences of nature. For instance, from Bodin to Montesquieu, one of the main justifying principles was of a mesological order, or the idea that historical evolution is determined by the environment.[13] The notion of contingency was more thoroughly considered in the nineteenth century. In his *Considerations on the Progress of Ideas and Events in Modern Times,* published in 1872, Antoine

Cournot argues that history is a "special modality of the connection between phenomena that mixes order and chance." Indeed, history cannot be a series of events that "derive necessarily and regularly from each other by virtue of constant laws." In that case, we would be able to tell the future. Nor is history "a series of events that are without any connection between them" like the random results of a lottery that can never constitute the foundation of a historical narrative. History, for Cournot, is situated between the two, between necessity and contingency. To be more precise, chance is no longer the form taken by our ignorance of causes. Instead, it becomes the meeting point, the unpredictable interference of "two independent causal series" that are connected through a process that is either partially or entirely random. In this way, he introduces the idea of a contingent causality: in a complex causal system, an accidental cause, a minor cause, can determine the chain reaction that profoundly modifies the whole.[14]

This tension between determinism and contingency reappears periodically, as it did in France, for example, a few years later during the controversy between the methodical school and the Durkheimians at the beginning of the twentieth century. Historians Charles-Victor Langlois and Charles Seignobos defended history as a study of the contingent and the singular, in opposition to the natural sciences that sought above all the establishment of laws. On the other side, the Durkheimian sociologist François Simiand, in his polemical article "Historical Method and the Social Sciences" published in the *Revue de synthèse historique* in 1903, attacked the French historians of the methodical school because, in his view, they were clinging to a description of contingent facts while refusing to understand their true causes. Simiand attempted to promote "causal research," which had a strong influence on the Annales school.

A tension of a different order between continuity and rupture in history also structures historical discourse. The writing of history was largely dominated up to World War II by linear narratives, based on a presupposition of continuity between historical facts. One of the first attempts to challenge this schema was proposed by Fernand Braudel, who drew upon the whole range of the human sciences—sociology, geography, economics, anthropology—which, contrary to history, focused on continuity rather than change.[15] Braudel questioned the idea of a linear succession of historical facts by revealing the temporal rhythms: short, medium, and long term. But in so doing, he made it difficult to analyze change and to reconsider the event. Another challenge to linear history was offered a few years later by Michel Foucault and his exploration of discontinuity in history.[16] Foucault intended to break with the history of ideas that prevailed at the time: a subdiscipline that remained focused on an analysis of continuities and the diffusion of ideas through concentric circles around men and their works. To the contrary, Foucault proposed an archaeology of knowledge with the aim of thinking about change and transformations through ruptures and cracks that led to brutal reconfigurations of new discourses and new social roles. This analysis of discontinuity allowed for the apprehension of newness. It also allowed one to understand new objects such as the history of emotions, of the senses, or representations more broadly. These processes are not linear and thus are not part of a mechanical causal logic. Historians can therefore identify phenomena of emergence and contemporaneity while respecting the critique of establishing causal links between two contiguous or synchronous historical phenomena.

A COUNTERFACTUAL THEORY OF CAUSAL ARGUMENTATION: MAX WEBER

This rapid presentation seeks to show to what extent the questioning of causality, old and new, has been abundant and varied. In each case, however, even if it is not always explicit, it would seem that a form of counterfactual reasoning is mobilized in attempts to think about these relationships. This was the idea of Max Weber, who analyzed this process and integrated it into his construction of a scientific approach to history, which would examine "objective possibilities" in order to hierarchize causes. His counterfactual theory of causal argumentation explicitly inspired Raymond Aron, Paul Ricoeur, Cornelius Castoriadis,[17] Antoine Prost,[18] as well as many Anglophone counterfactualists and was presented in his second essay on the theory of science published in 1906.[19]

Max Weber reflected on causal imputation in history through the works of one of his contemporaries, the German historian Eduard Meyer, who emphasized the role of great men in triggering wars.[20] In his view, the outbreak of the Austro-Prussian War in 1866 was the consequence of a decision made by Bismarck. Meyer uses counterfactual interrogation to challenge this decision. Bismarck, he writes, "could have made another decision, and other personalities . . . would have no doubt taken another; as a result the course of history would have been entirely different." But he quickly adds in a footnote, "It is not at all a question of affirming or contesting that in this case the wars in question would not have taken place; this question is unanswerable and ultimately futile." Contrary to Eduard Meyer, Max Weber chose to take the counterfactual interrogation seriously and ask what would have happened if Bismarck had not made the decision to go to war. For Weber, this was not a minor issue, but rather fundamental to the extent that it concerned "the crucial element in the historical shaping of reality: within the totality of those infinitely numerous 'factors,' which had to be just like that and no different for *this* result to come about, what causal *importance* should really be attributed to this individual decision?"[21] Weber continues his demonstration unflinchingly: the success of history depends on the counterfactual approach. "If history is to rise above the level of merely chronicling remarkable events and personalities, there is no other way for it but to pose such questions. And ever since it was established as a science [history] has proceeded in that manner."[22] For this German sociologist, counterfactual analysis confers on history the status of a science; and historians—consciously or unconsciously—have always made use of this device.

He demonstrates this by examining Eduard Meyer's analysis of the two shots that provoked the great street battles in Berlin in March 1848. Meyer argued that the question of the origin of these shots was of no significance. "The situation was such that any incident could have set off the conflict."[23] This assertion implies that Meyer asked himself what would have happened without these two shots. His response was simple: the same thing. Based on this example from 1848, Weber affirms the importance of the counterfactual approach for determining what he calls the "historical meaning" of an event:

> Thus, it does, after all, seem to be of considerable value for determining the "historical importance" of a single historical fact [if one can make] the following judgement: *If* that fact, within a complex of historical determinants, is imagined to be lacking or [as having been] changed, then this *would have* resulted in a course of historical events that was different in certain *historically important* respects. And [such a judgment is of value] even though, in practice, the historian may only in exceptional cases—i.e. if that "historical importance" is in dispute—feel impelled to develop and justify it deliberately and explicitly. It is clear that this circumstance ought to have prompted an investigation into the logical nature of judgements of this kind, which state what the result "could have been expected to be" if an individual causal component of a complex of conditions had been removed or changed, and into the significance [of such judgments] for history.[24]

Thus, Max Weber developed a scientific model of counterfactual analysis. Unable to find sufficiently pertinent theoretical elements among historians, which he described as being troubled by such epistemological questions, or sociologists, he looked to the work of Johannes Von Kries, a psychologist who was one of the primary German theoreticians of probability and most notably forged the concept of an "objective possibility" used by Weber.[25] He developed a methodology by integrating historians' constraints and objectives. The researcher could not take into consideration all "causes": this was both impossible—since they are by definition infinite—and absurd, in the sense that the historian is only interested in explaining the phenomena that are of historical interest. Historians are therefore limited to choosing one or more determining elements within an infinite series. There remains, however, a major obstacle: how to prove the existence of a causal relationship between those chosen and the effects observed by the historian. This is where the counterfactual approach enters in, which he named *Gedankenprozess,* a thinking process that allows one to develop a more sophisticated conception of causality. This thought process is founded on a series of abstractions, that is, modifications, or one or more "of those components of 'reality' that actually existed."[26] To do this, he proposed the creation of "imaginary pictures" (*Phantasiebilder*) by removing one or two historical facts and then drawing out a new unfolding of events. The analysis of these possibilities allows the researcher to identify causes as well as to untangle and hierarchize them. Thus, according to Max Weber, a historical event is a fact *that contains consequences,* that possesses the capacity to provoke change. The method of building alternative hypotheses must take into consideration rules of experience, empirical regularities that can be identified within reality: in general, certain elements produce certain effects, what Raymond Aron refers to as "consecutions that conform to known generalities." These retrospective calculations of probability allow one to discern occasional or accidental elements that cause change. This counterfactual methodology was reformulated by Raymond Aron—one of the key figures for introducing Weber into France—who updated it, no doubt with historians in mind, in his *Introduction to the Philosophy of History,* published in 1938.[27]

This stimulating counterfactual method does, however, pose a few problems. First, if one considers that the degree of probability is the foundation for a hierarchy of causation, how does one concretely attribute a suitable degree of probability for each "objective possibility"? It is easier to proceed with the "elimination of candidates for singular causality" than it is to "crown any particular one."[28] Moreover, one of the primary difficulties resides in the choice of one or more of the most pertinent antecedents, particularly in the choice of the precise moment that marks the beginning of the counterfactual investigation, the famous turning point. For example, for the case of triggering the French Revolution or World War I, it is possible to imagine a number of turning points.

> However well founded the scholar's decisions may be, they are rarely the only ones possible: the question might have been put at another time, for the evolution is continuous and one rarely gets back to the very beginning; no certain choice of antecedents nor any certain analysis of the effect is categorically prescribed.[29]

The same problem poses itself for the level of analysis: Is it necessary for any given event to analyze a given agent or, to the contrary, to examine structural phenomena? Raymond Aron offers another point of resistance to Weber's theory. The counterfactual approach assumes the existence of "constant causes" in history, while historical conditions are in constant evolution. The risk is that one becomes limited to a mechanical causal schema by studying the "consequences" of an event or of a situation rather than its "transformations."[30]

Nonetheless, one of the great merits of Weber's analysis and its developments by those who followed, is that it highlights the logical importance of counterfactual reasoning in the search for causality: one cannot think about relationships without imagining more or less plausible alternative outcomes. Different currents of research, more recently, have been interested in these "paths not taken" and have also attempted to model them.

LOGICAL AND MATHEMATICAL MODELS OF COUNTERFACTUAL REASONING

Counterfactual analysis was at the origin of one of the principal conceptions of causality developed in the twentieth century, formulated by an American philosopher in his 1973 publication *Counterfactuals.*[31] David Lewis reduced the relationship of causality between two phenomena to the existence of a causal chain constituted by a finite series of events. One could say that event C depends causally on event A if the following two counterfactuals are true: if A had taken place, C would have taken place; if A had not taken place, C would not have taken place.[32] As an analytic philosopher, David Lewis systematically explored the implications of modal logic: counterfactuals allow one to reflect on events that didn't happen in our world but which, under different conditions, could have taken place elsewhere. The definition of these possible worlds, causally separated from one another, allows the researcher to pursue comparisons and to draw more certain conclusions that distinguish between truth and falsehood. From this perspective, these other worlds are not imaginary constructs, but constitute other realities.[33]

Lewis's work was widely discussed, soliciting a certain number of critiques, but also interest among philosophers and literary specialists.[34] Its usage is more challenging in the social sciences, which are distrustful of the idea of a reality structured by self-contained modal logics. The real—be it shared, imagined, constructed, naturalized, or suffered—is the object of any investigation and remains a horizon of expectations to be discovered rather than a realm that is already preestablished.

There has been another, mathematical form of modeling. Here the aim is to establish demonstrable simulations between clearly defined elements. It is not surprising that work using mathematical or statistical tools explicitly poses counterfactual questions, to the extent that it is, de facto, produced by the approach itself (serving as the element that is inserted or removed in order to prove the researcher's demonstration).

Without returning to the cliometric or demographic simulations discussed earlier, Gary King and Langche Zeng were inspired by this mathematical approach in their work on processes of world democratization, causal effects of democracy, and the consequences of UN peacekeeping operations.[35] These American researchers created a database on the opening up of markets, the rates of infant mortality, degrees of democracy (autocracy, partial democracy, complete democracy), the percentage of the active population involved in the military and legislative efficacy.[36] This quest for plausible counterfactuals requires sophisticated calculations (at least from the perspective of nonspecialists). King and Zeng have proposed a mathematical formula in order to distinguish between counterfactuals "produced by the model" (independent of the data) and those corresponding to available empirical data.[37] This formula allows one to refine the former analysis and scientifically demonstrate the weakness of the probability that Saudi Arabia will become a democracy and that Canada will become an autocracy. More convincingly, they have been able to deconstruct the results of other works in political science, notably those focused on the effects of peacekeeping operations led by the UN. According to King and Zeng's formula, all the results are "model dependent," and are therefore useless.[38]

Nonetheless, and elaborate as it is, this approach still has its limits—that recall the methodological debates around the problem of arithmetizating the social.[39] First, within the context of "what-if" analysis, the number of cases independent of the model prove to be rather weak, similar to its conception of historical change: the categories for classifying the countries are not precisely defined, the relations between them are not necessarily causal, and even if they are calculated by year, time is not a dynamic feature in the model, because it remains unmodified. As a result, these tools prevent one from thinking about democracy as a historical process, just as they avoid a whole series of local, social, and cultural factors that play an equally important role. In this case, the counterfactual test nourishes an extremely positivist—in the restricted sense of the term—apprehension of the social world.

While not formally stated, there is still a close relationship between modeling in general and counterfactual analysis: all modeling, when it statistically or empirically defines a path to be followed, relies by definition on this type of reasoning. The researcher evaluates—in some cases even implicitly—what should have happened if certain conditions were met. Thus, in economic and social history, all analyses centered on path dependency, on development (as we shall see in chapter 8) or, for example, on the Industrial Revolution, that define a singular path for France or the German *Sonderweg* assume some form of counterfactual reasoning. The German debate on this notion is representative. In his monumental social history of Germany, Hans-Ulrich Wehler attempts to depart from the historical idealism of the 1920s–1940s that nourished the thesis of a particular path, according to which: "since there never was a 'bourgeois revolution,' as there was in England, the United States, or France, apparently through their classical revolutions, the bourgeoisie never succeeded in overtaking the princely states on its own. Freedom (*Freiheit*) was always understood as liberty (*Libertät*), guaranteed and protected by a strong state."[40] Wehler opposes this current with a comparative social history that depends upon a "norm" of political modernization grounded in rigorous observation of French, English, and American societies. The tensions between the nobility and the bourgeoisie, as well as the time period of 1867–1870, prove to be, according to him, more influential than the Revolution of 1848:

> What was decisive for the German *Sonderweg* in the end was the system of political domination with the constellation of social forces that supported it. Together, they created the fatal spiral that made the derailing of German politics up to 1945 possible. The Empire led to a

German *Sonderweg* because its structure of political and social domination, to employ the terms of Max Weber, allowed the authoritarian bureaucratic state with a parliamentary façade to deprive the mass of citizens of their liberty and be governed like herded animals, instead of participating in the government of the state.[41]

The definition of a Eurocentric norm as well as the idea of the specificity of the German bourgeoisie have since been criticized.[42] As for the *Sonderweg* thesis, even if it has lost some of its interpretive power, it continues nonetheless to be used in attempts to understand the German catastrophe as well as the reunification of 1989–1990.[43] In the end, if these modes of reasoning can be useful for opening up comparisons, they turn away from the complexity of particular situations and the causal chains that constitute them. Debates between these two tendencies persist up to this day.

ANTI-DETERMINISM AND "EXPLICITATION"

One means of deconstructing all-encompassing categories that can reify perception of societies is also to paradoxically make use of counterfactual reasoning, in order to disrupt implicit causal connections. This is what Kenneth Pomeranz proposes, for example, in an article that builds on the comparative analysis of economic transformations in Europe and China,[44] in his *The Great Divergence.*[45] To demonstrate that in the eighteenth century the Chinese economy in the Yangtze Delta and the Pearl River was not less developed than the English economy, he proposes a series of original counterfactual hypotheses that touch on both China and Europe (a modification of available carbon resources, other scientific developments, the absence of the opium wars). He takes particular care to avoid imposing a European model on China, showing the fundamental role that energy resources played as opposed to cultural factors: if the coal mines had been less numerous and less well located in England, the differential in economic development between Great Britain and China would have been reduced. The comparison of counterfactuals forces a reconsideration of common historiographical assumptions (the "xenophobia" of the Chinese Empire or Confucian conservatism that closed off possibilities of technological innovation) and suggests that an analysis founded upon the "industrial revolution," as a primarily European phenomenon, must be reconsidered. Ultimately, counterfactualism can be mobilized toward a critique of commonly established a priori connections and challenge deterministic historical schemas.

A century earlier, one of the first to grasp the potentially subversive power of the counterfactual approach was the historian Paul Lacombe in his work *History Considered to Be a Science* (*De l'histoire considérée comme science*), published in 1894. Lacombe referred to this approach as "imaginary experience":

> Think through a series of events based upon a turning point other than the one that took place, reconsider the unfolding of the French Revolution for example. Many minds will undoubtedly find that this constitutes a vain, if not dangerous, enterprise. I do not share this feeling. I see a more real danger in the tendency to believe that historical events could not be otherwise than they were. On the contrary, we must instill in ourselves a sense of their true instability. Imagining a different story serves this purpose above all.[46]

This was precisely Raymond Aron's point in his *Introduction à la philosophie de l'histoire* published in 1938. The first and most important contribution of counterfactual history, in his view, was to fight determinism: "the investigation of cause by the historian is directed not so much at tracing the broad outlines of the relief of history as at preserving for or restoring to the past the uncertainty of the future."[47] He later added in his work on *Dimensions de la conscience historique*: "The unreal constructions must remain an integral part of science, even if they do not move beyond an ambiguity of similitude. For they offer the only way of escaping the retrospective illusion of fatality."[48] Historians elaborate causes that a posteriori confer necessity on the unfolding of events, contradicting "the contemporary impression of contingency."[49]

In the same sense, and explicitly inspired by Raymond Aron, the philosopher Paul Ricoeur insisted on the necessity of reconstituting past horizons of expectations by updating probable possibilities in order to reproduce the uncertainty of the event:

> We must understand that the imaginative operation by which the historian assumes in thought that one of the antecedents has disappeared or been modified, and then tries to construct what would have happened in accordance with this hypothesis, has a significance that goes beyond epistemology. The historian acts here as a narrator who redefines the three dimensions of time in relation to a fictive present. Dreaming of a different event, he opposes "uchronia" (a timeless time) to the fascination with what once was. The retrospective estimation of probabilities thus contains a moral and a political significance that

> exceeds its purely epistemological one. It recalls to the readers of history that the "historian's past has been the future of the characters in history" (p. 184). Due to its probabilist character, causal explanation incorporates into the past the unpredictability that is the mark of the future and introduces into retrospection the uncertainty of the event.[50]

In this instance, usage of counterfactualism participates once again in causal research, but it is more a process of opening up the field of causality than determining a hierarchy of causes.

While philosophers of history have attempted to apprehend the question of causal imputation, the issue has remained problematic for historians. The ancient historian Paul Veyne is one of the few to have tackled this problem head on in his *Comment on écrit l'histoire.* He bases his analysis on a simple observation: since historians only have access to a tiny part of the information necessary for understanding the past, "as far as the rest is concerned, it is a question of filling holes."[51] He refers to this process as "retrodiction" and illustrates it with a simple historical hypothesis: "Louis XIV became unpopular due to an overwhelming tax burden." This assertion may emerge from two very different forms of reasoning. Either the historian learns through sources (but which ones?) that taxation was the source of the sovereign's unpopularity. Or the historian has access to two distinct types of information: he knows that there was a large tax burden and that Louis XIV became progressively less popular. In this case, the researcher embarks upon a retrodiction, that is, he traces the unpopularity back to a proposed cause, excessive taxation. The problem of historical discourse resides in the constant and oftentimes tacit movement from one form of reasoning to another, without the status of proof ever being clearly made explicit.

Even if Paul Veyne, like Max Weber, borrowed the notion of retrodiction from probability theory, he emphasizes the irregular, partial, and restricted nature of causality in history, titled "sublunar causality," because each historical situation is specific and the historian can never take into consideration the entirety of all causes. In his study on retrodiction, Veyne senses that the counterfactual method, which he refers to as "historical prediction," may increase the historian's understanding:

> An example of historical prediction: let's ask ourselves what would have happened if Spartacus had defeated the Roman legions and had become the master of southern Italy. Would it have brought an end to slavery? A shift toward a superior form of relations of production? A

> parallel suggests a better response, that everything we know about the period would seem to confirm. Since we learned that a generation before Spartacus, during the great revolt of the Sicilian slaves, these rebels gave themselves a king and a capital, we can guess that if Spartacus had won, he would have founded one more Hellenistic kingdom in Italy, where, undoubtedly slavery would have existed, as it existed everywhere in the period.[52]

Paul Veyne does not develop the counterfactual question any further, preferring to establish the conditions for an effective retrodiction. The approach becomes less precise when the historian distinguishes between those situations in which retrodiction may be effective, because there are certain constants (customs, linguistic codes, violence, and so on), and those for which it might be less effective (art history or the history of ideas). It would no doubt be possible to contest this division. Veyne later preferred the terminology "explicitation" rather than "explication" of situations.[53] With this method, the researcher is always in a position to reveal the abundance of ungraspable causal relations. By revealing these connections and showing an attachment, as much for the singularity of the phenomena as their connections, the historian contributes to reestablishing the complexities of the past. The historian is invited to decenter as well as question his or her own categories of analysis. This approach, adopted by numerous historians, and often inspired by the cultural anthropology of Clifford Geertz, is stimulating. It has the advantage of avoiding the difficult problem of causality while encouraging knowledge about past societies through a constant return to sources, an analysis from the point of view of the actors, and the interpretation of the researcher. Nonetheless, the explanatory question remains and cannot be dismissed.

CONFIGURATIONS, BIFURCATIONS, AND NONLINEAR REALITIES

More composite approaches to causal chains or historical explanation have been proposed that attempt to rearticulate regularities and changes, stability and irruptions, groups of relations and heterogeneities. The counterfactual, possibilities, and unrealized outcomes seem to play an important role in these analyses.

It may seem surprising to begin with the work of Norbert Elias in this context. Of course, his processual model has existed for some time, and it has difficulty integrating events, ruptures, and other "turning points." Moreover, the sociologist firmly opposed causal explanation as early as 1939 in response to a remark made by Raymond Aron. Traditional causal research, one of the dominant modes of reasoning, supposes implicit value judgments:

> We think therefore that we have "explained" the courtly love ballad when we say that it came from lyrical religious poetry (or perhaps also from contact with Arab culture). But we do not examine the reasons for the movement through which lyrical religious poetry (or what it could be) is transformed into courtly lyrical poetry. And hence one risks perhaps misunderstanding my argument which makes the claim that certain aspects of the civilized Western code of behavior first developed within the circles of courtly nobility and then were taken up, assimilated, reworked within bourgeois circles—in particular in France. Indeed, one runs the risk of understanding that I think that the courtly nobility was the cause or the initiator of the wave of bourgeois civilization that followed. . . . The process that we have before us resembles . . . certain chemical processes where, in a liquid that is engaged in a process of molecular restructuring, for example, crystallization, the crystalline form first impacts a small central core to which the crystals attach themselves. Nothing could be more incorrect than to assume that the core was the cause of the crystallization process.[54]

This does not mean that he refuses any explanation. The causal analyses with which he was familiar, appeared too one-dimensional. He preferred to put forward the relationships between the elements of a society, as well as their dynamics. This is what he referred to as a "configurational" and later a "figurational" approach to highlight that all of the different elements do not have same the relationship to one another: the sociologist must grasp a given state of these interrelations. His famous "civilizing process" illustrates this perfectly. It designates a series of dynamics that feed off of one another from the sixteenth century onward: the development of the state in its "modern" form (monopoly of violence and fiscal power), the growth of interdependencies tied to the differentiation of activities, and the emergence of a new psychic economy characterized through more effective self-control. All of these processes are concomitant, without any single one serving as the sole "source" of the others. One may also note that such an approach does not ignore the event. In this perspective, an "event" (and this is what defines it as such) modifies the prior relationship between the elements and the dynamics in order to propose a new organization or a new "configuration."

In doing so, the Eliasian configurations are not closed off to the question of possibilities of the past, because they describe dynamic power relations whose outcome, without being entirely accidental, is not predetermined. It is a question, he often repeated, of an "unplanned process," following a given direction, but which can change. A leitmotif in his analysis, where he attempts to combine scientific rigor with political awareness, may be understood in the following terms: if people had known better or knew more (thanks to processual sociology) about the situation of interdependence in which they found or currently find themselves, they would have made and would continue to make better choices. Without this knowledge, they risk limiting themselves to bad decisions, threatening the civilizing process.[55]

In the same vein, during the 1980s Norbert Elias showed an interest in the question of utopia. In one of his articles, the German sociologist explained that when Thomas More developed in 1516 his famous *Utopia,* he was proposing a mental response to a social, political, and also technological situation, which corresponded to a particular moment in the civilizing process: a moment when hope and fear were not only manifest in such realms as hell or paradise, but nourished a mental disposition where one begins to imagine that it is possible to change the world.[56] In the twentieth century, he observed, the utopias proposed by such figures as Huxley or Orwell were not positive, but negative: they expressed a fear and a threat. And yet they revealed a paradox to the extent that human beings now have the technical means to resolve a great number of problems with which they are confronted. For example, they may go to the Moon or potentially resolve the problem of world hunger. These new but poorly understood possibilities generate a sense of responsibility that leads to anxiety and a peculiar sense of insecurity. Human beings do not know what to do with their unprecedented capacities to realize utopia. As always, Elias historicizes his subject and inscribes it both in time and in changing social, cultural, and political contexts. The scale of possibilities, which has varied over time, appears maximal today (this may also provide an explanation for the current development of counterfactual thought). In fact, when Elias's configurations are inscribed in the *longue durée,* they allow us to understand both a vast realm of historical constraints and historical possibilities. This dimension may also operate, according to Norbert Elias, at the scale of the individual: "It is in the nature of societies that demand a fairly high degree of specialization from their members that a large number of unused alternatives—lives the individual has not lived, roles he has not played, experiences he has not had, opportunities he has missed—are left by the wayside."[57] In this sense, he proposes a kind of embedded counterfactuality in the sociohistorical process, a fruit of interdependencies that belong to any given society. While the modalities of application are not entirely spelled out, this approach, which may be applied as much to the individual case as to an entire epoch, remains stimulating.

Other perspectives that break with more classical modes of causal explanation have also been developed. This is the case for sociological analyses that function along the lines of "bifurcations" and which combine the regularities of given social spaces with the possibility of shifts, according to a heterogeneous logic.[58]

The study of life cycles, developed within interactionist sociology in the United States in the 1950s, is at the origin of this perspective. These works consider that over the course of a life, the same individual operates within coherent social universes, with the necessity of integrating their norms and dispositions. Each individual can shift from one to the other (from high school to university, from university to the workplace, from one social milieu to another).[59] This supposes an adaptation that requires both action and a certain attitude, and even ways of thinking. Studies of this type are numerous, concerning the world of elites and those of delinquents. For the latter, work has shown the importance—within these complex paths made up of little jobs and petty crime—of certain events (marriage, a steady job) or turning points that allow people to modify over the long term their situations and their behavior.[60] If such an event takes place, then a person is thrown into another framework and a radically different set of actions. In this case, the paths—notably ascendant—are multiple, even if their number is limited, in particular based on the organization of the labor market. At the same time, such an approach may be difficult to apply to history, since it is so difficult to master the full range of sociological information that is necessary.

This approach is also useful for understanding events, considered more and more, as we have seen, to be moments full of possibilities, in which the weight of the past remains, even if it operates differently. Though these works may draw upon the perspectives proposed by Niall Ferguson's approach toward counterfactual history, it is in order to criticize them: this method, by proposing scenarios that excessively stylize other possible outcomes, miss the essential point, that is, the plasticity of structures within any given event.[61] Having said this, the reasoning put forward for thinking these moments may be interpreted as counterfactual. And this subtlety remains important.

We may also turn to William Sewell's analysis of Mark Traugott's study on the June 1848 massacre. According to Traugott, the fact that a portion of the workers were on the other side of the barricades with the insurgents while others were with the armed forces, ready to attack them, cannot be explained by their specific trade or guild, but by the specific organizations to which these individuals belonged between February and June 1848 (either the national workshops or the armed forces). "Had the government maintained the Workshops in existence and kept Thomas as their director, the insurrection probably would never have happened." But "Traugott's embrace of eventful temporality does not mean that he has abandoned sociology for narrative history."[62] There is a slight difference here from the analysis presented in the previous chapter. Traugott, he suggests, proposes an analysis that is at once "path-dependent," causally heterogeneous and contingent, in which social action plays a decisive role in the reconfiguration of structures. According to Sewell, what is essential for the "eventful sociology" that he proposes is to identify the constrained possibilities and nonlinear causalities. From this perspective, while counterfactualism is not explicitly mentioned in this approach, such reasoning remains an integral part of the analysis, in addition to an analysis of structures from a dynamic perspective.

The sociologist Andrew Abbott is probably among those who have pushed such an approach to causality the furthest within the social sciences.[63] A specialist in the sociology of professions, and then academic disciplines, combining at once Goffmanian interactionism and the Braudelian *longue durée,* Abbott employs sophisticated statistical tools before subjecting them to critique. One finds in his work the same critiques discussed above: the categories are debatable, the relationship between the different elements remains constant, time and context remain absent. While he recognizes the real contribution of "traditional" statistical methods and a certain type of coding of variables, he refers to the type of reality that they produce as a "general linear reality."[64] Abbott therefore attempts to navigate the tension between quantitative and narrative approaches, between causality and temporality, and between formalization and interpretation. The "present" in his view may be defined as a moment when nothing changes, with its structures and regularities that can be observed by the sociologist. This moment, however, is also inscribed in larger changes, which may be observed at different scales. The structure and the regularities may also be inserted into slower transformations, and the like. All of this defines the unfolding of "presents" which are associated between themselves, offering the possibilities and impossibilities that evolve over time. Abbott explains this approach with the example of the invention of the exploding grenade harpoon by the Norwegian Svend Foyn between

1860 and 1880.[65] A number of versions of this type of harpoon had been developed in the 1820s. Nonetheless, Foyn's won out because it fit into the structural transformation of whale fishing with the arrival of mechanical boats and increased market pressure and so on. Had it been proposed earlier, the "invention" would have failed. Introduced at precisely this moment, however, it transformed fishing practices. The sociologist therefore combines the possibilities offered by large structural transformations and the way in which they may or may not be realized at the level of individual lives.

In a methodological essay, Andrew Abbott turns to counterfactual reasoning, which he associates with the work of Robert Fogel, as one of the "strategies" that allow one to more effectively think through social problems.[66] The scaffolding, he suggests, is somewhat elementary. Nonetheless, the question of unrealized paths or of "possible futures"[67] remains central to his broader conception of real, discontinuous, and historicized causalities. This perspective is elaborated in a text on turning points. Here he discusses the diversity of moments of bifurcation that constitute longer- or shorter-term processes and may engender radical breaks or slow transitions from one regime of probability to another.[68] The key point, however, lies elsewhere: in his view it is necessary to consider that "change is the normal state of affairs" and the fact that permanence is a construction to be questioned. From this, Abbott develops his thinking with "configurations"[69] that considers the articulation of complex singularities, which resemble what we commonly refer to as "structures" when they acquire certain regularities. While they generate a certain inertia, they are also constituted by tensions. They evolve and draw out structural possibilities of change, which may be mobilized or not by individuals or groups in a given set of circumstances. Abbott compares the action of these individuals and social groups to a key, and the situation to a lock. From this perspective, change is a part of social structure, and the turning point is a short moment that leads to the reorientation of a process. A limited range of possibilities are therefore included in the structure itself.

The value of Abbott's approach is in its refusal to abandon the imperative of modeling. He elaborates a statistical tool called optimal matching that allows him to gather the available data through this conception. Based on this software, the technique uses a system of slipping between trajectories and the evaluation of frequencies to allow the research to propose sequential probabilities and improbabilities. Optimal matching thus allows one to determine coherent sequences and mobile relations within a complex and uncertain social reality.[70] Used in a variety of ways, it helps to define a space of possibilities and constraints that offer a more capacious definition of situations. This idea has been employed by Claire Zalc in her study with Nicolas Mariot on the "991 Jews of Lens."[71] The study shows how, over time, the room to maneuver was reduced and subjected to increasingly arbitrary logics. Coupled with a study of trajectories, this tool offers an opportunity to visualize more clearly the moving set of possibilities to escape deportation or not.[72] Using this tool along the lines of this study thus allows one to determine the field of other possible outcomes and to see how they were modified, even if they never came to pass. As Abbott himself explains, optimal matching hardly provides an exact vision of "reality." It is yet another means for treating a given problem and complex sets of information. This method may also be used qualitatively when the available information is spotty.

This stimulating approach has also been the target of certain critiques. For example, Abbott does very little with language, the process of transforming facts into words and meanings. Similarly, there is little discussion of the process of internalization, by actors or social groups, of previous and future experiences that did not happen and may have modified possible outcomes and their uses. At the same time, Abbott has attempted above all to integrate in a scientific way that which does not come to pass and the potentialities of change in the social structure itself: this is what he refers to as "narrative positivism." Causality in his work is thus at once regular and irregular, micro and macro, historical and sociological. In such a framework, the counterfactual approach is more controlled and may participate in the determination of heterogeneous social causation, which is at once historically variable and inscribed in the processes of plural determinations. As a result, it no longer appears to be a tool imposed from the outside, but rather is an element included in the social world that researchers are attempting to objectify.

Other proposals have emerged from a similar critique of traditional statistical methods, offering a sophisticated explanatory model. They have also integrated the uncertainties of research as well as the possible outcomes of the societies under study. They provide a more explicit account of their relationship to a counterfactual scenario and the question of unfollowed paths. Qualitative comparative analysis (QCA), developed by the American sociologist and theoretician Charles Ragin, focuses sociological and historical examination on a specific number of cases and the configuration of causes that produce them.[73] Through a rigorous use of comparison, this method draws out combinations of fixed and variable factors in a given moment or situation.[74] Counterfactual hypotheses are explicitly mobilized, notably to overcome the gap between necessarily limited data available in the social world and those that the researcher needs in order to explain it. Their usage, controlled by the researcher, is presented as essential for comparison, the discussion of theoretical models, and the elaboration of the most pertinent causal combinations.[75] In Ragin's work on social inequalities, he developed what he calls "possibility analysis," or "the conditions under which the particular event that is of interest will occur."[76]

"Viability theory," developed by the demographer, sociologist, and historian Noël Bonneuil, provides for an even greater systematization. The development of this "concept" grows out of two requirements. First, it once again attempts to overcome the weaknesses of the probability model most commonly used in the social sciences, which use past statistical regularities to predict the future (in the past or the present), and works poorly for the apprehension of human societies wherein one small change in the trajectory can modify the entirety of the situation. It also attempts to integrate the progress achieved within the natural sciences in the analysis of complexity, while taking into consideration the specificity of studying human societies. With regard to chaos theory, for example, Noël Bonneuil notes that physicists have had to work with nonlinear determined systems that can be unstable and "sensitive to initial conditions." While in the human sciences on the other hand, "systems are by definition undetermined as a result of their lack of regularity, ignorance (of the researcher), contradictory choices, irrationality, heterogeneity, errors, illusions, and the immense variety of decisions taken by the human actors within these systems."[77] He attempts to find a scientific analytical model of complex and dynamic systems that are applicable to human societies.

To do so, he borrows from Jean-Pierre Aubin's mathematical theory of viability that brings together three elements: constraints (material or other structures that limit possibilities of action), demands (the variety of strategies that actors or groups of actors have at their disposition), and the "viable core" (the "*noyau viable*," or the aim of these strategies).[78] When this technique is joined with a robust capacity for mathematizing social processes, one is able to determine the variety of possible trajectories within a moving system and integrate into it the modification of possibilities based on the choices made. The researcher is not confronted with a single choice, but a myriad of possible strategies, one of which was chosen. The case of the Persian Basseri tribal nomads, studied by Fredrik Barth, has been used to demonstrate the value of this approach.[79] Faced with difficult ecological conditions, these populations seem to shift from one lifestyle to another (sedentary or itinerant shepherding) based on their situation and a precarious equilibrium. Noël Bonneuil's proposal (in which the rate of human predation of animals is written as c(t)e [cmin, cmax][80]) shows how these populations maintain their "viable core" in a dynamic and complex game between different strategies. Far from a fatalistic adaptation, these behaviors are a product of a construction that puts the actors, their organization, and the environment into play. The whole set of offerings, choices, new opportunities, and constraints may then be expressed in a form that renders their actions more comprehensible: in this way, "the decision or the transactions of social actors can be perceived to be particular moments in the struggle for survival, in a space of perpetually changing possibilities."[81]

The Medici family of fifteenth-century Florence and Norwegian fisherman at the end of the twentieth century have been studied from the same perspective.[82] The analysis is enriched through a consideration of the interactions between "states" that develop within a dominant trajectory among "viability domains." The analysis may be further elucidated through the example of the cat and the mouse: this method allows one to study all the sites where the mouse may escape from the cat, those where the cat may catch its prey, and the relations between them. The "discriminating domain" of the little rodent consists of all the sites where, depending on any given action on the part of the cat at moment *t*, the mouse may respond in order to stay alive for a given length of time.[83] The advantages of this approach are evident: it offers an interactive model that is not deduced from a theory but is built on available information. Centered on the spatiotemporal contexts of the object of study, it integrates contingency, recognizes the possibility of success or failure, and renounces predictive logics as well as fictional narratives. At the same time, it does not explore the causes and trajectories of a phenomena, but rather the range of possibilities leading to a given result, and all of those possibilities introduced by a given change within a "ocean of processes." There are some key similarities and differences with regard to Abbott's approach: they both focus on process; nonlinear connections; relationships between actions, events, and structures; and the question of unrealized futures. In this approach, however, which is more thorough and systematic, the bifurcations and the unrealized possibilities are neither decisive elements nor revealing aspects of the research. Counterfactual analysis and the examination of possible outcomes that did not come to pass appear to be interesting but relatively unimportant, because they tend to concentrate the researcher's attention on one alternative instead of the whole set of possibilities. In this case, it is instead a question of defining the "cognitive maps of pasts and futures," the two types of maps being "nonetheless inequivalent." One may use them "to understand what was at stake, what actions were possible, which were viable, which weren't, and how the chosen actions conformed or not to what was necessary." And "history may be about not only what was, but also about what processes were involved and what opportunities for change were available at each moment."[84] When we take into consideration plural pasts and futures, the similarity with the previous examples becomes more obvious. This approach also has its difficulties: the question of language and the ways of seeing the world (and thus of defining the ends of actions) is perhaps, here as well, less thoroughly considered. It demands above all a capacity to generate a formal equation, a creativity, and a mastery of the philosophy of the social sciences which is rare among researchers and risks limiting its application. The counterfactual or the consideration of unrealized outcomes may also, more modestly, constitute a means of testing this plurality of pasts and futures, which this approach suggests may be a realm of social scientific investigation in its own right. Whether unrealized outcomes are central or secondary to a given approach, they emerge within the heart of those sophisticated and dynamic analyses of causality that integrate the specificities of human societies and the documentation that they produce.

One should not be surprised by the diversity of the uses of counterfactual reasoning and possible futures in the research of causality, whether they be determinist or contingent, linear or multiple, inscribed within a common temporal schema or articulated across discontinuous scales. The counterfactual approach is by definition a relational mode of thought; as a principle, it is undetermined and allows one to reflect anew on these questions. It is therefore also possible to identify less useful ways of using it: those that tend to reduce a situation to an overly simple cause; those that suggest a given set of causes are always equally active; those that depend upon one theory and are too removed from context; those that assume to the contrary that everything is up to chance—in other words, any approach that imposes a crude and impoverished vision of causality. In a general way, the radical opposition between determinism and contingency does not make much sense. The most important issues are played out between them. While the tool of counterfactualism is not the only one, it often proves indispensable, to the extent that it is tied to the ability to grasp interrelationships in time. Whether it be intuitive, implicit, patched together, or sophisticated, it may also be used to consider the causes of a given phenomenon; to clear away categories and explanatory schemas that are too common or routine; to draw out networks of causes that are historically situated; to test the spaces of possibility based on available information; and to seek out relationships between theoretical perspectives and proposals of action. Its value depends on the researchers' ability to mobilize their skills toward the scientific ambition of their discipline, with a clear awareness of the goals they want to achieve. Imagination is useful here as well.

One should not be surprised to hear echoes from the previous chapter, nor to discover parallels between some of these approaches (including thought experiments, the elaboration of hypotheses, relational approaches, spaces of constraint and of possibility). As we suggested, interpretative imagination and scientific deduction can interact and interpenetrate across a wide range of approaches in which they are neither one and the same nor entirely opposed. Thus, at the close of these last two chapters we see that two poles emerge, which spread from a hypothetical deductive approach to a more hermeneutical practice. These two uses of counterfactual reasoning and the variety of possibilities they cover reveal uncertainties at the heart of the social sciences between a model founded upon abstraction and the elaboration of hypotheses, on the one hand, and a recursive reasoning that relies on narration and interpretation, on the other.[85]

Interlude

THE DOMINION OF FACTS IN THE SOCIAL SCIENCES

At this stage, a more general epistemological question may be posed: Does counterfactual reasoning belong to a "non-Popperian" realm of social scientific reasoning as elaborated by Jean-Claude Passeron?[1] Let's briefly introduce the key elements of the problem at hand. For the philosopher of science, Karl Popper, induction is a myth in the realm of science. Refutability is the central characteristic that allows one to distinguish between science and pseudoscience; theory must precede observation. The key issue is that the status of history and the social sciences is not entirely clear in this framework. On the one hand, history and social sciences can claim to be scientific under certain conditions (the establishment of facts based on a critique of sources), but on the other hand, and notably in their efforts toward generalization, they cannot deliver on this claim. The domain of the social sciences does not obey the laws of the physical sciences (laws that are true always and everywhere), and this is the essential point: thanks to this condition, the liberty of human action is preserved. Predicting the future, Popper argues, the futures of the present as well as of the past, is an unfounded and dangerous ambition that supposes that human reality is subject to immutable laws.[2] Note in passing that the past futures we have discussed here are not designed to be predictive and certainly do not aim to make this a dominant ambition within the social sciences. The uncertain status of the social sciences long nourished an implicit hierarchization between the human and the natural sciences.

Jean-Claude Passeron argued to the contrary that the social sciences possess their own scientific space. Their reasoning cannot be confused with research into laws and absolute truth. Instead, they multiply theories and modes of description, based on empirical inquiries, in an effort to regulate knowledge of the social world. The case of counterfactual analysis, one must highlight, is hardly clear in such a space. On the one hand, as we have seen, it is lodged in the heart of the modes of understanding developed by the social sciences. On the other, it seems to reach beyond this field of analysis. Sociological knowledge, Passeron insists, rests on "what happened" and on observable data. Historian Carlo Ginzburg outlines a similar approach. Distrustful of the idea that historical narrative is above all fictional, he opposes on numerous occasions the two levels of discourse, to denounce the dangerous use of imaginative fiction or "invention."[3] The historian, he insists, may only rely on facts and works based on them. By definition, counterfactual analysis stretches beyond this framework by exploring what could have happened, and thus does not appear to be an appropriate area of research.

The problem becomes particularly crucial in the realm of history, with its discontinuous, heterogeneous reality wherein the true, the false, and fictional intermix. For Siegfried Kracauer, for example, recourse to the "possible outcomes of a crisis" is one of the unworthy tools of historical reasoning. But it is one of the ways one "orient[s] oneself in the jungle the historian must navigate." This approach cannot here be separated from the judgments, hypotheses, and instincts of the researcher and therefore reveal the particularly ambiguous and uncertain nature of the historical investigation.[4] Nonetheless, such hesitations are widely shared, pushing the counterfactual approach to the edge of this space of reasoning. This unique position explains the uncertainty that characterizes the approach and its reception.

Three points however plead for pursuing counterfactualism within the social sciences. First, either in its mathematical logic or interpretative forms, the counterfactual belongs to the descriptive languages mobilized by social sciences. And, in purely logical terms, one cannot grasp "what comes to pass" without thinking about what did not. Or, in the words of Arnaldo Momigliano, "any question posed by any historian on any past subject implies the possibility that what he thinks happened could not have happened."[5] Finally, it is necessary to revisit the question of the domain of "facts" studied under the heading of the social sciences. The realm defined by Passeron, like the one identified by Ginzburg, is vast: "anything that is a part of social reality," including fabulations, myths, and rumors. Shouldn't the possible also be included this realm?[6] Should one employ a strict definition of "facts" or a broader one that includes relations, possibilities, dispositions, and potentialities? From this perspective, don't possible futures represent an extension of the factual (albeit one that is difficult to grasp)? The entire problem is that of knowing at what point such explorations leave the realm of facts. Counterfactual analysis is situated precisely on the porous borders of the dominion of the social sciences, which explains why it is so easy to enter and exit, with all the risks such a passage poses for researchers. It is then not so much "counterfeit" or "against the facts" as it is an exploration of the potentialities of what was taking place. On these blurred margins, an appropriately critical approach is required for the examination of documents, approaches, interpretations, and discourse. In this sense, its explicit usage may be atypical, but it is acceptable (and perhaps even necessary) from the perspective of the social sciences. Even so, it remains to be seen if it is not too dependent on a certain conception of the real, of time, and of history. It is to this question that we now turn.

CHAPTER 7

The Past Futures of Others

COUNTERFACTUAL REASONING AND HISTORICITY

> I leave to various future times, but not to all, my garden of forking paths. This web of time—the strands of which approach one another, bifurcate, intersect or ignore each other through the centuries—embraces every possibility.
>
> —Jorge Luis Borges[1]

> We are in the habit of studying the *gesta* of these societies, that is the actions they performed in their own present. For some time now, historians have taken an interest in their *memoria,* that is the ways in which they construct their own pasts. . . . But we should also take an interest in their *futura,* that is the way in which these past societies projected themselves into the future, the future that we are a part of.
>
> —Jean-Claude Schmitt[2]

Our investigation has thus far left a specific set of problems unresolved: Can one find the counterfactual approach everywhere, and can it be applied to all times and all places? Is this reasoning—and even the cognitive reflex that consists of "what if"—part of all human societies, a sort of quasi-invariant, or is it a predominantly Western type of reasoning, with its roots in what we have generally referred to as "modernity"?

As we have seen, the approach may be formally defined through its relationship to time (the acceleration of an outcome), to a scientific idea (the model of the "natural" sciences) and the natural world (an objectified, distantiated world). Employing this mode of reasoning in the ways we have discussed therefore generally relies upon a series of presuppositions: a temporal succession of elements connected by a simple or complex causal relationship;

the notion of an event or fact; and finally the idea of the future in its "modern" sense, that is a temporal field with a long duration.

There is, then, a certain conception of time that structures the counterfactual approach. As a result, we enter a realm of historicity that designates how history emerges within the consciousness of the actors, or more generally, the articulation between the past, the present, and the future. It is a question of treating the different ways of "inhabiting time" and their material, social, and cognitive translations within a given society.[3] Thus, even if this type of reasoning as we know it took shape in the "regime of historicity" that emerged in Europe in the eighteenth century, there is no guarantee that the perceptions of past futures or the idea of other possible histories is not specific to this conception of space-time, nor that it might not take other forms elsewhere.

In short, does this approach depend on a mode of modern and Eurocentric thinking that is inoperable for the study of ancient or non-Western societies? Or is it also of interest for those societies that have developed a different system of thought and perception?

ARE THERE CONCEPTIONS OF TIME THAT RESIST COUNTERFACTUALISM?

Georges Duby's study of July 27, 1214, may help us pose this problem.[4] On that day, better known as the "Sunday of Bouvines," Philip Augustus's royal French troops defeated Otto IV's Anglo-German-Flemish coalition. This victory led to the fracturing of the Holy Roman Empire, undermined John Lackland's ambitions over France, and reinforced Philip Augustus's position within his own territory and in Europe more broadly. Writing against positivist history, Georges Duby noted nonetheless that "the outlines of the event may not be effectively interpreted without first being placed within the cultural system that experienced them." This system included knightly culture as well as the emergence of a new culture of time. The book not only recounts the French victory, but also the social construction of the notion of the event, its relationship to a historically situated mental universe, a specific mode of social organization, and a perception of history that makes such an apprehension possible. Thus, the constitutive elements of counterfactual reasoning, along the lines of those discussed above, seem to be inscribed in a specific perception of temporality.

To explore this question, it is necessary to explore "distant" societies, first by mobilizing classical ethnographic and anthropological studies that have uncovered different systems for understanding the world. By focusing certain aspects of their inquiries on discussions of "time and space" in these studies, we may gain precious insights. We should note at the outset that these works provide both an introduction to other cultures of time and enlighten us on the ways non-European historicities were conceived at a given moment, which is another way of exploring the problem at hand. In order to stake out the territory of this investigation, we have set our sights on examples from four continents outside the European peninsula: China, Soudan, today's Arizona, and New Guinea. Again, our ambition here is merely to examine the arguments presented in these classical works.

China: Symbolic Time (Temps emblématisé)

We may try to imagine the immense and multimillennial Chinese Empire with the help of Marcel Granet's classic work from 1934 *Chinese Thought* (*La Pensée chinoise*).[5] The sinologist notes in the chapter on time that in his view the Chinese do not conceive of time as a "monotone duration and succession of similar moments."[6] Rather, time is cut up into eras, seasons, epochs, while space is divided into domains, climates, and points of orientation. Space and time are associated and assimilated to attributes: white, for example, symbolizes war, fall, and the West.

There did not exist, then, in "Chinese thought" prior to the nineteenth century an abstract notion of time and space, that is an idea of something detached from a perceived or measured world and which might serve as a standard for the existent or the becoming. Time refers instead to a game of symbols and concrete attributes that are at once discontinuous and associated with specific qualities. *Che* therefore does not signify time as such, but the "occasion," or the "circumstance,"[7] just like *fag* does not express "space," but rather "direction" or "site." Within this cosmology, time is not linear: it is considered instead to consist of revolutions, in the first sense of the word, that is, as a series of returns, cyclical eras, from a temporary point of emergence.

The question of power in its relation to time becomes essential in this account. According to Granet, time is ordered to follow seasons as well as dynasties. Each new dynasty produces a new calendar, as a sign of its power over the cosmos. Historical time participates in this same logic. It is necessary to reinscribe events in the framework of a rhythm and a liturgy. It is incumbent upon historians to find the right framework, the precise point of emergence: they are the guarantors of this temporal order, which gives them a tremendous power over the order of things. Marcel Granet emphasizes the force contained within this conception, which "provides the framework for a kind of total art": effective symbols—a season, color, body part, virtue—partake in an ordering of the world, which is inspired by Chinese society.

We are thus confronted with a temporal scheme that is closed, cyclical, and based upon symbols. The notion of the event exists, but not the unfolding of time, most notably of the future. The idea of a different future that would emerge from a bifurcation appears absurd. This relationship to time does not require a formal articulation between facts and does not establish a directionality within historical change. The problem for ancient Chinese historians is not to establish key moments, a pertinent succession of facts and information, or an understanding of ways of seeing, but, more fundamentally, to find the center of a given coherent period, bringing what is outside the frame back into it. The counterfactual approach and its consequences appear to be opposed to this very way of seeing.

The Nuer: Structural Time

Let's turn to the African continent, or more precisely to the Nuer people of Sudan, made famous by E. E. Evans-Pritchard's work in 1937.[8] This monument of ethnographic analysis proposes a study of pastoral populations whose lifestyle is described as "ordered anarchy": the expression refers to the idea that these societies without a state, without a chief, and without status are not without order, but founded on complex relationships between lineage segments and a specific mode of conflict resolution between equals. The work challenged earlier ethnographic analysis, such as English social anthropology, which was concerned with the description of groups more than their relationships, as well as studies within the discipline that analyzed "societies without a state." In his chapter entitled "Time and Space,"[9] Evans-Pritchard makes a distinction between two kinds of time: one related to the milieu, which he calls "oecological," and those bound to society, which he calls "structural," the two being related. The periods of time pertaining to shorter durations and a given year are "oecological" and the longer periods of time are "structural."

According to oecological time, which is the first point of reference, the year is divided into twelve months (which do not exactly correspond to our months), and two seasons of six months, a rainy season and a dry season. The dating of events is elaborated within this division, but also depends on important activities during the year (harvests, and so on). Evans-Pritchard provides an important insight for our study: time does not have the same value all year long. Moreover, he argues there is no Nuer expression for speaking of "time" as such that does not also imply a distantiation, and it is not something that can be "gained" or "lost." Events are connected between themselves according to a logical order, but they are not inscribed in an abstract system. In other words, the relationship between two events exists, but the lapse of time that separates them is impossible to evaluate: there are no hours or a specific date, only a period of reference.

To orient themselves in the depths of the past, the Nuer use "structural time," that of society: within this practice, time is the order of events that a group (family, village, tribe) considers important. In this sense, there are as many temporal frames as there are groups. This fundamentally social conception of time is therefore associated with relationships between groups, like the structure of the group itself. One locates oneself, for example, within one's age group or one's family tree.

From this perspective, the idea of temporal movement seems incomprehensible, since the structure of reference remains constant and the perception of time is elaborated within this structure. Another consequence is that "its time depth appear to be limited." It does not reach back more than a century, while the distance from what is defined as the origin of the world appears inalterable.

This coherent temporal system of the Nuer is founded upon a relationship to time that is complex and highly socialized: it appears to be a sort of bubble that is constantly reproduced in a changing universe, while it is maintained through the perception of a point of origin. The notions of unfolding, the future, or the event have little meaning in this structure, which is at once fixed and constantly recomposed. Imagining "what-if" reasoning in this context, with a point of bifurcation and the description of an alternative future appears once again incongruous.

Hopi Native Americans: Sentient Time

The case of the Hopis of Arizona, studied by Jamake Highwater, is equally interesting.[10] The author, purportedly of Native American origin, was adopted by a family of European descent. Rediscovering what he claimed were his Native American origins relatively late in life, he became a man of letters, a journalist and an anthropologist who specialized in Native American culture. His work, *The Primal Mind,* is a surprising text. It is less an account of ethnographic immersion than an effort to reconstruct the conceptual framework of the first inhabitants of North America.

In his chapter on time, Highwater insists on the relationship between time and language.[11] The Hopi language does not have an expression that specifically refers to time or those elements that are associated with it (past, present, future, permanence, duration, movement, and so on). While the Hopi do use the distinction between night and day, Highwater highlights their singular conception of time, characterized by an intrinsic aesthetic of everyday life. Everything that is lived, thought, and experienced is taken together. The objective and the subjective are not distinct. The Hopi perceive the future, but it is bound to these emotions and to that mode of perception. Instead of the future, Highwater prefers an attitude of expectation, or a desire. Hence, the Hopi Indians insist on the generative dimension of things: there is no equivalent of "coming" and "going," and these phenomena are rather apprehended as apparitions. Moreover, there is not a temporal future, a notion of succession or distantiation. The Hopi establish an immediate relationship between a given detail and the Great Whole. Reality is grasped in its immediacy. The separation between the past and future proves to be inoperable. It is no doubt in such a context that counterfactual reasoning would be the most inconceivable.

THE TIME OF OTHERS OR THE TIME OF HUMANKIND?

The possibility of counterfactual reasoning does not appear universal. But we should be cautious about the works we have used, since their disciplinary frameworks are dated and they propose a structural and dehistoricized analysis of the societies they study. What moment or period, for example, does the Chinese thought discussed by Granet refer to? The chapters called "Time and Space," which are characteristic of this descriptive mode of presentation (a preliminary approach to static "conceptual frameworks"), may in fact be quite poor guides. There is a real risk of falling into an ethnographic trap, denounced in the 1980s, which consists of artificially reconstructing the "time of others." This is the ambition of Johannes Fabian and his colleagues' famous critique.[12] For Fabian, these accounts are a violent reconstruction. Caught between the moment of ethnographic immersion and the scientific reconstruction of the information, they exaggerate the distance between "us" and "them" in the temporal register, caging these societies inside their foreignness. The anthropologist is therefore "allochronic," in that the elaboration of a distance between the two worlds justifies his scientific perspective. In reality, the mere immersion of the anthropologist into the society he or she is studying, through continuous interactions, proves that these individuals share a common time. This co-temporality should be, in Fabian's view, used more effectively by researchers and can serve as a foundation and a redefinition of anthropological practice. Fabian's work generated a strong reaction, most notably on the part of Claude Lévi-Strauss and Claude Lefort, who challenged the critique's excessiveness.[13] Indeed, it would seem important not to throw these earlier works out too quickly, since they are part of the first substantial Western descriptions of these societies, with their systems of representation and organization that are so different from our own. Nonetheless, the risk of "allochronic time" is real. Thus, for example, the historian Prasenjit Duara recalls the great diversity of regimes of historicity that characterize the Chinese world, in the present and the past.[14] During the early centuries of the Common Era, when the Chinese supposedly understood time to be purely repetitive, entire sectors of the social body developed a progressive and innovative conception of time.[15] Even if we place ourselves within this other "temporal culture" and accept the radical simplifications it imposes, the temporal context still remains deeply complex. This has been demonstrated by the philosopher François Jullien, who explores different "folds of thought":[16] while the West conceived of autonomous time, marked by a beginning and an end, with series of ruptures and stable identities, as well as an importance accorded to the event (understood as an exceptional moment that unsettles a situation), China does not have a thought of "time" as such. The Chinese focus their attention on "silent transformations," gradual shifts from one form to the next within continuous transitional processes that are shaped by a back-and-forth of different phases.[17] In this conception, an individual may seize opportunities offered by a "moment," and instead of analyzing the point of rupture, may explore the beginning of change (the *ji*), the moment when "the unpredictable mixes with an opportunity within a still indefinite tendency, . . . and [when] the seeds of new possibilities are planted."[18] In other words, within Chinese culture there is a conception of lost opportunity, of past possibilities, that resides within a language and a conceptual framework that is difficult for us to imagine. Moreover, one finds on the African continent societies whose relationship to time is more sensitive to the future. The Dogons of Mali, studied by Marcel Griaule,[19] offer an example of a dynamic conception of the world, with succession and continuity, in which they recognize liberty of action. The function of time is different, however from our own, to the extent that the population needs to ensure that they are going "in the right direction."

With this in mind, is it not possible to reverse the question and ask if the capacity to project into a future situation or a different future, notably through the evaluation of one's present situation, is not a universally human characteristic? The counterfactual would in this case be part of the human condition. This has been suggested by certain works in psychology and the cognitive sciences. The psychologist Jean-Pierre Boutinet, for example, argues that it is doubtful that there are societies "without projects."[20] According to works in psychology, even living organisms orient their behavior with regard to external events; and for humans, this dimension, acquired through learning, is essential. One must not oppose different human societies, but distinguish the relationships between forms of projects, among which Boutinet defines four: the project as vital necessity (the project allows all living organisms to be drawn toward the ultimate aim of its survival); the project as a cultural fact (its role and its function vary according to the society—industrial society, for example, gives this project an important place); the existential project (which allows the individual to orient him- or herself and give meaning to a feeling of chance or existential absurdity); and operational projects (which are directly tied to the realization of action and taking into consideration limits imposed upon the real). The relationships between them are multiple. In this context, the "what if" of the present is necessary to the lives of animals, and the "what if" of the past is necessary for human learning, no matter his or her life context. Work in the cognitive sciences has gone even further. Recent research on regret, defined as the permanent evaluation of difference between what is and what should have taken place, indicates for example that it is a fundamental disposition of human beings. Moreover, it may be located in the brain. Analyses of the brain place it in the orbitofrontal cortex, in the front of the prefontal cortex behind the eyes.[21] The objective of this research is to demonstrate the role of emotions in different forms of evaluation and calculation, but as a result they also suggest that counterfactual reasoning may be characteristic of humans because it is a function of the human brain.[22] Other work on decision-making or learning have developed this idea further, to the point of exploring counterfactual reasoning through neuroscience:[23] they emphasize that counterfactual reasoning (understood as the taking into consideration of what could have happened through recourse to alternative, fictional, and hypothetical outcomes) may be situated within the prefontal cortex, prior to the emotion that gives it meaning. It is involved in a number of decisive cognitive situations, and its deficiency can be correlated to a certain number of pathologies (depression, addiction, and so on). Because it employs imagination and calculation to tackle complex problems and adjust behavior, counterfactual reasoning is for some researchers a characteristic of the human species that can therefore be found in all societies. The risks of such observations are obvious: they are often founded on a series of generalizations and debatable parallels. Is any regret merely a rational calculation? Do the images that have identified the zones of brain activity actually reveal "rational calculation" as it is understood by researchers themselves? Are the varieties of social meanings embedded within these cognitive reflexes truly without effect? The ambition of the neurosciences to speak about humans in general and to situate activities in precise sections of the body is stimulating, but it may prove problematic when one denies historicity and the freedom that accompanies human transformation.[24] Indeed, researchers have reflected on the interactions between biological dispositions and sociocultural environments.[25]

In the entirely different register of language, the literary scholar George Steiner also evokes this potential universality: "Since language contains conditionals, optatives, counterfactuals and future verb forms, grammar is utopic. . . . We know there are many languages that do not possess verb tenses. . . . But we know of no language on the planet that is incapable of expressing the future, futures."[26] He then continues: "The human heart, humanism, seems to be that capacity to think and to articulate, I don't want to separate the two, in terms of propositions such as 'if': if this were, if this weren't, to propose sentences of a counterfactual order." The observation contains a moral element: the projections into other futures contradict the idea of the inevitability of the material order of reality; they bear the trace of the perfectability of humans and their desire for freedom. It is difficult once again to articulate the perspective in a precise empirical investigation, even if one may note that it does not contradict sociocultural constructions with a specific relationship to time. For the moment we are no doubt forced to leave such conclusions open, along with the search for invariants that underscore them.

In this context, it would certainly seem prudent to consider both more modest and more dynamic approaches. In the case of Georges Balandier,[27] for example, the problem is not that of opposing societies in time and societies outside of time, cold or hot, modern or traditional: all societies are in fact divided between order and disorder. In societies referred to as "traditional," the apparent stability of situations is in fact the product of a dynamic process. From this perspective, what characterizes these societies would be the search for a certain harmonization of temporal registers. And the modernity of Western societies does not appear as the only perspective in a linear development toward the future but rather as a set of contradictory temporalities, like a moment of confusion, fragmentation, and contrast. Such a dynamic perspective, which does not exclude the existence of multiple relationships to time, would seem more accurate. Moreover, it is increasingly used by researchers, to such an extent that one may speak of a new anthropology of time.[28]

Obviously, this does not necessarily invalidate our initial observations on the diversity of ways humans inhabit time. Works about Oceania, one of the regions that has generated the most vibrant research on the subject, offer important insights. In an article on the Hulis of New Guinea, entitled "The Workshop of History,"[29] the Australian anthropologist-historian Chris Ballard examines an expedition across the island's highlands by two brothers, Jack and Tom Fox, in 1932 that became famous after World War II. The explorers described their voyage in a travel journal. They forgot, however, to mention that their intrusion led to the massacre, rape, and hunting of a great number of people. Nonetheless, this expedition remained relatively important because it was one of the first forms of Western contact with these societies. It is difficult, Ballard notes, to establish the "facts" of the story in a society in which memory is truncated (our own) and a society in which is it largely oral (that of the Hulis). For, outside the massacre itself, what is interesting is the manner in which the Hulis took note of the event without transforming it into a history.[30] During their voyage, the Fox brothers were taken for divinities called "Dona," with peculiar characteristics: they could take on any appearance; their existence in the sentient world was only expressed through their impact on it. Thus, no memory of the Fox brothers' visit was conserved, and the Hulis only preserved the memory of the material traces of their passage (blood, marks on trees, footprints, and so on). Moreover, while the direct witnesses who met the author remembered the expedition, and in spite of their apparent importance, their passage was not entered into history or formalized within any narratives developed afterward that might have circulated the visit beyond those immediately involved. For the Hulis, the expedition was not an "event." In their more formal historical narratives, the Hulis did not pay much attention to the facts themselves, but instead concentrated their research on origins and responsibilities, following a logic marked by trade and principles of compensation. Ballard thus attempts to show that an event is not necessarily a given in itself and that it depends on the categories of perception as well as the ways of ordering reality.

Thus, even within a dynamic analysis that explores the variety of temporal experiences and suggests a relationship to time that is constructed and potentially changing, counterfactual reasoning may seem inoperative or delicate. In a society that accords no importance to the event, what is the value of an approach that mobilizes notions of causation, relies on turning points, and imagines another future? How then might one proceed? These long detours allow us to call into question sloppy distinctions between societies and open a few new directions for thinking about these problems.

CHALLENGING THE NARRATIVE OF THE SPANISH IN AMERICA: CAUSAL REVISIONISM

The problem is obviously less pronounced for the "scientific" hypothetical-deductive approach than for the interpretative ambitions of hermeneutical counterfactualism. Even if the two poles are not irreconcilable, the "scientific" version remains pertinent from the researcher's perspective. By definition, it establishes a distance from the object of study. Its methodological tools are recognized as pertaining to a "modern" and "universal" mode of thought, which facilitates its usage in all times and places. As a result, this approach may be used in the context of anthropological modeling, such as theoretical models built on fieldwork, which is then subjected to tests and verifications (kinship structures, repartition and transmission of property, organization of powers, anthropology of networks, and so on). One finds a particularly sophisticated form within structural anthropology, with its focus on deep structures of understanding. The forms of kinship explored by Claude Lévi-Strauss, for example, elaborated a register of possible combinations, some of which were actually realized while others were not. Thus, "far from turning its back on history, structural analysis pursues a list of possible pathways in which history alone determines which one will effectively be followed."[31] One finds a similar idea in the work of anthropologists who have continued this line of research with an interest in the transformations of human societies. In his recent study of the evolution of the early human societies, founded on a remarkable reevaluation of proof and causal reason, the anthropologist Alain Testart frequently uses this type of reflection to demonstrate the power of the "law" of development or structural logics that resist a simplistic evolutionary conception. Chinese royalty, for example, which combines "despotism," cosmology, and monumentality, "could have given birth to step pyramids and I think that it is only the very peculiar development of Chinese architecture that prevented it." Most of all, the project consists once again in studying the "potential forms which a given society may take," when considering the "virtual innovations," those inventions that could have given birth to massive technological applications known in other societies, but which didn't develop (such as the wheel for the Incas).[32]

Counterfactual reasoning can also be mobilized in the context of inquiries on the indigenous perception of facts, notably in historical anthropology. It serves as a precondition for discussing the supposed chain of events and creates a rupture in the official narrative. This allows the researcher to attempt to reconstruct the mental universe of the populations under study. This approach has been suggested by the specialist of the Aztecs, Ross Hassig.[33] Counterfactual reasoning is not only understood here as the fictional projection of possible trajectories of the past, but also as the present evaluation of alternatives. The efficacy of this usage rests on certain initial conditions: a simple variable, a significant fact in a system of thought shared by all the actors, a potentially important transformation, and minimal rewriting. Once established, the anthropologist recalls the value of this "theoretical comparison" for analyzing the Western conquest of Mexico in the sixteenth century. If one seeks to discuss the importance of the superiority of Spanish armament, for example, it is possible to explore the battle of Tlaxcala in 1520 and mobilize a simple version of counterfactual reasoning. This battle ended with the victory of Cortés's men over the Aztecs. Spanish guns have often been presented as decisive in this "success." However, had the battle lasted a few more days, Hassig writes, the Spanish, who were running low on powder, would probably have lost. Other arguments may also be put forward: during the flight from Tenochtitlán later on June 30, 1520, the Spanish fell into a trap and abandoned their canons. This did not prevent them from attacking and winning once again. The weapons were therefore not the determinant variable.

There remains, according to the anthropologist, a major problem with this form of reasoning: counterfactualism does not generally weigh the facts, but the causes, which require one to know the versions, the reading patterns, and the norms of reception of the actors who are involved. Each culture, however, registers, elucidates, or ignores an event differently, depending on the significance it has been granted. But in the case of the Spanish conquest of the sixteenth century, the data is too sparse: Aztec societies left few direct traces, and the Spanish sources are too partial. While we may know with some certainty the effects, causal reconstitution is more difficult and runs the risk of being incomplete. Hassig proposes then another form of counterfactual reasoning that he calls "causal revisionism." The principle is simple: it is not a question of modifying the cause to imagine other effects, but of keeping the same effect and changing the initial cause. The example of the massacre of Chololian of 1519 provides an illustration: during the conquest of Mexico, Cortés allied with the Tlaxcalteca, marched toward the city of Chololian, where he had been authorized to enter. However, an Indian woman who was accompanying the expedition, Marina, learned that Chololtecas were planning to massacre the Spanish with an Aztec army of fifty thousand men hidden in the city. She alerted Cortés, who took the advantage: he gathered the Chololtecas in their central courtyard, blocked the exits with the Spanish army, and ordered the massacre. Instead of asking "What would have happened if Marina had not been informed of the plot or had not told Cortés?" Hassig posed a different question: "And what if the Chololtecas were not planning to attack the Spanish and kill Cortés?" The plot, which is supported by Spanish sources, remains uncertain: Montezuma II did not have tens of thousands of soldiers to send to Chololian in the middle of the farming season, and the Aztec army probably was not present. The presence of barricades and stones in front of the city, due to the fear of the neighboring enemy Tlaxcala, was no doubt misinterpreted by the Spanish. In fact, there was indeed a massacre, but it was most certainly an intentional act on the part of Cortés: it was necessary to destroy the most powerful city in the region in order to warn the other cities. Moreover, it was an enemy of their Tlaxcaltec allies. And Chololian is situated on the road between Vera Cruz (the Spanish base) and Tenochtitlán (the home of the Aztecs). There was the risk that the city would sever the connection to the Spanish base that housed the army. The decision to go to Chololian and to perpetrate the massacre therefore appears more political: for Cortés, it was a question of securing his supply lines and striking fear into the hearts of his allies' enemies.

This credible hypothesis also suggests that the Spanish version, which sought to justify the actions a posteriori, is either false or must be reconsidered. To arrive at this conclusion, it is necessary to add a specious causal connection to explain the known historical result. In so doing, Hassig explains, counterfactual reasoning loses the predictive dimension that is oftentimes considered problematic. Since it does not alter the result, documentation can be used effectively in the process of interpretation. It is a question of filling in the blanks of the historical narrative through analysis and imagination, which, in spite of the absence of direct sources, relies on knowledge of the "social context, a wider cluster of events and conditions than those historically or intuitively evident from the immediate documentary record."[34] Counterfactualism may therefore break with the evidence of the official interpretation and include in its explanation and the inquiry's objectives the logic and the points of view of the actors. This stimulating proposal allows one to reenvisage how one reads archives and integrate a different perception of the world—and therefore of time and of history—in the search of a more refined understanding of causation.

FOLLOWING THE EXPECTATIONS OF OTHERS: COOK WITHOUT THE STORM

We would like to formulate another proposal that is closely related to our initial question: it is a question of reconstituting "past futures" understood as past projections of societies under study (and not in the form of Western-centric causal chains). In order to do this, it is necessary to explore, in the words of R. Koselleck, "horizons of expectations" and "fields of experience." We must remember that the first notion expresses the cognitive elements of projection as well as the expectations and the fears formulated by the group; the second refers to social, political, and material structures that render these horizons possible, translate them, but are also out of sync with them.[35] Having taken these elements into account, it is then possible to proceed toward the work of projection, that is, to follow the possible futures of societies defined as "other." Given that mastery of all the constitutive elements is impossible based on the cultural information available to the researcher, these fictional explorations may give more heft to the ways of seeing time, and provide a better grasp of their thickness in spite of the missing pieces of knowledge. In this way, they may improve our understanding. Since they are more remote and the documentation is rarer in the case of these societies, recourse to hypotheses seems more frequent and the "strangeness" of the approach is reduced.

It is possible to illustrate this approach through Marshall Sahlins's study of James Cook's "discovery" of Hawaii.[36] The story is well-known: Cook arrived in Hawaii at the beginning of 1779, and while he was immediately considered a god by the inhabitants of the island, the British Captain James Cook was killed a few weeks later by those same inhabitants following his return to the island. This dramatic shift in attitude led to a whole range of analyses and conjectures; Sahlins offers in this famous text his own detailed study of available information. In January 1779, Captain Cook, a famous explorer who had already discovered the Australian coast and New Caledonia, disembarked for the second time onto the island. He was greeted with open arms and invited by the king, who offered him his throne. Then Cook participated in a whole series of rituals and libations, leaving with pieces of the temple where the ceremony had been held. Sahlins explains that Cook was taken for the god Lono, god of nature and fertility, who was celebrated each year according to a ritual cycle. The arrival of the explorer fit directly into this cycle. There was therefore a literal actualization of the myth, or at least, what we refer to as such: if for Westerners the event was the discovery of the island, for the Hawaiians it was the realization of a predetermined cultural structure: there was, according to Sahlins, "a structure of the conjuncture."[37]

Sahlins's objective, with this study, is therefore double: it is a question of understanding the death of Captain Cook, killed after having been taken for a god; and then grasping the logic of the Hawaiians in order to discuss the classic opposition between structure and history, repetition and the succession of facts. The idea here is not whether or not structures have a history (he never doubts this is the case), but rather that history itself, and even the event are modeled on cultural structures.

This critique is addressed toward anthropology, but also history, which Sahlins considers too attached to the contingency of facts. He mocks a historical approach by reproducing a counterfactual logic: "If Cook hadn't done this or that, then . . . Then what?"[38] It was written, for example, that Cook was killed because he had taken a piece of the temple. One is tempted to ask in this case, "And what if he hadn't taken it?" But according to Sahlins, the point of departure of the hypothesis is false: the rite of Lono, the ritual of renewal, ends with the destruction of the building for the festival and the god must leave with the ruins from the site. The anthropologist criticizes historical interpretations that are obsessed with the examination of microfacts and minor bits of information. The myth of extreme contingency is, in Sahlins's view, absurd, since what is essential is the cultural structure that emerges. The event is instead "a unique actualization of a general phenomenon,"[39] the moment when the underlying structure realizes itself in history.

Returning to the end of this extraordinary story, after revealing the logic of the structure and the events at work, there remained the question of why Cook was killed. All was going well for him when he left the island on February 3 in conformity with the indigenous rituals. The ritual continued with a symbolic battle on the island between the god Lono and the king, before the execution of the first by the second in order to set off a new cycle of life. Then an unexpected event took place, a case of bad luck: blocked by a storm that damaged the mast, Cook was forced to return to Hawaii after a few days. On the island, the cycle of Lono had come to an end and that of the god Ku, king of war, had begun. The return of the god in the person of Cook provoked a grave political and cosmological crisis. It was at this moment, on the occasion of the third arrival, that the god "died" for the Hawaiians. The tensions among the warlords increased. In response to the theft of a rowboat, Cook took the Hawaiian king Kalaniʻōpuʻu hostage, replaying the drama of the struggle between the king and the god in reverse. Cook was then killed on the beach: since the myth was destroyed, it was necessary to kill the imposter. For Sahlins, it was the break with the cultural structure that explains this behavior, which, in spite of what was long argued by Europeans, was very logical.

Nonetheless, the dramatic ending of the meeting still emerges from a contingent fact: the storm. "It was chance," notes Sahlins,[40] "or in the Western scientific metaphor the intersection of the independent chains of causation." Sahlins seems forced to admit, while still insisting on the importance of structure, that the weather and the poor construction of the Western boat played a role. There is then a turning point in Sahlins's study that is neither bound to Cook's arrival nor the steps of the ritual, but rather his failed departure. Sahlins's reasoning depends upon the idea of a successful ceremony. His analysis invites us to proceed as if there had not been an incident, in order to avoid searching for some problem within the ceremony, and to the contrary reveals its overall logic.

Let's explore this point further. If Cook had been able to leave as he intended, he would no doubt have returned to Europe. He would have recounted his voyage and perhaps changed the perception Europeans had of the Hawaiian populations, even though we may never know for certain. As for the Hawaiians, Cook's arrival and his return to Europe would have been digested by the Hawaiian cultural structures. Perhaps they might even have reinforced the power of representations by conferring on them a heavy dose of reality, although this may not have been the case since Sahlins indicates in another text that the form in which the god appeared was of little importance.[41] In any case, the event would have become an element in itself in the ritual perception of time that, without being profoundly modified, could not have been exactly the same.[42]

Following this cultural logic, there would not have been other futures, or even other events, but a permanence. The future of the past, in this case, is the (re)production of the past. This counterfactual game coincides with Georges Balandier's suggestions, which show how a tradition is constructed and how permanence persists in dynamic processes. This understanding is inscribed in the extension of Sahlins's reasoning. The hypothesis of "Cook without the storm" reveals one more element in the cultural logics undergirding the perception of time and the processes in the production of the "past futures" of local populations. Placed alongside the actual history, the counterfactual approach renders more apparent the mutual incomprehension between historicities and the processual dimension of their elaboration. In its attempt to provide a more comprehensive approach, it offers the opportunity to test different relationships to time more concretely.

COUNTERFACTUAL TIME

The counterfactual hypothesis for societies that have a very different relationship to time from our own may therefore focus, nonetheless, on a "real" turning point as well as processes for reconstructing the past. It does so by interrogating, for example, how a "bifurcation," a history, a past, or another world is understood, as well as the terms in which they are said or thought. It implies that one must embrace ways of seeing that are foreign to the notion of the event, of a historical "turn," or a succession of facts, and then decipher within this temporal culture what may generate movement, change, and displacement. Thus, it is possible to historicize the counterfactual and its implicit underpinnings. In these conditions, history is not "contrary to the facts," but "contrary to a certain idea of the facts." The approach may therefore prolong the ways that anthropology enriches historical investigations and at the same time also inform the work of history and anthropology.[43] This detour through distant shores also comforts the idea that our societies are marked by a peculiar relationship to the event, which partially explains the interest that is currently focused on counterfactualism in the social sciences as well as literary and artistic production.

It also suggests that what we call the relationship to time or the Western "regime of historicity" is neither unique nor singular, but is rather plural.[44] There are always, in the same moment, many ways of representing or experience the "future." Counterfactual reasoning, understood as an experiment in our relationship between time, can be one of the ways of revisiting this multiplicity: rupture in time, construction of persistence, survival, resonance, specters, cycles, short-term futures, perspectives of "progress," and so on.

It would seem difficult to assign a place or unique location to counterfactual reasoning, to say that it is part of all human societies or characteristic of a specific spatiotemporal sequence. The forms that we are familiar with are subject to the regimes of historicity of the nineteenth and twentieth centuries in the West. Thus, the usages that may be contested are those that do not define the types of counterfactual that are employed (hypothetical-deductive or interpretative) or that impose, in spite of themselves, Eurocentric temporal schemas. Nonetheless, there are numerous alternatives, and, as a technique of questioning, counterfactualism may help reveal the diversity of relationships to time. Such variety should hardly be surprising: the counterfactual hypothesis—the "what if"—seems bound to experience and to the very perception of change, no matter what its content, as well as the symbolic forms and the material manifestations that allow it to take shape. This is why there is an oscillation between invariance and history, a capacity to incarnate a "modern" relationship to becoming while also revealing the diverse "ways of being in time" of human societies.

CHAPTER 8

Political Uses of Counterfactual History

> The historical materialist thus . . . regards it as his task to brush history against the grain.
>
> —Walter Benjamin[1]

A final question remains: Does counterfactual history not have an ambiguous relationship to politics? Since it attempts to imagine possible worlds by positioning itself in relation to established facts, does it not reveal the ideologies—either assumed or implicit—of the author? The Anglophone debates of the 1990s are a testament to this. According to the most virulent critics of this approach, counterfactual history is conservative by its very nature.

In fact, counterfactual history, which may valorize contingency or determinism, mathematical probabilities, and literary creativity has served Marxists, radicals, liberals, and conservatives. Nonetheless, this particular form of reflection on what has happened and what was possible possesses a fundamentally political dimension. The counterfactual researcher who is forced to intervene explicitly in the narrative therefore must recognize the specificity of his or her point of view. He or she must begin by deconstructing the historical narrative, setting aside turning points, reformulating the question of causality, reinterrogating sources, and developing a strong awareness of the effects of the new narrative.

In this beginning of the twenty-first century, the diversity of possible political uses of counterfactual history appears almost endless: ideological instrumentalization, demands for reparations for past injustices, moral arguments to sway public opinion, and a means of social critique. It is necessary to analyze these different modes in order to identify some of the political and ethical dangers that exist within counterfactual reasoning. On the other hand, is it not possible to open interesting new directions, in particular at this moment when historians' social role would seem to be changing?

LEFT OR RIGHT? REACTION AND REVOLUTION

Is counterfactual history necessarily conservative or on the political right? Conservative use of the counterfactual method has a relatively long past: in 1931, during his years out of power, Winston Churchill described a world in which the South had won the Civil War and a historian set out to write a counterfactual history about what would have happened had the Union won.[2] More recently, over the last fifteen years, the counterfactual approach seems to have become the mark of a group of conservative and neoconservative historians who have attempted to reassert the role of contingency in historical development.[3] The volumes of essays edited by Niall Ferguson and Andrew Roberts, who popularized the genre for a wider audience, opened with a direct attack on Marxist historiography, stigmatizing its supposed historical determinism.[4] This direct attack on leftist intellectuals served to legitimize their approach: "It seems to me that anything that has been condemned by Carr, Thompson *and* Hobsbawm must have something to recommend it," Andrew Roberts wrote.[5] Niall Ferguson employed counterfactualism in the service of his historical revisionism. In his case, the "what if" constituted an effective means of raising awareness of the importance of the British Empire in modern history. For this neoconservative intellectual and defender of the American interventions in the Near and Middle East, the American Empire is the inheritor of the "benevolent" British Empire, to such a degree that his portrayals would seem to provide a caricature of the historical past. In his television programs for the general public, for example, he imagines that if the United States had maintained its confidence in McCarthy, totalitarianism would never have taken root in North Korea.

Ferguson's epigones published a book perfectly illustrating the neoconservative interpretation of the counterfactual. *What Might Have Been,* published in 2004, brought together eminent members of American republicanism, including Conrad Black, a historian and wealthy newspaper owner and financier who was convicted of fraud. He asked what would have happened if the Japanese had not attacked Pearl Harbor. David Frum, former writer for George W. Bush, imagined Al Gore's mandate if he had won in 2000 (an odd counterfactual when one considers that he actually did win the election). Conservative sympathies appear as soon as it is a question of showing how the world would be better off if it were "relieved" of a few more revolutionaries and radicals. The editor of the volume, Andrew Roberts, wrote on the promising perspectives for Russia in the twentieth century if Lenin had been assassinated before his arrival in Petrograd in April 1917. John Adamson asked what would have happened in England if Charles I, a supporter of absolutism, had won the civil war against Oliver Cromwell. The military historian Robert Cowley attempted to respond to the question of what would have happened had the British won the American War of Independence. These essays also show that the course of history would have been much worse had the progressives been more successful, for example in the case of "President" Al Gore in the wake of September 11, 2001. This counterfactualism remains a source of fascination for those neoconservative politicians who have willingly tried their hand at it. The Republican Newt Gingrich, former professor of history at the University of West Georgia and Speaker of the House from 1995 to 1999, penned a counterfactual trilogy on the Civil War that has become a leading example of the genre in the United States.[6]

This affinity between counterfactual history and neoconservative ideology has been sharply criticized by historians on the left. Richard J. Evans, a professor at Cambridge University, offered a response that was as scientifically grounded as it was politically motivated. This specialist of feminist movements, the working class, and Nazism, who trained within the school that gathered around the "History Workshop" and then engaged in the movement against Holocaust denial, attempted as early as 2002 to uncover the ideology that this Harvard "H(*historian*)-Bomb" (Niall Ferguson) was hiding behind the smoke and mirrors of pseudoscientific *chaostory*.[7] At the same time, the London historian with ties to New Labour, Tristram Hunt, explained in his article "Pasting over the Past" in *The Guardian* that counterfactual history, far from being an inoffensive intellectual project, participated in the ideological program of the right. Hunt concluded this virulent critique against counterfactual history as the standard bearer of the right as well as being fundamentally individualist and antimaterialist:

> But "what if" history poses just as insidious a threat to present politics as it does to a fuller understanding of the past. It is no surprise that progressives rarely involve themselves, since implicit in it is the con-

tention that social structures and economic conditions do not matter. Man is, we are told, a creature free of almost all historical constraints, able to make decisions on his own volition. According to Andrew Roberts, we should understand that "in human affairs anything is possible." What this means is there is both little to learn from the potentialities of history, and there is no need to address injustices because of their marginal influence on events.[8]

The attack is crude and Hunt is incorrect: counterfactual history cannot be reduced to its use by a few Anglophone conservatives. To the contrary, it does allow one to do precisely what this Labour intellectual calls for, that is, reconnect with the "potentialities of history."

Undoubtedly, the categories "right" and "left," as well as "conservative," "liberal," and "progressive" vary, in some cases considerably depending on time and place. Nonetheless, the attitude of historians on the left, in the largest sense, and notably researchers with affinities for Marxism in the 1950s–1980s (or those inspired by a Marxist conception of history) have generally been distrustful. On the whole, this approach appeared to them at once to be an instrument designed to bolster a liberal conception of history and a game reintroducing the role of great men and chance at the expense of the masses. It therefore was understood to turn its back on the researcher with a more scientific conception of history who aimed to uncover the socioeconomic foundations of social transformation. E. H. Carr's 1960 attack at Cambridge in response to Isaiah Berlin also targeted the diffusion of a liberal conception of history. While rarer in France, such critiques have emerged on specific occasions. In 1954, the historian of the French Revolution Georges Lefebvre led the charge against a work of "alternative" history, *Probability in History: The Example of the Egypt Campaign* (*De la probabilité en histoire: L'exemple de l'expédition d'Égypte*), by the physiologist and defender of probability Pierre Vendryès.[9] Even if "the role of chance had no doubt never been so great," Lefebvre condemned this "metaphysical inspiration":

> Like Valéry, M. Vendryès, reduces history to a narrative of events that are only superficial. We should abstain from insisting once again that such a narrow conception is unacceptable . . . , it is undeniable that in both instances [knowledge and history] determinism is not to be a metaphysical truth, but a working empirical hypothesis which gives scientific research and humans themselves their raison d'être.

The historian and socialist intellectual concludes: "Would we sow seeds of grain if we did not think that we would have a harvest?"[10] During this period, "determinism," it must be remembered, was a scientific doxa and benefited from positive connotations. "Serious" history was supported by evidence that allowed one to establish social, political, and cultural determinations: historians did not have time to waste with dubious, fantastical, false, and ideological accounts.

Such rejection was not characteristic of all "left" intellectual traditions. Republican Charles Renouvier invented the word *uchronie* (uchronia) in the 1850s to express the liberty of history and thought against a providential religious conception. Revolutionary currents in Europe employed it as well. Indeed, the conservative genealogy invented by Niall Ferguson in *Virtual History* pasted over numerous other uses. One famous usage, most notably because it inspired Walter Benjamin, was pursued by the revolutionary Auguste Blanqui. This was not a political tactic or insurgent strategy, as one might have expected, but rather a socialism that might have been considered "metaphysical." He wrote his last work in prison, *Eternity by the Stars: An Astronomical Hypothesis,* at once an astronomical, poetic, and political meditation on modern society. Applying the cosmogenic hypothesis of Laplace to history, Blanqui imagined an infinity of parallel worlds, innumerable other worlds where history was different:

> At bottom, humanity's eternity by the stars is melancholic; sadder still is this imprisonment of brother-worlds by the inexorable barrier of space. So many identical populations that pass each other by without having ever suspected their mutual existence! Until now, at least. It has finally been discovered in the nineteenth century. But who will want to believe it? Moreover, until now, for us the past represented barbarism, and the future meant progress, science, happiness. This is an illusion! On all of our twin- or double-globes, this past has seen the most brilliant civilizations disappear without leaving a trace, and they will disappear yet again without leaving any more of a trace. On billions of earths the future will once again see the same ignorance, the same foolishness, the same cruelty of our previous ages![11]

There is an ambivalence in this theory of possible worlds. The fraternal idea of "brother-worlds" expresses Blanqui's revolutionary heritage and his pessimism at the end of his life, when he was overwhelmed with failure and disillusion.[12]

Perhaps the most important work on this question, posed along these lines, is that of Karl Marx, though it is not without its own contradictions. There are at once mechanistic claims that appear to corroborate a historical fatalism, such as: "But capitalist production begets, with the inexorability of a law of Nature, its own negation. It is the negation of negation."[13] Elsewhere, one finds an interest in a more "open" history that takes a counterfactual direction. The excerpt cited in the first chapter of our book is illustrative:[14]

> Why did the Paris proletariat not rise in revolt after December 2? The overthrow of the bourgeoisie had as yet been only decreed: the decree had not been carried out. Any serious insurrection of the proletariat would at once have put fresh life into the bourgeoisie, would have reconciled it with the army, and ensured a second June defeat for the workers.[15]

This counterfactual reasoning allows Marx to envisage other possible options—for the proletariat as well as for their enemies—and to compare them. This is a conception of history that consists of undetermined class relations, where struggle plays an essential role.

One would be wrong to attribute this difference to the type of texts in which these passages appear (a theoretical text and a piece written in the heat of revolution). Marx's thought is complex and shifting, allowing for different readings, some dominating others depending on the period. One of these readings maintains the primacy of the economy over all other aspects of social life, the succession of the three phases (feudalism, capitalism, socialism), and attention to repetitive cycles in history. Broadly speaking, this interpretation, which inspired researchers from the 1950s to the 1980s, is not incorrect, but it removes any room for other "possibilities" in the German philosopher's thought.[16] For example, one can find questions of contingency (chance, social contingency, historical possibilities), a conception of revolutions that are inopportune in a given moment, or revolutionary expectations. The concepts are often ambivalent and subtle. Michel Vadée has emphasized this point with regard to "historical necessity." This mode of argument is often cause for confusion: while the term is used to employ the strength of social determinations, it does not establish a fatality. The adjective "historical" as opposed to "natural" is to be understood in its fullest sense: "historical necessity" refers more generally to the emergence of a historically situated need. From this perspective, it does not rule out other possibilities. "What we refer to as 'historical necessity,' is also the 'historical possibility' of new social relations and a revolution that is realized through a historical action that generally requires force, or even violence."[17]

It should also be noted that these clarifications explain why Marxist historians might reject counterfactual history and focus on an analysis of socio-economic structures without ignoring the importance of uncertainty and historical possibility. "Historical determinism" was neither univocal nor absolute.

This reading of Marx has recently been reevaluated. The philosopher Daniel Bensaïd has shown, for example, that Marx was consistently opposed to historico-philosophical theories that imposed a general direction on a given people, even those inspired by his own work. To the contrary, "articulating temporalities that are heterogeneous to one another, Marx inaugurated a nonlinear representation of historical development." And in this conception, "at each instant the rational and irrational confront one another, as do possibilities that are realized in actual history and those that are provisionally or definitively eliminated. Only struggle sets them apart."[18]

This perspective reveals a close relationship between revolutionary thought and counterfactual reasoning. Slavoj Žižek notes in response to the wave of conservative counterfactual history from the 2000s: "The counterfactual is situated at the heart of the Marxist revolutionary project."[19] The philosopher asks how it is possible to imagine radical transformation of reality without understanding that historical reality is only one of the possible results of a situation that was initially open. One might imagine that any analysis of social change implies counterfactual reasoning. By increasing our understanding of historical situations and freeing us from a "fascination with what once was,"[20] we are able to explore possible and desired futures and increase our capacity for action in the present. Žižek offers a startling reversal of perspective. For a Marxist, the present world is in fact the fruit of an alternative history that we are forced to live in because, in the past, we were unable to seize the revolutionary moment.

> So, contrary to the misleading first impression, the actual revolutionary situation is not a kind of "return of the repressed"—rather, the returns of the repressed, the "symptoms," are past failed revolutionary attempts, forgotten, excluded from the frame of the reigning historical tradition, whereas the actual revolutionary situation presents an attempt to "unfold" the symptom, to "redeem"—that is, realize in the Symbolic—these past failed attempts which "will have been" only

> through their repetition, at which point they become retroactively what they already were.[21]

Not only is the counterfactual no longer conservative, it becomes profoundly revolutionary in this case.

Ultimately, counterfactual history conforms to a diverse range of political orientations. Thus far we have explored the two extremes of the political spectrum, but one must keep in mind the plurality of political options within each country and the possible uses of counterfactual history: center-right, center-left, Christian democrat, not to mention, of course, political ecology, and so forth. In the end, employing this type of history allows one to revisit the classic debate between necessity and liberty, in its fully political dimension. In this sense, this history may also be mobilized in a variety of ways depending on the context, the conflict, or the desire to delegitimize one's enemy.

COUNTERFACTUALISM IN THE AGE OF THE "END OF IDEOLOGY" AND "GRAND NARRATIVES"

These debates have taken place in an expanded social and political context that displaces the initial problem. We have already mentioned the reasons for the current explosion in the production of counterfactuals in a wide range of areas (historiographical developments, an interest in simulations, revolutions in entertainment, and so on). Among these reasons there is also the increasing discredit of political ideologies in the West at the turn of the millennium. Ideologies referred to as determinist, such as communism, were almost unanimously condemned by other political movements, including by intellectuals on the left, Marxist or not, who criticized grand narratives through postmodernism and favored instead a more relativistic conception of history and a more ironic perspective on historical facts. Counterfactualism drew inspiration from the new attention that postmodernists paid to dissident or silent voices of history, provoking a range of new possibilities. An anti–"what-if" zealot like Tristram Hunt argued that postmodernism provided the matrix for counterfactualism: "The rigorous, data-based study of class, inequality, work patterns and gender relations has fallen away in the face of cultural history and post-modern inquiry. . . . One history is as good as another and with it the blurring of factual, counter-factual and fiction. All history is 'what if history.'"[22] This ideology of the "end of ideologies" was reinforced by the collapse of communism at the end of the 1980s and the rise of the idea of the end of history.[23]

In this context, the trend toward counterfactual history was favored by the development of an increasingly ambivalent mix of confidence and insecurity. Confidence in liberal democracy, persuaded many that its triumph was ineluctable. With counterfactualism, however, one could envisage what the twentieth century would have been without liberalism. At the same time, one could imagine the emergence of new threats (a renewal of nationalism, religious fundamentalism, global terrorism, environmental destruction, and so on), in the form of highly mediatized—and almost immediately counterfactualized—events (September 11, 2001, the nuclear disaster of Fukushima, and the like). These moments of political, financial, and military crisis favor this type of speculation. Is this to say that counterfactual history has become a specific trait of liberal democracies that are simultaneously in doubt and self-assured at the same time? It is worth noting that the early modern historian Jeremy Black has observed the absence of counterfactual history outside of democratic societies. The emergence and development of counterfactual history, he argues, requires an open society built on freewill individuals and public liberties, while societies founded on fatalism and providence cannot produce such texts. Thus, he argues without hesitation that the reinvention of the origins of Islam would be considered blasphemous in Muslim societies and would condemn the author to death.[24] His observation is too shortsighted, however. We have already seen that counterfactual reasoning was mobilized by non-European populations. But one may ask if authoritarian regimes hinder this kind of thinking or if, to the contrary, they generate them as forms of resistance? At the very least, one might imagine that in such states, the official ideology constitutes a kind of historical game that constantly remodels the past and leaves little room for a publicly proclaimed counterfactual analysis. While one should not neglect the international circulation within the media of the uchronic models discussed above, political frameworks also play a role in the expression of counterfactual narratives.

Lastly, the success of counterfactual history in democratic societies may rest on the development of a new set of social demands bound to "presentism." The term designates the affirmation of a new relationship to time in which contemporaries have difficulty projecting into the future and have little interest in the past, preferring to concentrate on the present.[25] The traces of this are numerous, either in technology (acceleration of transportation, circulation of information, interconnectedness, and so on), psychology (insisting on individualism and the immediacy of experience), or culture, with, for example, the current affirmation of the "duty to remember" that connects the past to the present through subjective expectations. While it is obviously not totalizing, this tendency also favors the production of counterfactuals by inviting individuals to judge the past through their present values, or to approve or criticize the present through the past.[26] Political uses are multiple in this case. Whatever the reason, it would appear that there is a particularly propitious political climate for the counterfactual right now.

That's why in recent years this mode of reasoning and expression would seem to have moved out of the realm of history and become a social phenomenon of a particular type. It can lead to moral judgments that place the "professional" historian in a delicate position. The current trend toward judicializing history provides an excellent example of this complex situation.

PREVENTING A BETTER WORLD, OR COUNTERFACTUAL HISTORY AS A MORAL SCIENCE

As we have shown, alternative history as a literary form that attempts to imagine what could have taken place, by elaborating long-term developments from a given point of bifurcation, does not lead to a better understanding of the stakes of history. It can, however, entail an ethical dimension.

The growing recourse to counterfactual history is partially involved in the "criminalization" of history and the search for "reparations" for past crimes. In order to understand the recent multiplication of demands for indemnification for these "historical wrongdoings," one must return to the process of the "judicialization of history"[27] that has taken place over the last sixty years.[28] As Antoine Garapon has argued, one may distinguish three phases. The first moment in the criminalization of the past began with the Nuremburg and Tokyo trials after World War II; then there was the shift from this penal justice to a "reconstructive" justice, pursued most notably by the "truth and reconciliation" commission in South Africa and Rwanda. Here, it was a question of bringing together the population and producing a new national cohesion. Finally, starting in the 1990s, we entered a new period, that of a justice of "reparations": this justice attempted to compensate for past crimes by privileging the infralegal level (backroom bargaining, debates in the media, and the mobilization of public opinion).[29]

The question of returning Nazi gold from Swiss banks to the victims of the Holocaust offers a good example of this third phase, as well as its connections to counterfactual reasoning. The claims on the part of survivors or Jewish associations, which has been formulated with little success since the postwar era, acquired an unprecedented importance in the 1990s. Beyond the sociocultural context, there are many other reasons, such as the declassification of numerous documents from Eastern Europe and the end of the Cold War that rendered the politics of neutrality less "evident." In 1995, numerous class-action suits were initiated in the United States against Swiss banks; the most important of these suits was by the Brooklyn World Jewish Congress. Confronted with resistance by the banks, this federation of Jewish associations was able to establish political connections, in particular with the New York senator Alfonse D'Amato, who publicly denounced the hundreds of millions of dollars stolen from Jews and still hidden in Swiss banks. Faced with increasing pressure, the Clinton administration asked Stuart Eizenstat, undersecretary for commerce and international trade, to draft a report on the truthfulness of the accusations. Bolstered by extensive historical research in the American archives (under the supervision of Stuart Slany, chief historian of the State Department), the Eizenstat Report was delivered in 1997 and had a massive effect. It confirmed the accusations and demonstrated that the Swiss and other neutral countries had received money stolen from Nazi victims and had benefited from trade and commerce with Nazi Germany, "while the Allied nations were sacrificing blood and treasure to fight one of the most powerful forces of evil in the annals of history."[30]

One of the strongest critiques, mentioned in the introduction of the report, was against neutral countries, and Switzerland in particular: "the fact that they pursued vigorous trade with the Third Reich had the clear effect of supporting and prolonging Nazi Germany's capacity to wage war."[31] This critique was quickly clarified in its counterfactual form by newspapers as well as experts over the course of the investigation:[32] if Switzerland had not engaged in trade with Germany, the war would have come to an end more quickly. This argument strengthened the accusation by revealing the technical and financial considerations and pointing toward a more general responsibility on the part of Switzerland. This was one of the essential points of the controversy that developed between Switzerland and the United States between 1997 and 2000 and gave birth to a virulent debate within Switzerland itself. The government recognized its responsibility in 1997 and the banks created a Holocaust Fund in order to reimburse the victims. But the amount within the fund and the estimations of the "sleeping accounts" remained an object of debate. International commissions were put into place at the request of the parties involved in order to treat the most delicate issues in the case. Set up by the Swiss government in 1996, the Bergier Commission, named after the economic historian Jean-François Bergier, studied the historical question of the relationship between Switzerland and Nazi Germany. Composed of Swiss, Polish, Israeli, and American historians, it generated a large synthetic historical report that was delivered in 2002. The report corroborated the accusations (the deposit of Nazi gold in Swiss banks, and the request to stamp a "J" on Jewish passports, and so on) but it refuted the responsibility of Switzerland in prolonging the war. This theme was treated in a subsection at the end of the volume: "Nor can one draw the conclusion that the war would have ended earlier without Switzerland, given the reserves remaining in the German economy and Germany's resolve to fight to the bitter end. That is not to say that access to Swiss currency and the generous loans granted for certain areas of Germany's war economy were of no significance."[33]

This claim was accepted by international institutions. And as the amount in the Holocaust Fund came closer to the initial estimates ($1.2 billion was transferred in 2013, following an international plan established in 2000[34]), the question of Swiss responsibility was slowly set aside. In this novel situation, it was precisely the usage of counterfactual reasoning—independent of the more fundamental underlying question—and then its ultimate abandonment that increased the historical and moral responsibility of Switzerland and, after an extensive pursuit of historical research, gave the country the opportunity to save face in the eyes of the international community. Switzerland could thus continue to honor, officially on its own initiative, the sums that were claimed.

Over the last fifteen years, acts of compensation of "historical damages" have increased across the world. Counterfactual history has mobilized lawyers, NGOs, and administrations, in order to defend the claims of a variety of victims: victims of the genocide against the Jews, victims of South African apartheid, stolen generations in Australia (British children removed from their parents in order to populate the British territory), Native American populations who were expropriated in North America, and so on. In the context of this "global-moral enterprise," massive media campaigns have been launched with logical arguments that build on counterfactual history.[35] The political scientist Ariel Colonomos drafted an inventory on the questions posed by "moral enterprises": if the European and American banks had boycotted South Africa, the apartheid regime would have collapsed before 1991; if De Beers had stopped buying diamonds in Angola and in Sierra Leone, civil wars would have come to an end earlier, and so forth. These counterfactuals invite public opinion to imagine how actors could have behaved more virtuously. To establish these accusations, their authors do not hesitate to ask economists or historians to consider their plausibility. Thus, through its counterfactual dimension, history becomes a true "moral science": "These acts take on their meaning through the imaginings of a better world of which the victims were deprived."[36] Thus, some doctors, demographers, and militant pacifists go so far as to calculate what the rate of infant mortality would have been if the UN had not imposed the embargo on Iraq in 1990. This counterfactual allows experts to determine a plausible figure for the number of children who die as a result of international sanctions.[37]

These considerations, which aim to raise awareness in public opinion and international organizations, can also constitute a more direct scientific foundation for material reparations. Such is the case for reparation campaigns on damages tied to the slave trade. The phenomenon of these campaigns began in the 1980s and then mushroomed, mobilizing associations, militants, lawyers, academics, international institutions, elected officials, journalists, jurists, and so on. Counterfactual reasoning is at the heart of these claims, which have contributed to the formulation of a "counterfactual conception of compensation." Inspired by the work of the philosopher Robert Nozick in the 1970s, this notion was used in the context of reparation campaigns in the 1990s–2000s.[38] It merits particular attention.[39] These campaigns were supported by American academics, like Ronald W. Walters, who was a civil rights militant and professor of political science. He strongly criticized, for example, the impact of slavery that deprived captives and their descendants of possible lives in which they could have realized themselves:

> What is missing in Africa and the Diaspora is that which was taken away from Africans through centuries of oppression. The consequence of Racism, both in the Americas and in Europe, as Pierre Jalée[40] said, placed Africans "outside of history" and prevented them from amassing the kind of resources that would have made it possible for them to become captains of industry, builders of national and international institutions, masters of their own individual destiny on par with other peoples. In short, what was taken away was the ability to create new personal situations, even new worlds consistent with their imagination, something which cannot be quantified.[41]

The lawyer Robert Brock, another leader of this movement, aimed to recover for African Americans the payments that they should have received from the slave ancestors by giving them a portion of the national wealth that they would have possessed if they had been treated like other immigrants.[42] This posed the obvious question of the amount of reparations: How might one calculate the amount generated by such counterfactuals? According to Brock, the American government should offer $500,000 to each of the thirty-five million African Americans (over $15 trillion).[43] Interpretations diverge on how exactly to make such calculations. Thus, George Schedler, philosopher of law at Southern Illinois University, rejects the notion of unpaid salaries and a "free-worker standard" and proposes instead another form of reasoning to measure the loss suffered by African Americans.[44] The counterfactual reference, the basis for the calculation, should be a "world without injustice," a hypothetical world in which American slavery never existed, or, rather, a world in which slavery has been replaced by salaried work.[45] It is necessary to measure the amount of compensation by evaluating the opportunities and the joys of which an individual was deprived because of slavery.[46] This argument has also been mobilized by other campaigns, such as those claims for reparations caused in Africa to Africans. The first claims were made within the Organization of African Unity, which put into place in 1992 an International Panel of Eminent Personalities tasked with exploring the extent and nature of reparations. One of the proposals consisted not of giving money, but of intervening on the debt of African countries. The international African conference in Accra, Ghana, in April 1998 and the world conference against racism in Durban, South Africa, in September 2001 asked for a restructuring of the debt as a form of reparations for the slave trade and colonization. Once again, counterfactual reasoning was used to support the claims. It focused on the labor that was denied to the African continent. The political scientist Daniel Tetteh Osabu-Kle made a claim for the immense demographic losses generated by the slave trade: "there is no reason why polygamous Africa with its enormous endowment of plant medicine should have a population lower than Asia. . . . The population difference between Africa and Asia therefore provides a reasonable estimate of the present cost in human life to Africa arising from the enslavement of Africans."[47] He estimates that slavery caused the loss of more than one billion lives. Translated into human cost in dollars based on the Warsaw convention, which considers that the damages due for the loss of human life in an airplane crash is $75,000, the total damages should be $75 trillion, to which should be added $25 trillion for the African diaspora. As Daniel Tetteh Osabu-Kle notes:

> In response to enormous super profits, various banks sprang up, grew, and expanded their activities in Europe and, particularly, in England. The expanded activities of the banks enabled the financing of manufacturing experiments, ventures, and industries of all types, which increased their profit volumes. . . . African resources made the West rich and great! If Europeans were not greedy, Africa would have had the peace to develop on its own without being underdeveloped by anyone. While Africa was plundered to make the West rich, it became underdeveloped![48]

This Canadian political scientist from Ghana used, like many who have pursued reparation campaigns, the notion of "underdevelopment" and was inspired by the works of the historian and activist Walter Rodney, who tried to show that the level of development in the "Third World" resulted from the slave trade and colonial exploitation. In his work published in 1972, *How Europe Underdeveloped Africa,* Rodney drew upon counterfactual history to evaluate the impact of the slave trade on African demographics. He based his argument on the difference to normal demographic growth, what he referred to as the "distortion of the African economy":

> Because it is so much a question of what might have happened, hypothetical questions such as "what might have happened if . . . ?" sometimes lead to absurd speculations. But it is entirely legitimate and very necessary to ask "what might have happened in Barotseland (southern Zambia) if there were not generalised slave-trading across the whole belt of central Africa which lay immediately north of Barotseland?" "What would have happened in Buganda if the Katangese were concentrating on selling copper to the Baganda instead of captives to Europeans?"[49]

The slave trade and colonization shook the normal course of history, preventing the development of intra-African trade and accelerating the economic development of Europe. Only counterfactual analyses allows one to imagine the normal historical development of Africa. Researchers and experts are thus tempted to measure the gap between present-day underdeveloped Africa and a counterfactual Africa that is not underdeveloped, in order to calculate the amount of compensation. The counterfactual approach has also allowed Walter Rodney to denaturalize the incomparable "development" of Great Britain in the eighteenth and nineteenth centuries by inverting their historical roles: "What would have been Britain's level of development had millions of them been put to work as slaves outside of their homeland over a period of four centuries?"[50] The counterfactual proposal of an underdeveloped Great Britain is designed to generate a form of identification on the part of the European reader. This intellectual operation ultimately allows one to deconstruct the concept of "underdevelopment" and to clarify its counterfactual nature. This inversion of the roles has also been tried in literature. The African American author Steven Barnes published two alternative histories of the United States, *Lion's Blood* (2002), *Zulu Heart* (2003), and the movie *Black Panther* (2018), which favored a new awareness within public opinion during the media campaigns on reparations in the United States and Africa.[51] The question of reparations for the slave trade and slavery are testimonies to the circulation of counterfactual reasoning across academia, the media, civil society, and literary fiction.

What results have been achieved by these claims? Few it would seem. Counterfactual claims have generated controversy among jurists as well as legal philosophers. If counterfactual reasoning is part and parcel of legal arguments and has been formalized as such in the United States, it remains subject to caution. Many have criticized its lack of "positive" foundations. First of all, there is a practical problem: How might such sums actually be reimbursed? But there is also a logical issue, and even some partisans of the reparations themselves have denounced the "absurdity" of such reasoning. The philosopher Rodney Roberts estimates that counterfactual proposals based on a world without slavery is counterproductive:[52] without a system of slavery, one might imagine that African Americans would have been far fewer than they are today. As a result, such counterfactual reasoning suggests that African Americans should be grateful to the slave traders who sent them to the United States! Such reasoning, in his view, are the result of a vulgar hypothesis that has little place in the world of law. Concretely, the few cases that made their way into the courts in the United States in the 1990s all ran up against the impossibility of establishing the factual foundations and the amount of reparations.[53] As for the claims on the renegotiation of the debt, as we know, these have not been pursued either. While the courts were brought in, this judicialization of history remained primarily symbolic. In the end, its audience was the court of public opinion, which might push national and international organizations (US Congress, United Nations) to action. Nonetheless, its unprecedented nature makes it one of the most powerful international debates of the early twenty-first century, revealing the full extent of the social dimension of counterfactual history.

In the face of such a movement, the situation for researchers is delicate to say the least. While professional historians participate in these question, many are uncomfortable with the instrumentalization involved in this type of reasoning. The malaise is at once well-known and unprecedented: these claims correspond to the "political uses of history" along the lines of numerous studies of the last thirty years (high demand for memory and memorialism, public interventions on the part of nonhistorians). And yet there is something new about this situation, particularly for researchers: global approaches to history, monetarization of past wounds, and so on. The tension between these forms of reasoning and the foundations of the historical profession are patently obvious: What can the social sciences do when faced with demands like these that inscribe the past in expectations of the present and aim to regulate historical events in a juridico-moral mode, when such sciences are supposed to be grounded in documents, methodological interpretation, and a search for truth?[54] Whether or not the historian believes in the legitimacy of the claims, the historian is ultimately powerless. And when the historian is called upon, the analytical distance necessary for the pursuit of his or her knowledge is inaudible in the face of the intensity of emotion and the demands for justice that are expressed. This is no doubt one of the new challenges the discipline will face in the years to come. These challenges, on the moral and social plane explain some of the "natural" mistrust of historians with regard to counterfactual reasoning. The phenomenon is patent among those who have already been faced with the demands of remembrance, like "pasts that don't pass": one response on the part of historians has been to reaffirm the documentary, scientific, and critical foundations of the discipline.

ON THE HISTORY OF THE VANQUISHED AND THE OPENING OF PAST POSSIBILITIES

Other uses of counterfactual reasoning or unrealized futures may also be imagined in this context. This is the case for the original conception of history developed by Walter Benjamin between 1910 and 1940, which has recently undergone a renaissance—no doubt because of its resonance with many important issues in our present. This approach is founded on the quality and on the discontinuity of time rather than quantity and its linearity (the idea that time is a measurable entity that progresses). This perspective is expressed in the famous thesis IX from 1940, which begins with these lines:

> My wing is ready for flight
> I would rather turn back
> If I stayed everliving time
> I'd still have little luck.
>
> —Gerhard Scholem, *"Greetings from Angelus"*

> There is a picture by Klee called *Angelus Novus.* It shows an angel who seems about to move away from something he stares at. His eyes are wide, his mouth is open, his wings are spread. This is how the "Angel of History" must look. His face is turned toward the past. Where a chain of events appears before *us, he* sees one single catastrophe, which keeps piling wreckage upon wreckage and is hurled at his feet. The angel would like to stay, awaken the dead, and make whole what has been smashed. But a storm is blowing from paradise, and it has gotten caught in his wings; it is so strong that the angel can no longer close them. This storm drives him irresistibly into the future, to which his back is turned, while the pile of debris before him grows toward the sky. What we call progress is *this* storm.[55]

Benjamin is a theorist of "revolutionary messianism." He opposes the conception of progress as it was understood in the nineteenth century and which can be found in some of Marx's texts: the idea that historical causality connects a chain of events. To this, he substitutes an attention to relationships between the past, present, and future: the present is no longer a zone of passage from the past to the future, but the place where one redeploys the direction of history. The principal argument—which has been the subject of multiple interpretations—suggests the following: history, as we know it, is told by the winners, who advance by "destroying everything in their path," in particular the unrealized outcomes of the past. The true historian must avoid being enlisted in this illusory movement. He or she must use the present as his or her starting point and notably the conflicts and the crises in which he or she is currently immersed in order to uncover past conflicts, their possible outcomes, and the vanished hopes of the vanquished. It is by pursuing a connection between the past and the present that one "grasps the constellation into which his own era has entered, along with a very specific earlier one."[56]

There is no cycle of eternal return. Benjamin spent long hours meditating on Blanqui's *Eternity by the Stars* in order to elaborate this new perspective. In his account, the historian corrects the errors of the past, saves what has failed, and opens new possibilities for the present. Nor is there a passive acceptance of progress or cyclical historical evolution. Rather there is the work that results from the choices of the historian, which is part of an authentic political act. A time of necessity is replaced by a time of openings, qualitative and sentient, a "time of possibilities."[57]

This conception manifests itself in an original description of historical situations: the history that it generates is discontinuous, founded more on ruptures than on the succession of periods. Without a clear line of progression, the historian has only scraps of evidence to work with. One must reconstitute the "historical index," which may then be portrayed in its singularity (for example, that of Baudelaire, who captures the modernity of the Second Empire in France). In this way, the historian must attempt to rediscover unique constellations, those that may exist before progress destroyed them and imposed its values. This understanding depends ultimately on a theological perception of time and a search for "Redemption," a term that designates a humanity that has entirely recovered its past or—while waiting for this moment—provides a way of living the future in the present.

Benjamin's proposal is not counterfactual, as such. He did not imagine an alternative future to the extent that such possibilities of the past remain, in his view, contemporary: they exist in the present, and it is merely a question of reactivating them. But the proximity with the approach is clear: outside an attention to what has not been accomplished and what is possible, the apprehension of an "unrealized future" implies the possibility of another history. Without adopting the entire conceptual architecture (notably its theological dimensions), a number of historians have recently developed this thought and modified their historical approach in order to break with what they consider a linear reading of historical becoming. Thus, Michèle Riot-Sarcey practices such discontinuous history by using "traces" to reconstitute multiple interpretations of the past. These "lost understandings" have continued through an "underground continuity" of history and may return depending on the moment.[58] The revolutionary moments of the nineteenth century are precious clues, as demonstrated by the demands for political equality for women that were resurgent, vibrant, and then evacuated. The same may be said of the utopias of the early nineteenth century, as they were presented following the July Revolution of 1830.[59] This approach allows one to rediscover how past political projects were envisaged and then erased from history by the establishment of a liberal and capitalist order.[60] Ludivine Bantigny has also used the idea of revolutionary messianism—with the renewal of unrealized past possibilities and the perception of the immediate presence of the future—for the second half of the twentieth century.[61] The events of May–June 1968 in France generated a sense that the current formulas were out of date, coupled with new demands for the future. It was also encouraged by the sense that the great unsuccessful struggles of the past had been overcome: 1848, the Paris Commune, 1936, and so on. In order to grasp this specific form of the present future among the actors and the full reality of the moment, Bantigny reconstructed these futures, based on the writings of the period, until the final moments rendered the presence of such futures unreal and unthinkable.

In another register, the medievalist Patrick Boucheron discussed his use of the Benjaminian approach to define his understanding of the historical profession:[62] "to pursue the work of the historian does not mean knowing 'how things really happened.' It means instead grasping a memory as it surges forth at the moment of danger." This obligation too must be situated within an original conception of time. The historian must take pause before the traces, seize their singularity, the moments they contain, and break with the illusory sense of temporal continuity and the succession of periods. The researcher must bring forward the "between-time," the singular moments when the official connections do not function.[63] The deconstruction of the current foundations of our conception of "origins" or "identities" and knowledge of the past thus go hand in hand. This attention also invites historians to detect the "cracks" in the past and, in so doing, to develop a sensitivity to the poetic and tragic aspects of history that alter the reassuring story line of the "present."[64] This reference to Benjamin, with its discontinuities and its possibilities, participates in numerous ways in the interrogations into what could have been or did take place. It is part of a perspective that is explicitly critical and at the same time stimulates the search for lost detours in history.

What about today's histories that claim greater serenity? They are not necessarily apolitical histories, but part of a discipline that is more defined by its vocation for objective knowledge and civic function in the service of democratic debate. The angle has changed. In the face of denials of many sorts and new questions brought about by memorial demands, professional historians have, for the last forty years, multiplied the efforts to redefine their "social role" and the principles of their "responsibility." Thus, for Bronislaw Baczko, while historical discourse remains uncertain, swinging between facts and fictions, the "moral responsibility" of the author remains above all in the service of truth:[65] not so much to achieve it as to constantly strive for it. Many other historians, such as François Bédarida, have emphasized the risks of these "social demands" that are so difficult to define and to satisfy. The historian should be suspicious of the quick, superficial success such opportunities may bring and maintain a more scientific attitude, even if it is less gratifying: remaining attached to principles of historical critique and the establishment of facts.

> The exercise of responsibility on the part of the historian in his own sphere implies two conditions. First, independence, either political or intellectual, social or financial: this is the price of liberty. Then a scrupulous and detailed respect for the canons of the discipline: such are the demands of truth.[66]

As far as the moral and political demands are concerned, history can here put forward its scientific nature. Its social functions consist of displacing, with the help of documentation, the certainties of the present no matter what their stakes in society.[67] From this perspective, does the most common counterfactual approach not appear to be fundamentally distinct from the moral demands of historical practice? To be sure, many counterfactual narratives pose a problem: those that do not explicitly state their register, that claim to offer another "true" history or those that attempt to play off facile success in the media. One of the sources of this suspicion most notably is tied to the connections that seem to exist between historical fallacies and denial. Doesn't counterfactual history, that is, "against the facts," provide arguments for historical negationism? In fact, it provides an ideal counterexample: by definition, counterfactual history cannot be negationist, since it admits from the beginning that it is engaged in imagining another, different path from the one that actually happened, while negationism simply presents a falsehood as truth. Such a blanket condemnation therefore cannot apply. The validity of the counterfactual approach, it must be repeated, lies as much in its plausibility as in the pact with the reader. By definition, it is supposed to state what it is—a path that did not actually happen—and present its role within the process of historical reason (compare, evaluate, entertain, or meditate, and so on). This detour is entirely assumed, through words (announcing a counterfactual passage), textual indicators (use of the conditional tense, absence of quotations for words that might have been said, and the like), or even a certain tone. At these points in the demonstration, the historian must abandon his or her certainties (which ensure that things "necessarily" happened in this way) and enter a hypothetical register. By filling these conditions, the approach can offer a useful tool among others without breaking the moral (in this case) rules of the historical profession.

Having said this, the fictional detours that make up the counterfactual remain interesting on moral and political grounds. Their exercise can, as we saw in the previous chapter, help reveal the historian's presuppositions and facilitate setting aside one's own subjectivity.[68] This space "beyond facts" can also cultivate an area of debate between historians and impresarios of morality or actors who supposedly are responding to "social demands." Hence, on the question of reparations for the slave trade and slavery, a Benjaminian historian might study in great depth the oppression of the slaves, the vigor of their struggle, and their arts of resistance[69] in order to make them resonate with the oppression in the present. In so doing, the historian would reveal through this lived history of the vanquished, the incongruity of collective "claims for reparation," which are mediatized and relayed by elites and expressed exclusively in financial terms. A historian who mobilizes and is familiar with the counterfactual could more easily deconstruct this approach in order to renew the tensions at play in history that all too often appear univocal: the revolts and struggles within slave societies of the eighteenth and nineteenth centuries, the strength of the opposition within metropolitan societies, or the economic and cultural growth of certain regions of Africa. In this way, it shows to what extent the counterfactuals that are mobilized in public debate remain prisoner to European colonial discursive frameworks (Africans "deprived" of history) and thus sets aside the complexity of the dynamics at play, inscribing this history within multiple temporalities and forbidding an a posteriori Manichean reading. The horror of these moments—from our perspective—appears even more forcefully because it no longer appears to be an absolutely incomprehensible phenomenon but instead the product of the history of human societies, grasped in its full range of possibilities.

Above all, these historical counterfactuals can, more generally and dynamically, contribute to a break with the unquestioned politics that researchers have in mind, sometimes in spite of themselves. Giovanni Levi has made this point through an analysis of the historian who imposes current conceptions on the past and naturalizes their effects. Thus, the modern state or capitalism come to appear so "inevitable" and "necessary" that imagining a different development appears extravagant.[70] Among other tools (like microhistory, in Levi's case[71]), recourse to the counterfactual and other possible outcomes often appears necessary for deconstructing categories and denaturalizing points of history that appear obvious. Counterfactual history in this case clearly has a political significance, in the largest sense, distinct from any relationship it might have with a given ideology. The stakes of such a perception of the past are perhaps more decisive. In order to understand them, it is necessary to return to the approach proposed by Paul Ricoeur, already cited earlier:

> We must understand that the imaginative operation by which the historian assumes in thought that one of the antecedents has disappeared or been modified, and then tries to construct what would have happened in accordance with this hypothesis, has a significance that goes beyond epistemology. The historian acts here as a narrator who redefines the three dimensions of time in relation to a fictive present. Dreaming of a different event, he opposes "uchronia'"(a timeless time) to the fascination with what once was. The retrospective estimation of probabilities thus contains a moral and a political significance that exceeds its purely epistemological one. It recalls to the readers of history that the "historian's past has been the future of the characters in history."[72]

After having evoked the analytical dimension of the approach, Ricoeur insists upon its moral dimension. This perspective allows one to undermine any fatality in history by considering the articulation between history and memory: history, by restituting the past that was, including its hopes, fears, and unrealized futures, provides memory with the possibility of rediscovering and then reliving the futures of the past. Ricoeur elaborated this point in a later text:

> When history strives to reconstruct and reconstitute out of the past a way of living, a perception of the world, a way of interacting with others, one thing must be kept in mind: individuals of the past had a future that we could call the future of the past, which is part of our past as well. And yet, major portions of the future of the past were never realized. Individuals of the past had dreams, desires, and utopias that constituted a reserve of unrealized meaning. An important aspect of the reading and the revision of traditions that are transmitted consists in discerning the unkept promises of the past. The past is not only what happened, what actually took place and cannot be changed—an impoverished definition of the past—but remains alive in memory, I would say, thanks to arrows of the future that were not released or

> whose trajectory was interrupted. In this sense, the unrealized futures of the past constitute perhaps the most elaborate part of a tradition. The mutual deliverance of this unrealized future of the past is the major benefit that can be expected from bringing together memories and exchange of narratives.[73]

In this moment of presentism and a supposed "crisis of the future," opening up possibilities of the past, even to a small extent, may effectively contribute to opening those in our present. This is no doubt another great contribution of this approach. Far from renouncing its vocation as part of the social sciences, it constitutes a workshop that is propitious for reflexivity, education, and uses of a critical mind that are essential to this form of knowledge. It is then up to the reader to assume his or her choices and to defend them in "his" or "her" present. It is in this way that one discovers at once the scientific and the critical potential of this approach.

This path has already been taken by some historians. Speaking of "the age of possibilities" that characterized Jerusalem in 1900, Vincent Lemire has noted that this "history of possibilities takes into account the different horizons of a given period" inviting us to be mindful of hardened identities defined a posteriori at the same time that it offers resources for thinking about the present. The "alternative scenarios" and "contingent futures" of Jerusalem in 1900 "can be the point of departure for a shared historical reference point, at the same time that the Holy City finds itself in a new moment of torment in its history."[74] In the more radical register of calling capitalism into question, the medievalist Jérôme Baschet notes that "calling forth other possible (noncapitalist) worlds accentuates the relativity of our present state of affairs and frees up a source of energy susceptible to shaking its supposed invincibility. Refining critiques of what exists and giving consistency to alternative universes are complementary means of shaking and weakening the dominant modes of the production of reality."[75] While they are only one means among many, future possibilities of the past clearly have a role to play: challenging the symbolic blockages that encircle the perception of the present and threaten our ability to act.

COUNTERFACTUAL REASONING AND HISTORICAL POSSIBILISM

We have tried to clear out the brush from under the counterfactual approach. As a result, we have a better understanding of what might cause concern for historians, in particular when the analysis or narrative is not sufficiently controlled or carried to its extreme: generating an abstraction that can remove historical complexity or a dubious mix between fiction and history. In this "place of dead roads," any excess can threaten the foundations of the discipline. And yet we must take that chance, considering how fundamental the approach is to history and the social sciences.

Counterfactual analysis, which is by its very nature undetermined, has proven to be useful and even necessary in treating fundamental questions in which the stakes are constantly being redefined: for example, the relationship between history and fiction, determinism and freedom, event and actor and structure, and so on. Among these questions, the problem of the potentialities and historical virtualities merit reflection. They constitute an important challenge since the category of the possible is no doubt "one of the most difficult to conceive historically, for those who have decided not to turn to fiction (for example, Cleopatra's nose)."[76] And yet, taking up this challenge has become urgent in the face of social transformations and recent historiographical developments.

As we have discussed, history has undergone an epistemological shift in the kinds of questions asked since the 1980s, like other social sciences have in France, Germany, Great Britain, and the United States. The clearest sign of this shift has been the different epistemological "turns" (critical, spatial, historical, linguistic, imperial, global, and so on) frequently invoked by authors. Growing numbers of researchers have renounced analyses of grand (social, economic, or mental) structures, often founded on predefined categories (such as savant or popular, for example) and specific methods (serial analysis and the like). They prefer a more reflexive approach that focuses on the construction of categories and are sensitive to the experiences and the representations of the actors themselves, attentive to the variations of scales of analysis (from micro to macro) or the elaboration of new forms of cross-fertilization between quantitative and qualitative approaches or history and literature. New subjects and new questions have appeared in the wake of this "constructivist" perspective: overlapping temporalities (continuities and discontinuities); considerations of historicities (the articulation of the past, present, and future); examinations of more ambitious spatial connections (colonial, imperial, transnational, global history); reevaluation of the relationships between nature and culture (history of the environment, history of science and technology); and, within this more relational and comprehensive understanding of the past, the problem of uncertainty and possibilities. Many studies have made this shift. This is the case for a synthesis of historical sociology entitled

Remaking Modernity. Sociologist Elisabeth Clemens concludes that there have been styles and successive waves in the social sciences.[77] These terms serve to identify the common horizons shared by diverse works. One of the waves, at the beginning of the twentieth century, was characterized by research that took as its framework the study of societies and national spaces, considered as a whole, which were the product of relatively linear histories of Weberian inspiration. Since the 1980s a new wave has formed that englobes the notions of multiplicity, agency of actors, spatial connections, plural temporalities, and the reflexivity of the researcher. This research posed a new question: "How does the available repertoire of practices or schemas shape the space of possible actions?" This does not free the researcher from all constraints, since in a given society, Clemens argues, "not all things are possible, but more than one trajectory of change is conceivable."[78] In France as well, the ideas of indetermination and uncertainty have become central within numerous currents in economics, anthropology, and sociology. Pragmatic sociology, one of the dynamic branches of the discipline, places indetermination at the heart of its definition, as well as "the methodological present" (the reminder that actors do not know what is going to happen and that they organize their world as a result of their possibilities and their beliefs).[79] As for historians, the growing use of the terms "possible" or "potentiality" in their narratives also indicates a new set of interests. Some have even recently called for a renewal of the perception of historical change by insisting on "the virtualities of historical development and irreducibility of the event."[80] These different paths outline a stimulating historiographical conjuncture, even as it remains difficult to construct.

Within these perspectives, counterfactual analysis has proven to be a precious tool for proceeding toward an analysis that remains delicate in many instances. To do so, it is necessary to take a certain number of precautions: make the contract with the reader explicit as well as signal within the writing through the proper use of paratextual indicators. Second, one may shift from the indetermination of counterfactual reasoning toward historical reflection of connections and possibilities. Thus, it is not so much a new attempt to theorize accidents in history, but instead to take into consideration the possibilities lodged within the configurations of mobile constraints, temporalities, and perceptions of plurality. This is why we have adopted the expression "historical possibilism." Finally, it is important to consider these incursions into the counterfactual as a way of using fiction—this is the least costly and the most effective choice—whatever the methods or the sources (statistical, personal judgment, documentary assumptions, and so on). These fictions, which are mobilized in order to increase our capacities for knowledge and interpretation, can therefore allow us to explore further that which cannot be otherwise investigated.

It becomes possible at this point to specify the uses that would seem the most pertinent for counterfactual reasoning and unrealized possibilities. We have determined six, which may be combined:

1. The first usage is that of a "reflexive" counterfactual that may provide new insights into work that already exists. It allows one to clearly formulate the implicit counterfactuals that are contained through numerous considerations, typical chains of reasoning, and historiographical categories (such as the notion of "underdevelopment"). It becomes possible to put them at a distance or to openly accept them in order to improve the analysis of a given society.
2. Other uses are more directly tied to the actual work of research. The second one has its origins in the banal observation according to which we cannot understand what was without considering what wasn't. This is a classic counterfactual reflex, nourished by the available historiographical knowledge. It is a counterfactual of contextualization, which concerns the approach of sources as contexts.[81]
3. The third usage touches on the objective evaluation of relationships or the absence of relationships between facts, dynamics, or situations. This is the counterfactual of causalities and interdependencies. It corresponds more directly to statistical treatment or ambitions for modeling in historical research. These forms can be more or less elaborate: from hypotheses based on a given theory to the reconstitution of interactive and complex configurations, or the simple evaluation of a relationship within a constellation of facts and processes that is difficult to grasp. The counterfactual allows one to think about possibilities and impossibilities, probabilities and improbable trajectories.
4. The fourth usage also concerns chains of reasoning, but in their narrative dimension. It is a literary counterfactual that assumes its experimental dimension in another way. It serves to test the usual narratives and flush out implicit schemas of historical discourse. It can also suggest other modes of articulating facts and phenomena, facilitating expression, and then creating distance between the author and his own subjective position. In a different register, it can favor the conception

and interpretation of fictions that may fall between the cracks of documentation.

5. The fifth usage is part of what we may refer to as "unrealized futures" or "past futures." It is a question of exploring the way that actors perceive their own future, whether it be in specific moments—wars or revolution—or in their everyday lives. There are two aspects to be considered in this case: either an examination of how contemporaries perceive the futures of their past, that is, of the fact that their world could have been different; or the ways the contemporaries perceive their futures in the present, in considering the futures that aren't—or are only partially—realized and can nonetheless have an impact on how they see, anticipate, or act on their moments. The two can be bound to one another. Finally the futures of the past can be articulated to more refined studies of past experiences and the development of forms of anticipation in the social, political, material, or technological environments that give them form.
6. The last usage, which is the most delicate, is also important. It allows one to apprehend the possibilities of the past, that is the "real" virtualities of past situations. It is elaborated based on a knowledge of the situations that are understood as the actualization of constraints and potentialities put into play, and in so doing, allows for a better understanding of the complexity of the dynamics of past societies. It necessitates great prudence, that is a systematic evaluation of the exact status of the fiction, an explanation of the choice of the point of departure and the documents employed, and a minimal exploration of the future that did not happen. These forms may vary as well. The potential change can be a mere suggestion, as is often the case—and it is up to the reader to make the leap into the imaginary. Or the change can be made more explicit, the projection allowing one to reject more strongly the certitude of what actually happened. One might criticize this approach for being too rigid to the extent that it only explores one or two possibilities in a far more rich set of potential situations.[82] But at the same time, this usage also allows one to make manifest, and therefore to problematize, what generally remains implicit or silenced in a given analysis. Having taken these precautions, the analytical gains are far from negligible: this usage proposes a space of observation where perceptions, practices, and material conditions can be debated at the same time that pluralities of temporalities are revealed and events and

> opportunities as well as the routines and reflexes of social constraints are confronted. Above all, it enriches the repertoire of the social sciences by pushing it into the domain of the imaginable and the possible. Its field of application appears vast: individual trajectories, events, situations, the ensemble of social fields and interactions, *longue durée* social processes, historical movements that shape global history. These perspectives also allow one to call into question certain automatic categories of analysis used by historians ("crisis," "industrial revolution," and so on) and to authorize a more uncertain apprehension of historical change that is more open.

Whether it is a point of departure or arrival, this technique may therefore accompany the researcher who attempts to understand these new forms of analysis. The results seem to be at once modest and quite promising—modest because it is simply a question of adding an element to the already rich toolbox of the social sciences; promising because this approach invites us to grasp the halo of possibilities that surround facts, situations, configurations, and perceptions of the past. This is a domain that historians and researchers in the social sciences have been familiar with for some time, without ever feeling entirely comfortable with it or being able to clearly present it. Portrayed as it is here, the counterfactual approach is sensitive to unrealized outcomes and offers a more firm discovery of a history of possibilities.

Finally, these remarks do not invalidate the current counterfactual practice (along the lines of "if such and such an event had not taken place, then this would have happened"). Instead, it attempts to clarify its contribution: while there are more elaborate and convincing methodical forms of counterfactualism for the exploration of past possibilities, the "popular" version remains valuable as long as one is conscious of its fragile scientific and methodological status. It remains precious, indeed, to the extent that this "mental exercise" is operational for the historian, while at the same time remaining a simple and easily understandable mode of thinking. It reminds us of the ludic and pedagogical dimension, which has been evacuated here in favor of a more sober inquiry. No doubt it is important at this stage to associate the results of research, the reader's participation in the analysis, and the pleasure of discovery.

PART THREE

Experiments

> The world (by which we can understand our theories about the world) must have room in it for "the big stone Fedora and the little Fedoras in the glass globes. Not because they are equally real, but because all are only assumptions. The one contains what is accepted as necessary when it is not yet so; the others, what is imagined as possible and, a moment later, is possible no longer" (Calvino, 32).
>
> —Howard S. Becker[1]

It is now a matter of putting this experiment into practice, using these proposals to explore concrete issues based on available sources and existing historiographies. The following essays are clearly designed to be experimental: exchanging the projector with a magnifying glass in order to discover whether or not this approach is merely a pleasant form of entertainment or if it opens up new perspectives.

We use the tools forged in the previous chapters to explore two distinct areas. First, we explore the field of global history by adopting a macroscopic historiographical approach followed by a study of China at the beginning of the twentieth century. We then revisit a classic historiographical site and object of counterfactual analysis, the Parisian revolution of February–June 1848, employing a more microhistorical approach to revisit the event and the possibilities contained within it. We then return to the question of the modes of transmission and dissemination (or contestation) of knowledge, leaving more room for the reader. The immersive and participatory dimension in this approach may be useful for teaching history or research in a lively exchange with the public. Entertainment, pleasure, dialogue—such are the (equally important) benefits of this technique.

CHAPTER 9

Testing Empire

REVISITING WESTERN DOMINATION THROUGH COUNTERFACTUALISM AND POSSIBLE FUTURES

Castile, it has been said, won America in a lottery; only in a manner of speaking, for Castile had afterwards to turn her acquisition to account and this was frequently a mundane matter of balancing input and output. Furthermore, if the New World had not offered easy access to gold and silver mines, western Europe's need for expansion would have found other outlets and brought home other spoils. In a recently published study, Louis Dermigny suggests that the West, by choosing the New World, where almost all facilities had to be created by the Old, may possibly have neglected another option—that of the Far East where so many facilities already existed, where wealth was more accessible, and perhaps other options too: the gold of Africa, the silver of central Europe, assets momentarily grasped but soon abandoned.

—Fernand Braudel[1]

Two complementary questions have always dominated discussion of the economic consequences of empire: did possession of colonies benefit the metropolis and what consequences did subordination have for the dependencies? The main difficulty in answering either of them, apart from limitations of data, is that they involve a counterfactual. How different might things have been had the metropolis not possessed colonies or the dependencies remained independent? That immediately brings one into the realm of hypothesis.

—David Fieldhouse[2]

They talk to me about progress, about "achievements," diseases cured, improved standards of living. *I* am talking about societies drained of their essence, cultures trampled underfoot, institutions undermined, lands confiscated, religions smashed, magnificent artistic creations destroyed, extraordinary *possibilities* wiped out.

—Aimé Césaire[3]

> The Empire owes us both at least a tablet in Westminster Abbey, for had we not met and worked together, the British dominions would not have been extended to Tanganyika.
>
> —Letter from Harry Johnston to Cecile Rhodes[4]

At the beginning of the twentieth century, the Indian subcontinent was home to the greatest world power, the Bengali Empire, which dominated Europe politically and culturally. The Indians reshaped the map of the world and renamed the Mediterranean the Meti Pond; Switzerland was known as Chhachhurabad, Bordeaux was Booze-Shop, and Manchester was named Nimta. British schoolchildren studied how Bengalis peacefully civilized a weak and divided Old Continent. European governesses carefully served their Indian mistresses, while many British men adhered to the values of the Indians and imitated their colonizers: men wore *dhotis*[5] in the United Kingdom at the risk of catching pneumonia, and the English willingly darkened their skin with an amber-gray powder in order to conform to Bengali aesthetic ideals. A British nationalist movement developed, and certain militants envisaged the creation of a European Union to fight against their Asian oppressors.

This uchronic portrayal entitled *The Scripture Read Backwards,* published in 1929 by the Bengali satirist Rajshekhar Basu—Parashuram was his pen name[6]—staged a role inversion that revealed the very essence of forms of colonial domination: symbolic violence through toponymy, production and diffusion of the great imperial narrative, circulation of new cultural practices, and the emergence of new social and political identities. Nonetheless, by transforming the colonized into colonizers, by looking to update the foundations of the Raj, the novelist avoided two decisive questions: Was Indian domination possible? Would it have been different from British hegemony? The obviousness of Western supremacy may be called into question through counterfactual analysis and the study of possible futures. Imperial and global historiographies have explicitly mobilized the tools of counterfactualism—from the most hypothetical-deductive to the most interpretative—in order to study the "causes" and the forms of Western domination over the rest of the world, to examine the net results of colonization in the metropoles and the former overseas possession, to deconstruct the categories of the grand narratives of European expansion, to rediscover the capacities for action as well as the possibilities for colonized populations, and finally to apprehend the future fears and hopes envisaged through the counterfactuals formulated by contemporaries. Turning toward this usage, uncovering the functions and the issues at stake, thus has clear benefits. Our aim is to use it in a slightly different way for its capacity to bring to light implicit categories of historical understanding and to decenter our gaze.

IDENTIFYING THE CAUSES OF COLONIAL EXPANSION: THE DEBATE ON THE SCRAMBLE FOR AFRICA

Historians have focused on factors that favored colonial expansion at the end of the nineteenth century: "The debate on the new imperialism is essentially the result of conflict in the ordering of causes."[7] The search for causes (political, economic, strategic, social, psychological, cultural) of colonial conquest has generated numerous studies that implicitly or explicitly mobilize counterfactual analysis.[8] Most of the time, it is a question of identifying necessary causes and demonstrating that in the absence of certain factors ("negative counterfactuals") history would have been different. This has been the approach for studies, which affirm that the development of new techniques constitute a sine qua non condition for colonization. Daniel Headrick's *The Tools of Empire* suggests the determinant role of technologies, "by making imperialism possible where it was otherwise unlikely, or by making it suitably cost-effective in the eyes of budget-minded governments."[9] Without the gunboat, the repeating rifle, the Maxim gun, and quinine, colonial expansion would no doubt have been limited. Gandhi said little more than this when he spoke of the European railroad, the symbol of colonial oppression, cause of famine, and vector of epidemics: "But for the railways, the English could not have such a hold on India as they have. . . . Railways accentuate the evil nature of man."[10] According to Lenin, "imperialism" was the result of rivalries between capitalist powers.[11] Even in the absence of other historical factors, contemporary colonial expansion could have taken place due to the economic dynamics of Europe. This general thesis was revised by Ronald Robinson and John Gallagher, who considered that the new imperialism of the late nineteenth century had its origins precisely in the contingent evolution of the European imperial geopolitics: "Without the occupation of Egypt, there is no reason to suppose that any international scrambles for Africa, either west or east, would have begun when they did."[12] Great Britain would have unilaterally set off the process of African partition through its military intervention in 1882. According to the two historians, this campaign was part of the ambition to secure the Suez Canal and thus pushed the French to extend their influence in West Africa in order to compensate for the loss of Egypt. Leopold II then appropriated the Congo, and the Germans entered into the territorial competition as a result. In the end, the partition of Africa was an "accident" that logically followed the occupation of Egypt, and was tied to the strategic errors of the British.[13] This particular negative counterfactual (as opposed to the general form of reasoning rooted in capitalism or technology) allows the researcher to understand the appearance of a phenomenon in a specific location at a precise moment and to underline the importance of contingency in historical change.

The causal analysis of Robinson and Gallagher on the shift of 1882 was quickly called into question by Jean Stengers, whose objection also relied on counterfactual reasoning:

> Without the occupation of Egypt, would history have been different in South Africa and the Sahara? If the Egyptian question had not inspired a desire and a need for vengeance, would French opinion have embraced the Brazza cause in the way that it did? When it is a question of mobilizing collective passions, the "what would have happened if . . ." questions are almost always asked in vain: when it comes to playing on passions, there are always too many imponderables that escape analysis.[14]

While the Belgian historian would seem to be making concessions to the skeptics, he immediately responds, "But the scramble was also founded on economic reasons. And in this case, there is no possible doubt: Egypt or no Egypt, the economic factors would, in any case, sooner or later have set off the movement."[15] By focusing on the event, Robinson and Gallagher's study does not tell us why this phenomenon did not happen before or after, or here or there. According to Stengers, the economic penetration into Africa began before the occupation of Egypt and thus would appear to be irreversible. This use of counterfactual reasoning resituates the Egyptian event in the global context of the second half of the nineteenth century and expands the geographical focus of the comparison. Gallagher and Robinson, it is argued, too quickly set aside the existence of a new imperialist mindset in Europe at the end of the nineteenth century and the scrambles that took place elsewhere at the same moment, especially in Oceania. For Stengers, the decisive turning point is not the British occupation of Egypt but, the same year, the ratification by the French Parliament of the Brazza-Makoko treaty and the politics of the protectorate pursued in West Africa after 1883. The rival powers of France therefore anticipated what was to come: "To stop Brazza, to prevent these annexations, the only way was planting one flag in front of the other."[16] Stenger concludes: "But whether it was by Leopold II in his initial phase, or by Goldie, or whether it was by the French targeting the Benue River, Africa in the 1880s or, more accurately, the internal market of Africa was given over to a commercial competition that could have led to the scramble. And this would have been the case even if Egypt had not existed."[17] Thus, the ambition to access the new markets was a sufficient cause for the scramble in Africa. This counterfactual analysis reduces the importance of contingency and lessens the weight of specific events. Antony Hopkins confirmed a few years later that French expansion into sub-Saharan Africa was not a response to the British occupation of Egypt. Not only had the French been preparing the colonization of West Africa since 1879,[18] but because of their deep involvement in Algeria, Tunisia, and the peninsula of Indochina, they celebrated the British intervention, which guaranteed their economic interests and their cultural influence that prospered in Egypt after 1882. According to Hopkins, the Egyptian occupation could not be considered the reason for the partition of Africa but instead an event in the "long causal chain" inscribed in the social and economic transformations of the second half of the nineteenth century.[19] In 1882, just as it had throughout this sequence of New Imperialism, interimperial cooperation was as important as competition.

"Great men" no doubt played a determinant role in the process of conquest and partition of the continent. Such is the opinion of Pierre Renouvin, one of the founding fathers of the French school of international relations, who explained the collective imperialism of the end of the nineteenth century:

> The statesman did not create from whole cloth: he only knew how to recognize the possibilities that became open to him. But he was the one who benefited from them. The "partition of the world" would have been done with the same rapidity if, in the large majority of states capable of leading a politics of expansion, men had not almost simultaneously made the same effort for their country into colonial conquest or "spheres of influence."[20]

Unless it was actually a question of the men on the spot—military, businessmen, administrators—who were actually present on the African terrain.

This was the suggestion made by the colonial explorer and administrator Harry Johnston in a letter he wrote to the magnate Cecil Rhodes on October 13, 1890: "The Empire owes us both at least a tablet in Westminster Abbey, for had we not met and worked together, the British dominions would not have been extended to Tanganyika."[21] This counterfactual operation authorizes the two men to assume the principal responsibility for colonial expansion. Through this example, one measures the necessity for the historian to take into consideration the counterfactual reasoning produced by the contemporaries themselves. In the case of the scramble wherein each colonial power anticipated the ambitions of their competitors, counterfactuals would seem to have become a motor of history.

Juhani Koponen has synthesized these different analyses by proposing that the causes of the African partition must be interpreted as a process of interactions between the structural conditions and the personal motivations of actors in Africa as well as the metropole: they constitute an interdependent whole of "necessary" and "sufficient" causes. From the counterfactual point of view, the structural conditions appear indispensable: "It could have hardly happened without the expansionary economic pressures and the increased political rivalry created by the breakthrough of industrial capitalism."[22] But the form and modalities of the process resulted from other factors, notably the role of European actors abroad. "It is impossible to imagine that the map of Africa would have become the same without the initial activity of these private agents."[23] One must also add the decisions made by political individuals and high civil servants in the metropole who, at the outset, attempted to avoid any extensive engagement in Africa. In Europe, the overseas actors were driven by representations that were sometimes very different from the African reality: "the Africa they had before their eyes was a mirage."[24] This sequence of colonial expansion as presented by the Europeans created political entities that were much greater than most of the autochthonous units. Each colonial possession englobed numerous societies and local cultures, sometimes with great differences between them. According to Koponen, then, the initial "mirage" was transformed into reality when the nationalist movements reclaimed these entities that had been artificially created by the colonizers. "Given the premises, what else could the outcome have been?"[25] Though he doesn't answer the question, the Finnish researcher suggests that the analysis of historical causation must push beyond the traditional opposition between "necessity" and "contingency."

The counterfactual approach thus appears to be useful for determining causes as well as distinguishing the motives for the means and the conditions.

It stimulates the reflexivity of historians by inviting them to bring to light the implicit counterfactuals of their historical reasoning. Nonetheless, the examples discussed above also demonstrate the superficial nature of counterfactual analysis, which is all too often simply a means of reformulation of ordinary factual analysis based on mechanistic conceptions of causality.[26] Researchers often have recourse to counterfactualism because of its suggestive rhetorical or even aesthetic sway. They use it less often to call into question their own analytical framework. Thus, the different authors discussed here have adopted the point of view of the colonizers and forgotten one of the principal causes of colonial expansion: the relative weakening of the powers, kingdoms, and indigenous empires, which was not originally related to the European incursions. As a result, these historians have avoided a stimulating question: "And what if the Europeans had not colonized Africa in the second half of the nineteenth century?" This question, posed at the political and moral level by those who have pursued campaigns for reparations and damages caused by colonization, has pushed researchers to investigate the indigenous societies on the eve of colonization. In the immediate aftermath of decolonization, the historian Henri Brunschwig, without entirely escaping the evolutionary and essentialist assumptions of his moment, pointed out the potential of sub-Saharan Africa in the nineteenth century:

> Black Africa was shifting and modifying, like Europe based on the inventions and discoveries that were bringing it out of the Middle Ages. And like the Europe of old, it was slowly changing. Across this period, it was up to the Blacks to accept the rhythm of evolution, to accept or refuse these novelties: the African did not have the sense of being dominated or constrained. In general, he dealt on an equal footing with foreigners and did not feel pushed toward a path that did not suit him in spite of himself. This development could have continued. It was interrupted in the last quarter of the nineteenth century.[27]

The African continent was therefore denatured by colonization, in conformity with the thesis of "underdevelopment." Moreover, the comparison between a colonized Africa and an alternative noncolonized Africa sheds light on the limits of effective domination exercised by the colonizers, notably the limits of their territorial control. Thus, in the colonized regions during the period of the scramble, the colonial presence was extremely weak, as for example in Uganda in the 1890s, where a few dozen Europeans administered two million inhabitants. Here, counterfactualism has a heuristic vocation. It reveals the counterfactual dimension of factual history that has taken for granted flattering cartographic representations of colonial territories and official imperial discourses, when in fact key aspects of the conquests of this period were largely fictional.[28]

TAKING STOCK OF THE ECONOMIC IMPACT OF COLONIZATION: APORIAS AND PERSPECTIVES

Historians have investigated the contributions of colonial expansion in the economic growth of European countries and the "underdevelopment" of Third World countries. As the historian David K. Fieldhouse has noted, "The main difficulty in answering either of them, apart from limitations of data, is that they involved a counterfactual. How different might things have been had the metropolis not possessed colonies or the dependencies remained independent? That immediately brings one into the realm of hypothesis."[29] As early as the middle of the twentieth century, authors of anti-colonialist Third World inspiration set aside the determinist nature of colonization in the development of the West. Frantz Fanon was the elegant spokesperson for this thesis:

> The wealth of the imperialist nations is also our wealth. At a universal level, such a statement in no way means we feel implicated in the technical feats or artistic creations of the west. In concrete terms Europe has been bloated out of all proportions by the gold and raw materials from such colonial countries as Latin America, China, and Africa. Today Europe's tower of opulence faces these continents, for centuries the point of departure of their shipments of diamonds, oil, silk and cotton, timber, and exotic produce to this very same Europe. Europe is literally the creation of the Third World. The riches which are choking it are those plundered from the underdeveloped peoples.[30]

The historian Eric Williams attempted a few years earlier to demonstrate that the accumulation of capital through the slave trade and slave economy as well as the colonial outlets constituted a necessary condition to the British Industrial Revolution.[31] Numerous historians then attempted to minimize the role of colonial possessions in the process of European economic development,[32] or to update the negative impact of an empire that would have slowed the economy of the metropole.[33]

Bouda Etemad highlighted the importance of counterfactual reasoning in the Anglo-American historiographical tradition referred to as "imperial accounting": "This is an exercise that consists of asking what would have happened if the economies of the metropoles had not had the outlets, sources of provision, and colonial profits. In a world deprived of empire, would they have won or lost?"[34] This is an indispensable method for treating these questions, and even those who have not used it themselves, such as David K. Fieldhouse or Bernard Porter, recognize its potential.[35] The latter recognizes that an analysis of the impact of the empire on British society necessitates a counterfactual approach. But he considers such an exercise—What would Great Britain have become without its empire?—to be simply too speculative.[36] Some historians employ this method in order to relativize the role of colonies in the economic development of the metropoles. Thus, Jacques Frémeaux turns to this method on multiple occasions in his comparative study of European colonial empires:

> If it [colonization] favored "good business" for such and such an enterprise, to employ Jacques Marseille's expression, there is no guarantee that the intelligent businessmen would not have benefited from a different situation. As for power, the smaller colonial states, Holland, Portugal, or Belgium, were not able to extract any supplementary strength in moments when they were tested. Great Britain and France did not have any advantage over Germany, which they would have sacrificed had they been reduced to the resources of their metropole.[37]

The counterfactual approach has also been used to reassert the decisive role of colonial expansion in the development of national economic and political models, while historians often think, to the contrary, that colonial empires are more or less a product or the projection of national stereotypes. Thus, the "industrious" British would be understood to have prepared the entry of North America into modernity, while the "lazy" Spanish would have condemned South America to pauperism. Southern Europeans would be considered intrinsically inferior as a result of their violent predispositions and the Catholic superstitions that prevent innovation. John H. Elliott has attempted to deconstruct these stereotypes by highlighting the contingency of colonial expansion: at the beginning of the sixteenth century, the Spanish conquered Mexico, which possessed an effective system of extracting resources and impressive quantities of precious metals, while the British, in the following century, colonized the far less wealthy North America. Thus, Elliott reveals the role of the massive influx of silver in the political development of the Iberian Peninsula as opposed to the British:

> If Henry VII had been willing to sponsor Columbus's first voyage, and if an expeditionary force of West Countrymen had conquered Mexico for Henry VIII, it is possible to imagine an alternative, and by no means implausible, script: a massive increase in the wealth of the English crown as growing quantities of American silver flowed into the royal coffers; the development of a coherent imperial strategy to exploit the resources of the New World; the creation of an imperial bureaucracy to govern the settler societies and their subjugated populations; the declining influence of parliament in national life, and the establishment of an absolutist English monarchy financed by the silver of America.[38]

Some authors have pursued the line of counterfactual reasoning that Elliott suggests, arguing that under these conditions, Henry VIII would not have needed to confiscate the monasteries' property and thus would not have converted the country to Protestantism, while the emperor Charles V would have no doubt ignored Spain, allowing Protestantism to develop, since it would have been deprived of silver from the New World.[39]

Bouda Etemad has proposed a counterfactual analysis that nuances the impact of colonization on metropolitan economies.[40] He poses the following question: "Would Manchester have existed without Liverpool?" In other words, would British industry have been able to develop without the resources of colonial commerce? This question cannot easily be answered, the economic historian argues. Etemad insists that economic expansion cannot be reduced to colonial conquest and takes varied forms. This poses a question of defining empires themselves: Is it necessary to take "informal empire" into consideration? To do so, it is necessary to study the precise chronology and to analyze separately all the major dimensions of colonial trade. The provisioning of colonial products played a major role—notably for the development of the cotton industry—even as the sources of supply gradually diversified. As of the middle of the nineteenth century, the colonies offered more and more outlets for metropolitan products—nonetheless, there remained primarily a handful of settler colonies that maintained a relatively egalitarian relationship with the metropole. Lastly, if the colonial profits were significant in certain sectors, globally speaking, they only represented a small part of the national revenue. Moreover, the constitution of Britain's second empire (Asian and then African) only intervened thirty years after the beginning of the first Industrial Revolution in Europe. The Netherlands underwent an important economic development starting at the end of the nineteenth century, at the moment when the share of the Dutch Indies declined in terms of foreign trade. More generally, Bouda Etemad demonstrates that during the modern period the development of exchanges between Europe and its colonies coincided not with a period of massive economic growth, but, to the contrary, with periods of depression and protectionism, at the end of the nineteenth century and the 1930s. The portion of the colonies in foreign trade in Great Britain and France culminated in the aftermath of World War II following more than a half century of economic decline vis-à-vis competing powers. In the end, "the British economy's launch would have taken place without the advantages and gains generated by the slave trade, colonial commerce and the slave system of the American plantations. Manchester would have existed without Liverpool."[41] The slave trade and colonization therefore did not constitute a necessary condition for the Industrial Revolution, but were one "contribution among others." Bouda Etemad demonstrates, to the contrary, a lag between the size of colonial profits coming from an inflow of precious American metals, for example—notably into Portugal and Spain—during the early modern period, or the forced labor in Africa during the same period in the twentieth century and the weak impact it had on European economies. The profits were often monopolized by certain social groups and not invested in the economic development of Europe. On the flip side, many countries possessed few or no colonies—such as Germany and Switzerland—and still developed rapidly in the nineteenth century. Therefore, the colonies could, depending on the region and the period under study, provide the necessary energy to create a temporary or durable dynamism in certain economic sectors, constituting a "shock absorber" that supported activities during periods of crisis. These may have been useless during periods of growth, but they helped create a "cushion of laziness" that maintained activities without a future and ultimately slowed development. Nonetheless, the colonies, in Bouda Etemad's estimation, may not be considered one of the determining factors of decline: the imperial preference was merely the reflection of the weakness of internal economic dynamism.

Counterfactual analysis is also used to measure the impact of colonization on the conquered territories and populations: Did it facilitate or prevent their development? "What would have become of Black Africa without colonization?"[42] This question provides the foundation for the recent research of Elise Huillery on the history of the development of French West Africa. It is, however, an enigma without a response, "because history immediately confronts us with a radical impossibility: no counterfactual exists, all of the African countries were colonized. . . . We therefore will never know what would have happened to Africa without colonization." Most specialists of the economic history of colonial empires are not of this opinion, however.

In the camp of the propagandists of imperial Britain, Niall Ferguson, in his best-selling *Empire,* imagines what would have come of the world today if the British Empire had not existed:

> To imagine the world without the Empire would be to expunge from the map the elegant boulevards of Williamsburg and old Philadelphia; to sweep into the sea the squat battlements of Port Royal, Jamaica; to return to the bush the glorious skyline of Sydney; to level the steamy seaside slum that is Freetown, Sierra Leone; to fill in the Big Hole at Kimberley; to demolish the mission at Kuruman; to send the town of Livingstone hurtling over the Victoria Falls—which would of course revert to their original name of Mosioatunya. Without the British Empire, there would be no Calcutta; no Bombay; no Madras. Indians may rename them as many times as they like, but they remain cities founded and built by the British.[43]

The historian assumes his taste for the counterfactual method, of which he has become one of the principal supporters. According to Ferguson, in the absence of the British Empire the world would not have experienced the process of economic and cultural integration, the "anglobalization" at the origins of modernity. "The question is whether there could have been a less bloody path to modernity. Perhaps in theory there could have been. But in practice?"[44] The world would have been far worse off, in his view, if the French, Portuguese, Spanish, Dutch, or Moghuls had taken the place of the British in the seventeenth or the eighteenth centuries. For those empires, he argues, were more oppressive or less developed, as can be seen "[i]n dilapidated Chinsura, a vision of how all Asia might look if the Dutch empire had not declined and fallen; in whitewashed Pondicherry, which all India might resemble if the French had won the Seven Years War; in dusty Delhi, where the Mughal Empire might have been restored if the Indian Mutiny had not been crushed; in humid Kanchanaburi, where the Japanese empire built its bridge on the River Kwai with British slave labour."[45] Worse yet would have been the total absence of empire, which would have plunged the world into a dark "apolarity," anarchy, and extreme fragmentation of power.[46] Ferguson's counterfactual justifies the ancient theory of civilization and emancipation of colonized peoples by the European powers. Empire becomes a necessary condition for the modernization of the world. Niall Ferguson fits within a long intellectual tradition that has promoted the effects of the colonial enterprise from John Stuart Mill to Hilferding to Marx and Engels: founded on a narrow conception of development, exclusively measured as a function of growth, it considers that without European intervention, the colonized territories would have stagnated economically, in the image of an India that remained "semi-barbarian."[47] It is useful then to analyze the capacity of indigenous societies to develop on their own. In order to do so, the supporters of empire compare the colonized countries to those that remained independent and that are considered similar. They conclude that the latter (Liberia, Ethiopia, Haiti, and Afghanistan) have experienced a relatively weak development compared to the former: "There is little evidence to show that continued home rule would by itself have made any difference."[48] The reasoning is specious, however. When the major part of the continent or even the hemisphere has been colonized, "the impact is such that even the independent countries like Ethiopia cannot evolve as if there were no colonization."[49]

Those who despise the colonial enterprise have attempted to show to the contrary that the stagnation and sometimes the economic regression of a large part of African, Asian, and American countries resulted from the colonization of territories that were originally endowed with assets for their development. At the origins of this anti-colonial tradition was none other than Adam Smith, who, preferring commerce to colonial monopoly, considered that European expansion caused problems for the natural process of overseas development.[50] Within this critique, revisionist Marxists have attempted to demonstrate the pertinence of this phased development model, affirming that some autochthonous societies, at the moment of the first contact with the colonizers, were experiencing a level of development that was equal to or superior to the colonial societies.[51] Without European colonial domination, the Asian and African countries would have pursued their transitions from feudalism to capitalism. As proof, these authors invoke the example of a country that remained independent and followed the model of European economic development: Japan.[52] The results of these studies on the balance sheet of imperialism bring to light the socioeconomic logics and evolutions that were destroyed by the colonial period. Nonetheless, they would seem less convincing, since they depend not only on the definition given to the concept of development (growth versus human development and economic autonomy), but also the counterfactual necessary for such research. More stimulating is no doubt the reflection of Aimé Césaire, who accused colonization of the destruction of possible futures in colonized countries: "They talk to me about progress, about 'achievements,' diseases cured, improved standards of living. I am talking about societies drained of their essence, cultures trampled underfoot, institutions undermined, lands confiscated, religions smashed, magnificent artistic creations destroyed, extraordinary possibilities wiped out."[53]

The debate on the economic impact of colonial expansion has been profoundly renewed by the work of Kenneth Pomeranz. He displaced the discussion onto the ecological terrain by proving that the "Industrial Revolution" would not have been possible, or would not have been as far-reaching without the raw materials coming from the colonies.[54] Pomeranz uses Europe as a "real world counterfactual"[55] to explain the absence of the "industrial revolution" in China. The comparison with China allows one to understand the factors of European domination. From a methodological point of view, it is a comparative history without a benchmark. He considers that the most advanced regions in Europe (Great Britain and secondarily the Netherlands) and Asia (the Yangtze River Delta and the Pearl River in China, the Kinai and Kant Plains in Japan, the Bengal Plain in India) possessed, in the middle of the eighteenth century, a roughly equivalent level of socioeconomic development: high population density, comparable life expectancy, dynamic economic institutions (property rights, free markets, and so on), significant agricultural productivity, protoindustrial activities, and monetized economies. These factors, which are traditionally put forward by the historiography, are insufficient to explain the growing power of Europe. He concludes that during this period, no single element allows one to predict the economic and geopolitical hegemony of Britain. This observation leads one to imagine that it is illusory to look—as Karl Marx or Max Weber did—for the origins of European capitalism in age-old particularities, prior to the eighteenth century. Capitalism could just have easily developed in Asia as it did in Europe. But at the end of the eighteenth century, economic development and demographic growth in Europe, as in Asia, ran up against a number of obstacles: the production of wood and textiles would seem to have been too limited, and only Great Britain was able to escape this constraint by using coal and focusing on American agricultural production. The coal reserves were located near the cities of Great Britain, while in China the mines were largely situated in the north of the country, far from the Yangtze Delta, which remained the economic heart. Moreover, China and Great Britain maintained very different types of relationships with their peripheries. Therefore, the regions of the zone of influence of the Middle Kingdom, notably the dependent states of East Asia and Southeast Asia, which developed thanks to rice growing and trade, were too similar. By contrast, European expansion led to the construction of an economic system founded on complementarity between the metropole and the plantation societies as well as the settler colonies and those intended for exploitation. Indeed, Great Britain took advantage of the colonial imports of sugar, as well as grain and meat, which encouraged demographic growth. East Asia, on the other hand, remained economically dynamic but lacked the food resources necessary to pursue its development. The American colonial possessions developed through forms of agriculture (cotton and cane) that were intensive in human labor and soil exhaustion, thereby freeing up British agriculture from these constraints: the colonies brought to the metropole vast amounts of "ghost acreage," that is, lands that the metropole would have had to use for agriculture if they had not had their Atlantic empire.[56] Thus, Great Britain preserved its lands and dedicated its capacities to work in industrial sectors, while the Yangtze Delta continued the intense land exploitation.

The cliometric use of counterfactualism by Pomeranz corresponds to his neo-Malthusian bias, which focuses on access to food and raw materials. His work therefore necessitates complementary studies on social and cultural questions, but, from a historiographical point of view, it magisterially restores the role of empire within British economic development, and in so doing updates Eric Williams's theses, after having been highly criticized in the 1960s.[57] On the level of epistemology, he offers a powerful tool for denaturalizing classical categories of historical understanding, which assume the "superiority" of the West in general and "British exceptionalism" in particular. In this way, building on histories of colonialism, the tool of counterfactualism has been adopted over the last fifteen years by specialists of global history.

DECONSTRUCTING THE GRAND NARRATIVES OF IMPERIAL EXPANSION

Pomeranz's analysis shows very well how the grand narratives for the explanation of the domination of Europe rely on hidden counterfactuals that researchers must bring forward. Theories of social change explain the failure of modernization of certain countries, like China, through the absence of certain historical factors. Thus, Max Weber, who understood the city to be the driver of modernization, considered that administrative and political autonomy had fallen short in an overly conservative China.[58] The Middle Kingdom did not possess a true urban tradition: the Chinese were only ever intermittent city dwellers who belonged above all to their village. The urban development of China was therefore a history of failure. A failure compared to what? Compared to European urban civilization, which, since the medieval commune, had been founded on political autonomy and the development of a dynamic urban class. Through the identification of such hidden counterfactuals, one can see the epistemological and political frame of reference of any number of researchers. It is in this light that Christopher A. Bayly grasped the counterfactualism inherent in postcolonial studies:

> The postmodernist works, therefore, usually conceal their own underlying "meta-narrative," which is political and moralizing in its origins and implications. For example, many of these accounts appear to assume that a better world might have evolved if such historical engines of dominance as the unitary state, patriarchy or Western Enlightenment rationalism had not been so powerful.[59]

The best way of bringing out these hidden counterfactuals is to restore the different events and sequences studied in global history: "All histories, then, even histories of the 'fragment' are implicitly universal histories. Writing world history can therefore help to uncover a variety of hidden meta-narratives," writes Bayly. Global history and counterfactual approaches would seem to be intimately linked. One of the founding fathers of world history, Patrick Manning, argues that historical sources can be interpreted very differently based on the researcher's implicit or explicit counterfactuals:

> The historian has a counterfactual in mind when making any interpretive statement. Selection of a relevant counterfactual and comparison to the historical record provide a systematic basis for evaluating interpretations of the past. To put it another way, many of the disagreements among historians are not disagreements about the facts, but disagreements about the counterfactual. When making a judgment on the past, it is helpful to give an explicit response to the question: "Compared to what?"[60]

The counterfactual examination, like global history, undertakes such a comparison.

This method offers the means to deconstruct the categories of historical understanding: countries, centuries, great men. Immanual Wallerstien applied it to respond to the question: "Did India exist?" In order to respond, he proceeded with the counterfactual idea that between 1750 and 1850 the French succeeded in their ambitions on the subcontinent by colonizing the Dravidian cultures of southern India, giving it the name Dravida, while the British only succeeded in colonizing the northern half, known as Hindustan. No one today would have used the term "India" to refer to the subcontinent. Scholars and researchers would have produced innumerable works showing the ancestral roots of the two regions, Hindustan and Dravida, filled with two fundamentally different peoples and cultures:

> My question then is, how could what historically happened between A.D. 1750 and 1850 have affected what historically happened between say the sixth century B.C. and 1750, presently conventional dates for "pre-modern India?" It can do so because what happened in the distant past is always a function of what happened in the near past. The present determines the past, and not vice versa, as our logico-deductive analytical frameworks try to force us to think.[61]

The borders of India have not been predetermined by the history of the region. Not only could India have been different, but the word "India" covers over, by its very nature, extremely different realities that cannot be brought into one coherent unit. Following Wallerstein, Meghnad Desai imagined an India that could have been different, consisting of a variety of countries colonized by different foreign powers and inhabited by multiple peoples: Francophone Tamils, Lusophone Maharashtrians, Anglophone Bengalis, and so on.[62] This counterfactual is not all that improbable, since Southeast Asia did experience this process: the region that had a similar population and territory to India was governed by the Dutch (Indonesia), the British (Burma and Malaysia), the French (Indochina), and the Thai (Thailand). This approach also allows one to avoid the reflex of using "the century" as the privileged chronological framework for historical analysis, as Daniel S. Milo proposed when he counted the years following the Passion instead of Christ's circumcision.[63] The role of prominent historical individuals can be relativized through the same process. For example the global historian Ian Morris has invited his readers not to overestimate the historical impact of Muhammad:

> Arabs had been inventing new versions of monotheism and forming their own states in the desert for some time before Gabriel visited Muhammad. Byzantium and Persia were in desperate trouble well before

> Muslim war parties started crossing their borders, and the Mediterranean had been coming apart since the third century. If Muhammad had made different choices, seventh-century Christians might only have had one another to fight, rather than the invading Muslims. Maybe without Muhammad, Western social development would have recovered faster after 750, and maybe it wouldn't, but it would still have taken centuries to catch up with the East.[64]

Morris comes to the conclusion that great men could not have radically changed the course of history: they only accelerate or slow down historical change.[65]

In this way, new historiographical enterprises—world, global, connected, and so on—that attempt to free themselves from methodological nationalism and eurocentrism are attempting to build another narrative of world history by changing the scale of analysis and restoring other points of view, other relationships to history (historicities). In principle, they are opposed to historiographical conventions in which the researcher privileges the study of the West by attempting to demonstrate the natural character of its domination over the rest of the world.

WHY NOT THE OTHERS?

Counterfactual operations are situated at the heart of the central preoccupation of global history: Why was the world conquered by Europe "and not by some other civilization or even culture?"[66] Braudel posed this question early on in his first article published in English, which focused on the relations between European expansion and capitalist development. Only the Chinese and the Arabs, in his view, possessed the capacities and experience to contest the victory that ultimately went to Europe.[67] China quickly abandoned its ambitions for expansion after the expeditions of Zheng He at the beginning of the fifteenth century. Islam would have been content with the Arabian Peninsula, which was dynamic and prosperous and would not have felt the need to conquer the rest of the world. It was therefore the inactions of others[68] that provided the conditions for European success, which, after the sixteenth century, unified and modernized the rest of the world.[69] Since Braudel, specialists of global history have continuously posed this question. Ian Morris has asked, "Why did British boats shoot their way up the Yangzi in 1842, rather than the Chinese ones up the Thames? To put it bluntly: Why does the West rule?"[70] He proposes a counterfactual exercise, imagining the triumphal entry of the Chinese in London in 1848 and the kneeling of Queen Victoria, who pays tribute and swears loyalty to the emperor Daoguang. The vassalization of Great Britain would have been the result of a long process. The Chinese were initially greeted with open arms by the British: they financed war against Napoleon and, after 1815, sold their products more and more cheaply in British ports to the point of ruining the textile industry of Lancashire. When the British decided to increase the tariffs, the Chinese attacked British ships, killing Admiral Nelson and plundering the ports of the southern coast. Counterfactualism in this case is a pedagogical tool that allows one to reveal the characteristics of British imperialism in Asia. Inverting the roles allows one to confirm the intrinsic superiority of the West. Similarly, most of the contributors to the work *Unmaking the West,* which intends to denaturalize Western supremacy, in the end do not call into question the linear process of Western ascension.[71] When Victor Davis Hanson envisages the possible destruction of Greek culture by the Persians in the fifth century BCE, he conceives of the Battle of Salamis as the last chance to prevent this irresistible ascent. Carlos Eire studies the consequences of the Roman decision not to crucify Christ by demonstrating that, without Christianity, Rome would have been more powerful. Similarly, according to Jack Goldstone, if England had remained Catholic, it would have accelerated overseas expansion. While Robin Yates and Kenneth Pomeranz imagine scenarios in which China offers greater resistance to European expansion, they never evoke the possibility of Chinese hegemony. Only Joel Mokyr considers the emergence of the "Industrial Revolution" to be contingent and, therefore, that the rise of the West was not inevitable. The editors of the collection were visibly disappointed by the results of their collective efforts, proposing in the introduction a series of serious hypotheses that call into question the power of Europe since the Middle Ages. Thus, in the middle of the fourteenth century, an even more deadly plague broke out that destroyed more than half the population instead of a third. Coupled with the possibility of a new wave of Mongol invasions, the European continent would have been considerably weaker. As a result, social and cultural limitations would have prevented the development of certain innovations—like the compass, three-masted ships, or heavy artillery on ships—without which the Europeans would not have been able to dominate the Asian seas, and they would have conceded to the Moghul and Qing Empires. In contrast, after the beginning of the nineteenth century and the industrial development of Europe, which from this point on controlled the major oceanic routes, it was in their view difficult to imagine a combination of factors that could have inverted the course of Western expansion.

The counterfactual approach can also be used to relativize the cultural, technological, or military superiority of Europe by analyzing the mesological foundations of domination. In this way, the geographer Jared Diamond attempted to respond to the following question: "Why didn't the Aztecs conquer Europe instead of the reverse?" He argues that it is due to the extinction of mammals in the Americas during the last Pleistocene. The absence of domesticated mammals is what characterizes the Amerindians in comparison to European societies at the end of the fifteenth and sixteenth centuries. Without this extinction, mammals would have provided the Amerindians with protein and the necessary means of transportation. Under these conditions, the great Aztec cavalry could have easily pushed back the handful of Spanish soldiers in 1519 led by Cortés. Moreover, instead of being decimated by smallpox, the Aztecs would have been more resistant to germs and would have transmitted fatal diseases to the conquistadors. Aztec civilization would have conquered and ravaged Europe. The destiny of Europe and America was thus played out in the Pleistocene.[72] The east-west orientation of the Eurasian continent therefore facilitated the diffusion of plants and domesticated animals, as opposed to the north-south orientation of the Americas. If the tectonic plates had developed differently, the Americas would have been oriented laterally and could have welcomed more mammals, giving Montezuma II a great cavalry. In this case, counterfactual analysis allows one to modify one's apprehension of colonial encounters by bringing to light the physical and biogeographical conditions that make conquest possible: mesological factors, which are generally invisible, are fixed or considered to be givens in classical analyses. Imagining an alternative space or territory shows how geography can be determinant in the history of human societies. Here the question is not about knowing if horizontal American continents was an actual possibility, but rather of uncovering the importance of continental orientation in the evolution of the environment and society. Counterfactual geophysics invites us to think about space as a field of possibilities.[73] Nonetheless, Diamond's analysis, which considers the environment to be the decisive criteria, is intensely determinist—like the analyses that consider the "European miracle" impossible without, on the one hand, the physical fragmentation of Europe that stimulated military and technological competition between different states and, on the other hand, the mountains, rivers, and forests that protected the old continent from the Mongol invasions while natural barriers were not present along the immense fertile plains of the Indian rivers (the Ganges) and China (the Yellow and Yangtze Rivers) and were thus easily conquered by foreign warring peoples.[74]

Numerous researchers have seen in the end of the maritime expeditions of Zheng He a turning point in world history, either in an effort to deconstruct the idea of the inexorable rise of the West or, to the contrary, in order to confirm it. In 1405, under the patronage of the emperor Ming Yongle, the Chinese admiral Zheng He, an Arab-speaking Muslim, like his seamen, set off on a series of seven naval expeditions in order to explore the unknown routes toward Southeast Asia, the islands of the Indian Ocean, Egypt, and Mozambique. Considering this situation, historians have asked why these overseas expeditions were not pursued and why they did not lead to territorial conquest—as in the case of the Portuguese, for example. It is "a strange episode and, truth be told, not very clear,"[75] according to Fernand Braudel, who did not see this adventure as being in opposition to the isolationism that has pervaded Chinese historiography—as if the alterity of the potential power of the other ensured the manifest destiny of the West. Pierre Chaunu ran up against "the basic impossibility of thinking about the motivations of Chinese expansion and moreover the collective abandoning of the enterprise at the height of its success."[76] It is a question of coming to a better understanding of the European miracle: "Nothing, better than failure helps explain success."[77] Joseph Needham sees in it a scientific expedition that distinguished the irenic civilization of China from the expansionist civilization of Europe.[78] Janet Abu-Lughod interprets the Chinese retreat as the end of a potential global hegemony and the opening of new overseas perspectives for Europe: "The question that has perplexed—indeed caused despair among—serious scholars for at least the past one hundred years is why, given China's position of supremacy at the time, she did not take the final steps to become the truly hegemonic power in the world system that had reached a level of integration not to be matched for another three centuries."[79] William McNeill affirms that, if the Chinese government had continued to finance the expeditions after 1433, its ships, by following the Japan Current, would have reached San Francisco bay a few decades before Christopher Columbus came to the Antilles.[80] According to Robert Finlay, if China had pursued this ambitious naval policy, "world history would have been strikingly different."[81] This expedition would no doubt have been irresistible: "If Zheng He's men had made it to Europe and settled on the banks of the Tagus River, their encampment would have constituted the second largest city in Portugal, surpassed only by Lisbon with a population of about 40,000 during the time of Prince Henry the Navigator."[82] Indeed, it has been estimated that approximately twenty-eight thousand soldiers embarked onto Zheng He's three hundred Chinese junks: it is impossible that this was a simple exploratory or diplomatic mission. Rather, it was clearly one of the most impressive military expeditions of the period (the four ships of Vasco da Gama contained seventy men). For traditional Chinese historiography, Zheng He has in fact been presented as a model of success. The great reformist intellectual and theoretician of the "new history" Liang Qichao was the first, in 1904, after the humiliating defeat of the Boxers, to develop an informed study of these expeditions. This patriotic focus on the eunuch admiral has led the contemporary government of the People's Republic of China to officially propagate a lie about Zheng He's exploits, in which he discovered the United States and Australia. In October of 2003, President Hu Jintao visited Canberra and suggested to the Australian parliament that, thanks to Zheng He, the Chinese presence in Australia preceded the Europeans:

> The Chinese people have all along cherished amicable feelings about the Australian people. Back in the 1420s, the expeditionary fleets of China's Ming dynasty reached Australian shores. For centuries, the Chinese sailed across vast seas and settled down in what was called "the southern land," or today's Australia. They brought Chinese culture here and lived harmoniously with the local people, contributing their proud share to Australia's economy, society and thriving pluralistic culture.[83]

The Chinese officials were inspired by the book published in 2002 by Gavin Menzies which claimed that a portion of the Chinese admiral's fleet arrived on the Australian coast as well as the West Indies by circumventing Africa, while another part crossed the Straits of Magellan and arrived on the western coast of the Americas. In this account, Zheng He even establish colonies on the American continent.[84] Menzies bases his argument on a map dating from the eighteenth century that he discovered in a used bookshop and which is supposedly a copy of a map made in 1418 drawn by Zheng He showing the existence of the New World. The historical community has come to agree that this map is a forgery and that Menzies's research is not credible.[85] However, the absence of scientific credibility has not prevented the sale of more than one million copies worldwide.

In contrast, for some authors, these expeditions represent an incongruity in the long history of the Chinese Empire that was above all turned inward.[86]

Bound to the expansionist emperor Yongle, they begin with his arrival on the throne and end with his death. Considering the technological, political, and maritime culture of these expeditions, if they led Zheng He to Europe and the Americas, the great Chinese discoveries would not have changed the face of the world. In effect, according to researchers, the Middle Kingdom, in spite of real capacities in the naval realm, never put much stock in the high seas. The maritime routes opened by the Chinese, like most of their great discoveries (gunpowder, paper, sea maps, a compass that allowed for high-seas navigation) would have served the Europeans more than the Chinese themselves.[87]

Finally, for other historians, this period does not constitute a failure or a missed opportunity but a possible world. Patrick Boucheron, in his *History of the World in the Fifteenth Century*, sees in this event one of the "possible becomings" of a world where "other globalizations were possible":

> Since the works of Joseph Needham and Fernand Braudel most notably, the comparative history of the respective "chances" of Europe and China on the eve of modernity has become almost a historiographical obsession. But one quickly comes to grips with the limits of such virtual histories: by asking what was missing in China in order to accomplish what Western Europe actually achieved, one remains within a teleological schema. There remains the fact that the sudden end in 1433 of Zheng He's navigations by the imperial power of China obviously brings uncertainty into world development.[88]

Here the counterfactual question does not require a response in the form of an alternative history organized around a European standard. By momentarily placing the rest of the history to the side, it points to a moment of possibilities that were forgotten after the fact. These moments when historically the future remains open,[89] these moments of hesitation, shifting, reversal, filled with projects, failures, lost causes, and abandonment fascinate specialists of global history.[90] They allow one to denaturalize Western domination over the rest of the world by restoring the indecision within a historical situation.[91] The historian of empire Fred Cooper has also explored "historical possibilities" in order to reveal the uncertainties of social and political processes: "Even more important is what one does not see: the paths not taken, the dead ends of historical processes, the alternatives that appeared to people in their time."[92] He analyzes the case of the trade union movement in French West Africa after World War II, which did not attempt to exit the colonial framework but instead exploit the potentialities of the colonial system, notably in the domain of social rights: "I have argued throughout this book for telling a story about colonialism with full attention to the shifting trajectories of historical interaction, to the range of possibilities that people at any time could imagine for themselves and the constraints on their imaginations and on their possibilities of realizing their imaginations."[93] In 2014, Cooper adopted a new approach in his work on decolonization in French Africa, where he uncovered the possible political forms that citizenship, sovereignty, the state, and empire could have taken through the development of federalism.[94]

WHAT IF THE BOXER REBELLION (1900) NEVER HAPPENED?

The counterfactual approach offers the possibility of revisiting the history of imperial wars and restoring agency to non-European populations, who are generally underestimated by historians of colonial powers as well as some nationalist historians of former colonies. The historian Sanjay Subrahmanyam explicitly used the counterfactual method to reveal the intensity of Asian dynamics during the moments of British conquest.[95] He recounts the trajectory of Nādir Shāh, former Uzbek slave, who became the head of a band of thieves, then shah of Iran in 1736 and founder of the Afsharid dynasty. He invaded India and succeeded in 1739 in defeating an army from the Moghul emperor Muhammad Shah and taking Delhi. Then, against all odds, Nādir Shāh decided to return to Persia in May 1739 with considerable loot before being assassinated in 1747. This stunning defeat considerably weakened the power of the emperor, who did not possess the means to challenge the British assaults over Bengal after 1757. Nādir Shāh's military campaign therefore indirectly contributed to the British conquest in India. But Nādir Shāh could have decided to stay in Delhi, as his Afghan and Iranian predecessors had done. Sanjay Subrahmanyam suggests that, faced with this new power, the British would have remained confined to the coastal enclaves. Indeed, the cavalry and the artillery of Nādir Shāh were effective, organized, and disciplined and far superior to the armies of the British and French companies. Nādir Shāh could have remedied the weakness of the Moghul state, thanks to his knowledge of administrative culture, language (Persian), and religion (Islam). Under these conditions, the British and the French would not have conquered Bengal, and its immense revenues would not have supported future conquests in Asia and notably the opium wars. So if Nādir Shāh had stayed in Delhi, Asia would no doubt not have been colonized by the British in the late eighteenth century or at least the process would have been much longer and more difficult.

The military confrontation between the eight allied powers and the Chinese in northeastern China in 1900, following the Boxer Rebellion, may also be subjected to a counterfactual analysis. The movement, which was essentially insurrectional, as its Western appellation implies, would have been quickly and easily crushed by foreign forces. In collective memory, like in traditional historiography, a decisive event captured the essence of the conflict: the siege of the Peking legations, immortalized in 1963 in the film *55 Days at Peking* directed by Nicholas Ray. The excessive focalization on the "heroic" resistance of those under siege, crowned by a splendid allied victory in the capital, as well as the capacity to transform military failure into glorious exploits (the Seymour Expedition) no doubt masked the complexity of the power relations on the ground and the difficulties met by the foreign troops. Counterfactual analysis and the exploration of possible futures—hoped for or feared—by the actors of the Battle of Peking provide the opportunity to revisit this canonical episode in the scramble for China. What if the impressive army of Shandong, led by Yuan Shikai, had attacked in June–July 1900 the foreign troops defending the foreign concessions in Tianjin? What if the Chinese soldiers had joined the Boxers in the attack on the Peking legations in July–August 1900?

These questions, which appear fantastical and anachronistic at first sight, actually played a role in structuring the reasoning of actors in the China campaign. They can be found in numerous archives, newspapers, and memoires of the contemporaries. Hence, the military doctor of the French legation at Peking proposed in 1903:

> The Chinese troops of general Ma and Nihe who were in Tien-Tsin and Pei-Tsang (August 4) held their ground and inflicted serious losses on us. They had perfect armaments; their artillery fire (Krupp, 1896 model) was remarkable. If the famous Yuan-che-Kai—today the viceroy of Tien-Tsin—had obeyed the emperor's orders, if he had marched his excellent Chan-Toung army against us, not only would the Allies have taken Tien-Tsin, but, as early as July, they would have been thrown into the water. The quality of these troops, trained in a European style, was a cruel surprise for the Allies.[96]

This analysis echoed the counterfactual anxiety of those under siege at Tianjin. On July 4, 1900, as the situation became increasingly difficult and the bombing continued, a French officer wondered, "If the armies of Yuen-Chi-Kai lend a hand to those of Ma and Nieh, then perhaps we will need to evacuate."[97] If the Chinese Empire truly wanted to crush the legations and prevent the foreign intrusion, then why was it defeated? The *Revue de Paris* confirmed this idea, in the heat of the moment during the summer of 1900: "It is remarkable that the war itself has been a series of surprises. The conquest of Tien-Tsin revealed the unexpected strength of the Chinese army. Europe therefore felt the need to put forth a tremendous effort: more than 100,000 men needed to be sent to China, it was argued, and even then, will 100,000 suffice? If all of China rises up, then even this will certainly be insufficient."[98] The viceroys of the center and the south of China possessed powerful, well-equipped, and well-trained armies. Nonetheless, they were hostile to the Boxers so they remained neutral with regard to the great powers and did not pursue the conflict. Witnesses to the events underline the uncertainty that reigned in June–July 1900. The young Georges Weulersse wrote in August 1901:

> In any case, China—we are told—will never be a great military power. . . . But next to the old Chinese army, another one is forming, which is of a higher quality. There is, in Wuchang alone, many thousands of men who are well-trained and would offer a strong resistance to the European troops. The government of Shandong has 10,000 men—infantry, cavalry and artillery—against which, according to a French officer who has done a special study of the organization and saw them maneuvering, it would be foolish to lead a war. These troops have not been mobilized against the Europeans. The Allies, in order to go to Peking, have only had to crush the bands of Boxers and defeat the army of Petchili, which is greater in size but has less military capacity than Wuchang. Their victory has nonetheless been acquired at a high price. . . . The international flotilla of Pei-ho, has taken the forts of Takou from behind and suffered thirty-seven casualties and seventy-four wounded; the combat lasted more than six hours; two canons out of six were damaged and without the powerful canon shot of the Lion that blew the powder keg, there is no certainty that we would have taken the forts on that day. In twenty or thirty years, when Europe and the US have complacently armed them, who will prevent

the Chinese, on their own day of choice from throwing the Westerners into the ocean? They almost succeeded already in Tientsin![99]

Pierre Loti, who stayed in Tianjin just after taking the city, was equally impressed by the Chinese military potential: "My God! The day when China, in the place of its small regiments of mercenaries and bandits, shall arm en masse for a supreme revolt its millions of young peasants such as I have recently seen, sober, cruel, spare, muscular, accustomed to every sort of physical exercise, and defiant of death, what a terrifying army it will have, especially if modern instruments of destruction are placed in its hands!"[100] In the capital, where in contrast to Tianjin the regular imperial troops did not attack the legations, the observers also adopted a counterfactual point of view. Monsignor Favier, apostolic vicar of the Zhili province declared in 1901, "In Peking itself, the new government is far from having the entire population and the entire army on its side, and this is very fortunate for us, since if the entire city rose up without hesitation in favor of revolution, we would be crushed."[101] General Frey, commander of the French troops in China, reflected along similar lines: "There is no doubt that if the attacks upon the legations in Peking had been executed with the same vigor by infantry and with the shooting and artillery skills that were shown in particular against the train station of Tien-Tsin, at precisely the moment when the concessions were defended by more than 10,000 Allies, the legations would not have been able to resist for more than one or two weeks."[102] In the minds of the contemporaries, the event was not a victory but the nondefeat of the allies.

A study of the siege of the Battle of Tianjin (June–July 1900), a major event that struck the minds of contemporaries and was generally underestimated or avoided by historians, demonstrates the capacity for resistance and the efficiency of the Chinese troops. These soldiers, who were war-ready thanks to numerous domestic conflicts (Taiping in 1850–1864, Nian in 1851–1868, and so on) and thanks to lessons learned following defeats by the French in 1885 and the Japanese in 1895, had progressively modernized between 1860 and 1900. The city of Tianjin was transformed into a center of excellence and innovation, with its famous military academy and its arsenals that crafted weapons and electric mines.[103] Newspapers and memoires of allied soldiers described the Chinese soldiers as courageous and tenacious.[104] British soldiers, formerly stationed in southern Africa, saluted the merits of Chinese artillery, which they considered superior to the Boers'. The effectiveness of the Chinese was so impressive that they forced the allies to wait a month in

Tianjin after their victory in order to gather strength before marching on Peking. One might consider this difficult victory on the part of the allies in Tianjin to have been a key moment in the Boxer Rebellion. Indeed, if the Chinese troops had taken possession of the foreign concession, since they could have "defended the Dagu Forts, it would have been difficult for these forces to land."[105] With interimperial competition in full swing across the world, it was not at all evident that the foreign powers would put their differences aside and unite to invade China with one hundred thousand soldiers: the concretization of the union of foreign powers only took place at the Battle of Tianjin in order to free the besieged city from the Boxers. The allied victory at Tianjin thus opened the path to Peking and the repression of the Boxer movement.

The counterfactual interrogation "What if the Chinese had won the war with the Boxers?" forces us to reread the sources in a new way and to focus on the pieces of evidence that escape the reasoning of those who won. The Swiss Cäcilie von Rodt, who traveled through Tianjin after the war with the Boxers, noted that the victory of the allies during the battle of Dagu was the fruit of a contingency: "The cracks in the walls of the fort recalled the fierce combat of June 17, 1900. A French shell exploded the Chinese powder keg and the Japanese benefited from the confusion wrought by the disaster in the Celestial army to take the forts. Without these circumstances, the European gunboats, anchored in the Peiho, would have had a difficult time; the Allies would not have come and Peking would not have fallen into their hands."[106] The allied soldiers regularly recounted the opportunities missed by the Chinese and notably their inexplicable retreats, when in fact they possessed a military advantage. During the siege of Tianjin, July 2, 1900, "after an hour of intense gunfire, the Chinese withdrew without any obvious reason."[107] The same things happened the following day. And on July 4, "the Chinese, mesmerized by the idea of divine intervention, gained ground. But suddenly, around 8pm, at the moment they were going to overcome us, they stopped and abandoned without reason. Why? The enigma of all things Chinese!" After this destabilizing maneuver, the commander Alexis Daoulas and his second recognized the luck that had blessed them through counterfactual reasoning:

> One fact is entirely obvious to us: we owe our lives to our enemy's lack of boldness. If the Chinese had been taken away, at the right moment, by their officers and we had launched an assault, the station was lost,

> we were massacred in our trenches and forced back to the concessions. The incomprehensible indecision of the regular army served us once again beyond all hope and we consider ourselves lucky. There is certainly not a well-commanded troop who, having arrived two hundred meters from enemy lines, does not attack and engage.[108]

On July 11, a third confrontation opposed the Chinese and the allies in the neighborhood of the train station, where more than one hundred allied soldiers were killed in the trenches: "The strange incoherence of the Chinese has revealed itself once again to the allies and has saved them once again from a particularly difficult situation. Instead of benefitting from their tremendous and evident superiority, and pushing their attack, the assailants, to the contrary, diminished their efforts. Without any apparent reason, their fire slowed, artillery quieted and soon, across the Chinese front the guns came to a total stop; the combat is now over."[109] The allies were persuaded that the combat around the train station, which was very challenging, was the decisive moment, because on that day the Chinese almost won the Battle of Tianjin: "We are saved! We are victorious; but it was not without difficulty and we were within a hair's length from having to evacuate the train station. This would have been a defeat, war in the streets, and without a doubt, a general massacre in the concessions."[110]

One observes similar behavior in Peking, where Sir Robert Hart, the Chinese imperial inspector general of customs since 1863, affirmed that at the end of 1900, the Chinese deliberately spared the foreigners in the concessions:

> Indeed, the number of assailants was far inferior to the one the Chinese government could have deployed; moreover, the attack was never pushed to its end, and it always stopped at precisely the moment when the besieged feared that they would meet with success. And if the military that surrounded the Europeans had pushed their attack to victory and with it generated a real domination, it is obvious that they would not have been able to resist even a week, and perhaps not even a day.[111]

Why didn't the Chinese troops exploit their advantage by massively attacking the foreign armies? Perhaps because the government's objective and the Chinese strategy was not to win provisional military battles but to maintain and restore social order over the long term.[112] "In the old China, war was too complex a matter to be left to the fighting man, however well trained he might be. Its object was not victory but the reestablishment of order, and for this the arts of peace were equally necessary."[113] This Confucian idealism that dominated among Chinese mandarins was redoubled by a strong pragmatic tendency. Some high-level officials, like Li Hongshang, thought that victory against the allies would only be ephemeral: the foreign troops would return in greater numbers, even more well armed and organized.[114] Thus, in the face of strangers, the Chinese government hesitated constantly between military resistance and nonintervention (neutrality or retreat). The Chinese political elites never committed an irreparable action and did their best to economize their most effective military forces who did not all take part in combat. From this point of view, the Battle of Peking, in its interstate dimension, never truly and fully took place in spite of the declaration of war by the dowager empress on June 21, 1900. The allies continuously stated that it was not a "war" but rather an international expedition that put down a "revolt": the French diplomats spoke of the "events of 1900,"[115] while the Japanese evoked the "Boxer disorder."[116] This is why, in common accord with the Chinese and the foreigners, the famous protocol of September 7, 1901, between the allied powers and China that brought an end to the "disorder of 1900" took on the appearance of a diplomatic agreement rather than a peace treaty.

Finally, the counterfactual question "What if the Chinese had won the Boxer Rebellion?" pushes the historian to reconsider the traditional understanding of a war that separates the winners from the losers. Indeed, beyond the military aspects that were explored earlier, the idea of "victory," like that of "defeat," is relative. In China, the foreigners in the wake of the entry of the allies into Peking often complained that the Chinese did not behave as if they had been defeated. Here we shift from counterfactual interrogation to the study of the production of counternarratives by the Chinese themselves, which have been entirely omitted from the western historical record.[117] Hence, "Boxer posters" continue to flourish in the Chinese cities, relating another history of the war through images and recounting "imaginary victories." In Shanghai, before they were grabbed by the international troops, there were drawings with the following captions: "Victory of the Chinese at Tien-Tsin. As you can see in this drawing, the Japanese suffered extensively. Defense of the Tien-Tsin Fort. The French and the Russians were pushed back with losses. The engraving above portrays the greatest victory of modern times. The General To (?) annihilated the Allies on land and sea at Takou. His plan consisted of simply dressing the soldiers as fishermen, and letting the enemy come forward and then destroying the battleships."[118] These placards and posters fit into a "culture of fake," a regular state practice under the Qing.[119] Georges Weulersse suggests that such "lies" were spread throughout China:

> It would be difficult to exaggerate the Chinese power of illusion, and, I might say, the power of ignorance, when their national pride or rather racial pride is at stake. At present, there are certainly more Chinese convinced that China was victorious, than there are who admit that they were defeated. Did the Allies not evacuate Peking without any guarantee in exchange? This is not usually how Europeans treat those they have conquered. Was the emperor not safe in the middle of his Empire? Were there not powers that were anxious to negociate? Li-Hung-tchang himself acted arrogantly! . . . The modern history of China, recounted and repeated by the Chinese, is full of victories: and its soil is covered in pagodas in memory of these victories![120]

This caricatured presentation translates the frustration of the allied powers and the different perception of the facts of war. Li Hongzhang in Canton, and, similarly, the viceroys Chang Chih-tung in Wuhan and Yuan Shikai in Jinan hardly behaved as if they had been defeated, because they hadn't been defeated on the battlefield: autonomous and powerful, they ignored the declaration of war pronounced by the imperial government in Peking and continued their discussion with the allies until the signature of a sort of "separate peace."[121] Li Hongzhang himself used a counterfactual, if we are to believe his American friend Charles Tenney, the preceptor of his children, when he stated that he could have avoided the terrible months of war in Tianjin during the summer of 1900:

> Before the Boxer outbreak, he was sent to Canton as acting Viceroy, and was only brought back to his old post when the Court had fled from Peking, in order to straighten out the tangle which the folly of the Court had caused. I shall never forget my call upon him the morning after his arrival at Tientsin. He came tottering toward me (he was then only three years short of eighty) with both hands outstretched saying, "Ah, if I had only been here, this would not have happened." I feel strongly the truth of that remark. As it was, the influence of the old statesman prevented the spread of the movement. The Yangtze River Viceroys received a decree from Peking in the summer of 1900, ordering them to exterminate all foreigners within their jurisdictions. Before they acted, however, they reported the receipt of the order to Li

> Hung Chang at Canton and asked his advice. He telegraphed immediately: "Ignore the order." You will not find this in any history of the Boxer outbreak, but I know it to be true.[122]

The foreign victories over the Qing Empire, which were considered decisive and total, were understood by the Chinese to be insignificant and peripheral political and military events. The first opium war also generated different interpretations: while the British considered it a great victory of civilization, the Chinese of the nineteenth century did not pay much attention to this little border conflict with barbarian pirates. The conflict did not impact the functioning of the empire. Much later, Maoist historiography transformed it teleologically into a founding moment in the "century of humiliation."[123] The counterfactual approach and the study of possible futures therefore allow one to deconstruct classical historiographical schemas, both Maoist and "imperialist." The Chinese, who did little more than passively suffer the crushing domination of foreign powers, adopted multiple strategies of attack (Boxers), discursive resistance (counternarratives), accommodations (viceroys), and avoidance (the empress). Playful spirits and digging in archives shows itself to be indispensable for discovering the uncertainty of the situation in the Zhili province in 1900. The Battle of Tianjin became an event because the Chinese and foreign protagonists thought that other futures were possible. Counterfactual analysis may therefore allow researchers to update narrative schemas. A specific historical turn may only exist within the framework of a particular narrative and specific historiographical paradigm.[124]

CHAPTER 10

"Today, Only the Language of Dreams Can Translate History"

FUTURES OF POSSIBILITY, FEAR, AND HOPE IN 1848

The problem was not all that complicated: a parliamentary vote or a ministerial reorganization would have simplified it tremendously; a shift in the majority would naturally have resolved it sooner or later. But this was not the path chosen by those who lacked patience.

—Maxime Du Camp[1]

The first shots were decisive. . . . The thesis of a provocation was long argued. Today, we have returned to the hypothesis of an accidental shot. What temptation there is to be skeptical about the role of chance in history! One must nonetheless recognize that if chance decided the precise moment and the circumstances, it remained insufficient to create such an extraordinary tension between the monarchy and the Republic that their relationship could disintegrate at any possible moment.

—Maurice Agulhon[2]

Lest you forget, gentlemen of the monarchy, that it was not in order to remain slaves that we had our third revolution. . . . Since association is the only equitable institution to be found in nature, it is the only one that may give to the world, to all peoples, Liberty, true independence and universal peace. Without association, all of these beautiful speeches are little more than dead words that we read on our flags, but which have empty hearts.

—Placard signed Auguste Siberd[3]

Any event that significantly modifies power relations and the configuration of possibilities, is at once political and epistemological. In one single burst, overthrowing tyrants, hybridizing fields of meaning that have previously been distinct, and shifting the conditions of enunciation and the content of the declaration, such an event cannot be reduced to the elements of a preexisting storyline. To the contrary, it should be understood as an action that rips protagonists from a situation, a context or a temporality.

—Alban Bensa and Éric Fassin[4]

We now shift from the global scale to the street corner; from the succession of centuries to the cacophony of mere hours; from the international balance of powers to the overthrowing of a regime; from historiographical novelty to a "classic" of French history: 1848 in Paris. We embark on the study of the event, which is equally relevant for the approach of past possibilities. We are not referring here to an "event" in the everyday sense of the word (simply what happens), but in the sense of a rupture or a crisis that was perceived by actors as such and that was reconstructed after the fact, following particular narrative story lines. The event was "brought back" into the social sciences some forty years ago and continues to be a subject of study.[5] The revolutionary moment from February to June 1848 and the difficulty of establishing the Second Republic in France offers a particularly rich area of investigation for this field: the shots fired on February 23 on the Boulevard des Capucines have already been heard in these pages as one of the commonplaces for reflecting on accidents in history. 1848 was the year of the third revolution since 1789 and has generated ample scholarship. Moreover, the accusation that it was a mere "lyrical illusion," which is still leveled at this mid-nineteenth-century string of uprisings, would seem to make it particularly promising for such an analysis. In what follows, we mobilize the most promising and the less convincing forms of counterfactual reasoning (causal or interpretative analysis, futures that were imagined or possible, paths not followed, and evaluation of changes, counterfactuals on the part of researchers and actors, unique and multiple bifurcations). In so doing, we leave historiographical debates behind and focus our gaze on a more interpretative analysis that hugs the terrain. The reader may begin to interpret alongside us the sources and the specific contributions of this approach for an understanding of this moment. So let us start by following a few of the clusters of potentiality that constitute the "1848 movement."[6]

POTENTIALITIES OF THE "1848 MOVEMENT"

February 23, 1848*: The Reform*

At the beginning of 1848, a "banquet campaign" had been taking place for the last seven months across all of France, demanding that the king Louis-Philippe expand suffrage under the July Monarchy (1830–1848). It would have increased suffrage to more Frenchmen. On February 21, 1848, the final banquet, which was to be held in Paris, was forbidden for a second time by the head of the government, François Guizot, who feared its success. The day the banquet was to take place, and then the following day, February 23, a crowd gathered from the working-class neighborhoods and headed toward the city center. The bourgeois National Guard, which had come to act against the first gunshots, shouted: "Guizot resign!" and "Long live the reform!" Amid the growing threat, the king accepted Guizot's resignation, who had been in power for the better part of a decade and asked Count Molé to create a ministry. The news, which provoked an explosion of joy in the streets, has generally played a bit role in French political history of the nineteenth century because of the excitement of the events that followed: in particular the February Revolution and the republican regime that it brought forth for the second time in France. And yet it was an important moment, experienced as such by most of those who remembered it, including historians and journalists of the time no matter what side of the political spectrum they were on. Once the news spread, the moderate republican newspaper *Le Siècle* recounted:

> The struggle came to an end as quickly as it began. The troops who were stationed on every street and on all of the squares disappeared as if a spell had been cast; and at 5:30 we could freely circulate in the streets of the capital; the population appeared content. People approached one another to announce the struggle's happy end and the collapse of the retrograde and odious minister. When they heard the news at the stock market, the traders who were not known for being great patriots provoked an increase of forty centimes on the annuity.[7]

This narrative attempts to emphasize just how extraordinary the evening's events were. The political decision was nonetheless adapted to the situation and marked a turning point in the regime. At that point, the Revolution had not yet taken place, or at least this was the general perception of the authors we are about to discuss, including: Alphonse de Lamartine, a key figure in the events and their immediate aftermath, partisan of the moderate Republic and carried by the romantic thrust of the class unification; Daniel Stern (pseudonym of Marie d'Agoult), of a similar political tendency, author of an account of the revolution that has become a classic; Alexis de Tocqueville, deputy before and after the Revolution of 1848, a conservative and perceptive analyst of the social changes of the time; Maxime Du Camp, a member of the National Guard at the time, also a conservative and an insightful observer; La Rochejaquelein, a representative, head of the Legitimist Party, and reactionary; and to avoid an overly elitist vision, Louis Ménard, young leftist poet, republican, and socialist, who attempted to give a voice to the workers.[8]

In 1847, the conviction that other outcomes were possible was not widely shared. This is surprising considering the opening created by the French Revolution less than sixty years earlier and the gravity of the economic crisis since 1846. The idea of overthrowing the regime was not on the table. This was no doubt less true for the "republican party." But representatives like Marie or Dupont (de l'Eure) were not calling for revolution, and the republican secret societies were more energetic but also less numerous and under close surveillance by the regime. The socialists (Icarians, phalansterians, Fourierists), who flourished in the 1840s, were in a similar situation. Their utopias opened up spaces of reflection that nourished a dynamic workers' movement, while remaining distant from immediate and large-scale revolutionary practice. Their impact as a force for direct change was limited. The different forces came together and were carried on by a romantic *elan* that produced what Agulhon referred to as capacity for motivation.[9] The dominant idea however was that an equilibrium had been found after 1830 between national representation and royal stability, and that 1789 had come to its logical "resolution," even if the situation could have been improved. This position was shared by political elites and the general population. Looking back retrospectively, Louis Ménard recalled "the universal calm of nature that precedes the storm [and which] provides the image for the torpor of public opinion during the years of the monarchy." Among the numerous critics that developed during the period, including during the banquet campaigns, there were more often calls for "expanding" suffrage[10] than for universal suffrage. If the hatred for the regime was widely expressed, it continued to be expressed within a political framework: "reform" was the order of the day.

Was the outbreak of the revolution really the result of one gunshot on the Boulevard des Capucines, which in turn provoked a response by the soldiers? This mysterious shot, which according to Maxime Du Camp was fired accidentally by a Corsican sergeant of the 14th line,[11] has been the starting point for all narratives on the 1848 Revolution. Numerous scholars have explored the question of the causes of the 1848 Revolution. In a famous text by Ernest Labrousse, he argues for the importance of the economic and social crisis, to such an extent that in his view the popular and spontaneous revolutions took place in spite of the "average revolutionary."[12] Recent studies have placed more emphasis on the political and cultural dimensions of the event. For example, historian Vincent Robert has reconsidered the role of the banquet campaigns: outlawing a banquet, he notes, meant outlawing social freedom (celebrating together) and weakening any chance for hope. This in itself was a sufficiently strong motivation. The historian has also suggested that the revolution was "one of many possibilities" in 1847, a moment when the majority of elites and a good share of the population remained skeptical of revolutionary action. And then there was also the question of why these conditions conjoined in one direction or another: Was it the result of the gunshot? The relationship between the events and the realization of the deeper tendencies is always difficult to determine.[13] In any case, if we consider the potentialities of the evening of February 23, 1848, it is clear that the situation remained uncertain. There was still the possibility that the regime would survive, even if the tension in the air remained palpable. The new ministry should no doubt have responded positively to the calls for expanded political rights, progressively expanding suffrage toward the creation of a strictly parliamentary monarchy, without ever actually bringing an end to the opposition. Within this thicket of complex interdependencies, there remained a "cluster of potentialities."

February 24, 1848*: The Regency*

Next came the events themselves: after the gunfire on the Boulevard des Capucines, the transportation of the dead bodies on the boulevards strengthened the resolve of the working-class neighborhoods and the young students. The combats—we have forgotten how bloody it was—multiplied on the barricades that had been quickly erected on the night of February 23–24. The king Louis-Philippe hesitated, taking contradictory steps. Then, overwhelmed and probably remembering 1830, he abdicated in favor of his son, Louis-Philippe of Orleans, Count of Paris. It is surprising how quickly power shifts in these moments, when suddenly everything is slipping away.

Constitutionally speaking, a regency was still possible. On February 24, the Duchess of Orleans brought her ten-year-old son to the Bourbon Palace, home to the legislative body. A surprising episode began in which the regent was introduced to the representatives by the Orleanist André Dupin. At the same moment, the insurgents noisily entered the building, while another impressive crowd headed off for the Hôtel de Ville. At that moment, it was as if power, legitimacy, and sovereignty were suspended.

The idea of setting up a regency was not unthinkable. Alexis de Tocqueville's reasoning may have had its political biases, but its subtlety remains unquestionable. His *Recollections* propose an interesting perspective between the "first causes" and "chance." The first causes, he argues, are insufficient. At the same time, however, he notes that "chance accomplishes nothing that has not been prepared in advance"—a powerful formulation that effectively explains the relationship between constraints and possibilities and merits further consideration.[14] On that day, Tocqueville stayed on the benches of the National Assembly and observed that most of the representatives would have accepted the regency in spite of their divisions. Some would have favored a slow return to a more powerful monarchy, while others would have supported a clearer power sharing between monarchy and democracy. The archconservative royalist Henri de La Rochejaquelein would even have been open to such a compromise with extended suffrage. The insurgents dominated the situation within the parliamentary building. At the same time, however, Tocqueville notes the ambiguity of their political demands. The younger revolutionaries, the National Guard, the workers, and others spoke more in terms of democratic and social principles than rewriting the constitution. A compromise within such chaos was therefore possible.

The problem at that moment, Tocqueville continues, was that the most influential representatives had abandoned the parliamentary building for the Hôtel de Ville. This had been a mistake in his view. He highlights the symbolic importance of these institutions, which provided continuity, especially the Bourbon Palace, where the legislative body gathered. A decision made in this location would have been significant. "Had the deputies been able to proclaim the Regency, the latter might have triumphed, in spite of the unpopularity of the deputies." He observed the unfolding of a political configuration, in which the symbolic landmarks retained their effectiveness. Tocqueville's counterfactual reasoning is not a mere examination of unintended consequences. To the contrary, it provides for a reactualization of the uncertainty of the situation and the persistent influence of institutions even in moments of revolutionary action. Specialists of political crises have explored how certain landmarks can maintain their importance during such events.[15] In other words, one must not overestimate the structural force of institutions nor set their referential tenacity aside too quickly. This tension must be considered as such, as precisely what was at stake in this "elastic" moment on February 24. It is in this situation that one finds the second "cluster of possibilities": the regency could have succeeded.

The site of decision-making power had nonetheless shifted toward the Hôtel de Ville, creating a surprising spectacle of the dilution of power and its diffusion onto the streets. Lists were drafted opposing bourgeois republicans, liberals, and nonsocialists of the newspaper *Le National* on the one side and democrats who were interested in the social question of *La Réforme,* those won over by socialist ideas and numerous skilled workers who supported a "people's" candidate on the other. While the proclamation of a new government was made at the Hôtel de Ville, its legitimacy remained relatively weak. The word "republic," with its traditional connotations, was present in everyone's mind. But it was not immediately accepted. It was only after a show of force between the crowd and the new Provisional Government, some of whose members wanted to wait for elections and the creation of a new parliament. This new body, they argued, would have had the legitimacy to declare a republican regime or not.[16] The Republic was therefore a widely recognized semantic framework, filled with uncertainty.

After February 24: The Opening of the Field of Possibilities

But the scene had changed. In Paris and in the provinces, when people learned of the new revolution (sometimes with a delay of a few days) old republican practices reappeared: liberty trees were planted, people greeted each other as "citizen" in the streets, missives were signed "Health and Fraternity." A new universe took form. Clubs reopened in which orators rose up one after the other calling for the immediate satisfaction of their present demands, both traditional ("Liberty, Fraternity, Equality") and more recent (right to work, humanity, and so on). While the Springtime of the Peoples in Europe began boiling over, the Provisional Government in Paris was, by definition, only that—provisional. It was a time of ideals and expectations. In keeping with their opinions, under the pressure of the streets and the crowds at the events, the members of the government took decisive measures at the end of February and early March: universal manhood suffrage, abolition of the death penalty for political crimes, abolition of slavery, liberty of the press and association, and right to work. Breaking with the July Monarchy and its spirit, these decisions appeared extraordinary. They gave the contemporaries the impression of having opened a new field of possibilities. Without this, one cannot understand, for example, the revolts in the Pyrenean forests: in a regime now based on "liberty," the peasants hoped to "reclaim their rights" by reappropriating the communal lands or commons. The situation was similar for the series of machine sabotages that hit recently mechanized regions. Some of the destruction was done in the name of "customary right" (*bon droit*) against the (out)dated reign of "feudal industry."[17] For many, the coming of the revolution was indeed accompanied by a new relationship to time and a new way of participating in history. The past futures of the actors themselves seemed to open up once again. Those of former revolutions—July 1830, of course, but also the great Revolution of 1789–1793—seemed reanimated after an interruption of "unfortunate vicissitudes" (*funestes aléas*) as they were referred to it at the time. The references to the previous revolutions brought with them into the present of 1848 promises and possibilities of change that never came to pass—which could have, or should have, been realized, but never were.[18]

Among others, the republicans of the 1830s–1840s expressed this idea. G. Desjardins, former editor in chief of the *Tribun du peuple* and former president of a secret society, explained the end of the monarchical regime:

> Now that this government has fallen, we can agree that it was entirely in keeping with the political premises of 1789 that had begun the emancipation of the French people. . . . But this government of privilege of a minority could only have a temporary significance, a temporary efficacy, with regard to the social considerations and the general principles of a higher order than those clearly posed by the democratic period of 1792: principles that may not have been the order of the day in 1830 but that, without a doubt, would inevitably have reconnected with their traditions and their times because they remained alive in all tough minds, because they were a real progress over their forebearers, because in the end, the future belonged to them.[19]

"Reconnected with their traditions"—this is a perfect example of Walter Benjamin's "revolutionary messianism." These futures of the past that were made present once again, were not necessarily reproduced in exactly the same terms. For those who carry them, the idea is obviously to improve them in alignment with the spirit of the age. Some have insisted on the idea of a humanitarian revolution, which was achieved without any casualties (which was not exactly the case, since the confrontations in various places in Paris—

notably at Château d'Eau—were bloody). Most of all, it has been highlighted that a new Reign of Terror was avoided. Others have emphasized that this was the first social revolution, centered on questions of work and justice. In this view, the revolution continued the abandoned projects of 1793–1794, or even those of 1795–1799, more than those of 1791–1792.[20] But the change expected was of a different scale: "1793 and 1848," *Le Journal des travailleurs* recalled in early June "are two sisters who are closely related but do not look alike. . . . Our Republic is entirely social."[21]

This dual sensation of an acceleration of the course of events and a contraction of time seems to have been widely shared. It was as obvious for those who were directly involved as those who resisted the movement. One can see it in a variety of formulations, in *Le Siècle,* for example, as well as in the more conservative *Journal des débats.* The "broken lines" of past futures, as Sophie Wahnich eloquently put it, were plural. In the heat of the moment, their messianic dimension was equally patent; one could hear references to providence across widely varied milieus. Monsignor Sibour saw in this beneficial revolution the work of "he who reigns in heaven and to whom all empires owe their allegiance,"[22] announcing a more just world. The workers' club of Sedan recalled: "these memorable events which have been accomplished in our dear fatherland and that carry the visible mark of the HAND of GOD have finally given us the rights we are due as citizens and free men. For too long our rights have been unknown and even boldly denied; but they will inevitably triumph."[23] The bishop and the worker were clearly not expressing the same type of religious conviction. Nonetheless, these references attest to the unanimity of the moment and the almost sacred character with which it was infused. Present, past, and future melded.

How might one make sense of this baffling eruption? Historians have often evoked an essentially oral "underground memory" that tied together these events but escaped the archives. One must also draw attention to the disparate array of texts, images, monuments, signs, and rituals, which were polysemic and filled with anachronisms, creating virtual connections across multiple levels of interpretation.[24] In the words of Aby Warburg, there was a phenomenon of "survival" made up of overlap, reinterpretation, and slippage that prolonged the eruption of polyvocal meanings and therefore potential future actions. The latter remained latent and unstable, generally pushed underground below the normal course of events. They were not singular, nor were they tied to the events through a causal chain. Hence, the fracture provoked by the event also plays a role. Emmanuel Fureix has shown how the symbols of power (crosses, statues, effigies, and plaques) were literally "re-charged" with meaning during the events, notably in 1848 leading to specific gestures and actions.[25] It would be worth investigating the idea of sacredness further. In particular, it would be interesting to explore, beyond actual religious institutions, relationships to the perception of suspended time, the revolution's eschatological dimension, and, over the long run, what Alphonse Dupront referred to as the "phenomenon of the return" in Western history.[26] The framework for making sense of the world was modified. The subterranean potentialities of the past were subject to a variety of interpretations. In so doing, they created the backdrop of the situation, nourishing the idea that this was a moment of great change.

Instituting the Future

The fact is that expectations of other futures were not only a product of isolated discourses or acts. In a number of minds, they were the manifestation of a power (*puissance*), in the deepest sense. They contributed to the construction of a new world whose force seemed even more real since the actual organization of institutions remained uncertain.

The wave of petitions was one sign of this phenomenon.[27] Its development was remarkable because, after an initial phase of decline in the 1840s,[28] it vigorously gained steam again afterward. If one only considers the petitions that were received and registered by the legislature, the numbers went from five hundred per year between 1846 and 1848 to almost seventy-four hundred received by the Constituent Assembly between May and December 1848.[29] They were sent to the legislature by private individuals or collective groups from throughout France and different social groups. As of February, the demands were globally addressed toward bodies with some public power: the Provisional Government, the Luxembourg Commission (created on February 28 to manage the organization of labor), and then the Constituent Assembly and Executive Commission after the first elections by universal suffrage on April 23, 1848.[30] The extent of the demands for change sent to the sites of power is striking compared to previous ones. Such a practice may appear strange for those of us who live in societies with stable and professionalized liberal democratic institutions. There was already a tradition of sending petitions prior to 1848. Moreover, even if other opportunities to vote existed (in local elections, for example), this was the first time universal manhood suffrage was practiced at such a scale. The vote therefore took on a particular aura and appeared to be an act of fraternity and communion between the people and its representatives.[31] One can imagine the expectations placed in these institutions.

We will return to the workers' petitions further on in order to highlight the diversity of the demands; for example, the demands of colonization, which, in keeping with the previous chapter, show the importance of empire in the middle of the century. "We would like to submit to your wisdom and your patriotism," explained a petition from the Committee of Colonization of Eastern France, "a project whose execution will inaugurate a new era of power for the French navy, prosperity for our trade and grandeur for the French name. We ask for the colonization of Madagascar. . . . What we are proposing is nothing new, Citizen Representatives, it is merely reconnecting with the work of Richelieu, Colbert, Choiseul, the Convention and the Empire."[32] There were also petitions sent in favor of the "office employees," such as Ferdinand Jammes, who called for the creation of a philanthropic society on the model of an association: "This organized Association would put an end to all difficulties, would perfect professional education, provide the state with good employees, facilitate access to all positions that are currently reserved for a few privileged individuals, and would bring an end to the variety of solicitors and protectors who are a plague on government as well as the insatiable parasites within society."[33] A similar phenomena could be seen in the requests for improvement of the situation in the countryside, which were hardly forgotten.[34] Some seemed to use this tone and its formulations in a more instrumental way, since there seems to have been a kind of grammar of justification that was popular at the time. This is another indicator of how widespread expressing ideals for the future had become. The petition of banks and insurance companies provided numerical and juridical data as it responded to a bill discussed by the Assembly to put fire insurance under the control of the state:[35] "The minister's bill not only undermines private interest; it not only is an error and a financial illusion that will send the National Assembly in an onerous and fatal direction; it is an infringement on Liberty and Equality, which are your political symbols; . . . the respect for property without which neither the Republic nor Society is possible."[36] It would be interesting to analyze the tenses employed. One observes, for example, a relatively moderate use of the conditional, the future is common, and from time to time, the present is used, as if the new world were already there. In order to paint a more complete picture, it would be necessary to explore a larger range of projects and authors (individual or collective, elite or militant or the "people"). In any case, it is clear that this phenomenon was generalized, as attested to by the "dreams of police," proposals by citizens for reorganizing the police that were addressed the Parisian prefecture of police.[37] Attached to specific institutions, these futures that were hoped for, but never realized had a real capacity for projection in the eyes of those who wrote them. They bore witness to a moment when, to borrow the elegant formula of the *Journal des débats*: "today, only the language of dreams can translate history."[38]

Different claims, which seemed either fanciful or maximalist, had different chances of success. For example, the claim for political equality between the sexes met with fierce resistance. Women like Eugénie Niboyet, Jeanne Deroin, Pauline Roland, or Désirée Gay attempted to make their voices heard. Arguing for the extension of citizenship and the overcoming of social barriers, they made their demands for suffrage in the name of "true" equality: "The servitude of women must come to an end with the servitude of work. They, too, are able to provide good work; they, too, want to live in the center of progress, escape the numerous dangers of ignorance and misery."[39] The argument was strong but unsuccessful. These women remained political "minors," unable to vote, sometimes disagreeing among themselves, as indicated by the famous address of George Sand, who called for a staged[40] increase of feminine awareness. While their words, which reconnected with the feminist calls of the 1790s, challenged the established political and symbolic order, the established norms in this domain remained too powerful.[41] Public power therefore remained male. This was not to deny the importance of what the historian Joan W. Scott has referred to as a "fantasy echo," a mode of political awareness that links different moments and disrupts existing social orders.[42] Other requests may seem less pertinent. "L. L. T. V." from Saint-Brieuc thus called for a "Republic of fathers," where only fathers had the right to vote. The first paragraph of the proposed bill stated: "National sovereignty being only the natural and divine sovereignty of the fathers of families, under the universal sovereignty of God, the father of all, France declares itself a Representative Republic, rooted in the universal vote of national paternity." This would, according to its author, ensure a return of authority that could be combined with the demands of the new citizens while dismissing women who were seen as unimportant and youth who were considered impetuous. According to this logic, the dream was to create a solid basis for social order under the double law of nature and of God and a republican return to patriarchy.[43] This aspiration contained implicit notions of legitimacy. For example, the "republic of fathers" was first formulated in 1792 and continued up to the

Directory,[44] but in this case it was at once isolated and far from the preoccupations of its audience. At the very least, these hopes offered by L. L. T. V. make it possible to measure the extent of the changes that could be imagined at this moment and reveal how History (with a capital H) was constantly intertwined with the history of social groups and the more intimate hopes of individuals. Tensions and social differences were palpable, not to mention indifference and flat out refusal: in Marseille, which was politically "white" (that is, royalist), the unrealized outcomes of the Revolution, even in their milder form, generated distrust. But expectations and suspense prevailed.

These futures that were feared, hoped for, possible, and always plural were also complementary, competing, and antagonistic. They may therefore be considered together as a whole. First of all, this allows us to go back to these early moments of the Revolution, which constituted an exceptional moment of social communion and the promise of a bright future—a promise that continued in France as well as in Europe. It was the "collective effervescence" coined long ago by Durkheim,[45] a suggestive concept that should perhaps be exploited more often. Now that the rest of the story is known, this moment has often been referred to as a naïve time of "illusion." Interrupting the narrative, listening to alternative voices, pushing the movement beyond its standard account may therefore help reassess the dynamics of the revolutionary fervor, before the disenchantment that followed. Such an exercise does not take anything away from the suspicions, antagonisms, or strategies for escape. It does, however, offer an opportune insight into the tensions of this particular moment when, gripped by the shivers of reality, it was in the process of becoming possible. This exercise also makes it possible to feel the effects of the shock wave that spread across social organization, inviting one to consider the various forms of political awareness, or the way in which "ordinary" individuals or those excluded from fields of power hoped to participate in the production of history. Though difficult to uncover, such suspended moments deserve more careful analysis. As with other crises, it would seem that historians are somehow embarrassed by the slightly exacerbated and confused expression of hope. A second area of interest may be found in the relationships, at this moment, between these alternative futures and institutions (we have not discussed the local level, which is decisive). There is then a tension between the collective form of desire and the organizations responsible for making the social world function. In psychoanalytic terms, desire is the expression of a lack as well as a process of production of the real (and of oneself);[46] while the organizations depend on order or the capacity (real or supposed) to realize and guarantee the routines that reduce the margins of uncertainty. This also explains why these institutions can become formidable echo chambers of contemporary hopes and appear to be endowed with an original institutional force, and also why at the same time they already impose constraints and make limitations felt.[47] The stakes are high in this realm of uncertainty. So perhaps this may help us to better understand the troubled but vibrant feeling of living a key moment when the future remains open and slowly, over the course of weeks, becomes increasingly threatening and uncertain.

The Social Democratic Republic at Work

Some demands were voiced by groups or individuals that had greater ability to act at the same time that social divisions increased. The strongest and most visible demands emanated from the workers and popular circles of Paris. It must be remembered that this "class" did not imagine itself to be in opposition: these social milieus were rather trades that were unified and grouped together (typographers, locksmiths, shoemakers, tailors, and so on).[48] Social ties, an "ideological and cultural homogeneity,"[49] connected the most skilled workers and the most well-structured trades, united under the banner of the principles of association, social justice, the right to work, price controls, and so on. Louis Ménard gives a good account in his *Prologue* of this outlook and these ideals, which were also expressed in petitions sent to the Provisional Government, the Labor Committee, the Constituent Assembly, and the Executive Commission. The demands were at once very concrete (prices of fabrics for tailors, master-worker relationship among bakers, critiques of machinery[50] and so on), and at the same time draped in the generous and universalist rhetoric of the moment. Hence, a worker from Mâcon proposed to set up a "national labor bank" to improve commerce and keep cost of living down.[51] Or, for example, the declaration of faith in the "Manifesto of the Delegates of the Guilds of Luxembourg Commission," called upon the "sovereign people" to "Open your eyes and step out from your darkness to see the light! Unite your strength into a single force, come put an end to your misery through holy ASSOCIATION that the fortunate of this century, in their egoistic perspective, have the audacity to consider a utopia."[52] These were perhaps utopian opinions for the historian who looks at them from above, with the impression of being aware of the "reality of the situation." But by adopting the perspective of these groups through a comprehensive approach, and recalling the singularity of the context opened by the revolution and the first measures of the Provisional Government, these positions gain credibility. Above all, they acquired a capacity to bring people together, as groups of referents that structure expectations, actions, and policies. Beyond this diversity of positions, there was a silent undercurrent in favor of the "universal" democratic social Republic: the idea that one could not change the political order (the creation of the Republic and the exercise of popular sovereignty) without changing the social and economic order along with it (with the introduction of the right to work and the establishment of a fairer process of exchange between the producer and the consumer). This project would necessarily take the very concrete form of association between different "workers' guilds" (the term returns at this point), which claimed responsibility for implementing this true Republic and allowing for the emancipation of all, bourgeois as well as worker. The union of all classes remained the principal horizon of expectations.

Could these "February promises"—for example, a greater presence of workers within the executive, the implementation of proposals from the Luxembourg Commission, notably the right to work, which was granted for a brief moment and then withdrawn—have been realized? The hypothesis is not as wild as it sounds. Workers already occupied a place in the new political organization. The worker "Albert," who was a modeler, member of secret republican societies, and founder of the newspaper *L'Atelier* was part of the Provisional Government, which was in itself a considerable achievement. At the Luxembourg Commission, presided over by Louis Blanc, the speakers debating the new organization of work were for the most part representatives of workers' guilds. There was an increased working-class presence in Lyon as early as February 25. Moderate republicans like Joseph Bergier succumbed to the force of persuasion of the famous silk workers called the *canuts.* He therefore established a municipal commission dominated by "workers" in Lyon's Hôtel de Ville, waving a red flag. The experiment lasted for a few days until the arrival of the commissioner of the Republic.[53] These demands were part of a tradition, a social fabric, and a unique organizational dynamic. This was even more the case in Paris, the seat of power and revolution. At mid-century, 52 percent of the Parisian population lived on industrial labor.[54] There was a tradition of associationalism, which could be traced back to the eighteenth century[55] and was renewed in the 1830s and 1840s and then modified again in 1848 (this increased its strength and reinforced its credibility). There was a fabric of popular sociability on the streets, in the cabarets and the neighborhoods, whose roles were at least as important as the trades themselves.[56] Institutionalization, on the other hand, rose out of the effervescence of 1848 and was reflected in the vast creation of mutual-aid societies, corporations, associations of production and consumption, as well as the local committees that provided members of the Luxembourg Commission.[57] Like most of these bodies that operated in the form of committees or assemblies with blurry contours, proposals and decisions were part of a complex process of confrontations and exchanges. Sociologists have shown the mechanisms of these kinds of "decision-making arenas," operating through the multiplication of options, the alignment of collective scenarios, and their possible effects, in contexts where they have purchase.[58] The result was a vast, socially anchored, but also random and unstable movement that generated an active social force. This can also be found in other clusters of potentiality, which no longer appear to be simple "anecdotes of history." On March 17, for example, during the "walk of the two hundred thousand," the Provisional Government was saved by a thread thanks to Louis Blanc, who was at the head of an imposing popular demonstration. On April 16, nervous Parisian workers spontaneously organized a gigantic demonstration to demand once again that their claims be taken into account. The bourgeois National Guard reacted quickly, the workers' procession arrived, unarmed, at the Hôtel de Ville in front of one hundred thousand bourgeois guards. This radical potential among the workers, often neglected because of the focus on the events that followed—these were the people crushed in the June insurrection—seems credible. It would have been conceivable that, on one occasion or another, certain claims had been successful. The conjunction between future hopes, albeit plural and diffracted, and concrete possibilities for change was remarkable in this instance.

At this stage it is interesting to imagine a more social turn within the Republic if the Provisional Government had been more shaped by the presence of workers. The provinces (a range of cities and the majority of the countryside) would probably have rejected this particular form of republican government. While February had a strong following in these areas, the importance of conciliation as well as class unity is well known, especially across the varied modes of acceptance of the Republic in each of the French regions, cities, and villages.[59] A more social Republic would have been perceived as more aggressive. Moreover, the provinces could not impose their own vision of the Republic: before the elections, uncertainty was too great, and after April, the power of the National Assembly was still undermined by the other sites of decision-making power that maintained their legitimacy. Two solutions were therefore imaginable: a separation between Paris and the provinces in the shorter or longer term; or, more probably, a polarization of the opposition within Paris (between the advocates for a more direct democratic and social republic on the one side and a regrouping of the republican positions, moderate and frankly conservative on the other) and a rejection on the part of the provinces, except in a few places such as Lyon and perhaps Limoges. In this context, the Republic could have failed. It would have generated a wave of rejection, promoting the idea that "this isn't working," since the "the republican experiment," as we know, was carried out step-by-step. The relationship between the French and the idea of the Republic would have been changed. The Third Republic, which today is considered foundational, would not have existed in the form it came to take. Perhaps a constitutional monarchy would have been put into place, a change that would probably have had more general repercussions on Western countries and their empires.

We have obviously gone too far. Such "leaps into the void" are fun for the vertiginous thrills they provoke. But they also bring us back to our analysis. In the first place, they reveal a certain sympathy on our part for this democratic and social perspective as well as a disenchantment that seems to characterize the period when this chapter was written. Can we not also imagine that, by giving more institutional form and facilitating the associational movement that was germinating in the large cities, the democratic and social hypotheses, whatever their eventual limits, would have gained more credibility and legitimacy—along with the demands for popular sovereignty, the rejection of the "hoarders," or the development of more local rules of production? But these are once again subjective biases that generally underlie usual historical narratives and are precisely those that must be generally uncovered and set aside in order to further the analysis itself.[60] In the second place, this leap is a timely reminder that the Parisian situation was part of a larger political terrain that was taking a less malleable form (after which Paris no longer made revolutions by itself). This also suggests, therefore, the plasticity of political forms, which were not yet fixed. Finally, it encourages us to formulate new questions: Did the Second Republic not also succeed in establishing itself because it relied in part on a certain ambivalence and on the mobilization of slogans or previous institutional forms? In general, the opening of horizons is justly emphasized, but to imagine another probable future also underlines the role of the reappropriation of legacies necessary for the acceptance of any new political framework. On the other hand, if these workers' expectations had potentially more weight than in the Luxembourg Commission alone, is it not appropriate to ask, once again, about their imaginaries, the workers' expectations, their positions, and their organization? This would make for a fascinating object of historical study, often overlooked because these perspectives have not taken hold. It is also the result of a discourse that developed later, inspired by a certain Marxism, which has discredited these modes of action. These problems are more and more frequently addressed by historians.[61] But the counterfactual detour renders them more salient. The "forgotten" revolution begins to resurface.

Union and Disunion

No matter how likely it was or not, in the end the scenario was highly credible to the minds of many protagonists. The insistent demands on the part of the workers aroused a great deal of fear, enflamed discourses, and pushed them to share the perception of possible futures. A gap seems to have opened. This was the great anxiety from March to June 1848 for the leaders who were gathered under the term "communism." "Communism," said George Sand suggestively, is "the calumniated and misunderstood future of the people."[62] The debate began in February, when the labor commission was set up at the Luxembourg Palace to reorganize labor in the country, but also to remove the pressure (which weighed upon the slightest deed or gesture within the government). Afterward, it continued to grow.

Three points merit clarification. First, individual positions and commitments also varied according to given situations (lives can be transformed by the choices that are made or the events that are experienced); the effect of February, therefore, remained suspended, and the theme of the union of classes constantly chipped away at the sociopolitical divisions. Otherwise, it is unclear why a year later, in 1849, under the conservative Republic, Jeanne Deroin regretted that such high levels of class antagonism had returned at the expense of social union, appearing increasingly inevitable.[63] Finally, the situation changed as other institutional forms, including those sanctioned by universal manhood suffrage, were more firmly established. This was demonstrated on May 15, 1848. On that day the crowd of club leaders, workers, and curious people, who came to speak about Poland and then make their demands heard, invaded the National Assembly. Barbès, who joined the protesters, proclaimed the names of a new Provisional Government amid total confusion. The guard arrived, the protestors were evacuated, the leaders were arrested and then marginalized. Tocqueville, our privileged witness, noted that the tumult saved the Republic, either conservative or moderate, depending on one's choice. For "if Barbès had succeeded in voting his motion," the rupture of the tacit agreement that controlled the situation would have been achieved. The chamber would then have "had to show its true face" and the conflict would have broken out, unleashing popular anger, leading to the emergence of new possible outcomes.[64] The example confirms the potentiality within the workers' movement. But it also suggests that the possibility of bifurcation was based more and more on parliamentary speeches, which signaled the structuration taking place within the political process. The insurgents then tried to repeat the events and appoint a new Provisional Government at the Hôtel de Ville, amid mass confusion. The attempt failed. Acclamation was not enough to produce the event: its effectiveness depended on the context, and its time had perhaps already passed. The field of possibilities was thus modified piece by piece.

June 23–26, 1848: Was Class Warfare Avoided?

In May and June, frustrations and tensions were particularly high as a result of the persistent economic crises. They came to their climax, and a partial resolution, in the famous June Days (23–26, 1848). These terrible battles on the streets of Paris have long been considered to be the inevitable outcome of preexisting social tensions. Against the reading of "bourgeois" republicans and conservatives who spoke of a struggle of civilization against the expression of despair, chimeras, and even barbarism, Karl Marx described these events as the consequence of class struggle, naïvely masked by workers in late February. June 1848 was considered by Marx to be the first great battle between the two classes that divided modern society, and its beginnings were perceptible as early as the clumsy and unequal compromises of February.[65] Marx's analysis, which he presented in the heat of the event, later sedimented into an overly simplistic reading. We know, thanks to work by historians, that in June there were also two visions of the Republic opposing one another: a liberal, orderly republic supported by elites, conservatives, sincere republicans (like Cavaignac), and even many workers (either because they supported this vision or followed their company in the National Guard).[66] Facing this coalition was the democratic and social republic, defended for the most part by skilled workers bound by important neighborhood social networks. In some cases, they were more focused on defending their neighborhoods or on a particular conception of trampled dignity.

It is also important not to neglect, as we have seen, the role of evolutionary and unpredictable dynamic situations. This has been suggested by Mark

Traugott's analysis of organizations created in February. According to Traugott, three collective actors had an important role in mobilizing Parisian workers:[67] the Luxembourg Commission, the Parisian mobile guard, and the national workshops. We have already discussed the first. The second was set up on February 26 in order to provide work for workers and to secure a "popular" force for maintaining social and political order. It was composed of relatively young workers, who had been pushed out of the labor market by older workers. This guard was initially disobedient until military experience and effective management by the hierarchy succeeded in creating an esprit de corps among its members. The national workshops were created at the same time, also designed to provide work for laborers as part of the new right to work. The initial ambitions were quickly diminished, however, as the workshops started filling the role of containing the social crisis and unemployment, before becoming, at the end of April, a breeding ground of opposition and politicization once the workers' clubs and associations were crippled. To this should be added the democratized National Guard, and the important role it played.[68] Injected into political and economic dynamics, which were sometimes convergent, sometimes divergent (they were progressively path-dependent), these organizations, according to Traugott, exerted semidependent causal influences and thus participated in contingent outcomes. Counterfactuals are therefore necessary to clarify these heterogeneous relations: if the government had not provided uniforms to the mobile guard in time (this was an early object of recrimination), a revolt would certainly have taken place and the guards would not have marched against the insurgents in June. On the other hand, if the government had kept the director, Émile Thomas, at the head of the national workshops, perhaps the insurrection would not have occurred.[69] June no longer appears in this perspective to be the result of an inevitable movement of history, but rather a probable outcome among others, which makes sense in that particular context. Would the confrontation have taken place afterward? No one knows. The reasoning suggests, in any case, how sensitivity to unrealized outcomes can lead us to question categories of analysis that have become too rigid (the class struggle between "bourgeois" and "proletarians" as the engine of history), and how it can make the thickness of collective trajectories felt, without neglecting the reality of powerful social antagonisms whose explicit crystallization also depends on specific situations.

Once the fight was on, the tensions became more clear. According to specialists, the military balance of power remained indefinite during the early hours of fighting, especially as the military hesitated on the proper course of action. But the presence of troops, the bourgeois National Guard, the mobile and republican guards, commanded by General Cavaignac, left little room for the insurgents to express their despair. The massacre was horrible; all ambiguity disappeared. The "democratic and social" perspective, which had been the motor behind the revolution and fueled hopes during the first months of the Republic, would seem to have been closed. This time, the Republic, which had no doubt integrated some elements of social democracy, was to be parliamentary and moderate. The unfulfilled path, however, literally fed hopes for generations and had a profound impact on French political and social life.

1848–1851/1852: *The Elections, Parliamentary Life, and the Coup d'État*

After June, the elected Constituent Assembly became the key reference point. We could have insisted more on the elections of April 23, 1848, which would have made it possible to note that by definition, in a democratic parliamentary framework, elections are (or at least are supposed to be) a time of uncertainty: in spite of social, political, and geographical determinations, there is little room for maneuver, leading to results that are more or less predictable and decisive.[70] Moreover, the consensual nature of the electoral results was astonishing in this case, since moderate republicans occupied the majority of the Assembly. The parliamentary speeches that were organized after June were also part of a response to these same tensions. The debates on the inclusion of the right to work in the constitution, as studied by Thomas Bouchet, reveal, for example, the importance of the representatives' habits, paths, social and ideological positions, as well as the decisive impact of interactions, the mastery of eloquence, and the more or less local contexts in which they spoke (as well as very simply the number of people present in the Assembly).[71]

Let us now look at the presidential election of December 1848, which of course led to the overwhelming victory of Louis-Napoléon Bonaparte, the nephew of Napoleon I. It was indeed, for the majority of those who thought they knew public opinion, a surprise. If Lamartine, among others, represented a bygone moment, Louis-Eugène Cavaignac aroused real interest. Historiography has largely held him accountable for the June 1848 massacre, followed by the repressive policies that followed: the victor of June was the "villain" of history. But he was also "the most authentic and loyal example imaginable of a 'long standing' republican"[72] and had organized the killing of

Parisian workers in the name of universal manhood suffrage, which had just spoken in May. For him, the Republic, or *this* republic in any case, even with its faults, had been in danger. Maxime Du Camp noted in his *Souvenirs* that Cavaignac could easily have taken power after the June Days. The workers had been dispersed, the army supported him, his name was spoken with a sigh of relief. Moreover, the legislative chamber was a disappointment and Cavaignac presided over the government. He could perfectly well have set up a republican dictatorship (in the Roman sense, since the model was so present among these elites who bathed in the culture of ancient Rome) and maintained universal manhood suffrage for the election of the legislative chamber. This was yet one more possibility for the republican regime, another "cluster of potentialities."

But he did not establish a republican dictatorship, no doubt emboldened by the same convictions and respect for the institutions he had tried to save. So when he ran for election in December, he seemed to many the best guarantee of a republic of order and liberty. This was the position of most of our authors (Louis Ménard excepted), whether they were moderate or conservative republicans. Daniel Stern concluded her history of 1848 on this missed rendezvous with the one who could have been, according to the logic of the time, a "great man." Cavaignac lacked "a penetrating intelligence and spontaneity of action." If he had been elected, she continued, the Republic could have been what it should have been. And this perspective was a real option if one reads the newspapers and follows the political calculations of the moment.

However, it was also an error of analysis: if the rejection on the part of the workers was predictable, the vote in the countryside had not been sufficiently taken into consideration nor were the subterranean attachments to a Napoleonic figure (which Bernard Ménager reminds us was hardly discussed in the Parisian or regional newspapers[73]). Louis-Napoleon's skillfulness did the rest. But this time, the hidden and unexpected was clearly on the side of what actually happened.

The regime, under the influence of the "party of order," underwent a conservative turning point the following year. The elections of May 1849 produced a legislative assembly filled with tension. Debates were lively between the most conservative members and the *démoc-socs* (democratic-socialist) minority, who nevertheless had a strong presence on the benches of the Assembly (about five hundred "Whites" [conservatives], one hundred republicans, and two hundred "Reds" [far left]). Tensions also opposed, little by little, the parliamentary representatives from the party of order and Louis-Napoléon

Bonaparte. A majority of the former desired a return to the monarchy and had the means to attempt a restoration. Historians have had a tendency to chart the "other paths," which in general followed more or less what we would consider, the "right direction" (more democratic, more just, and so on). Nonetheless, the monarchical restoration, most likely with an elected legislative body, was still another possible outcome of 1848. The power of this dynamic, based on the disappointments of February, on a local anchoring that was still strong, though being eroded, and supported by a "red" scare after June, remained consistent. Probably based on a less expansive version of universal manhood suffrage, it would have been part of a set of deep social and cultural forces, which would have been reinforced at the same time, also changing the lines of opposition. The story scatters here into multiple vanishing lines. The restoration of the monarchy was avoided in part thanks to the president's cleverness, who began to break with his allies, as well as the organizational difficulties of the "Whites." There was also the weight of the republican idea, which was old and fragile, but remained present in the institutional dynamics at the most local level. This process of crystallization and progressive attenuation of certain options was also decisive. The movement alternated between expansion, retraction, and the displacement of opportunities.

A deadline was quickly approaching, however: 1852. According to the regime's constitution, a new president of the Republic needed to be elected (the president could not run for reelection) as well as a new legislative body. The game of representative democracy was set to be played: in the language of the time, it was the "deadline of 1852." For the republicans, it represented a real hope. In spite of the police pressures and the restrictions on universal suffrage (May 31, 1850), the movement for the diffusion of republican ideas had begun to spread. It was spreading within the popular culture of villages (carnivals and processions), building on secret societies and partially on the phenomenon of worker associationalism, which was benefiting from a strong resurgence. It was a vast extra-institutional movement. But many local leaders, often those close to the juridical community, made a choice in accordance with their principles to pursue the lawful route and privilege the vote. As a result, the election took on the character of a call for a truly republican political future. The singer Pierre Dupont captured this idea as early as 1850: "It is in two years, two years / That the Gallic rooster will sing / Come let your light shine / 1852." For the monarchists and conservatives, both moderate and radical, the challenge was to maintain a dominant position in order to avoid what was perceived as republican anarchy and to ensure a return to "natural" order. 1852 was therefore cause for concern. The famous propaganda pamphlet of Auguste Romieu offered a good illustration of this.[74] "The signs are accumulating: everyone can see them now; a brand of mute terror has chilled the bones of the smallest and the greatest; the Red Specter of 1852, which we have not wanted to see and that I bring before you once again, is revealing itself to a society in shock." The range of appreciations obviously varied. But the long-awaited "year of 1852," with its hopes, expectations, projections, positions, and tensions, suggests that the regime hardly collapsed of simple "old age."[75]

This year that had been the object of so much projection was interrupted by the coup d'état. After the failure of the constitutional revision, which would have allowed Louis-Napoléon Bonaparte to run for president a second time, it increasingly appeared to be the only option—although the president apparently took some time to accept it, according to his biographers.[76] The operation was well prepared and enjoyed the success that we now know. The republican opposition had been brought under control, especially in the provincial towns, through the campaigns of repression from 1849 to 1851. The Parisian workers did not intervene, or only very few did, feeling excluded from the political game since the June Days. As for the deputies, while Louis-Napoléon Bonaparte tried to control them, they met at the town hall of the 10th arrondissement on December 2 to declare the former president unlawful. Constitutionally speaking, they had a window of opportunity during this moment of suspension: Louis-Napoléon Bonaparte, who was in the process of taking power, was marginalized. The decision could have had an impact if the rogue president had failed or made a misstep. Up to that point any variety of political forms was still a possibility. But the chances of success on the part of the deputies were slim. The main opposition, as we know, came from certain parts of the countryside, which had become "red" (that is, republican) in the previous months, testifying to the extent of the growing process of politicization that marked the nineteenth century. The refutations, however, followed a complex path, mixing a variety of references and problematics. If a majority of the rebels were not looking to defend the Constitution but "to reclaim their rights," as the Republic of the Peasants promised in 1852, other motivations ended up being more surprising for historians. In the Dauphiné, the rebels called for the defense of the Christian faith, which they thought was under attack. In Ardèche, they imagined that they had been called upon by Louis-Napoléon to march against other provincial towns. Elsewhere, there were calls to avoid a return to the Old Regime.[77] On the ground, the differences were no doubt more subtle. But all these reasons combined with future hopes, which were coherent within the current systems of representation and provided opportunities for intervention. The new power in place also used them effectively: playing off the "fear of 1852" (a possible victory of the *démoc-socs* in the elections) and the specter of the jacqueries of the Old Regime, Louis-Napoléon acquired a new legitimacy by transforming these rebellions into threats against the social order. With time, the coup d'état became a canonical date in the history of contemporary France. By reintegrating it into the uncertain mutations of the years 1848–1851 and not simply waiting for the deadline of 1852, one understands better what a shock it was—a final jolt in a situation that had long been suspended and full of tension. After the crushing of the opponents, proponents attempted to impose a new reading of the event almost immediately. The din of 1848 had been quieted—and even silenced.

FRACTURED DIMENSIONS AND ECHOES OF THE "1848" THAT NEVER CAME

Some Problems of Interpretation

Such an exercise would seem to provide a series of tests of the events and offer a way of reading the situations experienced by the actors against the grain, opening up a myriad of new possible directions. It provides an opportunity to grasp, perhaps better than the standard historical narrative, the importance of the successive actualizations that modified the previous situation.[78]

In doing so, the exercise helps measure the extent of the displacements involved, regardless of the ultimate vanishing point. When faced with the uncertainty of the events, the conventional account of the 1848 Revolution generally focuses on the "end of the story": the slow creation of the Republic. The counterfactual approach, or possible futures, invites us to explore "as if" we didn't know the end of the story. It modifies the implicit hierarchy of the dynamics involved and pushes us to think differently about their articulation. It can thus make the revolutionary moment feel like a succession of situations with intermediate outcomes and plural meanings.

Thus, it builds on approaches to the event that have been proposed in other disciplines.[79] It is no longer a question of an analysis based on the outcome of the events, but from the perspective of the experiences they generate. These possible futures make it conceivable to experience concretely an evolving sociopolitical configuration, which is often the aim of researchers, by sharpening the corners. They help to take into account the problem of the opening of possibilities, of grasping the weight of shifting determinations and bringing into light forgotten or neglected episodes.

The approach also facilitates the apprehension of the perception by the actors. By showing the dynamics of coalescence, crystallization, disintegration, and rupture, it shows why 1848 appeared to the protagonists, direct and indirect, as a time of profound indeterminacy, where the routines and norms that organized social life seemed suspended. In particular, one understands the omnipresence in the newspapers, speeches, and correspondences, both among elites and more "popular" genres, of references to "eddies," "waves," or "sinking." Similarly, the approach helps to interpret the strategies of the individuals. Perceived afterward as illusory or useless, through this approach they become the motors of these mobile situations. As we have seen, it is not a question of calling upon some abstract rational actor, but of grasping the rationalities inherent in the "zero hour" of such events.[80] It is therefore necessary to add to the calculations and the ideological orientations the importance of social trajectories, formulations of hope, emotion, the experience of the sacred, and political awareness. At the same time, various forms of avoidance and indifference must not be forgotten. The approach helps us find an original point of entry into the logic and the specificity of the event.

There remain three aspects that must be considered. The question of the status of these possible futures, especially those on which we have insisted, is still a problem. Are they pure fictions? Yes and no. Michel Dobry's analyses of "situational logics," or Luc Boltanski's "regimes of action"[81] suggest that these nodes are virtual real worlds, from which thoughts, choices, ideas, actions, and groups are articulated. They are, in a way, "real" without having happened. As such, these interpretive fictions are at once the fruit of a risk on the part of the researcher at the same time that they give relief to the blanks within the sources and the unknowns of events.

No doubt it is necessary to avoid typifying the stories and actors in this process of exploration. Categories like "workers" and "monarchists" do not always favor a deep analysis, and there is a great risk of closing oneself off from the fundamental uncertainty of these moments.[82] The "possible futures" of workers are different according to whether we adopt the point of view of the educated and politicized Parisian typographer or the weaver working at home in misery. Moreover, there are multiple points of bifurcation that have been set aside here. It is unthinkable to grasp them in their entirety (a completely reliable analysis would imply an impossible total mastery of all the variables at play). These possible futures should be considered benchmarks to improve the analysis, or tools likely to prevent the mechanical use of categories, in order to open our eyes to a particular situation.

The last point touches upon modes of narration. These possible futures seem to offer an original way of restoring the specificity of the historical or revolutionary event. They propose a narrative form that is at least as appropriate as the classical ones for exposing what was happening. In particular, it allows a more fragmented, analytical, and kaleidoscopic appraisal, while avoiding chance and psychologisms.

There is nothing absolutely new in these remarks, either in the discussion of clusters, the writing of the event, or the opening of opportunities. Nonetheless, the paths of possibility allow these different problems to be articulated at the same time that they put into practice proposals that oftentimes remain at the level of theory: they therefore allow for a broader mode of analysis.

Evaluating 1848

What emerges when we expand the temporal horizon? It is useful, at this level, to consider the variety of possible bifurcations as a whole, in order to escape a simplistic schema (a cause, an event, a change). Global transformation is irreversible and obvious. But the ultimate result appears to be the product of negotiations, of reduced possibilities, and of a permanence that remains salient (institutions, personnel, political practices, perceptions, and so on). Thus, in 1851, the institutional, economic, and social extensions are as surprising as the reality with which the word "Republic" (with or without content) is endowed; and the shifting coordinates seem to undermine the foundations of old social structures, forced to adapt once again.

Can a more precise account of this transformation be provided? Another type of counterfactual, which would be less interpretative and more evaluative, might provide a response to this question. What was, for example, the impact of the 1848 Revolution in Paris on the European "springtime of peoples?" The international dimension has not been sufficiently treated in the analysis provided here. We are, of course, familiar with the progress of the revolutionary process: the movement in Switzerland in 1847, revolts in the Italian peninsula, and so on. Some have argued that these movements took two paths forward, one through Vienna and the other through Paris, before reverberating outward. For others, only the Parisian path was decisive and initiated the movement.[83] No doubt, the process was multifaceted. It may be argued that without the Revolution of February 1848, in the cradle of the French Revolution of

1789, the springtime of peoples would not have spread so widely. In this argument's favor, one may cite the circulation of slogans and French practices, such as the barricade, which could be found throughout revolutionary Europe.[84] Moreover, without the Viennese revolution, the impact of the Parisian revolution would probably have remained just as important. An examination of the dissemination of information and a comparison with the beginnings of the different revolutions would allow for a more elaborate set of conclusions. If 1848 was a polycephalic revolution, its organization was not without its own hierarchies or points of reference.[85] These explorations remind us that the Paris event also fits into a transnational framework.[86] The European dimension in turn influenced the Parisian and French dynamics, undoubtedly contributing to the reinforcement of the actors' beliefs. It reveals, in fact, a rich and complex system of interactions and co-definitions between these different places.

What about the economic significance of 1848? A broader look is equally necessary here. German researchers have recently reassessed the importance of the economic crisis of the years 1846–1848 in triggering or not triggering revolutionary episodes in Europe: "without the economic crisis of 1845–1848, which so obviously endangered the economic welfare of so many people and discredited the old regime so thoroughly, there would not have been the critical mass to support these new ideas. Hence, no explanation of the European revolutions of 1848 should neglect short-term economic factors."[87] The regional or national trajectories that followed were also part of this matrix. The French situation is well known: the 1848 Revolution took place in a context of crisis, while the beginning of the reign of Napoleon III in 1852 opened a period of prosperity. For example, according to Maurice Agulhon, the Republic accentuated the crisis by delaying essential investments (banks, railways, and so on)[88] because it was caught between so many contradictory crosswinds. The earlier ends to the crisis in England and other European states bear witness to this effect. In other words, if 1848 had not occurred, the economic trends would not have been fundamentally any different. Simply, the moment of economic growth would have come earlier and the social crisis would have been less pronounced. The impact here was therefore a question of lag time.

Politically, the recurrent question has been: Was the Revolution of 1848 and the Second Republic a "success" or a "failure"? The key question in response is: Compared to what? If the comparison concerns our current norms (a liberal democratic republic in a capitalist economy), the question is necessarily anachronistic. If it takes into consideration what could (or should?) have happened, it is engaging in a counterfactual that is moral rather than analytical. Picking up the question on a more social or cultural basis may be more helpful. The positions of elites, especially those with political power, survived the event relatively well.[89] While the Republic brought a new set of political elites onto the scene through universal suffrage and provoked shifts in power relations, the old structures seemed to return as early as 1851: socially speaking, the legislative body of the very young Second Empire closely resembled that of the July Monarchy (a majority of civil servants, rentiers, and businessmen). The shake-up of 1848, in this case, was not as pronounced, nor were the continuities that helped consolidate Napoleon III's regime. Was the experience of 1848–1852 merely a parenthesis then? Obviously not. As Philippe Vigier has shown, the perception of social relations shifted, clearly modifying their base and the ways they were maintained.[90] Similarly, without 1848, universal male suffrage would not have been instituted, or at least not as early as it was. And after the event, it was never called into question again. The Republic had also come into existence, had been invested with hopes and concerns, had shown it could be real, and became a memory enriched with its own set of values, heroes, and events.

We could continue this line of reasoning, whether for the growth of the state or for socialist thought[91] or the accentuation of a national culture. 1848, as we know, also played a decisive role in the awareness of the importance of the nation and in the will of nations to assert greater control over national identities.[92] In this sense, 1848 does appear to be a tipping point.

What emerges from this investigation, therefore, are the economic, social, and cultural permanencies, as well as the real power of the event, which disembeds, suspends, or displaces them for a moment or for a longer period. One comes into contact here with the creative dimension of the event, which profoundly reorients previous lines of development. The result is an irreversible and uncertain ensemble between the short and the long term, latency and potentiality. One comes then to an original type of political form, inscribed in the *longue durée* of French and European history, that develops with a coherence that may be retraced afterward, without being predictable: the face of republican and then imperial France appears anew, while having been drawn by its old features and unrealized expressions.

Regrets and Anger

These periods, which were also experienced by the actors in a mode that bordered on counterfactual reasoning, left echoes in their memories in the form of other futures past. There is then a history of these unrealized '48s. The memory of the new regime constantly employed the imagery of the Second Republic and the dangers that France would have faced if it had been abandoned to "parties" and "systems." This memory fits into the "temporal discordance" that characterized nineteenth-century modernity.[93]

The "what if" is also systematic in memories, memoirs, and histories. We have already mentioned those of Stern or Tocqueville. It can also be found in Louis Ménard and Maxime Du Camp: "If the Republic had been possible in France, it would have been founded by Cavaignac," he noted regarding Cavaignac.[94] A careful reading of these texts invites us to take another step: generally speaking, the events are analyzed from the angle of a "lack," or a fault—Alphonse de Lamartine even speaks of a "betrayal of the moment": "Great services were rendered, mistakes were made," he said in his conclusion. "I ask God, my contemporaries and posterity to pardon me."[95] The sense of regret and the feeling of having deviated off course are by definition modes of counterfactual reasoning: we compare the situation to what could have been. Everything happens as if there had been a gap between what the Revolution carried within itself (good or bad) and what it became.

The counterfactuals produced after the fact by the actors themselves then makes it possible to study their aims and political ideas, especially since we are dealing here with subsequent narratives that clarify uncertainties. This implies a certain shared perception of historical development: we discover once again the modern "regime of historicity" that was peculiar to the nineteenth century, directed toward progress and heightened by the surprise of the revolutionary event.[96] No doubt this temporal relationship makes it possible to understand why the feelings of frustration were so strong. During this period, there was a particularly strong projective force in the very idea of a possible future, which may have faded today for those of us who are going through what some would call a "crisis of temporality." Restoring this impulse allows us to analyze how intense it was to live through these three years of transformation. In return, it legitimizes many aspects of the approach discussed earlier.

Revolution and Possibilism

One question remains: What relationship is there between revolution and possible futures? Is every revolution marked by possible futures, and can we identify specific developments from this perspective?

Moving forward in time, to 1870: after a period of stability, the Second Empire underwent an accelerated phase of liberalization, which was brutally interrupted by the Franco-Prussian War. Few moments have been the object of so many "what-if" reflections, even fleeting ones. Such analyses can be found among all the specialists of the period, French or Anglo-American.[97] These reflections are, moreover, necessary for bringing the Second Empire out of the republican narrative reconstructed in the 1880s, where it was presented as a kind of error in the irresistible advance of the (good) republican ideal.

Counterfactual reasoning usefully sheds light on the process that lasted from September 4 to March 18 in Paris, and then, following the "week of uncertainty" (March 18–26), to the election of the Commune. This week was marked by intense negotiations between the mayors and deputies of Paris, the Assembly of Versailles, and the revolutionaries who occupied the Hôtel de Ville.[98] As opposed to February 1848, the advent of the Commune was in this sense a "slow journey," which, according to Robert Tombs and Jacques Rougerie, invites us to relativize a priori political and sociological readings.[99]

The approach would be equally relevant for the Commune itself. Once the revolutionary moment began, the scene changed, in line with the discontinuity discussed earlier: the actors, the words, and the referents were revived. The idea of unrealized futures made its return, those of the Great Revolution, of 1830 as well as 1848 and 1851: the democratic and social republic was present once again. Changes also unfolded in a confused brouhaha. The Paris Commune of 1871, like the ephemeral communes of the provinces, was more positivist, more bound to workers, more bellicose. At the same time, the will to build a new world and to eradicate the traces of the old remained intense (this time the city was fully in the hands of the revolutionaries). The unanimity of the moment, however, was less apparent.

The possibility of variation was perhaps no longer the same. The Commune itself did not really represent an alternative: it maintained a distance from elected power, it had relatively little following in the provinces (even if we now have a better sense of the cities that, during the few weeks before and after, followed the movement[100]), and did not have the military means to impose itself. Regrets that a Communard offensive had not been carried out before the mobilization of Versailles were numerous, but the Communard army itself was not structured at that point. The paradox of the Commune may be then combining the expression and the implementation of a profound change of political forms and social relations, which ran deeper in some senses than in 1848 (with a resurgence of the social democratic expectations that had been disappointed in 1848), and, unlike 1848, a lesser capacity for mobilization and transformation. Not that the situation of the insurgent Paris wasn't gripped by uncertainty, but there was little immediate grasp on the whole of the French or European political future. The force of change may have been playing out elsewhere at that stage, in the legislative body, in the provinces, or in the army, and so on. What appeared was another political space of possible alternatives, that operated on a more national scale and resulted from the social, political, and cultural changes of the 1860s. The Commune revived the revolutionary experience while at the same time updating it. Its failure weighed upon memories for a long time to come. The revolutionary idea then continued in the French political field of the 1900s and in the redefinition of the workers' movement.[101] It was transformed, adopted other modes of expression, and became more organized before resurfacing elsewhere later. We are thus witness to the burial of a field of possibilities (and constraints), those of the first half of the nineteenth century, and the emergence of another. It remained marked by the reinvigoration of previous moments, while remaining offbeat and following other lines of force.

There would seem to be a historicity to the relations between revolution and possible futures, and the use of the approach must adapt to concrete situations. This is another way of extending the analysis of the revolutionary phenomenon. The moment of crisis, and then of revolution when it takes place, is by definition the crisscrossing of time, the heterogeneity of cases, the suspension of power relations. At the same time, these power relations do not disappear. Crisis or revolutionary moments resist the ordinary approaches of historians, who often struggle to bring these different dimensions together. Distanced observation and observation from within, comparative historical sociology and the study of lived experience do not always work well together. They make reference to very different phenomena: long-term social mutations, anthropological transformations of the relationship to time, transnational circulation of revolutionary experiences, rupture within the revolutionary and counterrevolutionary idea, the cycle of forms of violence, the resurgence of political projects and repertoires of action, the thickness of local situations, experiences, and the emergence of the previously unknown. What these pages would like to suggest is that the "what-if" approach offers an original way of articulating these dimensions, their connections, and disjunctions, without imposing a predetermined fixed relationship.

These remarks, then, make it possible to return to the perspectives drawn by different historians, such as Martin Malia, American specialist of the Soviet Union and revolution in the twentieth century.[102] In his last work, published shortly after his death, he proposed a vast study of revolution defined as a phenomenon peculiar to European political lifestyles from the fourteenth century to 1989. A "revolution," in this long-term perspective, is a generalized revolt against an old regime. In this context, 1848 and 1871 are not revolutions, but rather echoes, reverberations of 1789: 1848 marks the end of a lyrical moment; 1871 is an anachronism. The real relationship was the one shared by 1789 and 1917. This perspective has the merit of offering significant points of comparison for the analysis of the two revolutions. Nevertheless, since it is entirely focused on 1917, the analysis tends to blur the revolutionary moment itself, its intensity, its capacity to shift—even just a touch—the contours and finally its echo within memories and policies. To the contrary, the approach discussed here pushes us to take them into account. More precisely, in this case it is a question of reevaluation: the relationship between the time of the crisis and the revolutionary upheaval, which is only one of the possible outcomes; suspending the "end" of the event to explore the displacements or the role of dispersed fragments; apprehending the compression of the experiences and the fluidity of crisis situations; rediscovering the variety and vigor of political expectations; returning to the role, the meaning and the functions of violence; integrating into the analysis the latency of social, mental, and material constraints, as well as the role of contingency; penetrating into the thick web of pasts, presents, and futures; thinking about the spatial connections and the complex temporal leaps that can tie these experiences together. This is a different kind of reading. One that invites us in return to leave room for the upsurge or the unforeseen in the most constrained or established social orders (whatever one's judgment on it may be). This is partly what we learned from the round of revolutions during the Arab Spring of 2010–2012 and, in another register, the Maple Spring of 2012.[103] What emerges is a form of history that is less certain about its closures.

By definition, the events and, in particular, crises and revolutions are moments of "what ifs," be they actors, situations, readings after the fact, or distant observations. It therefore seems logical to use a mode of reasoning that follows the characteristics of its object.

By examining the tensions between what has happened and what has not happened, this approach compels us to reject perspectives that hover too distantly at the same time that it can help us distance ourselves from present perceptions. For a long time, revolutions have appeared to be engines of history, moments of desire and fear that shake worlds. Then, with the changes in the relation to time and shifts in the post-1989 geopolitical situation, the revolutionary experiences were eroded, sometimes even erased from history—with the exception of 1789. This approach, with its artful exploration of setbacks and connections, offers a way of approaching and restoring anew a phenomenon that still seems to undermine many of the implicit elements of the historian's narrative, either modern or postmodern.

Through this approach, stimulating perspectives await for reconsidering more classical sets of problems, such as the events and processes of social transformation, the entanglement of temporalities and temporal experiences, the lived and the situated, the closed and the opened, the naturalized and the possible.

CHAPTER II

The Console and the Chalkboard

REPLAYING HISTORY, A "SERIOUS GAME"?

> You are Captain B. J. Blazkowicz, the American War Hero. After emerging into this world of darkness, you must launch an impossible counter-offensive against the monstrous Nazi regime. Only you dare stand up against an unstoppable army of Nazi robots and hulking Super Soldiers. Only you can stop Deathshead. Only you can rewrite history.
>
> —*Wolfenstein: The New Order*[1]

> WWI games are very rare, and tend to sell poorly. I've heard it argued that this is because of how entrenched/static the war was, and how limited it was compared to WWII. But the Eastern Front, Middle East, Balkans, and German invasion of Belgium were all fairly fluid at times and didn't have the same trench system the Western front did. Between the trenches in the plains of France, the sheer scope of the East, the Alpine Warfare in Italy, the deserts in the Middle East, and the limited wars in Africa/the Pacific, I believe there is enough diversity to create an interesting game.
>
> —Alternate History, Forum[2]

> There is still a reluctance to the playful functionality of mimesis, or rather the idea that there is an incompatibility between knowledge and the practice of immersion.
>
> —Jean-Marie Schaeffer[3]

Up to now, our discussion has been quite serious. And yet we are all familiar with the playful and participatory dimension of counterfactual reasoning, which operates on two levels. First, when choosing the bifurcation point; there is the moment when the reader enters the "workshop of history" (François Furet): in general, the researcher must justify his or her choices, report on his or her hypotheses, discuss the sources, assume the fragility of his or her knowledge, and invite the reader to accompany him or her. Then there is the question of the counterfactual account itself: whether it is suggested or substantiated, insofar as it supposes a particular implication on behalf of the reader, who must compare the information of what happened with the proposals of what didn't. To this may be added the feeling of transgression of a given temporal order, which can generate a sense of vertigo and anxiety as well as amusement. The audience of successful counterfactual history experiences such feelings. Would it not be possible then to mobilize them more fully in a history that is more concerned with investigation, interpretation, and interaction with the audience? Knowledge of the workings of counterfactual reasoning and its implications makes it possible to approach more calmly questions of exchange and emotional involvement, which are decisive at a time when so-called scholarly history can struggle to find an audience. At the same time, many would seem passionately engaged in "their" past, and participative practices like reenactments have become forms of sociability. Moreover, might the approach not also be of educational interest? We must therefore study the playful, pedagogical, and critical uses of the counterfactual, placing us this time more on the side of the reader, the listener, and the historical enthusiast.

RECREATIONAL AND INTERACTIVE PRACTICES IN HISTORY

In reality, many areas of activity have already made effective use of counterfactual narratives without bothering with more scientific questions. To be clear, it is not a question here of judging these practices as professional historians (the authors and the practitioners are not terribly concerned with such assessments), but rather with gauging the uses of the counterfactual that have been developed as forms of entertainment. Recreational practices of history, which themselves have a long history,[4] experienced a remarkable expansion in the 1980s. History spectacles provide evidence of this booming interest, like, for example, the historical theme park Le Puy du Fou, which has inspired numerous similar initiatives in other countries. Created in 1978 by the French nationalist Philippe de Villiers, it welcomed 1.7 million visitors in 2010 alone.[5] The phenomenon of historical reenactments, especially in the context of "living history" is of particular interest for our purposes. The most visible part of this trend has been very large events, often related to national or international commemorations. In Russia, the Battle of Borodino, during which the Russians resisted the Great Army of Napoleon I, was reenacted for the bicentennial in September 2012, with nearly three thousand "historical actors" and an audience of more than three hundred thousand spectators, including Vladimir Putin. In Germany, the Battle of Leipzig, which also took place in the context of the Napoleonic Wars, was reenacted by nearly six thousand volunteers in front of thirty thousand spectators.[6] The phenomenon has met with similar success in Quebec and the United States, for the Revolutionary War, the American Civil War, or World War II.[7] In 2013, one study estimated that Americans spent about $1.4 billion a year on living history events related to the Civil War (twice the annual income of all Broadway shows).[8]

The phenomenon not only concerns major national events, however. In France, many associations and theater companies frequently perform reenactments of the past on a local scale, that of a city or a village, which is considered more accurate: European gatherings for military reenactments at La Neuville-sur-Essonne, ancient games at Bédarrides, medieval festivals at Provins, the Great War of 1914–1918 in Pressins, as well as the reenactments of the meeting between Catherine de' Medici and Nostradamus at Salon-de-Provence.[9] While the means employed vary tremendously, these practices share the same historical ambition: the objective is to achieve the most "authentic" reproduction of these historical moments, as a result of sometimes very sophisticated studies of the unfolding of the event, as well as the costumes, the weapons, the artisanal techniques, the culinary practices, the lifestyles, and so on. Exchanges on Internet forums play a key role in this elaboration. The phenomenon concerns the four great historical periods (with a preference for the Middle Ages and the two world wars) and not only deals with specific battles but also camps, fairs, or village life. The interviews with "reenactors" by journalists also indicate that, more than the "great men," it is the ordinary individuals, the people who, with the aim of creating a more "authentic" experience, arouse the most interest. This form of incarnated history, sometimes described as a reaction to the skepticism of postmodern globalized societies, is also a means of creating specific modes of sociability or highlighting local histories. Historians are mistrustful of those practitioners who dispense with their expertise: the consensual scenes of the past tend to set aside the tensions that unsettled these former societies and often subordinate the past to the political stakes of the present. To which the "reenactors" oppose the image of a living, popular history that is closer to the lived experience of the populations and is more interesting than elitist and boring scholarly history filled with jargon.

Be that as it may, uchronia, counterfactualism, and possible futures are generally not present in these manifestations. Although everyone recognizes that these reenactments never offer an identical reproduction of the past, the search for authenticity and accuracy is directly opposed to the idea of a version that has somehow strayed from the course of history. Nonetheless, counterfactuals can be found from time to time in the form of a game in the annual rehearsal of reenactments, a recreational activity that allows for a little fantasy and humor. Accustomed to famous reconstructions in the Vaucluse, the village of Lauris thus put on in 2010 some uchronic scenes: "What if Hannibal had passed through Lauris?" "What if Napoleon had returned from Elba through Lauris?" "What if Prosper Mérimée . . . ?"[10] There is also space for seemingly less fanciful alternative outcomes in some battle reenactments, particularly in the United States and the United Kingdom. These generally follow a strictly planned scenario and stick with the "real" course of history (minus the deaths and bodily harm). Some, however, leave open the battle's outcome.[11] The choice is sometimes made by the organizers to be less faithful to the exact unfolding of events, leaving more room for the game itself. To the contrary, it can even participate in a desire to restore the uncertainty of the battle to make it more vibrant. The possibility of the alternative favors, in this case, the very project of the resurrection of the past. The new outcome, whether the same or different, is then the subject of discussion on the forces at play, the tactical choices, the weather, and so on, especially within the local press.[12]

These considerations bring us closer to the practice of role-playing games. This is also a relatively old activity that has emerged since the 1970s, reaching a plateau over the last ten years (a few thousand versions are sold a year for the most well-known, developed on the Internet and in new specialist magazines). These playful simulations, organized around another world, characters, and scenarios prepared in advance, are generally structured around a distinction between a game master, who ensures the smooth running of the game, and the players themselves.[13] Playing within a fictitious environment with clearly defined characteristics, the players react to different missions, trials, or battles during games that can last several hours. These other worlds are often borrowed from science fiction or medieval fantasy, as in the case of the most famous of them, *Dungeons and Dragons,* created in 1974. There are also historical role-plays, which contain moments of alternative history and incursions into fantasy worlds. In recent years, such games have ventured off more directly into the uchronic and the counterfactual. Such is the case for

Khaos 1795, for example. This history follows our own until 1794, the moment when Fouquier-Tinville condemned Robespierre to death: "That day, a gigantic eye appeared over Paris, and Fouquier-Tinville became the high priest of the supreme being. Under his yoke, France lived a regime of Terror while the presence of the eye deformed animals and created chaotic change of whole areas throughout northern France."[14] The players are members of one of five revolutionary groups (the National Guard, the Citizen-Corsairs, the Jeu de Paume, the Age of Enlightenment, the Shadow Cabinet) who fight against the supreme being and his clergy.[15] The presentation of Uchronia 1890[16] is even more revealing of the expectations placed on such historical distortions:

> At first glance, the world of Uchronia is familiar to you, since it is the same as our own at the end of the nineteenth century: it is the era of Queen Victoria and Arthur Conan Doyle, the time of the great empires and great inventions. The context mentioned above is only a decoration, or even a trompe l'oeil. Beneath its falsely historical exterior, the universe of Uchronia hides a number of unsuspected mysteries, secrets and oddities that players will discover through the adventures of their heroes. The first of these decisive differences concerns the Great Threat that weighs on the future of this uchronic world. . . . Since the beginning of the 1880s, a race of beings from another planet has been preparing the invasion of the Earth and the extermination of Humanity. . . . It goes without saying that the Secret War between the Club and the Machine seriously compromises the "normal" unfolding of the history of the world. . . . From the moment the game is launched, everything becomes possible, and the Chronicler is free to modify the course of History according to his imagination, but also according to the events that occurred in his scenarios: thus the successes and the failures of the players can have a real impact on the future of the world, contrary to what would have happened if history were already written.[17]

The alternative or uchronic story is therefore primarily for the pleasure and thrill of the player. It mobilizes, in an unbridled way, the formidable imaginary conveyed through history. Moreover, being linked (in spirit) to the "real" history, it gives more weight and impact, even in terms of imagination, to the actions of the players in the world. As a result, the game has more impact. These technical advantages are not negligible: as noted by commentators of specialized sites,[18] uchronia proposes a consensual world that mobilizes common historical references, allowing the game master to focus on the scenario more than the universe itself, thereby facilitating the immersion of the player.[19]

This instrumental dimension is also essential in the realm of video games. Here we enter into a completely different domain, since for the last fifteen years it has been the first cultural industry in the world: 1.2 billion players (or approximately one-seventh of the world's population) and a commercial growth of more than 50 percent between 2010 and 2011, a figure that hit $70 billion in 2013. In spite of the economic crisis, the prospects for growth continue to be optimistic, thanks to the explosion of mobile and multimedia platforms.[20] The sector is booming, with a multiplicity of forms and numerous ramifications, and it is impossible to present in just a few lines the diversity of this activity and everything that is at stake economically, politically, and socially. It is important to note, however, the role of historical modification, possible futures, counterfactualism, and uchronia that are commonly mobilized. On the surface, it would appear to be a question of historical contexts that are more or less faithfully reproduced, where gamers modify the initial point of departure without necessarily provoking serious historical change. This can be a simple change in the background, as in a number of war games, especially FPS (first-person shooter) games. It can also be a more sophisticated framework for action, as in the series *Assassin's Creed,* known for its meticulous historical reproductions (in one of the latest versions, which is set in revolutionary Paris, Notre-Dame Cathedral was recreated at a scale of 90 percent accuracy). In this game, the user intervenes in a so-called systemic universe, that is to say, a universe that has its own independent movements (five thousand characters can be displayed at the same time), and which reacts to his or her actions: the assassin can set off the movements of the crowd, kill one of the characters, modify the decor, and so on.[21] He or she therefore acts, alone or with others, within a space of shifting determinisms and modifies the historical situations. That said, it never upsets the official course of grand historical narratives: Louis XVI is always still guillotined.

There is also another, deeper level in which the game is more profoundly uchronic. In this case, the game takes place at a moment that comes long after the point of divergence. As in role-playing games, this can be a purely fanciful event: in the *Wolfenstein* series, considered to be a pioneer in FPS, launched in 1981, the Nazis managed to bring the dead back to life through their scientific experiments. The hero, B. J. Blazkowicz, is an American soldier who fights German soldiers and other supernatural creatures.[22] Beside these fantastic forays, which are also found in the sagas *Command and Conquer: Red Alert* and *Resistance: Fall of Man,*[23] other games propose historical divergences and uchronic universes that are designed to be more realistic. *Turning Point: Fall of Liberty* is therefore anchored in the accidental death of Winston Churchill, then a little-known British diplomat, crushed by a taxi in 1931 (the consequence after a series of bifurcations is Nazi victory).[24]

There are also games that take place before the point of divergence, where the action of the player can send the story in one direction or another. This narrative technique exists in some FPS-type war games, but also in more ambitious strategy games, such as *Europe Universalis, Total War,* or the more famous *Hearts of Iron* and *Civilization.*[25] In *Civilization,* the famous series created by Sid Meier, the player takes the place of a leader of a "civilization" (Caesar, Montezuma II, Napoleon I, and so on), who is in competition with others and must lead his people from the Stone Age to the conquest of space. To do so, he or she controls a number of parameters (natural resources, cities, settlers, technological research, armaments, diplomacy, and so forth), which must be combined in the most effective way. Following a series of critiques and requests from commentators and players, the later version refined the dimensions of the game in a less bellicose direction (ideology, culture, pacifism, commerce) and proposed scenarios that were located in more specific historical contexts (African colonization, for example). The recourse to artificial intelligence (AI) since 2010 has increased the game's potential.[26]

Here we find once again the characteristics of a return to history and alternative history discussed previously. We must not be fooled, however: the players of these games, as the sites and forums that specialize in them show, are most interested in the richness of the gameplays, the fluidity of movements, the realism of the situations, the multiplicity of options. Nevertheless, these latest games come closest to being fun exercises of historical simulation, a feature that contributes to their reputation and has earned them numerous prizes. The award-winning game *Civilization* has been considered by some to be the most inventive in the history of video games.[27] The advocates of this form of cultural practice use it willingly to demonstrate the learning capabilities of video games (the player is immersed in another world of authentic characters and places, not to mention that he or she must acquire knowledge of cultural, ideological, and geographical factors susceptible to modify the course of history). Professors in the United States have not hesitated to use these resources in class in order to introduce students to world history or stimulate student interest.[28]

It is hardly surprising then that Niall Ferguson has participated in this world of entertainment, considering his ability to adapt to new questions as well as modes of communication. The Harvard historian showed an early interest in video games. He even participated in 2007 in the creation of a game of strategy and historical simulation developed by the company Muzzy Lane, entitled *Making History II: The World of War,* wherein the player takes on the role of the leader of a nation involved in World War II. A number of scenarios build off of key dates (1933, 1936, 1939), which allows the player to intervene in the diverging directions and configurations inspired by history. This game also uses artificial intelligence in order to combine data; some outcomes that would be too improbable were then eliminated in a later version. The game was relatively poorly received at first (there was too much information, the combat was not sufficiently dynamic, and so on). So the developer added a series of modifications, proposing a new version that has drawn the attention of specialists. The game was then nominated for Strategic Game of the Year organized by the site Games Industry in 2010. Beyond strictly financial considerations,[29] the objectives of these projects were clearly stated by Ferguson in a number of articles and interviews. It is first and foremost a form of entertainment aiming to draw on a large public with an interest in history. "Gaming history is not a crass attempt to make the subject relevant to today's kids. Rather it's an attempt to revitalize history with the kind of technology that kids have pioneered. And why not? After all, the Game Boy generation is growing up. And, as they seek a deeper understanding of the world we live in, they may not turn first to the bookshelves."[30] Moreover, the game also contains a pedagogical interest that teaches history in a pleasant way and is adapted to a new public in the Internet age. Ferguson, for example, has stated on many occasions his support for history games for learning purposes:[31] "These games offer invaluable insights as well as entertainment, not least because they remind players that the unfolding of historic events really is more like a game than the linear and predictable narratives offered by traditional historians."[32] Finally, Ferguson suggests that this game, through its simulations, allows one to refine their historical knowledge:

> I was able to put some of my own Second World War counterfactuals to the test, exploring ways in which (for example) a different Axis strategy in 1941–42 might conceivably have won the war. What if Hitler had attacked the USSR before the west? What if the Japanese had attacked the Soviet Union rather than the US? These are the kinds of

> question that a serious game such as Making History—which is based on meticulously accurate historical data and a superb artificial intelligence system—really can illuminate.[33]

One should no doubt not take such claims by the designers and the players literally when they speak of disseminating historical knowledge. These games are designed above all as distractions and are not without their commercial and ideological ambitions, either explicit or not. The conservative vision of Niall Ferguson's world is entirely accepted.[34] As for the strategy games discussed earlier, in spite of the cultural and social correctives that have been added as forms of potential power, they propose a reading of history that is bound to long-term linear outcomes (in spite of the sophistication that is claimed to result from the ramifications), driven by relatively trite mechanisms (science, war, diplomacy, and so on) and marked ultimately by a will to domination. More generally, they propose combinations between stable elements—"nations," "civilizations," and the supposed characteristics they contain—that lead one to neglect the role of exchange, connections, and hybridizations that operate within dynamic social formations over time. In the end, they set aside the question of the plural ways of seeing and thinking about the men and women of the past.

It would nonetheless be an error to push such a critique too far, at least from the perspective of this book. Returning to those who are targeted by the games and the types of knowledge that are diffused by them (these numerical discussions create interesting "closed publics," in which people speak directly and knowledgeably through the common language shared by the given group, but which are also accessible to a wider audience). A number of players, clearly adults, explain on these sites how they have discovered the existence of Aztec societies, the role of Winston Churchill, or the dates of World War I. Beyond the elements of self-display involved in these exchanges, these observations indicate that the information considered minimal by teachers or the "educated" public circulate through these games beyond the usual circles or educational institutions. Moreover, the designers and the users are perfectly aware of the limits of these tools. As Ferguson suggests, "To be sure, even the smartest game can offer you no more than a simplification of the possible futures the world faced in 1941. Yet, like the models used by economists, serious war games are a wonderful aid to thought about complex causal systems."[35] Similarly, teachers that use *Civilization* are very clear that it is only one element among many others in their pedagogy, which is aimed, above all, at stimulating the interest of students who would otherwise be indifferent to the subject at hand. Moreover, these games allow people to take an interest in the question of simulation as a way of ordering information;[36] this also applies to video games, cinema, graphic novels, or books: the political underpinnings are not necessarily adapted as such by the players who are looking for a form of entertainment, just as they are often multidimensional. Hence, for example, *S.T.A.L.K.E.R.: Shadow of Chernobyl* is a uchronic video game that denounces the dangers of nuclear power.[37] And one should not forget, even if these examples have tended to draw from more serious games, there has been a growth in games designed to inform citizens, notably youth, about humanitarian and environmental threats, often with the support of major international organizations (United Nations, World Bank).[38]

There is one last type of game, referred to as ARG, or alternate reality game, which is more closely related to social networks.[39] One of the most famous, *World Without Oil*, was created in 2007. It simulates a grave oil crisis. The players find themselves in a plausible counterfactual scenario. They can increase the realism of the experience by sending videos or producing worlds of sound. Above all, the players must work together to exchange information and find solutions to the situation. The underlying idea (based on principles of collective intelligence) is to find democratic and collective solutions to contemporary problems, which makes it, according to the designers, an experience of "transforming the future."[40] The example indicates the specificities of ARG, which is not necessarily organized through a video game: it takes place in the real world, is collaborative, and the outcome is not defined in advance. Historical uses exist, such as *Tecumseh Lies Here*,[41] designed by a team at the University of Western Ontario,[42] which aims for a "subversive commemoration" of the War of 1812, a conflict that marks the birth of the nation in the narrative of American history but which was also a war of conquest of Native American territories. The game is based on the Shawnee chief Tecumseh, a British ally who fought against the United States and was killed in mysterious circumstance in October 1813. This approach proposes an interesting open-ended dimension.

In summary, the ludic dimension of the counterfactual approach has clearly been mobilized by different industries and practices that have benefited from its hybrid character between history and fiction as well as its immersive potential and its interactive capacity. The most common have certainly made use of the successful approaches presented in the first part of this book, whether it be a simplified conception of history born in the nineteenth century (around great men and great dates), or using one's imagination, such as steampunk. Here we find a vast current of influence that does not pose a problem in itself, but which must be used delicately when it comes to rethinking the ways of pursuing and disseminating historical knowledge. However, we are now better equipped to weigh the risks and the potential value of such fictional forms. Could we not imagine, for example, a video game (not necessarily a war game) based on highly accurate audio and visual reconstruction, with probable outcomes, which would be more in keeping with the frameworks previously discussed, or would explicitly signal its deviation toward more fantastical imaginings? There is no guarantee that such a game would be a success, but it would at least help recall from within these digital worlds that there are several uses of history, and that historical reasoning in itself does not belong to a given media form, which would be considered outdated: it remains active—and essential—whatever the form through which it is delivered.[43] It is also possible to draw inspiration from these experiences to rework the counterfactual narrative itself, when one wants to develop it: its ability to motivate the users facilitates the process of "bringing the past to life." In this case, it would be necessary to work on developing scenarios with game designers to take advantage of some of the literary techniques that are useful for counterfactual historical narratives. In the previous example of the possible futures of 1848 ("the promises of February"), it would be possible to provide a different approach to "leaping into the imaginary" of the democratic and social Republic. After clearly signaling the shift away from historical analysis, one could imagine going further in a more participative writing process, whether it be reproducing associations' visions of the moment, playing with the reader on the political imaginary of the present (for example, imagining a world without financial speculation), or simply creating an imaginative "pause" in the analysis. To be well done, this would require careful writing in a narrative register with clear markers of change. It is true that historical writing has long been successful in immersing its readers in the past in order to elaborate refined analyses. But the way in which these stories mobilize reasoning, imagination, or affects and thus contribute to putting the reader "in the place" of the historical actors deserves attention. Other uses of counterfactual reasoning and past futures can be addressed, especially in a school setting.

A PEDAGOGICAL TOOL?

The question of the pedagogical uses of counterfactual reasoning or unrealized outcomes in history that have not occurred in history has been the subject of an abundant literature consisting of books and articles, as well as blogs written by students, researchers, and teachers who have shared their experiences. Most of these blogs have been in Anglophone countries, in particular the United Kingdom, Australia, and especially the United States.[44] There are signs that there is a process of formalization taking place and a market that remains timid, but which is growing among publishers, colleges, and universities with the increasing draw to ICT[45] and the development of pedagogical excellence.

These works bring together the same body of arguments, articulated in different ways. The first is based on the work of neuroscience or experimental psychology.[46] We have already indicated the problems posed by these scientific methods; the mechanisms they bring to light are worth mention. Neuroscience shows the role of past alternative issues in the work of attitude adjustment or the processing of information.[47] Mobilizing imaginary alternatives would play a vital role in the sorting of experiences and in the process of accumulation and internalization of skills. Experimental psychology, with its emphasis on typologies (between strictly counterfactual, conditional, hypothetical futures, and so on), has shown the correlations between play, simulation, and the use of counterfactuals in learning processes (the counterfactual is in a way an "adult" version of child's play), while the work on childhood psychology suggests that as early as four years old, children known how to conceive of alternatives, to develop coherent causal chains, and perfectly distinguish them from reality (thus without risk of confusion).[48] Here we touch upon fiction as a "shared play of feigning," as developed by Jean-Marie Schaeffer, which appears decisive in the apprehension of the surrounding world.[49] So why not use counterfactual reasoning for learning, especially history?

Painting a somewhat gloomy picture of teaching in the discipline of history, based on various European and American surveys, the second argument is based on two observations:[50] the knowledge of history appears weak beyond what is learned in school; and history teaching, in the form of a story proposed by the teacher and then a regurgitation of raw facts, is perceived as boring. This observation is certainly forced for the purposes of promoting a new method. But the idea is that, in a dual objective of civic engagement and adaptation to the youth of the twenty-first century, this teaching of history must be transformed.

The last argument specifically notes the growing development of computers, the Internet, and new media in the search for information and in the way of shaping it. It mentions the emergence of serious games, simulations designed to improve student awareness, work in teams, and develop learning skills. The practice is growing—well beyond the "humanitarian" version presented above—especially in diplomatic, military (flight simulation), technical, and trade and management professions, this time translating a very instrumental and strategic vision of social life, driven by a search for efficiency.[51]

According to these texts, these three arguments—cognitive, playful, and sociotechnical—have therefore tended to legitimize using counterfactualism since the 1990s. When faced with the potential risks for historical inquiry, professors argue that the mode of reasoning may be less useful for research and more useful for teaching.[52] Indeed, the mobilization of emotions and attention facilitate the acquisition of content and push the student to reproduce and to better control, through games, modes of historical reasoning (search for sources, sensitivity to contexts, attention to ways of seeing, mastery of plural historical causalities, and so forth). The expectations expressed are diverse, however: some authors insist more on the dimension of historical simulation, starting from the examination of military facts or the study of processes (scientific for example), with the risk of proposing a relatively fixed conception of history, reduced to a sum of interactions between entities. Others note that in order to establish probable alternatives, it is necessary to become familiar with the culture and ways of thinking at the time (knowledge, habits, technology, desires) and to establish the mental horizon, the modes of being in the future, or even the "historical consciousness" of the populations under study. This last comprehensive version seems more attractive,[53] but also less easy to implement in the classroom or lecture halls. We have chosen to present here three more practical, class-oriented propositions concerning both the secondary and postsecondary levels. Because of the initial level of knowledge, the types of reasoning envisaged, and the expected proximity of the world of virtual play, teachers believe that these educational experiences should concern students who are twelve and older.

The first example concerns the use of video games in history classes. Some businesses have specialized in this sector, such as Muzzy Lane, mentioned earlier.[54] Aaron Wechtel, a PhD in history and a professor at Washington University, offered an interesting account of his experience using *Civilization III* and *IV*.[55] The author begins by recalling the value of using video games in teaching history: it promotes interaction and exchange between students, invites the use of content as well as modes of historical reasoning, and helps to motivate the most passive students in the classroom, a phenomenon that has been confirmed by a recent study.[56] Lastly, *Civilization* makes it possible to test the nonteleological dimension of history (by exploring other historical trajectories) and encouraging the adoption of a non-Eurocentric perspective (by choosing, for example, non-European civilizations). The value of this analysis is also to point out the weaknesses of these games, even when they are elaborate, in order to make them an integral part of the course and to transmit a richer and more relevant vision of historical processes. Among these flaws are the evolutionist nature of technical, social, and cultural change, the implicit presuppositions of the game that increase the players' chances of winning with a "modern" democratic and capitalist republic, or the rigidity of definitions and "national" traits that are largely a product of the nineteenth century (Americans, for example, are presented as being industrious and expansionist as early as the Neolithic). Several possible course activities are presented. We have highlighted the most reflexive: inviting the student to play a certain number of rounds and then making him or her compare the fate of his or her civilization with the real development. The goal is to raise the student's awareness of the assumptions of these games, but also to improve his or her knowledge of the chosen civilization. It also aims to raise awareness of the contingent nature of history by showing the impact of certain choices—military or social—on historical trajectories. Concretely, the students choose alone or in groups the same civilization, then play until the end of the game. The professor can use this experiment to complement course content, but it can also serve as an optional exercise outside class time. In the process of this activity, students must increase their gaming experience by offering specific readings on the "civilization" or sociohistoric formation chosen, while being advised by the teacher. The final result takes the form of a written or oral presentation that discusses the accuracy of the portrait of the civilization chosen in the game and tries to explain how and why the game and the real historical development have diverged. It then gives rise to a debate between the teacher and the students on these different aspects.

Another proposal is more similar to role-play. It is more commonly used in the classroom, especially in Germany and the United States than in France, for example.[57] It has been the subject of ambitious official projects, such a *Reacting to the Past,* created in 1990 by the historian Mark Carnes, with support by Barnard College (Columbia University) and supported by a group of universities gathered in the Reacting Consortium (set up in 2001). The program offers a series of games in the form of debates, in which students must interpret roles, which they learn using classical texts of a period or books in the history of ideas. During these debates, they can "change the past" (underlined in bold in the presentation). The project includes a book series[58] written by specialists and teachers at Barnard College: *Charles Darwin, the Copley*

Medal, and the Rise of Naturalism, 1862–1864; Confucianism and the Succession Crisis of the Wanli Emperor; Defining a Nation: India on the Eve of Independence, 1945; and *Henry VIII and the Reformation Parliament.* The material consists of a game book for students (which contains the main elements of the historical context, the premises of the debate, and rules), a teaching manual (with a more precise description of roles), and a set of historical texts and sources. The sessions take place in class, in four stages: first, a traditional course, in which the teacher gives the key informational elements of the period, presents the actors and the intellectual issues of the time. Then comes the preparation of the game, where the roles and functions are distributed (the teacher becomes a game master). From there, students need to learn about their roles, research collaboratively, and prepare and write arguments using textbooks. The actual game session takes place in the classroom. It is organized by the students. The teacher largely guides and advises. Once started, the debate continues until the game master brings it to an end. Winners are determined in the next class, when students return to their normal "roles" and discuss collectively. The assessment takes into account both written work and oral presentations. The program's interest lies, moreover, in the explicit mobilization of counterfactual history: according to the "general instructions," this type of reasoning helps stimulate the pleasure of participation (students have an impact on the course of history) while sensitizing the students to issues around historical causality and emphasizing the role of individuals and their agency in history. The students have face-to-face interactions as well, at the same time that their actions are shaped by "great" historical forces, which are learned more thoroughly because they are studied in the process.[59] In doing so, "it seeks to draw students into the past, promote engagement with big ideas, and improve intellectual and academic skills."[60] Winner of the Theodore Hesburgh Award for Pedagogical Innovation in 2004, the game has been supported by numerous foundations (Carnegie Corporation of New York, the National Science Foundation, Teagle Foundation) and has been the subject of numerous reviews.[61] It is currently used in almost three hundred colleges and universities in the United States.[62]

The third possibility explores the opportunities offered by ARG. This has been shown by the experience of the Arcane Gallery of Gadgetry created in 2011 by a team of researchers and teachers with a group of students between thirteen and fifteen years old.[63] The starting point is the year 1877 and the fire of the Patent Office, considered to be the "temple of inventions" (from 1836 to 1932): the fire destroyed 12,000 patents and damaged another 114,000. In the game, an encrypted document escaped the fire and recounts the existence of a mysterious "curiosity cabinet" that was missing. The students are members of a secret philanthropic society, Jenius (referring to the Junto Club that was actually created in 1727 by Benjamin Franklin), and must reconstruct the possible contents of the cabinet. They play the roles of archivist, cryptographer, inventor, and supervisor. For fifteen days, with researchers and the help of codes, maps, and/or research (in libraries, museums, or on the Internet), they reconstruct a coherent account of the facts, a picture of the period and its possibilities, striving to recreate plausible inventions. Compared to other historical ARGs, the Arcane Gallery of Gadgetry's interest is in frankly blurring the lines between fiction and reality and explicitly mobilizing counterfactual reasoning, as noted by the designers in their account of the experience. Immersion in the alternative world imposes a constant critical distance and constant recourse to questions such as "What if . . . ?" The website argues that this mode of reasoning is a powerful tool for learning that develops capacities for investigation in a wide range of disciplines, such as history, science, or business. In more strictly historical terms, it would help to counter arguments in favor of historical inevitability, as well as to clarify the distinction between fact and historical interpretation. "Our goal was to have players view historical events and artifacts as possibility spaces that needed to be actively interpreted and reconstructed, not inevitabilities that could simply be memorized and retold."[64] This review also proposes a discussion on ways to construct a relevant pedagogical counterfactual. Three elements are mentioned. One must first find a good historical object, which does not directly contradict historical knowledge, one of those missing pieces that is marked by constant uncertainty—such as a fire whose causes remain undetermined and in which patented inventions have disappeared. Next, it is necessary to clearly indicate the divergence between fact and fiction. Such precautions are all the more important since the uchronic space is generally "fed" by a wiki, a blog, and videos and therefore gains in credibility. In the 2011 experiment, teachers decided to let students pursue such a project, but the distinction was indicated by a series of markers: normal font for historical facts and italics for those that were invented, using classic sites on the Internet for the former and wiki for the latter; the creation of tables on either side of a line presented the historical elements and the divergent creations. The principle of ARG is indeed "TINAG" (this is not a game), and the very "realistic" character of the game can cause discomfort for some students (about 20 percent of them, according to the answers in a retrospective questionnaire). It is therefore appropriate to end with a debate designed to make students think together about the facts, the lies, the alterations, and the means of alteration in history. The experiment was not evaluated, however: the professors wanted above all to encourage the mobilization of creative and critical thought and to promote collaborative work.

The value of these three examples is what they offer in terms of concrete teaching situations. All note the participants' intellectual and emotional commitment, as well as the effectiveness of an investment-based approach. References to being a "detective" are common, which is not without interest for the type of knowledge required by historians. In a sense, it is a question of making the historian explore a playful place adapted to the level of the student. Finally, recourse to these activities is never disconnected from the content of the course. It serves to support it, to rewrite causality into history, and is always subject to discussion. This contrasting story allows the teacher to make his or her students reflect on the relationships between historical knowledge, with its unknowns on the one hand and inventions or lies on the other. In so doing, it emphasizes the importance of seeking accurate information, and, in counterpoint, the possibility, perhaps enhanced by new tools of communication, of deliberate or involuntary manipulation of discourses and facts.

In class it is possible to simply lead a counterfactual reflection without subjecting oneself to such elaborate devices (it should be noted in passing that they have a cost in terms of investment, time, and money[65]). This more "flexible" pedagogical practice has long been marginalized within stricter procedures of academic evaluation. According to the historian Bernard Eric Jensen, it was so badly perceived within Danish universities in the 1960s that the teacher who used it was discredited. And in the 1980s, the board of examiners refused to validate a course on counterfactual history proposed by Alexander Demandt.[66] It still plays a very modest role in extracurricular programs or the editions of textbooks. A "Learning Toolbox" (including a resource guide, a CD-ROM, twenty-two biographical dossiers) produced by the Library and Archives of Canada, on the Canadian prime ministers,[67] which may be adapted to school programs for students between fourteen and eighteen, contains, for example, a chapter on counterfactualism. The objectives are clearly stated:

> In this exercise, the student will
> — examine an event in Canadian history in which one or multiple Prime Ministers participated;
> — measure the importance of the factors that determined the outcomes of the event;

— analyze the repercussions of counterfactual scenarios;
— explain what the student has learned through a text written for an anthology of fiction.

This pedagogical practice is also the subject of a collection of American university textbooks entitled *Turning Points: Actual and Alternate Histories,* launched in 2005 by ABC Clio and edited by Rodney P. Carlisle, emeritus professor of history at Rutgers University and specialist in political and military history. Each textbook focuses on a specific period of American history (from prehistory to first contact, the Civil War era, the 1960s and 1970s, and so on). The course sequences are centered on a particular moment in American history and are organized along the same model: defining a turning point, presenting the real history, then the counterfactual history presented in gray, then a series of questions to which students must respond; for example, in the chapter on Nixon's "war against poverty": "Is poverty inevitable in a capitalist society like the United States?"[68] This is followed by a complete bibliography. It remains to be seen how widely these works are being used in university classrooms.

That said, this form of reasoning is no doubt frequently used in offhand ways in the classroom, in particular among students. Obviously, more confidential and equally well-prepared uses exist. We conducted an experiment in 2009, for example, that was much less elaborate than those just presented, as part of a course with high school seniors on World War I. Student interest and flexibility in their schedules made this experience possible over the course of fifteen hours during the methodology section of the class. The classical starting point was the assassination of Archduke Franz Ferdinand in Sarajevo on June 28, 1914. The course then developed in three stages. After an introductory course on World War I, the first hour was dedicated to the event itself. We discussed the reasons for the archduke's visit to Sarajevo, the particular context in the Balkans, the strained relations between Austria, the Ottoman Empire, and Serbia, the existence of the associations of the Black Hand and Young Bosnia. We also discussed the unfolding of the attack itself: a first bomb that exploded around 10 a.m., without success, before Gavrilo Princip was presented with an unexpected opportunity an hour later, in front of the Latin Bridge. This first step made it possible to quickly show the historical depth that can be hidden behind a canonical date, to present the Austro-Hungarian Empire, which is generally not very well-known, and to point to the imperial and global dimension of this triggering of the war in western Europe. Finally, it allowed us to underscore the fact that the assassination could have failed. Princip's unpreparedness is notorious, and the assassination is generally described as the consequence of a series of unexpected coincidences. What if Princip had gone to eat his sandwich somewhere else? And what if Franz Ferdinand had protected himself after the first bomb attack, and so on.[69] The question therefore exists: If Franz Ferdinand had not been assassinated, what would have happened?

The second hour was spent preparing the discussion on the issues of divergence. The class of thirty students was divided into two groups: one had to show that the war would still have occurred, the other that the war would not have occurred, and everyone had to consider the possible consequences of their outcome. Roles were distributed within each group: a team leader, information collector (at the school library or on the Internet), a scribe who prepared the arguments, and a speaker who led the debate. Each group had fifteen days to prepare. Papers were distributed to guide the preparation of the arguments (micro and macro elements, diplomatic, social, economic, cultural) as well as two texts (the conclusion from Christophe Charle, *The Crisis of Imperial Societies,* and an excerpt from Stéphane Audoin-Rouzeau on the culture of war and its anticipation before 1914). The texts and the arguments could be discussed with the teacher at the end of class or during the breaks.

Then came the debate, refereed by the teacher. One of the groups, drawn by lot, began (in this case the group "The war would not have taken place"), and the other responded by trying to adapt and articulate their arguments. At the end of the discussion, there was no winner. The next hour, the arguments were summarized and taken up as a group on the board.

Option: "The War Would Not Have Taken Place"

— Following the failure of the attack, the protection of Franz Ferdinand was reinforced, and the Austrians became more careful. There was never another opportunity of this kind.
— The system of alliances that united the nation-states and empires was as much a driving force toward conflict as a source of prevention. Peace conferences were also frequent during this period. There were precedents that had created resolutions (Berlin, Morocco, and so on). Moreover, the system of international law, which had been reorganized in the 1860s, did a good job of integrating the "civilized" European powers (and excluded the others, in particular the countries that had been colonized).

— The national trajectories were not entirely focused on the conflict. The famous debates in the French legislature on a three-year military service and the income tax in the summer of 1914 attest to this. While nationalism and xenophobia had a strong presence in European societies, each country was not entirely isolated from the other. Moreover, they had very different situations: the strength of the workers' movements across all European countries, tensions between parliamentary and authoritarian government in Germany, and so on. The "social configurations" (Christophe Charle) established fields of power with undetermined outcomes. It is possible that war would not have happened.
— Continuations: this does not mean that the tensions would have come to an end. There is no doubt that Balkan and colonial lands would have continued to serve as sites of confrontation (perhaps favoring the resistance movements of the colonized), while the United States and Germany were still asserting their position within industrial and commercial markets. What followed was therefore hardly an absolute ideal, but the world had changed (followed by a few clearly imagined forays into this "other" world in the form of a game).

Option: "The War Would Have Taken Place"

— The arguments appear to be more straightforward: once the mechanism was in place, any event would have set it off and led to the same outcome.
— Even if Franz Ferdinand was not killed, any attempt by nonnational conspirators or colonial conflict would have unleashed the same process.
— The alliance system mobilized the whole range of actors and their empires.
— The logic of economic competition favored the triggering of the conflict.
— In spite of the elements discussed in the previous option, nationalism was a powerful structural social force. The arguments for exchange did not work, precisely because it was the national identities that were the fruit of the circulations that paradoxically increased the sense of difference and the desire for opposition.

— The role of memories of previous conflicts remained strong; the weight of wartime expectations generated by conflicts of the 1900s (including the Russo-Japanese War, the subject of Olivier Cosson's thesis[70]) must not be neglected, nor the theme of the "war cultures" that affected societies of the period. In short, sooner or later the conflict would have taken place on a European and global scale.

— Continuations: since the trigger did not occur in Serbia, it did not primarily concern Austria-Hungary, and therefore the empire intervened at a different moment and the domino effect was not exactly the same, nor the forms of justification of the conflict, nor even perhaps the winners (followed by a few fantastical forays into this "other" world in the form of a game).

The last course consisted of feedback based on two questions. The first concerned methods of the historical discipline: the search for sources, the establishment of facts and interpretations, the question of potentialities in history, the examination of the moment of sliding toward invention, but also a debate on learning processes in a classroom setting. The second sought to determine whether the two options were absolutely irreconcilable. This allowed us to show how the event in Sarajevo triggered a series of dynamics that happened but were not necessary (*possibles*), that appeared inevitable after the fact. The students then made a connection, for example, to the events of September 11.

As a result of this example, it was possible to improve their knowledge of World War I, to increase the students' awareness of the relationship between structures and events, and to initiate an introduction to the notion of the event and its ability to rearrange situations after the fact. The scenario made it easier to capture these mechanisms, sometimes presented as overly complex, and then these notions could be mobilized later throughout the year.

Of course, in reality, the experience was not quite as fluid as it has been presented here. There was more uncertainty, which regularly risked falling outside the broadly defined field of teaching history. In our view, what was essential in this exercise was to prepare the framework and its ambitions, but also to be able to adapt them according to a given situation. In the previous year, we had watched in the final class Peter Watkins's *The War Game,* which imagines in 1965 a Russian nuclear attack on the United Kingdom, based on archival documents from other bombings. As a politically motivated director, Watkins sought to denounce the military practices that were used by Western countries during World War II and the reassuring speeches of the British government on its capacities to protect citizens in such cases. The realism and verisimilitude of the film disturbed the students, to the point that it was necessary to remind them of the elements in the previous course on the Cold War. It was necessary to adjust the sequence by emphasizing not so much Watkins's critical ambitions, but rather the question of lies, the means of historical falsification and its risks, in order to reestablish a clear distinction between facts and falsehoods in their minds. It is clearly necessary to adapt the purpose of the exercise to its organization. When all goes well, the teacher may discuss at the end of the experiment the question of contingency, configurations, and what is possible in history. If things become less clear, it is necessary to move to a discussion of truth in history and the risks of manipulating the past. The fine line between them has already been discussed in the previous chapter. But in both cases, the pedagogical aims may be accomplished.

This approach also seems to be in keeping with analyses and research proposals over the last twenty years in pedagogy. Summing up a synthetic paper published in 2008,[71] a number of these works point to three elements: first, the history course is a special course that transmits knowledge validated by research, but which is also subject to social demands and plays a clear role in defining citizenship as well as modes of "self-recognition." Furthermore, the verbal aspect of the course tends to rely upon the teacher's spoken word, as dialogue with the class tends to take place in pedagogical "micro-cycles" (question, response, evaluation, formalization, additions).[72] Historical reasoning itself is less commonly mobilized, which does not necessarily bother the students. The passive aspect of knowledge acquisition is considered by them to be a part of this type of course.[73] Lastly, studies that have investigated how "history is conceived" have found that students always mix elements of "natural" reasoning ("naïve" psychology and sociology, comparisons with personal elements drawn from the school setting, family or shared social conceptions, simple narrative frameworks, prevailing social values, spontaneous theories, and so forth) with forms of "scholarly" historical reasoning (criticism of sources, controlled comparison, generalizations, insertion into plural temporalities, hierarchy of causation, mobilization of the modes of narration, and so on). Above all, the phenomenon does not respond to a linear evolution going from the first type of reasoning to the second, between the kindergarten and the postsecondary, but it is observed throughout the learning cycle, even during the more advanced phases, and probably still in many adults (and researchers).[74] Analogy and anachronism are, in fact, constantly mobilized: for example, to understand the concept "absolute monarchy," students begin by associating it with a king—Louis XIV—and with a strong image (the Sun King). Later, in an effort to grasp the content of this idea, they appeal to the idea of dictatorship—embodied by Hitler and Nazi Germany—and democracy—from France or another country today. Looking back farther in time to clarify the institutional mechanisms involved, they pursue a "natural" comparison with other types of monarchy—English parliamentary monarchy from a relatively static point of view, and so on. The value of counterfactual reasoning and possible futures in such a context, when used in a controlled manner, is quite clear. Because it draws at the same time on common sense (Cleopatra's nose, teleology, "great men," good and bad) and historical reasoning (comparison, causality, awareness of temporalities, processes), it can be a real pathway from one to the other, creating a laboratory for more advanced learning. In addition, since it is a matter of following a line of reasoning, it is possible to discuss it and adjust it to each of its stages. Finally, it is based on the game, which avoids the boredom of exercises that are too elaborate and have the ability to mobilize students at very different levels. The role of the teacher here remains essential, as a provider of knowledge but also as a companion in intellectual achievement. Such a proposal is, of course, only one possibility among many, but it remains interesting in light of the observations discussed earlier.

Thus, through its immersive, participative, affective, and cognitive elements, the approach seems to contain numerous pedagogical virtues. It even seems possible to reconcile them with the scientific dimension of the discipline. This obviously depends on how it is used. To be relevant, one must maintain a deep awareness of the stakes that are involved, effectively prepare the exercises, tie them into the standard lessons, and be willing to take certain risks. At times, these interactive practices may appear to work at cross-purposes to the traditional modes of learning. However, these counterfactual techniques recall and illustrate the fact that historical reasoning may be taught in a variety of ways. Pleasure and play also constitute quite serious entry points into modes of historical analysis and critical thinking.

CHAPTER 12

Writing History Together

A REFLEXIVE AND PARTICIPATIVE HISTORICAL ESSAY (11/11/11, GRENOBLE, FRANCE)

> Look, look! The play has to be made. [*To the Director:*] But if you wish, and your actors are willing, we can soon work it out among ourselves.
>
> —Luigi Pirandello[1]

> "No! Not such tones! But let us strike up something more agreeable and more joyful!"—You would like to have it so, my impatient friends? Well! Who would not willingly accede to your wishes? My bagpipe is waiting, and voice also—it may sound a little hoarse; take it as it is! don't forget we are in the mountains!
>
> —Friedrich Nietzsche[2]

There are obviously a plethora of techniques to be invented. Admittedly, among those classroom activities discussed in the previous chapter, even the participants who were directly involved remained relatively "passive." Would it not be possible, then, to pursue a more direct and interactive form of exchange? After all, in this realm between "facts," "fiction," and the "possible," the researcher does not necessarily have to be looking down "from above." In this case, it is a question of establishing a more balanced relationship with the public, without denying the specific knowledge that such a public brings with it. By using such an approach, the counterfactual becomes a space for sharing considerations, understanding, and emotions and for developing a greater mastery of the issues involved in historical reasoning and its impact. It is therefore possible to talk together about knowledge, fantasies, accepted ideas, personal and family histories, political positions, beliefs, or utopias and how they relate to history. Risks and benefits go hand in hand: the historian's word becomes more fragile, but it is also more welcoming and open.

It was precisely such an experience that we wanted to explore in Grenoble, France, in 2011. Thanks to an invitation by Jeanne Moisand, Nicolas Delalande, Ivan Jablonka, and Florent Guénard, we were able to lead a collective discussion in the context of the forum "Remaking Society" on November 11–12, organized by the Republic of Ideas, a think tank based at the College de France. We prepared two turning points for our counterfactual narratives in advance, one within a long-term socioeconomic process (the absence of the Atlantic slave trade), and the other a specific event (a successful escape by the French king Louis XVI during the French Revolution in 1791). A PowerPoint presentation, with different slides projected on a large screen, was prepared to complement the discussion and present the problem at hand. It was based on historical work and social science research, as indicated in a bibliography at the end of each slide series. The purpose was to provide the participants with insights, develop their own alternative stories, and put them in discussion with other participants and ourselves. The question of the link between these past alternatives and the debate on the present was clearly posed by the theme of the forum. We have reproduced the exchanges here, leaving aside the initial presentation of the approach, as explained in the previous chapters, and adapting it, when necessary, to written form. Unfortunately, the images and the slides have not been conserved.[3]

The scene took place at the Cultural Center in Grenoble on Friday, November 11, from 2:30 to 4:00 p.m. The room, which contained about sixty seats, was set up as a square designed to facilitate interactions. Women and men of all ages sat in the orange chairs facing the screen. And we, "the authors" faced the public. The discussion was introduced by Jeanne Moisand. We then presented the approach, its risks, and the stakes involved.

CASE 1: A WORLD WITHOUT THE ATLANTIC SLAVE TRADE

THE AUTHORS

Why revisit the history of the Atlantic slave trade and slavery more broadly? First because the slave trade and slavery constitute a central part of modern history. In the Americas and the West Indies, planters needed a growing labor force for working the particularly labor-intensive crops, such as sugarcane, tobacco, and cotton, and because the indigenous peoples—the Native Americans—were insufficient in numbers. Between the seventeenth and the nineteenth centuries, an estimated 12–15 million Africans were deported as part of the Atlantic trade. Other forms of slave trade existed, of course, an intra-African slave trade involving 10–15 million captives) and the Eastern slave trade (6–17 million). However, the Atlantic slave trade had an incommensurable historical impact when compared to the others. The conquest of the Americas marked a decisive break with the global equilibrium, with the brutal collapse of Native American populations due to the microbial shock provoked by contact with Europeans and, on the other hand, the Atlantic slave trade, which permanently weakened the African continent. This trafficking induced a demographic reconfiguration of a large part of the planet, which has affected not only Africa and the Americas, but also, in the wake of abolition, indentured servitude, and free migration, the Indian Ocean, Southeast Asia, and Oceania. We also propose to revisit this history because it has relevance to our present. Slavery and trafficking are still taking place: it is estimated that today there are about 27 million people subjected to traditional forms of slavery, not to mention the 250–300 million enslaved children. Moreover, the legacy and the memory of slavery are still very present in the media and political discourse, especially in the Caribbean. For example, in 2005, Hurricane Katrina in New Orleans brought the issue of the slave trade and slavery forward once again in the United States. And France has witnessed the deeper long-term impact of its slave past in the political debates around the riots and the social movements in February 2009 in Guadeloupe. You can see on the screen a quote from the leader of the LKP[4] union, Élie Domota, in 2009: "We are not going to let a bunch of *békés* recreate slavery."

Finally, the issue of trafficking and slavery, since the 1980s, has come to the fore in Europe, the United States, and Africa in the reparation campaigns for damages suffered by slaves and their descendants. The organizers of these reparations campaigns—we will return to this point—have mobilized counterfactual arguments. So we would like to begin by posing an initial question:

Without the Atlantic Slave Trade, Would Africa Have Been More Developed?

THE AUTHORS
A vast question, that you undoubtedly have a few ideas about.

A WOMAN, sitting on the right
So, I'm just throwing out a few hypotheses, what I do know, is that for the ancient period, we generally say that slavery slowed economic development. In

any case, there are a number of theories that make this argument. We could try to adopt the same type of approach for America and consider that slavery basically delayed economic development because it provided cheap labor. Whereas, if this cheap labor had not been available, it would have made it possible to develop industry or other economic forms more rapidly with higher technical skills and with less manpower. So, one might develop a logic along these lines. It's not absurd. *(The organizers remind the audience that the question is focusing on Africa.)* Oh! I'm sorry, we are talking about Africa. In that case, I don't have anything to say. *(The speaker laughs.)* I misread the question. I was a bad student!

THE AUTHORS

This is an interesting remark because it is an argument that has been put forward to explain the absence of an industrial revolution in India. It is argued that India, in the eighteenth century, experienced a level of development that was comparable to Europe's, which is true, and then that India did not experience an industrial revolution in part because labor was so cheap, which prevented mechanization.

A SECOND WOMAN, *raises her hand*

A simple hypothesis—that is, a positive hypothesis—could be that the presence of a different population, through colonization, from Europe, may not have led to development, but may have opened the horizons of African populations, horizons that would not have existed without these new elements of contact in the form of colonization by drawing on their resources, of course, but also confronting them with the realities and values of another civilization.

THE AUTHORS

So your hypothesis is the opposite: without trafficking, Africa would have grown less. From a strictly economic point of view, there is a consensus among historians that trafficking was not a factor of economic development. The slave trade was at the origins of the development of colonial economies, based on the monoculture of cane and/or cotton and exports, which did not promote local economic development.

THE SECOND WOMAN

Very good! Then you have your answer!

THE AUTHORS

Not yet! We are simply responding to your hypothesis.

A MAN, on the left stands up

The question turns around the removal of African populations through the Atlantic slave trade. The question has been posed in the following way: If this removal had not taken place, how would the history of the African continent been different? This begs the question: Does development have a direct relationship to demography, or in any case, the population? In a very modest way, we might ask ourselves: Did a certain number of opportunities, of minds, forms of know-how, talents, which were removed from the African population through trafficking, not have an impact on cultural development?—because I think that this is perhaps where the drivers of development originate, before the actual economy itself. One might then make the assumption that a certain number of talents were sorely missing on the African continent, because they were obviously transported elsewhere, even decimated. Especially since unfortunately it is not simply a question of transport but also elimination through the very conditions of the slave trade. In this light, and I am going to make a bold assumption, but maybe not too bold. During the war of 1914, the disappearance of potential writers, researchers, captains of industry who were between eighteen or twenty and thirty years old between 1914 and 1918 could have had an impact on the cultural and economic development of Europe after the war of 1914. In other words, the question of demography, of the number of people, is not necessarily correlated to the quality of development. Having said this, I would like to hear what you think.

THE AUTHORS

Thank you very much for this response. We are largely in agreement with you. The first part of your analysis clearly picks up on a study by a political scientist Ronald Walters

(A quotation appears on the screen.)

He wrote:

> What is missing in Africa and the Diaspora is that which was taken away from Africans through the centuries of oppression. . . . The consequence of Racism, both in the Americas and in Europe, as Pierre Jalée[5] said, placed Africans "outside of history" and prevented them from amassing the kind of resources that would have made it possible for them to become captains of industry, builders of national and international institutions, masters of their own individual destiny on a par with other peoples. In short, what was taken away was the ability

> to create new personal situations, even new worlds consistent with their imaginations, something which cannot be quantified.[6]

Deprived of "new worlds": this is the idea you were talking about, and at the same time we agree with you that basically it is difficult to identify a causal relationship between demography and development. Most researchers today would say it is difficult, if not impossible, to answer this question. There is no reason to believe that, in the absence of trafficking, the increase in the population would have had positive effects on economic development. But there is nothing to prevent us from arguing that, in view of the African economic systems and the ecological fragility of certain regions of Africa at that time, these regions would have been unable to withstand such demographic pressure: under these conditions, there might have been cycles of crises of excess mortality. In fact, the crux of the problem lies in the lack of reliable data. Specialists do not have precise information on the demographic evolution of the African continent before the arrival of Europeans and during the slave trade. In particular, accurate data on the pace of population growth are lacking. In these circumstances, it is very difficult to give a definite answer to the question.

A THIRD WOMAN

This ties in to what you said previously. I am naïvely wondering: Could they [Africans] have not invented another model if they had been allowed to do so? Because in the end we imposed our system and they were brought into it. And so what is happening now is that they are trying to catch up with our model and enter our system, which has become global. So if we had not intervened, would they not have found other solutions and another model for the African continent?

THE AUTHORS

Yes, this is certainly a possibility. Such a counterfactual could, for example, push us to make the argument: without trafficking and slavery, there would not have been capitalism. However, we know that many of these African societies were monetized, like the indigenous societies of present-day Nigeria, with their famous cowries. In some cases, these companies were part of very dynamic commercial circuits, which would call into question the idea of a totally alternative model. There are, of course, very different indigenous economic models, but not necessarily ones that are radically foreign to European economic logics.

A SECOND MAN

Like many of us here, I do not know much about this subject. However, I am surprised to see that the trafficking is considered here to be a simple extraction of people. My reaction would be to say: We probably don't know what would have happened if there had been a very different demography. On the other hand, I imagine that the development would have been completely different: We annihilated initiative and responsibility and that has left its mark on centuries, so would Africa have been more and better developed? The next question is: What development? The same or some other form? Certainly there would have been some form of responsible development and not one that was imposed from the outside with the whole process of introducing currencies, useless wealth over there. So at some level it seems to me that there would have been a development that would surprise us today and that might have been very different from one country to another, but would have been responsible and positive.

A THIRD MAN

I would just like to add a historical variable that is missing in this debate, which is the other Arab-Islamic slave trade that also removed millions of Africans and sent them toward the Maghreb, and even farther east throughout the Arab-Islamic world. What new types of relations between the Western powers and the Arab-Islamic world could have arisen from a change of attitude of the Western powers with regard to the slave trade, if Africa had developed without this massive confiscation? How could Western powers have favored or disfavored processes of local development? And what would the effects have been on the interactions with the Arab-Islamic world, which, to my knowledge, removed several million Africans and sent them toward the Maghreb and farther east than the Maghreb? What would the end of the European slave trade have changed in the relationships between empires and development of Africa itself?

THE AUTHORS

We do not have a response to your questions, but it is important to discuss other forms of slave trade, the intra-African slave trade, knowledge of which is indispensable for analyzing the stakes for African history across the three to four centuries. There were forms of traditional slavery in Africa before the intrusion of Europeans. In reality, the progressive end of the Atlantic slave trade, with its abolition in 1807 and then of slavery more generally in Britain in 1833 and then in 1848 in the French Empire, paradoxically increased slavery in Africa since British and French merchants often took individuals to become slaves and captives who had already been slaves on the spot in Africa and there was no longer anywhere for them to be sold. Thus, in 1885, on the eve of the scramble for Africa, there were societies in West Africa wherein more than a quarter of the population were slaves. The indigenous forms of slavery were an endogenous factor that developed in relation to two other treaties, since the demands for captives aroused by the Atlantic and Arab-Islamic slave trades intensified intra-African trafficking. Without the Atlantic and the Eastern slave trade, slavery would never have developed to such an extent in Africa; it would have been mere residual slavery, but it would have been modest compared to the other parts of the world. During the same period, there were slaves in China, but they were a small minority. The same was true on the European continent.

A FOURTH MAN

I had another line of reasoning. If one looks forward, I wonder if the claims in the 1960s on human rights in the United States would have been possible if there had not been a slave trade. And might this not somehow serve as an example for Africans? That is to say, somewhere, a social movement making new claims with populations that originally came from African countries at a given moment allowed for the advance of the rights of man.

THE AUTHORS

Yes, but maybe not exactly in those terms. It is interesting to note that many historians have specifically asked this question: Without the slave trade and slavery, would US democracy have existed? Several researchers have argued that the slave trade and slavery in the United States helped unify whites against well-identified subalterns, that is Native Americans and black slaves. The concept of liberty by white Americans was coined in the context of slavery. Emmanuel Todd takes up this idea in his book *After the Empire* [*Après l'empire*] where he explains that US democracy was an "ethnic democracy," the democratic ethos basing itself initially on race. It is a stimulating counterfactual because if we develop this line of reasoning, this means that without the slave trade and slavery there would have been no Revolutionary War, because the whites would not have been able to gather among themselves to break off from the British; the United States would have remained a dominion like Canada; nor would there have been a Civil War, and so on. So there is, of course, a very strong link between slavery and politics in the United States.

A FOURTH WOMAN, *on the left*

I am not very familiar with the history, but I'm wondering about your comment that the Atlantic slave trade helped the development of trade and the market for slaves to develop in Africa. In fact, Africans were confronted with a horrible system. The so-called civilized world was treating them as if they were only second- or third-class individuals, and at the same time the Europeans brought with them the worst humanity had to offer. So the African leaders developed this model, the worst of what Europe and the Americas had to offer. My hypothesis is that this model followed the Africans who lived for centuries under forms of domination that continue to divide blacks and whites.

THE AUTHORS

Very quickly, moving on to the second question. There is no overarching answer to the complex questions you are asking. It is difficult to generalize. Indeed, the African continent is characterized by very different situations. For example, one of the first countries in the world to abolish the death penalty was the kingdom of Sotho in the middle of the nineteenth century, in what is now Lesotho in southern Africa. We could provide a whole range of examples.

A FIFTH MAN

What was the demographic evolution of Africa during the slave trade?

THE AUTHORS

Historians have different views on this subject. If we look at the eighteenth century, Patrick Manning, a historian of forced migration in Africa, considers that the African population was stagnating, that is to say that its development stopped at around 50 million; another historian, Dennis Cordell, says that the population of Africa was growing from about 70 to 85 million. That is, despite the trafficking, there was actually positive population growth. Why? Because of the recovery strategies that were put into place, including polygamy, which may have been a strategy for demographic recovery in situations of trafficking. That is, the slave trade removes males, and when there are fewer males and many females, polygamy can be a response to the gender disequilibrium.

Perhaps we can now address the second question:

Without the Atlantic Slave Trade, Would Europe and the United States Have Been Less Developed?

A FIRST MAN

I am not at all sure that there is a clear link between slavery and growing cotton. To draw a parallel, as you were talking about the recovery strategies, which seem very convincing to me, I was thinking in line with the discussion that has just taken place that the removal of men in Africa may have had less impact than we imagine. Difficult, dramatic, or limiting situations can lead to the search for solutions that would not have existed if such constraints did not exist. The historians in the room can confirm this, but I think I remember from my history classes long ago that if there had not been a continental blockade under the Napoleonic Empire, we would not have attempted—I am making a connection with sugar—solutions of substitution to acquire sugar, and Chaptal would not have invented the chemistry around the beet that led to the substitution of sugar from beets instead of cane sugar. This is a clear example of the situations that lead no doubt to the creation of solutions that would not have emerged otherwise. Or at least this is the hypothesis I am proposing.

A FIFTH WOMAN

I would now like to shift the problematic a little bit. Within the process of the slave trade, there are social actors, social groups who benefit, while others are victims of this trade, and I think that if we look at this from this perspective, we can provide more nuanced responses to these questions and pose the question differently. Who benefited from the slave trade in Europe and the United States? Who were the groups that benefited from the slave trade? The traders, of course, and the agricultural economy, notably the large plantations. Perhaps if these groups had not developed through the slave trade, other social groups could have developed. We can pursue a similar reasoning for Africa, where there are African populations who have been subject to trafficking. If we look at this from the point of view of social groups that are affected by the phenomena, we can provide nuanced answers to this type of problem. This my hypothesis anyway.

THE AUTHORS

Yes, indeed, one of the responses to this question is none other than that of Karl Marx as well as Keynes.

(Quotations appear on the screen.)

This is the thesis that trafficking and slavery are at the origin of the development of Europe and the United States, even at the origin of the industrial revolution. This hypothesis was updated in 1944 by the great Trinidadian historian Eric Williams, in a book entitled *Capitalism and Slavery.* He explains that the capital accumulated through the slave trade allowed for the financing of the industrial revolution. This thesis is very intellectually stimulating: it pinpoints the importance of colonization in economic development at a time when most historians thought that the development of Europe was solely due to endogenous factors. But, for the last thirty years, historians have challenged this interpretation by putting forward the arguments that you just presented. They have demonstrated that the trading economy had in fact played a very important role for the specific development of certain regions and towns: Nantes in France, and Bristol, Liverpool, and London in Great Britain, as you can see on the map.

(A map appears on the screen.)

We need to avoid generalizations on the scale of an entire country. It cannot be said, for example, that the slave trade was at the origin of the Industrial Revolution, based on the pretext that capital accumulated through the slave trade and slavery played a decisive role in certain sectors of the economy, in navy shipyards, the insurance industry, in the banking sector. Economic historians do not consider these assets to be a condition sine qua non for the emergence of the industrial revolution.

A SIXTH WOMAN

I would like to return to the first question. You said there was a recovery strategy that probably led to polygamy in Africa. And so, in light of this hypothesis or this observation, it seems to me that the African continent would have developed better, since women, instead of becoming to some extent slaves themselves by being forced to play the role of "machines of reproduction," might have stepped in and taken over African development. We are currently seeing that there are many development operations that are pursued by women. It is important to note that today there is extensive slavery of women, especially in the form of prostitution, which introduces a bias into the economy. So here is a hypothesis: If there had not been this massive displacement of males, perhaps the fate of Africa would have been more quickly guided by women.

A YOUNG WOMAN, in the second row, on the right, raising her hand

I would have thought that, above all, this would have slowed the development of the United States. The abundance of easy labor may have helped with the crops, but I think other solutions would have been found anyway. It would have probably been more expensive, more complicated to manage, and it might have been slower.

THE AUTHORS
When you speak of other solutions, what are thinking of specifically?

THE YOUNG WOMAN
I don't know. Perhaps more European immigration toward America, people who wouldn't have been slaves.

THE AUTHORS
What type of European immigrants could have done the work?

THE YOUNG WOMAN
I don't know, the Irish?

THE AUTHORS
Yes! The Irish could have replaced the black slaves. Because the Irish, from the sixteenth century to the eighteenth century, were considered by the British to be the "blacks" of Europe. They were considered "uncivilized" because they were Catholic, and therefore considered to be below Hindus and Muslims by the British, and so the Irish could have done the trick. This is at once counterfactual and factual. Since this also actually took place (*amazement and laughter in the room*). In the British West Indies, in Montserrat in the seventeenth century, 70 percent of the slaves were Irish. As in Barbados, the Irish were ubiquitous and they then mixed with black populations. They originally had the status of slaves. This began in the seventeenth century with Charles I and then James II—the Irish political prisoners were deported as slaves. Children and women, too. These were concomitant phenomena: England colonized Ireland at the same time that it colonized the Americas. At the end of the seventeenth century, an Irish slave cost (£5 sterling) ten times less than an African slave (£50 sterling). We do not find in this case the hierarchies that we expect; the traditional racial framework does not hold.

THE YOUNG WOMAN
In that case, since there were not as many Irish as there were Africans—I don't know, I'm just throwing this out there—this [the development] could have been less rapid. After all, there were fewer people to deport to the United States or else there would have been nothing left of Ireland (*laughter in the room*).

THE AUTHORS

We should signal that the transportation was much less costly. Precise studies have been done by historians. We have perhaps given the impression here that we are playfully entertaining wild questions, but researchers have worked very hard on questions like these. And the deportation of the Irish was cheaper than the African slave trade.

A MAN, in the next row over

I am wondering, beyond the problems of wealth, there is a moral issue. Indeed, there were people who became rich through slavery. There have obviously been economic benefits, and many people have benefited from them. But I imagine that most of the profits went to a small group. A small group that became influential and agreed to base their wealth and power on slavery. So at the level of social morality, just offhand, we could say that it prevented the emancipation of society as a whole. It ties in a little bit with what you were saying earlier: Has this been a good or a bad thing for human rights? But the fact that we initially accepted enrichment through barbarism, necessarily at the level of a given society, became a skeleton in the closet.

THE AUTHORS

We would tend to agree with you, but historians who have studied this question in detail tend to think the opposite. Indirectly, slavery would seem to have favored the emergence of American democracy as it exists today. If we read the eloquent quotation from the renowned black intellectual and professor of literature Gerald L. Early, he presents the paradox of slavery as an extremely violent experience that allowed the United States to be a great democratic and even "moral" power.

(A quotation appears on the screen, which presents Early's argument that slavery was a catastrophe for the United States and far worse for the people who lived through it. But for a whole set of reasons, the quotation suggests, the country has benefited from this great tragedy. Its moral strength and capacity to define itself as a democracy and as an inclusive society were dependent on overcoming this human calamity. It has made the country more human, he claims.)[7]

One could develop a similar analysis for British liberal democracy. What would British civil society, the British public sphere, have been or be without trafficking and slavery? It would be very different, because it was especially during the abolitionist struggle, starting in the eighteenth century and the beginning in the nineteenth century, that a civil society was created and developed through associations and petitions: hundreds of thousands at the end of the eighteenth century and then millions of people at the beginning of the nineteenth century signed petitions against the slave trade and then against slavery. Those living in the United Kingdom invented the boycott by refusing to buy Caribbean sugar, which was preferred to that of India, but supposedly produced under conditions less degrading to the dignity of workers. Some researchers, therefore, have not hesitated to make the link between trafficking as a long-term phenomenon and the emergence of new forms of political practice.

ANOTHER WOMAN

In this case we are suggesting that the revolution, in the positive sense of the word, in the United States was partly due to the fact that the situation of slaves was very bad. We needed a great misfortune to create a revolution to then lift us a little higher. When I look at the history of the United States, in the nineteenth century, slaves contributed to the economy. But when you look at what happened in the twentieth century, it created a very poor population. It created a split in the American population that has generated a permanent war, and then when we see certain neighborhoods—there are no doubt new hybridities—but nonetheless the former slaves were set up for a long time in the neighborhoods that were almost entirely filled with poverty and unemployment in the United States. Is that what we call progress? Perhaps at some point, but the result has hardly been one of progress thus far.

THE AUTHORS

We are going to grab this opportunity to end with a positive note. Ira Berlin, a great American historian, has offered a counterfactual: "If you put aside slavery, the music would be different; the language would be different; religion would be different; food would be different."[8]

Indeed, without the slave trade and slavery, a period of intolerable violence, there would have been no blues, jazz, Faulkner, Twain, civil rights movements, and so on. This period of the Terror was also a period of intense cultural creation.

ANOTHER WOMAN, *standing up*

I do not know if I have the time to say something. But since we are in a utopia, I was imagining. It occurred to me that slavery nonetheless has caused a great deal of pain in the minds of Europeans and Americans. There is a kind of guilt that always hangs over this history. And if the slave trade had been different, if we had proposed to the people of Africa the opportunity to come help in the development of another country by proposing a decent salary, that would not have been slavery, but on the contrary a contribution, a cooperation of mutual development, wouldn't the world be a better place today? The United States would not have this guilt, and blacks would have been helped for a long time already, if we had not gone through slavery but rather respected individuals by offering them a flourishing new land where there was plenty to do.

THE AUTHORS

What you are describing has existed, not in the idealized form you suggest, but in the form of indentured servitude, the so-called coolie trade. After the abolition of slavery in the British world and in the French Empire, the colonizers went to seek free contract workers. They first tried to recruit Africans to work in the Caribbean, but met with little success. And from 1834, it is little known, but the British appealed to the Germans, Maltese, and the Irish to work in the islands. When they saw that it was not working well, they turned to the large reserve of manpower that was available to them, India, which was part of the British Empire. Between the 1830s and the 1930s, 6.5 million coolies and nearly 25 million free workers left the subcontinent to work all over the world—in the West Indies, Africa, Asia, the European colonies. This explains why Mauritius and Fiji have a population largely of Indian origin.

The demographic reconfiguration as a result of the slave trade, labor contracting, and worker migration of Asians was planetary. The West Indies and Africa were not the only regions impacted by this question: it was worldwide. The work was done under duress, in often very difficult situations, but your hypothesis is pertinent.

CASE 2: JUNE 21, 1791—THE KING SUCCEEDS IN FLEEING FRANCE

THE AUTHORS

Before considering the following case, please allow us to make one remark. Many you of have opened your comments by saying "this is only a hypothesis." We would like to restate that this is also the case for us. In this game, we only have hypotheses. It is true that we may have additional elements to bring to bear. However, what is of interest to us today is leading a discussion that transgresses to some extent the separation between the expert—the historian—and the nonexpert. In this context, we learn that everyone has knowledge to contribute to the discussion. All assumptions are welcome, especially since these assumptions, as we have seen, have been a part of historical work for the last fifty years. We invite you to do the same with the second case, the "flight to Varennes"—as we say for the moment when Louis XVI tried to leave France during the French Revolution. Contrary to what we have been discussing, the case of the successful flight of the king of France is a pure event: in this case, it deals with the fact that an arrest did not take place. It is less a question of structural changes than of the classic problem of chance in history, a chance that falls within a set of actions that have not yet been realized. We therefore approach this counterfactual hypothesis very differently from the previous one. Let's start with some chronological reminders.

(The authors point to the screen that shows a timeline.)

A BRIEF TIMELINE

May 5, 1789: Meeting of the Estates General.

June 20: Tennis Court Oath: the deputies of the Third Estate gather to demand a constitution.

July 14: The taking of the Bastille.

Summer 1789: The "Great Fear": agrarian revolts in the countryside. The peasants enter the Revolution.

August 26, 1789: Declaration of the Rights of Man and of the Citizen.

July 14, 1790: Festival of the Federation.

June 21, 1791: The king tries to leave French territory. He is stopped at Varennes

The value of the example of Varennes is that it draws upon an educational background that we all share. We need to remember that in 1788 in France, a financial, political, and agricultural crisis forced the king to convene the Estates General. A part of the representatives of this Estates General met on May 5 and claimed, in a famous scene, that the Assembly should vote by head instead of by state. The king refused. The Assembly proclaimed itself the National Assembly and, at the Tennis Court Oath on June 20, asserted its sovereignty. The king yielded and a legal revolution ensued. The legitimacy of power no longer came from God or tradition, but from the people and a written contract. At the same time, popular revolutions erupted. The Parisians stormed the Bastille on July 14, and the fear of an aristocratic conspiracy, among other things, in the peasant world generated the famous "Great Fear," studied by the French historian Georges Lefebvre, which led to a series of revolts against seigneurial domination. These popular movements pushed the Assembly to adopt a series of decisive measures. On August 4, 1789, the Assembly abolished seigneurial privileges and rights, and on August 26, the famous Declaration of the Rights of Man and of the Citizen was passed. The change was tremendous: the French were no longer royal subjects but citizens before the law. The members of the new Assembly asked, What should we do now? At that time, a constitutional monarchy was being prepared in which the king and the representative legislature shared power: it was a question of combining the reassurance of tradition (the king) with the novelty of a parliament that would lead to a new vision of the future.

But on June 21, 1791, the king tried to flee French territory and perhaps join emigrated nobles abroad. He was arrested in the French town of Varennes and brought back to Paris by force. Historians believe that the break between the king and the people took place at this moment, or more precisely that a fissure emerged that only grew afterward. So: What if the king had managed to escape? This very probable hypothesis has been extensively studied by historians. All those who have studied the French Revolution have been obliged—if only to understand the importance of the event—"to follow the road to Varennes," to use the words of historian Mona Ozouf. In her book on the flight to Varennes, published in 2005, she writes, "No matter how allergic to hypothetical history, the historian is forced to travel the road to Varennes in spirit."

(The quotation appears on the screen.)

In particular, Ozouf recounts how "fatal minutes" were lost in different places: the king and his family stayed a quarter of an hour at the roadside stop at Orbéval, a half hour at Chaintrix, and so on. Without these stops, Louis XVI would have been able to make it to the border, where troops were waiting for him with the noble émigrés. He could have launched them against the young Assembly, which was not yet sufficiently organized, and at that moment the king could have regained his power. We are here in front of a bifurcation point that came down to almost nothing: fifteen decisive minutes in the history of the world.

Let's continue: Without the "flight to Varennes," what would have happened? We should take this moment to remind you that the king did not intend to flee to Varennes (*laughter in the room*)—he was, of course, fleeing the country. This is one of those now-classic formulas that actually doesn't make sense, the legacy of classroom teaching that was too quickly adopted. So let's make some suggestions, just to raise our awareness on the issue: without

Varennes in 1791, there is probably no "1792," no Republic, no Terror, so then there is no automatic relationship between the Revolution of 1789, the Republic, and the Terror. There would have been no opposition between right and left around the legacy of the French Revolution, which still divides our contemporary politics. One might even push a little harder and suggest that generally the years 1789–1793 constituted a kind of rupture, a switch between a before and an after (do we not speak of an "Old Regime"?). In the context of this counterfactual, with just fifteen minutes less, this entry into modernity could have disappeared. And the question still resonates in the present: in 1989, we celebrated the bicentennial of the French Revolution and, at the same time, witnessed the collapse of the Eastern Bloc. On this occasion, it was recalled that the founding date of 1917 appeared to be an echo of 1789, or rather 1793–1794. Without Varennes, this whole horizon, both implicit and omnipresent, disappears.

And yet the particularity of this example is that the historian has no choice but to take this question into consideration, because the event of Varennes constantly produces counterfactuals. Historical rationality runs up against the interpretation of what has happened: there is no separation here between play and analysis. Therefore, we are going to try to answer the following question: What would have happened afterward if the king had returned to the throne and put an end to the Constituent Assembly?

A MAN, in front

It still seems to me that the ideas of the Revolution were already there in 1791: the seeds were sown. So the return of the king and the absolute monarchy would not have changed much. First of all, because there was a return of the king anyway, with the restoration [from 1815 to 1830 the brothers of Louis XVI return to the throne] and it was well established with the Third Republic [1870–1940] that the return of the king was no longer possible. We could thus have had an English-style evolution, as historians have tried to imagine: it would have changed our entire relationship to democracy, a democracy that would no doubt have been more peaceful, less dominated by absolute and systematic conflict and resentment, so maybe it would have been better after all (*laughter throughout the room*).

A SECOND MAN

Your question supposes the king's success in Austria and Germany. The real question is: Is he still a warrior king? Is Louis XVI still capable, by his personality and the structure of his army, made of noble émigrés, of raising a sufficient number of men and reconquering France? This is a kind of counterfactual in the counterfactual: Perhaps he would not have succeeded because kings were no longer warriors?

A THIRD MAN, with vivacity

What would have happened after the return of the king? Nothing fundamental, I believe. Because my great-great-great-grandfather, had, just before the king's flight to Varennes, bought a tiny piece of land from the Duke of Polignac, who had emigrated before the king tried to leave. He never would have accepted that this piece of land be taken back from him. It had allowed him to move on to something other than the status of a quasi-slave—or at least slaving away for someone to whom he owed revenues from his work even if he never saw him. I think he never would have allowed the priest to intervene again in his personal life, in his family life. Besides, the priest in question was married (*laughter in the room*), so the question was already settled. He had married before the king had taken off for Varennes. On top of that, he would never have accepted to repay the tithe, to repay the salt tax, to repay all those taxes. So things were already decided. Maybe in appearance, constitutionally, for example, there might have been variations, but nothing fundamental, with regard to what I said about my great-great-great-grandfather, who never would have accepted a return to his previous situation.

A FOURTH MAN, raises his hand

Since the aim of the game is also utopic, one could imagine in the spirit of what has been said that the return of the king with an army would have aroused a very strong reaction, a resistance by the people and the peasants, and the rapid federation of the French people around the idea of a republic and greater equality. Because even if the king himself was not a warrior, behind him, many who were motivated to go to war could have gotten behind him and forced him into conflict.

A FIFTH MAN

I want to come back to the previous hypothesis on the question of confidence. I believe that the departure was above all the mark of a powerful individual who no longer trusted the people with whom he had established a contract. So the question of the return of the king posed that of the manner in which he would have attempted to recover the situation. One could imagine that he would have come back with the means of reinforcing the constitutional monarchy at his own expense, but that he would have had the ability not to oppose the democratic evolution that might have taken place. In any case, it seems to me that our memory of the event is marked by the terrible suspicion hanging over Louis XVI. So if de Gaulle had been arrested on the way to Baden-Baden in 1968, what would have been the impact of this event on our relationship to institutions? If the king had returned to Paris, would he have had the wisdom to recover power without despising the actors of the Revolution?

THE AUTHORS

Everything that has been stated is very interesting. A first line inquiry, which seems to be quite common, has been proposed: a temperate monarchy could have been established. This is the traditional hypothesis of nonrevolutionary historiography, ranging from conservative to moderate positions. If Louis XVI had indeed been kind, he would have understood and finally things would have developed more naturally. The remark about the warrior king is right: the noble émigrés blamed him for being too soft and hesitant. During the preparation of his departure, he spent as much time deciding how he was going to respond to the nobles who reproached him for not resembling a "true" sovereign, that is to say a warrior king. Louis XVI was perhaps already following another path. In fact, we must remember that the movement of change began before the Revolution. The so-called Old Regime was not fixed in time. The concepts of the general will, the nation, and sovereignty began to influence a nascent public opinion. The historian Roger Chartier speaks of "modifying the space of the thinkable." Philosophers such as Voltaire, Rousseau, and Montesquieu had already begun to modify the ways of seeing things. More deeply, dechristianization was discussed. These fundamental movements were already working toward something that no longer resembled the absolute monarchy but rather an administrative monarchy. And to this must be added the food riots of the previous years. In this new framework, we can easily imagine that if the king had returned, he would have had little choice: 1789 had taken place, the privileges had been abolished, and there was no turning back—you are entirely correct. So the "normal" path, the natural development, would have been the constitutional monarchy. In fact, here we come to the main debate on the French Revolution since World War II. In a word: from 1950 to the 1980s, a Marxist reading prevailed, with the idea that an economic bourgeoisie rose up and used the proletarian classes to oppose the old caste of the landed nobility. The revolution was therefore necessary in one sense: with or without Varennes, the social forces at stake were irresistible. Then another reading was imposed little by little, called the revisionist thesis, through the works of François Furet: he insisted on the role of chance in the event, while considering at the same time that the Terror was one of the possibilities opened up by the Revolution from the beginning. In his view, 1789 should have been able to lead to a temperate English-style monarchy. We see that these well-documented hypotheses mobilize counterfactual analysis and continue to structure our reflections on the Revolution. And the thesis that comes naturally to mind today is the "liberal" path. There remains a third hypothesis that has been mentioned, which is a bit like the first: that is, the Revolution would have taken place at a later date no matter what. From this perspective, one can read the entire nineteenth century as a repetition of a French Revolution that would ultimately have succeeded. We are then well within the framework given to us by historians who have studied these events.

A WOMAN

We may be in a utopia, but an English-style constitutional monarchy was not conceivable because the Parisians had already taken the Bastille and aristocratic privilege had been abolished. In my opinion, if the king had returned, he may not have seen the ultimate truth, but he would have thought twice. He would have noted that the army could not do much and would not have allowed him to take power back. So he might have decreed the abolition of the army, saving the French taxpayers a lot of money (*laughter in the room.*)

ANOTHER WOMAN

Indeed, if the king had returned, the constitutional monarchy would have been established, and Napoleon's empire never would have happened. This changes a lot, because it means that a number of achievements of the Revolution would not have spread across Europe, especially in the southwestern part of Germany. This changes the map of Europe a little bit. If the counterfactual is pushed further, perhaps there is no longer a European Union. The constitutional monarchy in France after 1791 would probably not have led to a retreat, but perhaps it would have modified the balance of European power.

THE AUTHORS

Let's return to the question of the army and the police: as early as 1789, the middle class and the bourgeoisie thought that the citizens themselves had to take over the police and the army. This principle existed, but it was only implemented by the actors of the Revolution. And during the revolutions of the nineteenth century, in 1848 as in 1871, the idea was that the citizens themselves should ensure their own safety, before the principle of a professional force became evident.

ANOTHER WOMAN

I was bathed in the Marxist dialectic and thus learned what you have just said: revolutions are the result of a quantitative accumulation and constitute a qualitative leap that is inescapable. So whether or not the king spent fifteen minutes here or there, there was a moment when the bourgeois revolution was inevitable. According to this approach, which seems relatively accurate, the continuation of the monarchy would probably not have changed the course of history. It would have delayed it ten years, or slowed it down. That's what I learned.

THE AUTHORS

We should no doubt remind you that researchers are still thinking about these questions. Moreover, this touches upon the delicate problem of the power of the event in history. Long-term processes may or may not emerge out of an event; and if they do, then the event remains a catalyst for change. Things are not necessarily ineluctable. This is one of the problems posed by the Revolution: it seized underlying transformations that were already present, gave them a form and a meaning that weighed on the future. If the French Revolution had not occurred, the course of things would still have been different, and no one can be sure that a revolution would not have exploded later. Historical reflection on the event has been profoundly renewed. In so many words, for a long time we wrote histories of great men and events, then we turned toward histories of deep social and cultural forces before rediscovering that the event and the actors also play a role in these longer-term constraints. The French Revolution, on this point, remains an open question.

THE SAME WOMAN

Yes, but do the revolutions profoundly change the structure of society?

A MAN

I was wondering if, in spite of all the political advances that we have seen, it would not be possible, with the return of the king, to restore a stable monarchy in certain regions that were traditionally royalist, like the Vendée [a region in western France] (*laughter in the room.*)

THE AUTHORS

It is true that historiography throughout the nineteenth century argued that the Vendée was a reservoir of royalists. The Revolution sharpened the counterrevolutionary reflexes in some regions like the Vendée, and then the memory of the wars in the Vendée reinforced this idea. In a way, the long-term development of royalism in the Vendée is also the product of the events and power struggles that emerged at this moment. Jean-Clément Martin has shown this through his study of this period: the counterrevolutionaries were full-fledged actors in the revolutionary process. They contributed to shaping it, and eventually reinforced the use of violence.

A MAN, on the left

I am wondering what would have become of France if the king had returned from Varennes, a constitutional monarchy was established, and Napoleon's empire never existed. Because I think I remember that before Napoleon there was not one language in France. It was in the years 1800–1815 that the state was set up, that an administration was created, a language, the *nation* per se more generally. My question is this: With the return of the king, would France have the same borders (I am thinking of regions like Savoy)? Would we live in one single state?

THE AUTHORS

You are asking the question of the nationalization of French society. In the 1860s, a good part of the population still did not speak French. In Brittany, interpreters were often needed in courtrooms. The situation was the same in the Var [a region in southern France], where love for the Republic in 1848 was expressed in Occitan. So the question of Napoleon's place in the process of centralization again pushes us toward a counterfactual question: centralization had already been going on for some time, and the disappearance of regional languages came much later, under the Third Republic. In other words, have we not overstated the role of Napoleon in the construction of the French nation? The counterfactual analysis pushes us to ask these kinds of questions, which makes it possible to reconsider elements of the story that strike us as natural. Napoleon played a decisive role in structuring French centralization, but he cannot be considered a starting point. Other dynamics must be taken into account, which were also developing on a European scale.

A MAN

I would like to respond to what was said earlier about the constitutional path. If France had adopted a monarchy on the British model, would the

French have adopted another attitude toward the nobility? I am speaking about this with some experience because I come from a family of Spanish nobility, and so I have an aristocratic name. It still happens sometimes that someone shows a certain respect for my name, though I make no specific claims (*laughter in the room*). I think that if France had maintained a more peaceful relationship to the monarchy, we would have solved a number of problems. In particular, the forms of power, for example, linked to the aristocracy, which have not yet been undone, contrary to Spain and Great Britain.

THE AUTHORS

We would like to take advantage of your comment to present a final hypothesis, especially since the international dimension has already been mentioned several times. Do these French events change anything on the global scale? The French Revolution is actually part of a much larger revolutionary context: the Glorious Revolution with the Bill of Rights (1689), the American Revolution (1776–1783), the Batavian Revolutions in the United Provinces (1783–1787), the revolt of the slaves in Santo Domingo (1791–1801), the more or less successful revolutions in Geneva, Belgium, Poland, Ireland, and so on. Not to mention all the movements that shook Spanish rule in Latin America, with the independence of Mexico (1810), and so on. The French Revolution was also one of many events. Here we fall into the question of structural analysis: was there not a long-term structural change already taking place? Under these conditions, do we not tend to overestimate the role of the French Revolution? This is what recent works have suggested. Historian Steven Pincus argues that 1689–1690 is the real moment when liberalism and democracy emerged in Europe. In this sense, in the absence of the French Revolution, "modernity" would still have occurred. What did the French Revolution bring about with regard to these longer transformations? It posed in an original way the republican question, the national question, and crystallized the elements underlying them. This work of global contextualization nevertheless makes it possible to place the canonical history of France back into a longer-term process. The French Revolution was a moment of great importance, but only one moment among others. This puts into perspective the importance of the hypothesis that we have proposed.

A MAN

It is obviously hard to see into the future. In addition to chance there is another important feature, as in physics or chemistry. I want to recall a few facts. First, England had already beheaded a sovereign—I do not know if it was James I or Charles I—and that did not prevent a monarchy from flourishing in England, where the king and the queen are relatively unimportant. Second, indeed, it was the Revolution of 1848 that then marked people's minds, because Marx wrote on the Revolution of 1848 and not, to my knowledge, on 1789. Third, about the "flight to Varennes": we say "flight" and not "counterrevolution." One can imagine that the king would have gone to the Germanic duchies, which were not yet gathered into Germany, and settled in Austria. In this case, he would not necessarily have returned to Paris with an army to chase the revolutionaries.

THE AUTHORS

On England, we follow your point. As for Marx, he wrote extensively about 1789, as a failed revolution for the people. Paradoxically, he also proposed a vast counterfactual rebellion along the lines of: why the revolution that should have taken place did not happen, and how to make it happen because historically the balance of power made it possible that it could have happened. It is also in this sense that he examined 1789, 1848, and 1871. On the subject of your last hypothesis, we agree. We had asked a colleague who is a specialist of the period. He thought that the king could have returned with an army, which he would have managed to bring together. But it is interesting to note that with the flight of the king, the National Assembly also lost some of its credibility. The arrest ultimately ended this movement, and we see that at this moment, in 1791, the figure of the king was not yet dead, far from it. The process was much slower.

To conclude, what does this type of exercise show? This mode of reasoning makes it possible to project all the dynamics involved in the event more clearly than if one sticks to the illusion that what happened was a necessity. The exercise also reminds us that revolution is a process, that is to say a political structure in motion whose realization depends on the balance of power and events. It is in this sense that we can articulate structure and event. Finally, this game reveals something about our political imaginary: basically the hypothesis that seems the most plausible to us today is that of the constitutional monarchy, that is the liberal version of François Furet. In 1945, the most credible might have been the Marxist hypothesis of the necessary revolution. In other words, if we attempt collectively to understand how to "remake society," we must ask ourselves from what political unconscious and ideological matrix we are reexamining these questions. Counterfactual reasoning makes it possible to explain them, whereas historical narratives may seek to hide them.

Thank you.

(*On the screen there were a number of bibliographical references that were mentioned during the discussion.*)

Introduction

Alain Boureau and Daniel Milo, eds., *Alter-Histoire. Essais d'histoire expérimentale,* 1991.

Rodney. P. Carlisle and Geoffrey Golson, *America in Revolt During the 1960s and 1970s,* 2008.

Alexander Demandt, *Ungeschehene Geschichte, Ein Traktat über die Frage, Was wäre geschehen, wenn . . . ?,* 1986.

Niall Ferguson, ed., *Virtual History,* 1997.

Geoffrey Hawthorn, *Plausible Worlds: Possibility and Understanding in History and the Social Sciences,* 1991.

Paul Lacombe, *De l'histoire considérée comme science. Introduction à l'histoire littéraire,* 1894.

Antoine Prost, *Douze leçons sur l'histoire,* 1996.

Case 1: A World without the Atlantic Slave Trade

Robin Blackburn, *The Making of New World Slavery: From the Baroque to the Modern, 1492–1800,* 1997.

Marcel Dorigny and Bernard Gainot, *Atlas des esclavages. Traites, sociétés coloniales, abolitions de l'Antiquité à nos jours,* 2006.

David Eltis, *The Rise of African Slavery in the Americas,* 2000.

Bouda Etemad, *De l'utilité des empires,* 2005.

Angus Maddison, *L'Économie mondiale. Une perspective millénaire,* 2001.

Patrick Manning, *Slavery and African Life,* 1990.

———, *Slavery, Colonialism and Economic Growth in Dahomey,* 2004.

Frédéric Régent, *La France et ses esclaves. De la colonisation aux abolitions (1620–1848),* 2007.

Nelly Schmidt, *La France a-t-elle aboli l'esclavage? Guadeloupe-Martinique-Guyane. 1830–1935,* 2009.

Ronald W. Walters, "African Reparations: Dealing with a Unique and Unprecedented Moral Debt," in A. Mazama, ed., *Africa in the 21st Century: Toward a New Future,* 2007.

Case 2: June 21, 1791—The King Succeeds in Fleeing France

Keith Baker, *Inventing the French Revolution: Essays on French Political Culture in the Eighteenth Century,* 1990.

Roger Chartier, *The Cultural Origins of the French Revolution,* 1991.

Marcel Dorigny, *1804: Haïti première République noire,* 2004.
Laurent Dubois, *Les Vengeurs du Nouveau Monde. Histoire de la Révolution haïtienne,* 2005.
Dan Edelstein, *The Terror of Natural Right: Republicanism, the Cult of Nature, and the French Revolution,* 2009.
François Furet, *Interpreting the French Revolution,* 1981.
Jonathan Israel, *The Radical Enlightenment: Philosophy and the Making of Modernity 1650–1750,* 2001.
Annie Jourdan, *La Révolution, une exception française?,* 2004.
Martin Malia, *Histoire des révolutions,* 2008.
Mona Ozouf, *Varennes, 21 juin 1791,* 2005.
Steven Pincus, *1688: The First Modern Revolution,* 2009.
Albert Soboul, *Comprendre la Révolution,* 1981.
Timothy Tackett, *When the King Took Flight,* 2004.
Michel Vovelle, *Combats pour la Révolution française,* 1991.
Sophie Wahnich, *La Longue Patience du peuple. 1792. Naissance de la République,* 2008.

Some lessons may be drawn from this collective exercise. First, it was fun, for us and obviously for the participants. It had "worked," we might say. The uncertainty involved in pursuing a uchronic analysis was immediately obvious, as evidenced by the participants caution ("I am just proposing a hypothesis," and the like). Researchers and participants therefore spontaneously situated themselves in a hypothetical register: in so doing, this type of gathering made it possible to bridge the gap between the historian and a wider public audience. So the experience tended to create a new equilibrium between the public and the historians, without calling into question the historians' competence or their social function. Admittedly, the audience had its own specificities. It was generationally mixed, from teenagers to the elderly. It was obviously a relatively well-educated public: high school students, secondary and higher education teachers—either practicing or retired—history buffs, civil society actors, political supporters, and activists. Some of the technicians even came over to speak to us afterward to propose their own hypotheses. All of them obviously had relatively sophisticated cultural backgrounds, were accustomed to debating, and attentive to contemporary issues. It was an "informed" civically engaged public, or, in more straightforward terms, the type of public that participates in this kind of event.

In the end, what might be the value of such an experience for the participants? First, a mass of information, including books and debates, were presented without overwhelming the audience. In addition, mobilizing shared knowledge, the public was able to participate concretely in the process of historical reasoning. This was all the more the case since many of their counterfactual hypotheses had already been mobilized by serious historians. Thus, each participant was in the situation of the researcher who is also anchored in his or her own time period, with his or her own doubts and questions, which are sometimes trivial, sometimes too general, but must be dealt with nonetheless. Finally, the participants were able to bring into play their imaginaries associated with these historical periods, and discuss impressions, suggestions, hypotheses, and personal stories related to their families or childhoods, of a kind that is rarely discussed in a traditional academic conference setting. On several occasions, we were invited to take more seriously such appropriations of the historical past that are generally considered "unworthy" by historians. But these appropriations cannot be entirely ignored by historians. To the contrary, historians may benefit from serious dialogue, based on these historical or memorial fragments, which are both forms of knowledge of the past and an important issue for the present.

For us, it was a wonderful experience. First of all, we did not entirely control the discussion: we were drawn toward questions, proposals, and analyses that we did not expect. It is a demanding exercise. The flames that are fanned by such propositions and hypotheses bring to life many elements that are known to the researcher, but they are rarely posed in a direct or obvious way. There are the political issues of the discussion, the fragility of the sources, the lines of questioning, and so on. One of the most unexpected points was, for example, the ease with which many people grabbed on to the notion of utopia to dream historically. This was the stated purpose of the workshop. It was also, however, the part with which we were the least comfortable. Such debates may "fail," drift off into relatively meaningless platitudes. Or, to the contrary, they may turn into philosophical considerations that are too far removed from a specific contextualized historical reflection. This was not the case here. These exchanges may in turn be useful for historical reflections. At least two elements should be highlighted. First, the public had no difficulty finding certain historical reflections that had been used by historians (determinist approaches, the role of chance and individuals, and so on). This fact, which is gratifying for the participants, may also suggest a certain lack of creative imagination on the part of historians. Another interesting point was no doubt, through the example of the French Revolution, the updating of a political imaginary that could hardly be considered "liberal," which seemed to limit the formulation of the "most wild" hypotheses, an imaginary that has its own history and that the historian carries in spite of him- or herself. This type of discussion allows a political imaginary to resurface and to be identified, in order to put it aside and begin a new analysis. There is a collective production of history, even if each individual only plays his or her role.

Hence, from a somewhat vague process of collective reasoning, we shifted to an approach, an object, and a technique. It would seem possible to use counterfactual reasoning and to approach possible futures in a way that is very different from the counterfactual, alternative, uchronic histories, with which it is most commonly identified.

These chapters are experiments: many of the elements treated can be discussed, other pathways explored (periods, objects, sites). And the problem of transmission, how the approach may be shared, no doubt merits further exploration.

These experiments are also meant to be invitations to embark on a voyage: people may use these propositions in order to realize or reject the possibilities. But it would appear that within the realm of research, these tools can help make analyses more precise, displace perspectives, or acquire knowledge. Concerning the question of exchange, which is fundamental in a period when scholarly knowledge would seem to be losing a portion of its public, these more playful approaches to history, at their own modest level, may offer a site where historical reason is not called into question but placed anew in a framework that is different from the one that is usually offered. In so doing, the use of counterfactuals and possible futures may constitute, in its own way, a site from which we may question and reinvigorate historical practice.

Conclusion

BECOMINGS IN THE WORLD

Happy the man who, like Ulysses, has traveled well,
Or like that man who conquered the fleece,
And has then returned, full of experience and wisdom
To live among his kinfolk the rest of his life!

—Joachim du Bellay[1]

There is no establishment of the truth without an essential position of otherness; the truth is never the same; there can be truth only in the form of the other world and the other life (*de l'autre monde et de la vie autre*).

—Michel Foucault[2]

The counterfactual approach and the analysis of possible futures opens a gap. One can easily get lost. One may consider it too risky, detect a certain vacuity, or proceed with some precaution. In this case, one discovers interesting lines of research, and perhaps more. It is now time to briefly summarize the main ambitions of this inquiry.

POSITIONS IN COUNTERFACTUAL REASONING

Counterfactual history and uchronia have developed in response to a certain zeitgeist whose characteristics we have highlighted (the end of ideologies, modification of the relationship between reality and fiction, a sense of uncertainty in a globalized world, and so on). From this has emerged a tremendous diversity in its variations, an inventiveness in the forms it has taken, a popular curiosity with regard to virtual history, and finally a vigorous debate that has animated the historical community. Under these conditions, it might seem more reasonable for the researcher to ignore such a precarious mode of investigation.

However, it quickly becomes apparent that this reasoning and its narrative or analytic expression are part of a larger space and an older story. They have been employed by human societies even more widely than might have been expected, as was clear in the beginning of this study. Their present-day ubiquity therefore seems less strange or new. Following this initial exploration, the historian—as researcher, teacher, and citizen—has been invited to take this counterfactual approach seriously, exploring old and still-relevant questions.

The counterfactual approach and the analysis of possible futures is not intended to constitute yet another historiographical "turn." Instead, it is a form of reasoning that may be added to a series of intellectual operations that are already well known to researchers (the cross-referencing of sources, immersion, interpretation, conceptualization, narrative design, and so on). Counterfactual analysis can play a role in these operations without necessarily taking center stage. One can, of course, do and read history without worrying about counterfactuals. On the other hand, we are convinced that the explanation and clarification of the problems involved in this process can enrich the "tool box" of the social sciences, that is, their critical and interpretative apparatus.

Within the terminological framework set up at the end of part 2, we identified six uses of counterfactual reasoning: reflexivity, contextualization, interdependence, plot making, unrealized futures, and past possibilities. We can now complete them by adding three temporalities: long, medium, and short. When the story of the unfulfilled outcome is pursued far beyond the point of inflection, and it appears in the form of a current world that is different from our own, it is operating in the register of literary creation, of philosophical reflection or moral judgment. While it appears perfectly legitimate within the wider public, among novelists, philosophers, or lawyers, this usage is less useful for the researcher who is looking to shed light on past and present societies. The case of an alternative outcome considered in a medium timeframe seems more appropriate to the formal modeling elaborated in sociological and economic analysis and international relations theory. These counterfactuals are more experimental, designed for sophisticated data formation, testing models and their concrete application. Finally, there is the approach that minimizes projection into the alternative future, in order to reduce the certainties of what actually happened and the implicit sequencing that supports its understanding. This short-term counterfactual is perhaps the most useful and easily mobilized in the social sciences, particularly for historians, who are often suspicious of theoretical systems. It responds to the demands of an inquiry, helps shift perspective, contributes to opening up new horizons, and enlarges the questionnaire. These three temporalities and six uses constitute a framework of analysis that makes it possible to distinguish between different forms of counterfactual reasoning, which has in some cases generated misgivings among historians.

As for the edges of history mentioned in the introduction, the outlines have become more precise and more complex. Starting from multiple entry points rooted in the realm of what has happened or in our incomplete knowledge of the past, its reach would seem unlimited. These paths seem uncertain, open to fantasy, metaphysical speculation, and futile political considerations. But they also appear to open up a space of knowledge: it is impossible to understand what has happened without analyzing what didn't. And because they circumscribe a field within social sciences, they allow one to grasp it better, to understand its architecture, mass, materials, colors, and tools of measurement from another perspective, as we suggested in the introduction.

SOMETHING POSSIBLE: A TERRAIN FOR HISTORY AND THE SOCIAL SCIENCES

If we synthesize our initial questions, we see that in the end the problem is not only an opposition between "scientific" history and "counterfactual" history in the sense of alternative history. It is rather the manner in which one is defined in comparison to the other. This is no doubt a part of the scandal caused by "popular" counterfactual history. It occupies a somewhat obscure zone within the historical terrain, that of "it could have been," in order to fill it with characters, events, and conceptions of history disconnected from academic research, mobilizing a powerful social imaginary that elicits public interest. But this zone is not outside of history, it lies within it, or on its margins. It forms one of the realities of this discontinuous and heterogeneous knowledge that makes up history. Herein lies the space of the relevant uses of the counterfactual that we have endeavored to hunt down, delimit, and explain in this fundamentally indeterminate territory. In so doing, the survey also shows how ordinary knowledge can provide resources for reasoning in the social sciences and thus be the subject of theoretical and methodological investment.

This work of uncovering was, of course, based on a certain definition of history that we must now return to. Throughout this investigation, we have been guided by a specific way of doing history or, more exactly, a certain desire to pursue a history that is social and cultural, relational and comprehensive, learned and nourished by social sciences, that assumes its literary and scientific dimension and remains aware of its social and political issues. This way of pursuing history is the product of the vast set of reflections, debates, and work of historians, sociologists, and anthropologists, to whom we owe a tremendous debt. This book is the result of this collective dynamic. In this context, we can specify the usefulness of what we have learned from the counterfactual. Three elements emerge, either in the form of tools, objects, or social uses.

The counterfactual approach and its applications have first of all appeared to be a valuable source of reflexivity. They constitute in a scientific, playful, and political mode an ideal tool to test the possible alliance between the theoretical requirement of the social sciences and the narrative freedom of fiction. Similarly, they can provide a relevant framework for further study of the relationships between truth, falsehood, and fiction that feed historical analysis, or those between modeling and narration, explanation, and interpretations that do not constitute two radically different modes of access to the social world. In another register, they have proven to offer a means of comparison. This can be pursued between established facts and outcomes or possible worlds constructed by historians. Such a recourse can appear particularly useful for updating categories of analysis and implicit interpretative schemas on the part of the researcher and the reader. Moreover, recourse to counterfactual analysis seems more common for equating the situations, entities, and actors, which may at first appear incommensurable. This comparison has been abundantly criticized in recent years: it has been disparaged in particular for reifying and freezing social phenomena that are in fact dynamic and uncertain. The current use of counterfactual reasoning recalls the importance of comparison in historical work, as well as the hierarchization of causes, the definition of singularities, or even comprehensive immersion.

This approach, then, has allowed us to isolate our object of study: the possible. For the counterfactual approach and unrealized futures leads almost inevitably to this crucial question for the historian. This old problem is of interest to a growing number of researchers today: possibilities that never came to fruition, potentialities, virtualities, divergent paths within the past are frequently signaled in works of history, sociology, or political science. They usually remain, however, at the stage of invocation or evocation. If counterfactual reasoning is, in the eyes of the "serious" researcher, an operation that is sometimes awkward and unworthy, it has the merit of taking a firm and conscious step onto this terrain. It makes it possible to confront concretely the question of methods and sources for experiencing a plurality of outcomes, future fears and hopes, feasibility, and conditions or spaces of possibility. It reveals that these possibilities of the past are not infinite, by highlighting the constraints, the mechanisms of reproduction, and the routines that organize the social worlds under study. It reveals the creative force of the event, decisive moments in the eyes of actors, which could quickly fall into oblivion. It recalls that the way societies think about the future and project themselves into it structures their organization. The manipulation of counterfactual reasoning is difficult, but it allows the historian to apprehend the possibilities of the past that, in spite of their fragile and uncertain status, are also part of the realm of historical fact. This analysis can then be deployed to answer at multiple scales studies that stretch from biography to the evolution of the world.

Finally, counterfactual reasoning and all the applications that we have explored create an original site of exchange and action. They are already commonly used outside academia, in playful, commercial, political, ideological, artistic, or scientific ways. Once the conditions under which this approach can be a reliable tool are defined, the researcher can push beyond his or her comfort zone, avoiding defensive reactions, which are often counterproductive. If we admit that the social sciences should not be content with the vertical, hierarchical dissemination of research, historians can exploit the playful and participative dimension of counterfactual reasoning that allows for enjoying games in the process of producing and recreating historical narratives while maintaining a strong methodology. Because it is also based on a common form of reasoning, counterfactual analysis also proposes a platform from which one may teach modes of historical reflection. The mastery of counterfactual reasoning and its devices makes it possible to intervene in public debates wherein alternative historical developments are frequently mobilized because of their rhetorical efficiency or their capacity to make moral judgments. This helps in avoiding the pitfalls of a retrospective judgment nourished by the values of the present. Above all, by uncovering a limited number of the possibilities that did not come to pass, the researcher avoids historical determinism. He or she avoids confinement to trajectories presented as irresistible and enriches the understanding of contemporary societies by pointing out the discontinuities that have produced them. By uncovering other possible outcomes of the past, the historian generates a means of action in the present. In this sense, the counterfactual allows us to open up our perception of the historical present.

THE INSTITUTION OF THE REAL AND THE REALS OF HISTORY

Joined together, these elements may enrich our historical practice. But the stakes, which stem from the very status of counterfactualism and possible futures, may prove even more decisive. They point toward a rather cloudy area, expanding the limits of historical knowledge, while at the same time reshaping them and challenging their quiet transparency. More than thirty years ago, Michel de Certeau noted that bringing to light the "shameful" elements that historiography attempts to hide allows us to see how the real is created, a real that is represented and that he referred to as the "legendary institution."[3] No doubt, counterfactualism and possible futures give insight into this realm as well.

With its very concrete anchoring and at times naïve questioning, the grand and in some cases timeless philosophical interrogations it can lead to, counterfactualism as well as its applications also reveal what history is through a series of contrasts. It emerges as a learned practice made of questions, a set of methods, and documentation with an ambition toward truth. It is a product of a professionalization with its rules, internal struggles, shared positions with regard to other social sciences, as well as the work of researchers, including their doubts, their passions, and their interests. It is a way of participating in debates and dealing with the questions of one's time. It implies the implementation of a philosophy, implicit or not, of science and historical development.

In so doing, the domain of the counterfactual that we have traced does not challenge the architectural structure of the discipline, nor does it abolish the boundaries that delimit the rules within which historians operate or their fields of action. Rather it tests the boundaries of the trade, bringing them into play, uncovering the most pertinent mechanisms and inconvenient difficulties. It helps avoid the rigidification of strict oppositions (objective and subjective, internal and external, real and fictional, and so forth). It also contributes to keeping the practice of history vibrant. This reasoned use of the counterfactual approach and of possible futures is not, therefore, opposed to the idea of a real that exists outside of texts. To the contrary, it recalls that there is indeed a historical reality that is external to the researcher and toward which he or she is oriented. But this reality is hardly fixed or closed in on itself. Rather it is plural and fragmented and enclosed within uncertain borders. It also shows that this informal material only reveals itself when the historian actually studies it. As such, it carries with it the perspective of the observer as well as a specific mode of analysis.[4] External realities and ways of knowing are indissolubly linked. Whether the historian likes it or not—this too is shown by counterfactualism, even if it is politically, methodologically, or epistemologically naïve—this mode of reasoning also shows that the historian participates in the effort to elucidate the past. The tension, and the process of distantiation, between the past and the present becomes fundamental. The areas to which counterfactualism may be applied shapes these very connections. In this sense, it has an almost existential dimension: there is something liberating about traveling across this territory, which invites more audacity and generosity in historical study. And at the same time, it demands greater methodological rigor on the part of the historian, and especially an increased awareness of his or her responsibility—an opportune attitude in a social world that seems increasingly encircled by plural and unrealized determinisms, a world in which the historian has a role to play in reminding us that, to put it simply, history is still full of possibilities.

Notes

PREFACE. THE DARK ENERGY OF HISTORY

1. "Uchronia," *Victorian Literature and Culture* 46, nos. 3–4 (Fall/Winter 2018): 928–930.

INTRODUCTION. ON THE EDGE OF HISTORY

1. Friedrich Nietzsche, *Writings of Nietzsche,* ed. Anthony Uyl, vol. 1 (Ontario: Devoted, 2016), 103.
2. Guillaume de Bertier de Sauvigny, "Quarante ans d'historiographie (1940–1980)," *Romantisme* 10, nos. 28–29 (1980): 84.
3. Niall Ferguson, *Virtual History: Alternatives and Counterfactuals* (New York, Basic Books, 1997).
4. "Without the breakdown of the pitot tubes, the accident would not have happened," declared the experts on flight 447 from Rio to Paris on June 1, 2009, who considered the primary cause to be technical and not human error. ("L'Accident de l'AF 447 aurait pu être 'évité,'" *Libération,* October 4, 2009.)
5. Pierre-Olivier Bédard, "La Mobilisation des savoirs scientifiques par les analystes de politiques québécois. Analyse de cheminement contrefactuelle et essai épistémologique d'interprétation causale" (PhD thesis in political science, Université Laval, Canada, 2013).
6. Wars in particular lend themselves to a consideration of possible alternative outcomes. For example, Ian Kershaw, *Fateful Choices: Ten Decisions That Changed the World, 1940–1941* (London: Penguin, 2013); Christopher Clark, *The Sleepwalkers: How Europe Went to War in 1914* (London: Penguin, 2012); Gerd Krumreich, *Le Feu aux poudres. Qui a déclenché la guerre en 1914* (Paris: Belin, 2014); Kees Schulten,

Waterloo (1815), la double incertitude (Paris: Economica, 2009). Works oriented toward a larger public audience are particularly well suited to this approach: Hyell Williams, *Days That Changed the World: The Defining Events of World History* (London: Quercus, 2014); Renaud Thomazo, *Les Pires décisions de l'histoire de France* (Paris: Larousse, 2013).

7. Pierre Laborie, preface to *L'Opinion française sous Vichy. Les français et la crise d'identité nationale 1936–1944* (Paris: Points, 2001).

PART ONE. INQUIRY

1. Paul Celan, from "Breathturn," in *Selections* (Berkeley: University of California Press, 2005), 97.

CHAPTER 1. IN THUCYDIDES' WAKE

1. Cornelius Castoriadis, *Ce qui fait la Grèce,* vol. 3: *Thucydide, la force et le droit* (Paris: Seuil, 2010), 180.
2. Stewart Flory, "Thucydides' Hypotheses about the Peloponnesian War," *Transactions of the American Philological Association* 118 (1988): 43–56.
3. Thucydides, *History of the Peloponnesian War,* trans. Richard Crawley (Avon: Floating Press, 2008), 869.
4. Robert Tordoff, "Counterfactual History and Thucydides," in *Probabilities, Hypotheticals, and Counterfactuals in Ancient Greek Thought,* ed. Victoria Wohl (Cambridge: Cambridge University Press, 2014), 101–121.
5. Titus Livius, *The History of Rome,* vol. 2, bks. 9–26, trans. D. Spillan and Cyrus Edmonds (London: Bohn, 1849), 582–583.
6. Tacitus, *The Annals of Imperial Rome,* bk. 2: "If he had been in sole control, with royal power and title, he would have equaled Alexander in military renown as easily as he outdid him clemency, self-control, and every other good quality."
7. Philippe Duplessis-Mornay, *De la vérité de la religion chrestienne. Contre les athées, épicuriens, payens, juifs, mahumédistes & autres in dèles* (Paris: 1581).
8. This method is used again by Le Sage in his *Aventures du chevalier de Beauchêne* (Paris: 1732), which offers a role reversal and imagines the discovery of Europe by the Native Americans: "Having discovered an unknown territory in the northwest, they would have said, we have resolved to descend and take possession in the name of the chief of our nation and to make them praise our gods." (vol. 2, Librairie commerciale et artistique, 1969, p. 65.)
9. Blaise Pascal, *Pensées,* trans. W. F. Trotter (Mineola, NY: Dover, 2003), 50 and 48.
10. H. F. McMains, *The Death of Oliver Cromwell* (Lexington: University Press of Kentucky, 1999).
11. Edward Gibbon, *The Decline and Fall of the Roman Empire,* vol. 5 (1776–1789; Memphis, TN: General Books, 2009), 221.
12. Françoise Micheau, "732, Charles Martel, chef des Francs, gagne sur les Arabes la bataille de Poitiers," in *1515 et les grandes dates de l'histoire de France,* ed. Alain Corbin (Paris: Seuil, 2005).

13. François-René de Chateaubriand, *Memoires from Beyond the Grave* (New York: Penguin/Random House, New York Review of Books Classics, 2018), bk. 9, 309–344.
14. Karl Marx, *Le 18 Brumaire de Louis Bonaparte,* in Œuvres politiques, vol. 1 (1852; Paris: Gallimard, Bibliothèque de la Pléiade, 1994), 529.
15. See chapters 8 and 10.
16. Aristotle, *Poetics* (Cambridge: Harvard University Press, 1995). This approach also concerns the works of Plutarch and Herodotus. See Claude Calame, *Pratiques poétiques de la mémoire. Représentations de l'espace-temps en Grèce ancienne* (Paris: La Découverte, 2006); Bérenger Boulay, "Histoire et narrativité. Autour des chapitres 9 et 23 de la *Poétique* d' Aristote," *Lalies* 26 (2006): 171–187; Cornelius Castoriadis, *Ce qui fait la Grèce, 3. Thucydide, la force et le droit* (Paris: Seuil, 2010); and, more recently, Wohl, *Probabilities, Hypotheticals, and Counterfactuals.*
17. Raymond Trousson, *Voyages au pays de nulle part, Histoire littéraire de la pensée utopique* (Brussels: Éditions de l'université de Bruxelles, 2001); Hinrich Hudde and Peter Kuon, eds., *De l'utopie à l'uchronie. Formes, significations, fonctions* (Erlangen: 1986; Tübingen: G. Narr, 1988), especially Henning Krauss, "Querelle des Anciens et des Modernes et le début de l'uchronie littéraire," pp. 89–98.
18. According to the timeline proposed by Éric Henriet, *L'Histoire revisitée. Panorama de l'uchronie sous toutes ses formes* (Paris: Les Belles Lettres, 1999), which constitutes the definitive work on this subject.
19. Louis Geoffroy, *Napoléon et la conquête du monde* (Paris: H. L. Delloye, 1836), 483–484. Louis Geoffroy, *Napoléon and the Conquest of the World, 1812–1832: A Fictional History* (Oklahoma City: Campaign Press Publications, 1994).
20. The full title was "Uchronie, tableau historique apocryphe des révolutions de l'Empire romain et de la formation d'une fédération européenne."
21. The word "uchronia," invented by Charles Renouvier in 1876, was first defined in the French Larousse dictionary (1904) as "the reconstruction of the history of a period based on imparted facts." Nonetheless, it never appeared in Paul-Émile Littré's *Dictionnaire de la langue française* or *Le Petit Robert.*
22. Avidius Cassius was a Syrian general who was victorious in the Parthian War. Marcus Aurelius charged him with governing the eastern part of the empire. After the false information about the death of the emperor, he was even proclaimed emperor by his troops in 175 and attempted to take power. He was assassinated a few months later by his legionnaires.
23. For a full critical interpretation, see Alain Pons, "Charles Renouvier et *l'Uchronie,*" *Commentaire* 47 (Autumn 1989): 573–582.
24. For the first two texts: for example, Lorenzo Pignotti, *Storia della Toscana sino al principato con diversi saggi sulle scienze, lettere e arti, Pisa, co'caratteri di Didot, 1813–1814.* Such projects came apparently a little later in Spain: "*Cuatro siglos de buen gobierno (novela de la Edad Moderna),*" in *La Ilustración Española e Iberoamericana* 44 (1883): 311–314.
25. The significance of this approach is explored in detail in the French edition by Jean-Clément Martin, *Peut-on prouver l'existence de Napoléon?* (Paris: Vendémiaire, 2012).

26. In Isaac D'Israeli, *Curiosities of Literature,* vol. 2 (Paris: Baudry's European Library, 1835).
27. Auguste Blanqui, *L'Éternité par les astres* (Paris: G. Baillière, 1872); *Eternity by the Stars: An Astronomical Hypothesis* (New York: Contra Mundum Press, 2013).
28. Castello N. Holford, *Aristopia: A Romance-History of the New World* (Boston: Arena Publishing, 1895).
29. Marcel Gauchet, *Philosophie des sciences historiques. Le moment romantique* (Paris: Seuil, 2002). This fluidity continued into the interwar period in a number of areas.
30. Reinhart Koselleck, *Future's Past: On the Semantics of Historical Time,* trans. Keith Tribe (New York: Columbia University Press, 2004); Jean-Marie Goulemot, *Le Règne de l'histoire. Discours historique et révolutions XVIIe–XVIIIe siècle* (Paris: Albin Michel, 1996); Gauchet, *Philosophie des sciences historiques.* For the social, political, and cultural implications in the nineteenth century, see Alain Corbin, "Le XIXe siècle ou la nécessité de l'assemblage," in *L'Invention du XIXe siècle. Le XIXe siècle vu par lui-même (littérature, histoire, société)* ed. Alain Corbin (Paris: Klincksieck et Presses de la Sorbonne nouvelle, 1999), 153–159.
31. Michèle Riot-Sarcey, *Le Réel de l'utopie. Essai sur le politique au XIXe siècle* (Paris: Albin Michel, 1998); Michèle Riot-Sarcey, Thomas Bouchet, and Antoine Picon, eds., *Dictionnaire des utopies* (Paris: Larousse, 2002); Thierry Paquot, *Utopies et utopistes* (Paris: La Découverte, 2007).
32. Paul Ricoeur, *Lectures on Ideology and Utopia* (New York: Columbia University Press, 1986).
33. Uchronia is therefore, according to Charles Renouvier, a "utopia applied to history."
34. See "Utopies/Uchronies," *Temporalités,* special issue, no. 12, 2010.
35. Peter Novick, *That Noble Dream: The "Objectivity Question" and the American Historical Profession* (Cambridge: Cambridge University Press, 1988).
36. Joseph Edgar Chamberlin, *The Ifs of History* (Philadelphia: Henry Altemus, 1907).
37. Among the numerous publications in this field, one may cite an article by James M. Beck, entitled "It Might Have Been" and published in January 1920 in the *North American Review,* or the work by Fossey J. C. Hearnshaw, *The Ifs of History,* published in London in 1929 by G. Newnes.
38. Arnold Toynbee, "The Abortive Birthright of the Far Western Christian Civilization," in *A Study of History,* vol. 2 (Oxford: Oxford University Press, 1934).
39. Arnold Toynbee, "The Forfeited Birthright of the Abortive Scandinavian Civilization," in *A Study of History,* vol. 2 (Oxford: Oxford University Press, 1934).
40. Ibid.
41. Arnold Toynbee, "If Alexander the Great Had Lived On" and "If Ochus and Philip Had Lived On," in *Some Problems in Greek History* (Oxford: Oxford University Press, 1969).
42. Arnold Toynbee, "Some Great "Ifs" of History," *New York Times Magazine,* March 5, 1961.
43. Daniel Snowman, *If I Had Been: Ten Historical Fantasies* (London: Robson Books, 1979).

44. John M. Merriman, ed., *For Want of a Horse: Choice and Chance in History* (Lexington, MA: Stephen Greene Press, 1985).
45. "Sheer chance found little place in the interpretation of such crucial events. . . . " Ibid., ix.
46. See our chapter 6.
47. Alfred H. Conrad and John R. Meyer, "The Economics of Slavery in the Antebellum South," *Journal of Political Economy* 66, no. 2 (April 1958): 121.
48. Robert Fogel, *Railroads and American Economic Growth: Essays in Econometric History* (Baltimore: Johns Hopkins University Press, 1964).
49. George G. S. Murphy, "On Counterfactual Propositions," *History and Theory* 9 (1969): 14–38.
50. Chapter 4 provides a more in-depth discussion of counterfactual analysis in cliometrics.
51. Robert Fogel, "Historiography and Retrospective Econometrics," *History and Theory* 9, no. 3 (1970): 256.
52. Patrick Gardiner, *The Nature of Historical Explanation* (Oxford: Oxford University Press, 1952), 107.
53. David Hume, *Philosophical Essays Concerning Human Understanding* (London: Millar, 1748), 124.
54. Geoffrey Hawthorn, *Plausible Worlds: Possibility and Understanding in History and the Social Sciences* (Cambridge: Cambridge University Press, 1991).
55. Ibid., 37.
56. Niall Ferguson, ed., *Virtual History: Alternatives and Counterfactuals* (New York: Basic Books, 2011), 79.
57. This method also allows one to measure the effect of determinist theories on the beliefs of the actors themselves.
58. Ferguson, *Virtual History,* 85.
59. See "Histoire et sciences sociales. Un tournant critique?" *Annales ESC,* no. 2 (March–April 1988): 291–293, for a French synthesis of this international phenomenon. See also amid an abundant bibliography in Marcel Gauchet, "Changement de paradigme en sciences sociales?" *Le Débat,* no. 50 (May–August 1988); François Dosse, *L'Empire du sens. L'humanisation des sciences humaines* (Paris: La Découverte, 1995).
60. Robert Cowley, ed., *What If? The World's Foremost Military Historians Imagine What Might Have* Been (New York: Putnam, 1999); Robert Cowley, ed., *More What If? Eminent Historians Imagine What Might Have Been* (New York: Putnam, 2001). The first volume appeared on the *New York Times* bestseller list, https://www.nytimes.com/books/00/10/08/ bsp/papernon ctioncompare.html [accessed 2010]. It was translated into Italian (2001) and German (2000, 2002). The second volume was translated into Portugese (2003).
61. Niall Ferguson, *Empire: The Rise and Demise of the British World Order* (New York: Basic Books, 2004).
62. Having said this, the reception of *Virtual History* was generally positive; the commentators considered the idea to be stimulating even if the final result was disappointing: *History and Theory* 38, no. 2 (May 1999): 264–276; *Social History* 28, no. 2

(January 2000): 51–52; "The Promise and Perils of What If," *Historical Social Research* [*Historische Sozialforschung*] 25, no. 1 (2000): 186–190; *Journal of Military History* 64, no. 3 (2000): 918–919; *Journal of Modern History* 72, no. 4 (December 2000): 990–991; *English Historical Review* 113, no. 452 (June 1998): 815–816; *Journal of Interdisciplinary History* 31, no. 3 (Winter 2001): 428–429; *American Historical Review,* 105, no. 5 (December 2000): 1692–1693. The critics of Niall Ferguson's *Pity of War, 1914–1918* (London: Penguin, 2012), which used this technique in an explicitly political mode, suffered a far more severe reception, most notably for its use of counterfactualism.

63. For example, the military and political historian Jeremy Black from Exeter University in *What If? Counterfactualism and the Problem of History* (London: Social Affair Unit, 2008).
64. Martin Bunzl, "User's Guide," *American Historical Review* 109, no. 3 (June 2004): 845–848.
65. Richard Evans, "Telling It What It Wasn't," *Historically Speaking* 5, no. 4 (March 2004).
66. Richard Evans, *Altered Pasts: Counterfactuals in History* (London: Little Brown, 2014).
67. Eric J. Hobsbawm, *On History* (London: Weidenfeld & Nicholson, 1997).
68. As demonstrated by a simple Google search focused on the year 2013. See also the on-line review of *The Counterfactual History,* edited by the historian Gavriel Rosenfeld, from the University of Fairfield, created in 2013, which provides information on the subject.

CHAPTER 2. FROM DELHI TO VIENNA

1. In what follows we have relied on a systematic study of the various publications on the subject, notably found in the major national libraries, including the Bibliothèque nationale de France, the British Library, the Staatsbibliothek zu Berlin, and the Biblioteca nacional de España. Outside the previously mentioned difficulties, language barriers also prevented an exhaustive survey.
2. Geoffrey Hawthorn, *Plausible Worlds: Possibility and Understanding in History and the Social Sciences* (Cambridge: Cambridge University Press, 1991).
3. Edward Hallett Carr, *What Is History?* (London: Penguin, 1961); Edward P. Thompson, *The Poverty of Theory and Others Essays* (London: Merlin Press, 1980). These were the George Macaulay Trevelyan Lectures, given between January and March 1961.
4. Isaiah Berlin, *Historical Inevitability* (Oxford: Oxford University Press, 1954).
5. Lewis Carroll, *Alice's Adventures in Wonderland,* ed. Richard Kelly (London: Broadview, 2011).
6. According to a precise definition: "Everything that happens has a cause or causes, and could not have happened unless something in the cause or causes had also been different." E. H. Carr, *What Is History?* (London: Penguin Modern Classics, 2018).
7. "The point is that today nobody seriously wishes to reverse the results of the Norman Conquest or of American independence or to express passionate protest against these events." Ibid.
8. Ibid.

9. Thompson, *The Poverty of Theory.*
10. Eric Hobsbawm, "Labor History and Ideology," *Journal of Social History* 7 (1974): 376–377. He continues: "For instance, in assessing the development of the British labour movement since the 1880s we can exclude the possibility that a mass Marxist party could have developed instead of something like the Labour Party, before or after 1920, and we can therefore criticize the SDF or the CP not for what they could not seriously hope to have achieved, but within the limits of what it was not so impracticable for them to achieve—e.g., greater success in local government elections."
11. Marc Bloch, *Apologie pour l'histoire ou métier d'historien* (Paris: Armand Colin, 1949), 49.
12. Niall Ferguson, "Virtual History: Toward a 'Chaotic' Theory of the Past," in *Virtual History,* ed. Niall Ferguson (Oxford: Oxford University Press, 1997) 1–91. He is targeting the linguistic turn with the last term in the series.
13. Sanjay Subrahmanyam, "Un '*Grand Derangement*': Dreaming an Indo-Persian Empire in South Asia, 1740–1800," *Journal of Early Modern History* 4 (2001): 337–378.
14. Amiya Kumar Bagchi, *Private Investment in India, 1900–1939* (Cambridge: Cambridge University Press, 1972).
15. In 2006, Irfan Habib published *People's History of India: Indian Economy, 1858–1914* (New Delhi: Tulika Press), which also employed a counterfactual analysis.
16. See also the reviews of the professor of political science from the University of Bristol, J. M. Lee, entitled "Australian Counterfactuals," for a general sense of the books discussed, *Pacific Review* 5, no. 3 (1992); Paul Burns, *The Brisbane Line Controversy: Political Opportunism Versus National Security, 1942–1945* (St Leonards, Australia: Allen and Unwin, 1998).
17. Stuart Macintyre and Sean Scalmer, eds., *What If? Counterfactual Essays in Australian History* (Carlton, Australia: Melbourne University Publications, 2006).
18. Stephen Levine, ed., *New Zealand as It Might Have Been* (Wellington: Victoria University Press, 2006). A second volume appeared in 2010: *New Zealand as It Might Have Been 2* (Wellington: Victoria University Press, 2010).
19. Signed in 1840 in Waitangi, New Zealand, between the representatives of the British Crown and the Maori chiefs of new Zealand, the treaty recognized the sovereignty of the British Crown over new Zealand, even if the terms of the treaty—notably in its Maori version—have been the object of intense controversy.
20. This is a reference to the environmentalist movements for Lakes Manapouri and Te Anau in the 1960s.
21. John H. Coatsworth, "Counterfactual Mexicos," *History Compass* 4, no, 1 (2005): 176–180.
22. Paulo Roberto de Almeida, "História virtual: Limites e possibilidades," http:// www.pralmeida.org/05DocsPRA/1075HistoriaVirtualIntro.html; Paulo Roberto de Almeida, "História virtual do Brasil: Um exercicio intelectual," *Revista Acadêmica Espaço da Sophia,* no. 9 (December 2007).
23. This led to the publication of an article of interest: Víctor Hugo Palacios Cruz, "La libertad y la comprensión histórica. Los límites de la historia contrafactual,"

presentation given for the *9es journées d'actualisation philosophique*. See also "Causalité et émergence. Dialogues entre philosophes et scientifiques," in *Pensamiento y Cultura* 7, no. 1 (2004): 79–89. The analysis of the implications of Ferguson's positions is affirmed. See also Carlos Vargas, "Historia virtual o el vértigo de la mariposa," *Cuadernos de Marcha*, no. 169 (January 2001).

24. "Pasados imaginarios," *Letras Libres*, Edición Mexico, no. 118 (October 2008).
25. Humberto Beck, "Presentación: Sobre la historia contrafactual," *Letras Libres* 10, no. 118 (2008), 14–15. On this space, see the contextualization proposed by Josue Barrera, "La historia contrafactual en la época contemporánea," https://www.academia.edu/603721/La_historia_contrafactual_en_la_%C3%A9poca_contempor%C3%A1nea.
26. Though they were very present in Mexico, the Jesuits were expelled in 1767 by the Spanish. The event has long been considered yet one more difficulty imposed on local populations in the spheres of education or (relative) protection against slavery. In 1847, the American army invaded Mexico and was confronted, during the taking of Mexico City, by a unexpected guerrilla force. The "Mexican War" appears to one of the factors in the American Civil War that began in 1861.
27. Niall Ferguson, *Historia virtual* (Madrid: Taurus, 1998). This translation helps explain the diffusion of his ideas in Latin America.
28. The first was emeritus professor at Columbia University, the second was the director of the Center for Democratic Transition Studies in Spain at the University of San Pablo—CEU in Madrid.
29. Ferguson's book was translated into Polish. See also Janusz Osica, Andrzej Leon Sowa, and Henryk Samsonowicz, *Co by bylo gdyby: Historie alternatywne* (Warsaw, Poland: Bellona, 1998); Dmytro Shurkhalo, *Ukraïns'ka "iàkbytolohiià": Narysy al'ternatyvnoï istoriï* (2004; Lviv, Ukraine: Piramida, 2007); Ø. Sørensen, *Historien om det som ikke skjedde: kontrafaktisk historie* (Oslo: Aschehoug Forlag, 2005).
30. "Quando la storia si fa con 'i se e con i ma,'" in a "Magistra Vitae" meeting organized in December 2005 in Rimini, Italy, dedicated to "storia controfattuale," and bringing together philosophers, journalists, and writers.
31. "La storia non si fa con i se? Ri essioni sull'identità italiana," organized at Ravenna, Italy, in 2006. The title of Gentile's conference was "Se Mussolini non fosse entrato in guerra nel 1940?" March 25, 2006.
32. Pasquale Chessa, *Se Garibaldi avesse perso: Storia controfattuale dell' Unità d'Italia* (Venice: Marsilio, 2011).
33. Ibid., 7–14.
34. This project was followed by Alberto Benzoni and Elisa Benzoni, eds., *La storia con i se: Dieci casi che potevano cambiare il corso del Novecento* (Venice: Marsilio, 2013).
35. Alexander Demandt, *Ungeschehene Geschichte, Ein Traktat über die Frage, Was wäre wenn?* (Göttingen, Germany: V & R, 1986; reissued 2001 and 2005), 7.
36. Friedrich Nietzsche, "Statement," in *Nachgelassene fragmente, 1875–1879*, vol. 4, ch. 1 (Munich: Dt. Taschenbuch-Verlag, 1999), 32.
37. Geoffrey Hawthorn, *Die Welt ist alles, was möglich ist . . . , Über das Verstehen der Vergangenheit* (Stuttgart, Germany: Klett-Cotta, 1994); Alexander Demandt, *History*

That Never Happened: A Treatise of the Question What Would Have Happened, If . . . ? (Jefferson, NC: McFarland, 1993).

38. A new edition appeared with the same editor: Alexander Demandt, *Es hätte auch anders kommen können: Wendepunkte deutscher Geschichte* (Berlin: Propyläen-Verlag, 2010).
39. Kai Brodersen, *Virtuelle Antike. Wendepunkte der alten Geschichte* (Darmstadt, Germany: Primus Verlag, 2000). See also Wilfried Nippel, "Die Geschworenengerichte der späten römischen Republik: Kontrafaktische Überlegungen," in *Gegenwärtige Antike—antike Gegenwarten: Kolloquium zum 60. Geburtstag von Rolf Rilinger,* ed. Tassilo Schmitt (Munich: Oldenbourg, 2005), 127–149.
40. Michael Salewski, ed., *Was Wäre Wenn, Alternativ- und Parallelgeschichte: Brücken zwischen Phantasie und Wirklichkeit* (Stuttgart, Germany: Steiner Verlag, 1999).
41. Michael Salewski, "Andere Welten, andere Geschichten: 'Verheißung oder Drohung?,'" in *Streifzüge ins Übermorgen. Science Fiktion und Zukunftsforschung Weinheim,* ed. Klaus Burmeister and Karlheinz Steinmüller (Basel: Beltz, 1992); Michael Salewski, *Zeitgeist und Zeitmaschine: Science Fiction und Geschichte* (Munich: Dt. Taschenbuch-Verlag, 1986); Uta Heimann-Störmer, *Kontrafaktische Urteile in der Geschichtsschreibung: Eine Fallstudie zur Historiographie des Bismarck-Reiches* (Frankfurt am Main: Lang, 1991).
42. Most notably, his book *Logic and Society: Contradictions and Possible Worlds* (Hoboken, NJ: John Wiley & Sons, 1978).
43. Joachim Losehand, *Die letzten Tage des Pompeius: Von Pharsalos bis Pelusion* (Vienna: Phoibos-Verlag, 2008).
44. Course of Jürgen Elvert, professor of the History of Modern Europe in Cologne.
45. "Counterfactual Thinking: 'Parlour Game' or Analytical Tool?," Centre for British Studies, Humboldt-Universität zu Berlin, November 27–28, 2008.
46. Roland Wenzlhuemer, ed., "Counterfactual Thinking as a Scientific Method" [Kontrafaktisches Denken als wissenschaftliche Methode], *Historical Social Review* [*Historische Sozialforschung*] 34, no. 2 (2009). The continuation and the reception of the work of Alexander Demandt presented as "philosophy of history" or "exercises de reflexivity," a testimony to this movement: *Endzeit? Die Zukunft der Geschichte* (Berlin: Siedler, 1993). See also the remarks of Juliane Schiel, "Was wäre gewesen, wenn . . . ? Vom Nutzen kontrafaktischer Geschichtsschreibung," *Viator Multilingual* 41 (2010): 211–231.
47. See the project's website at https://whatifkn.wordpress.com/ [accessed October 2020]. The historical section is edited by Bernhard Kleeberg, from the University of Konstanz. Bernhard Kleeberg, "Significance and Abstraction. Scientific Uses of Counterfactual Thought Experiments in the Early 20th Century," in *Counterfactual Thinking/ Counterfactual Writing,* ed. Dorothee Birke (Berlin: De Gruyter, 2011), 112–129.
48. Excerpts gathered by Béranger Boulay in "L'histoire au risque du hors-temps. Braudel et la Méditerranée" (article online on the fabula website, http://www.fabula.org).
49. Fernand Braudel, *The Mediterranean and the Mediterranean World in the Age of Philip II,* vol. 2, trans. Sian Reynolds (Berkeley: University of California Press, 1995), 660.

50. Ibid., 950.
51. Hervé Le Bras, "La population avec des si," in *Les 4 Mystères de la population française* (Paris: Odile Jacob, 2007), 19–46.
52. The approach is often invoked in the context of economic history, but its actual use remains sparse, as demonstrated by Jean-Charles Asselain, who evokes "the resistance of history" in the face of counterfactualism. Bertrand Blancheton, "Itinéraires et travaux scientifiques de Jean-Charles Asselain," in *La Croissance en économie ouverte (XVIII*[e]*–XX*[e] *siècles),* ed. Bertrand Blancheton and Hubert Bonin (Brussels: PIE Peter Lang, 2009), 451–456. Nonetheless, it sits at the heart of the vast analysis of Maurice Lévy-Leboyer and François Bourguignon, *L'Économie française au XIX*[e] *siècle* (Paris: Economica, 1986). It also appears in the works of economists interested in historical or critical approaches (see, for example, Frédéric Lordon's blog, https://blog.mondediplo.net/_Frederic-Lordon, where counterfactual "thought experiments" are sometimes used: *"Économistes, institutions, pouvoirs," Mediapart,* November 21, 2012; "BNP-Paribas, une affaire à géométrie variable," Diplo blog, https://blog.mondediplo.net/2014-07-08-BNP-Paribas-une-affaire-de-geometries-variables, July 8, 2014). Lastly, it is used in the context of the cliometry of Claude Diebolt, "The Cliometric Voice," *History of Economic Ideas* 20, no. 3 (2012): 51–61.
53. Jacques Revel, "Ressources narratives et connaissance historique," in "Les terrains de l'enquête," *Enquête* 1 (1995), 43–70.
54. Gérard Noiriel, "L'imagination historique," *Histoire, théâtre & politique* (Marseille: Agone, 2009), 175: "Using fiction allows one to do thought experiments on possibilities which one would not spontaneously have thought of when sources are lacking. This observation explains the recent development of connections between history and literature and the appearance of new areas of research such as virtual history, which attempts to explain what the world would have become if, for example, Napoleon had not lost the Battle of Waterloo." He also notes that it is used by authors of critical theater, such as Bertolt Brecht in *The Business Affairs of Mr. Julius Caesar.*
55. Alain Boureau and Daniel Milo, *Alter-Histoire. Essais d'histoire expérimentale* (Paris: Les Belles Lettres, 1991).
56. Daniel Milo, "Pour une histoire expérimentale, ou la gaie histoire," *Annales ESC,* no. 3 (May–June 1990): 717–734.
57. Robert Musil, *The Man Without Qualities* (New York: Vintage, 1996).
58. Milo, "Pour une histoire expérimentale," 726. Example developed by Daniel Milo in "Du possible en histoire. Le cas du calendrier républicain," in *Trahir le temps* (Paris: Les Belles Lettres, 1991).
59. "Exalter l'imagination libre de l'historien," interview with A. Boureau, *Le Monde des livres,* March 5, 2009.
60. Antoine Prost, "Écrire l'histoire avec des si," in *Douze leçons sur l'histoire* (Paris: Seuil, 1996), 174–187.
61. Paul Lacombe, *De l'histoire considérée comme science* (Paris: Hachette, 1894); Raymond Aron, *Introduction à la philosophie de l'histoire. Essai sur les limites de l'objectivité historique* (Paris: Gallimard, 1938).

62. Prost, "Écrire l'histoire avec des si," 176–177.
63. Ibid., 176.
64. Fabrice d'Almeida and Anthony Rowley, *Et si on refaisait l'histoire?* (Paris: Odile Jacob, 2009).
65. Jacques Sapir, Frank Stora, and Loïc Mahé, eds., *1940. Et si la France avait continué la guerre . . . Essai d'alternative historique* (Paris, Tallandier, 2010). Sapir, Stora, and Mahé, eds., *1941–1942. Et si la France avait continué la guerre . . .* (Paris: Tallandier, 2012).
66. "Et si . . . ? La cause du contrefactuel," *Labyrinthe, revue interdisciplinaire,* no. 39 (2012); "Réalité(s) du possible en sciences humaines et sociales," *Tracés, revue de sciences humaines* 24 (2013). We organized two seminars on the question "What if?": Contributions, Limits and the Significance of the Counterfactual Approach in History," seminar at the École des Hautes Études en Sciences Sociales, 2009–2010; and with Jean-Mathias Fleury, "Uses and Significance of Counterfactual Reasoning in History and the Social Sciences," Collège de France (under the chair of Jacques Bouveresse), 2010–2011. The seminar of Jean Boutier and Alain Trannoy, "Causality in Social Sciences," École des Hautes Études en Sciences Sociales, Marseille, 2010–2014, should also be noted.
67. Pierre Duhem, *La Théorie physique, son objet, sa structure* (Paris: Vrin, 1981). The "ample" mind has an easier time imagining groupings of complex phenomena; the "profound" mind is more oriented toward abstraction and generalization. In this sense, it corresponds well to the separation brought on by counterfactualism.
68. One of the strongest critiques concerns the notion of Britishness. J. G. A. Pocock, "The Limits and Division of British History: In Search of an Unknown Subject," *American Historical Review* 87, no. 2 (1987): 311–336.
69. See Johan Heilbron J., "Qu'est-ce qu'une tradition nationale en sciences sociales?" *Revue d'histoire des sciences humaines* 18 (2008): 3–14; Johan Heilbron, Nicolas Guilhot, and Laurent Jeanpierre, "Toward a Transnational History of the Social Sciences," *Journal of the History of the Behavioral Sciences* 44, no. 2 (2008): 146–160.
70. On the logics of importation of the social sciences in France, see Marc Joly, *Devenir Norbert Elias* (Paris: Fayard, 2012); and Mathieu Hauchecorne, "La Fabrication transnationale des idées politiques. Sociologie de la réception de John Rawls et des "théories de la justice" en France (1971–2011)" (PhD thesis in political science, directed by Frédéric Sawicki and Frédérique Matonti, Lille 2 University, 2011).
71. Gisèle Sapiro and Ioana Popa, "Traduire les sciences humaines et sociales. Logiques éditoriales et enjeux scientifiques," in *Translatio. Le marché de la traduction en France à l'heure de la mondialisation,* ed. Gisèle Sapiro (Paris: CNRS Éditions, 2008), 108.
72. Christophe Charle, "Les Références étrangères des universitaires. Essai de comparaison entre la France et l'Allemagne, 1870–1970," *Actes de la recherche en sciences sociales* 148 (June 2003): 8–19.
73. Jacques Revel, "Ressources narratives et connaissance historique," *Enquête* 1 (1995): 43–70.
74. This movement was paradoxically of French origin. French theory referred to the works of Deleuze, Foucault, and Derrida.

75. A *longue durée* analysis that brings together both dimensions can be found in J. Heilbron, "The Tripartite Division of French Social Science: A Long-Term Perspective," in *Discourses on Society, The Shaping of the Social Science Disciplines,* ed. Peter Wagner, Björn Wittorock, and Richard Whitley (Berlin: Kluwer Academic Publisher, 1991), 73–93.
76. Suzanne Citron, *Le Mythe national, l'histoire de France revisitée* (Paris: L'Atelier, 2008); Patrick Garcia and Jean Leduc, *L'Enseignement de l'histoire en France de l'Ancien Régime à nos jours* (Paris: Armand Colin, 2003).
77. Pierre Bourdieu, "Système d'enseignement et système de pensée," in *L'Inconscient académique* (Zurich: Éditions Seismo, 2006), 21–47.

CHAPTER 3. FROM PTERODACTYLS TO PICCADILLY CIRCUS

1. William S. Burroughs, *The Place of Dead Roads* (New York: Picador, 1983), 287–289.
2. H. G. Wells, *The Time Machine* (London: W. Heinemann, 1895).
3. P. J. Mergey, "En guise d'introduction, un peu d'étymologie," in *L'Histoire revisitée. Panorama de l'uchronie sous toutes ses formes,* by Éric Henriet (1st ed. 1999; Paris: Les Belles Lettres, 2004).
4. Thomas Pavel, *La Pensée du roman* (Paris: Gallimard, 2003). Revised and expanded in Thomas Pavel, The *Lives of the Novel: A History* (Princeton, NJ: Princeton University Press, 2013). See also Judith Lyon-Caen, *La Lecture et la vie. Les usages du roman au temps de Balzac* (Paris: Tallandier, 2006); and Jérôme David, *Balzac, une éthique de la description* (Paris: Honoré Champion, 2010).
5. Philippe Ethuin, "Présentation," in *Histoire de ce qui n'est pas arrivé,* by Joseph Méry (ArchéoSF/publie.net, 2012).
6. Joseph Méry, *Histoire de ce qui n'est pas arrivé* (Poissy, France: Imprimerie de Arbieu, 1859), 16.
7. Dolf Oehler, *Le Spleen contre l'oubli, juin 1848: Baudelaire, Flaubert, Heine, Herzen* (Paris: Payot, 1996).
8. Guy Dent, *Emperor of the Ifs* (Heinemann: London, 1926).
9. Raphaël Colson and François-André Ruaud, *Science-fiction. Une littérature du reel* (Paris: Klincksieck, 2006).
10. Henriet, *L'Histoire revisitée.*
11. Sarban, *The Sound of His Horn* (1952; New York: Ballantine Books, 1960), 61.
12. Richard Saint-Gelais, "Quelques avatars de l'advenu. Excursions en uchronie," in *L'Empire du pseudo. Modernités de la science-fiction* (Québec: Nota Bene, 1999).
13. Donald R. Bensen, *And Having Writ . . .* (New York: Bobbs-Merrill, 1978).
14. Jean-Claude Vareille, *Le Roman populaire français, 1789–1914. Idéologies et pratiques* (Limoges, France: Presses Universitaires de Limoges, 1994).
15. For the following analysis, see Saint-Gelais, "Quelques avatars de l'advenu."
16. Louis-Napoléon Geoffroy-Château, *Napoléon et la conquête du monde* (Paris: H.-L. Delloye, 1836), 273.
17. Pavel, The *Lives of the Novel.*
18. We would like to thank Jérôme David for this insight. According to this reading, the "real of novelistic realism" is, for example, defined by the obviousness of the ordinary

or recourse to scientific laws. The uchronic novel therefore provokes a game of mirrors that shifts this "real" from one space of reference to another, without ever abandoning historical or psychological laws: the ordinary loses its obviousness, but above all the principles and the biases that define the real of realism reveal themselves to be fully in this "other" fictional world. Out of this inevitably comes the *mise en abyme* described earlier.

19. Henriet, *L'Histoire revisitée.*
20. Paul Seabury, "The Histronaut," *Magazine of Fantasy and Science Fiction,* April 1963, 117–125.
21. The choice of certain turning points may also be surprising, such as those of Neil Comins, professor of astronomy, who asked in 1993 what Earth would be like if the Moon didn't exist, and then in 2010 what it would be like if there were two moons. Neil Comins, *What If the Moon Didn't Exist? Voyage to Earth That Might Have Been* (New York: HarperCollins, 1993); Neil Comins, *What If the Earth Had Two Moons? And Nine Other Thought-Provoking Speculations on the Solar System* (New York: St. Martin's Press, 2010).
22. See James Blaut, *The Colonizer's Model of the World: Geographical Diffusionism and Eurocentric History* (New York: Guilford Press, 1993).
23. The term "uchronia" is used with less frequency in English.
24. Gérard Klein, *Histoires de la quatrième dimension* (Paris: Librairie générale française, 1983).
25. See also the interview by Bertrand Campeis in March 2010, available on the Uchronies website: uchronies.com/Interview_003_Andre_Francois_Ruaud. html [accessed September 2018].
26. La porte des mondes, http://portedesmondes.noosfere.org/ [accessed October 2020]; Uchronies, http://www.uchronies.org [accessed October 2020].
27. Henriet, *L'Histoire revisitée*; André-François Ruaud, *Passés recomposés, anthologie uchronique* (Aix-en-Provence, France: Nestiveqnen, 2003).
28. Ugo Bellagamba, *Tancrède: Une uchronie* (Lyon, France: Les Moutons électriques, 2009).
29. See http://www.uchronia.net/bib.cgi/notes/anthology.html. First dedicated to creating a list of alternate history, the Uchronia website has gone from 150 entries to more than 3,000 in 2010. We have noted in our count the essays of historians and the works of non-Anglophones.
30. Martin Greenberg and Charles S. Waugh, eds., *Alternative Histories: Eleven Histories of the World as It Might Have Been* (New York: Garland, 1986). See also Robert Adams and Pamela Crippen-Adams, eds., *Alternatives* (New York: Baen, 1989); Gregory Benford and Martin Greenberg, eds., *What Might Have Been* (I Books, 2004); Gardner Dozois and Stanley Schmidt, eds., *Roads Not Taken: Tales of Alternate History* (New York: Del Rey, 1998); one may also add *Alternate Histories* (*Alternate Kennedys, Alternate Presidents, Alternate Warrior,* etc.) published by Hodder and Stoughton from 1995 onward.
31. Stephen Stirling, *Marching Through Georgia* (Wake Forest, NC: Baen, 1988).
32. Harry Turtledove, *The Two Georges* (London: Hodder and Stoughton, 1995).

33. It is worth noting that that this development has been confirmed with the development in France of the Actusf de l'Uchronie Prize.
34. This narrative technique allows one to present scenes lived by characters in the past, in other worlds, and in alternative universes.
35. *What If Spider-Man Joined the Fantastic Four?,* Marvel Comics, vol. 1, no. 1 (February 1977).
36. Kevin Wayne Jeter, *Morlock Night* (New York: Daw Books, 1979); Tim Powers, *The Anubis Gates* (New York: Ace Books, 1983); James P. Blaylock, *Homunculus* (New York: Ace Books, 1986).
37. The first computer was in fact created by Babbage, but it was never completed. The uchronia is therefore built on the proposition: "If the computer built by Babbage had actually functioned . . ."
38. Jay Clayton, *Charles Dickens in Cyberspace: The Afterlife of the Nineteenth Century in Postmodern Culture* (Oxford: Oxford University Press, 2003), 105–118; Herbert Sussman, "Cyberpunk Meets Charles Babbage," *Victorian Studies* 38 (1994): 1–23.
39. Francis Spufford and Jenny Uglow, *Cultural Babbage: Technology, Time and Invention* (London: Faber and Faber, 1996); http://www.sff.net/people/gunn/dd/ [existed from 1996 to 2017].
40. Fabrice Colin and Mathieu Gaborit, *Confessions d'un automate mangeur d'opium* (Paris: Bragelonne, 2013); René Reouven, *Bouvard, Pécuchet et les savants fous* (Paris: Flammarion, 2000); Johan Heliot, *La Lune seule le sait* (Paris: Gallimard, 2003). See also Dominique Kalifa, *Les Bas-Fonds. Histoire d'un imaginaire social* (Paris: Seuil, 2013), 331–333.
41. The French have taken an interest in this movement, as seen in Étienne Barillier, *Steampunk! L'esthétique rétro-futur* (Paris: Les Moutons électriques, 2010).
42. See http://www.mhs.ox.ac.uk/exhibits/steampunk/; Catalogue *Futur antérieur* (Paris: Le Mot et le Reste/Galerie du jour Agnès B., 2012).
43. In this work, Jesus is spared and the course of history is changed, giving the author the opportunity to engage in a wider set of reflections on literature, history, and theology.
44. The opening pages contain an excerpt from an interview by the author: "Building off the principle that the future, as we conceive it, is already part of the inventions of our past, I thought I would take the opposite path and reconstruct from the present what happened in other futures that had also already taken place, facts that didn't happen but which could have happened. Less real than a mere premonition, less diffused than a simple invention. It is possible time, with its own nostalgia." Haruki Murakami, *1Q84,* bk. 1 (Paris: Belfond, 2011).
45. It would be interesting to bring together this use of distantiation that Jean-Marie Schaeffer attributes to fiction in human culture within the process of adulthood and human development; see Jean-Marie Schaeffer, *Pourquoi la fiction?* (Paris: Seuil, 1999).
46. Saint-Gelais, "Quelques avatars de l'advenu."

CHAPTER 4. THE TEST OF THE SOCIAL (AND NATURAL) SCIENCES

1. Luc Boltanski, "Le Pouvoir est de plus en plus savant," *La Vie des idées,* August 28, 2011, 11.
2. Neal Roese, "Counterfactual Thinking and Decision Making," *Psychonomic Bulletin and Review* 6, no. 4 (December 1999): 570–578; C. Gustav Lundberg and Dean E. Frost, "Counterfactuals in Financial Decision Making," *Acta psychologica* 79, no. 3 (1992): 227–244; Elias J. Duryea, "Using Counterfactual Exercises to Enhance Decision-Making in Sexual Health," *Journal of School Health* 73 (November 9, 2003).
3. Neal J. Roese and Taekyun Hur, "Affective Determinants of Counterfactual Thinking," *Social Cognition* 15 (1997): 274–290.
4. Ibid.
5. Victoria Husted Medvec, Scott F. Madey, and Thomas Gilovich, "When Less Is More: Counterfactual Thinking and Satisfaction among Olympic Medalists," *Journal of Personality and Social Psychology* 69, no. 4 (October 1995): 603–610.
6. Ruth M. J. Byrne, *The Rational Imagination: How People Create Alternatives to Reality* (Cambridge, MA: MIT Press, 2005).
7. Laura J. Kray, Adam D. Galinsky, and Elaine M. Wong, "Thinking within the Box: The Relational Processing Style Elicited by Counterfactual Mind-Sets," *Journal of Personality and Social Psychology* 91 (2006): 33–48.
8. Keith D. Markman, M. J. Lindberg, Laura J. Kray, and Adam D. Galinsky, "Implications of Counterfactual Structure for Creative Generation and Analytic Problem Solving," *Personality and Social Psychology Bulletin* 33 (2007): 312–324.
9. Kai Epstude and Neil J. Roese, "The Functional Theory of Counterfactual Thinking," *Personality and Social Psychology Review* 12 (2008): 168–192.
10. Bruno Bais, Denis Hilton, Karine Mazurier, and Sébastien Pouget, "Psychological Dispositions and Trading Behaviour," *Cahier de recherches,* Institut d'Administration des Entreprises de Toulouse, 150 (2002).
11. Keith D. Markman, Igor Gavanski, Steven J. Sherman, and Matthew N. McMullen, "The Mental Simulation of Better and Worse Possible Worlds," *Journal of Experimental Social Psychology* 29 (1993): 87–109; Neal J. Roese, "The Functional Basis of Counterfactual Thinking," *Journal of Personality and Social Psychology* 66 (1994): 805–818.
12. C. G. Davis, D. R. Lehman, C. B. Wortman, R. C. Silver, and S. C. Thompson, "The Undoing of Traumatic Life Events," *Personality and Social Psychology Bulletin* 21 (1995): 109–124.
13. Antonio Pierro, Susanne Leder, Lucia Mannetti, E. Tory Higgins, Arie W. Kruglanski, and Antonio Aiello, "Regulatory Mode Effects on Counterfactual Thinking and Regret," *Journal of Experimental Social Psychology* 44 (2008): 321–329.
14. Neal J. Roese and James M. Olson, eds., *What Might Have Been: The Social Psychology of Counterfactual Thinking* (Mahwah, NJ: Erlbaum, 1995).
15. Rachel Smallman and Neal J. Roese, "Counterfactual Thinking Facilitates Behavioral Intentions," *Journal of Experimental Social Psychology* 45 (2009): 845–852.

16. Laura J. Kray and Adam D. Galinsky, "The Debiasing Effect of Counterfactual Mind-Sets: Increasing the Search for Disconfirmatory Information In Group Decisions," *Organizational Behavior and Human Decision Processes* 91 (2003): 69–81.
17. Laura J. Kray, Linda G. George, Katie A. Liljenquist, Adam D. Galinsky, Philip E. Tetlock, and Neal J. Roese, "From What Might Have Been to What Must Have Been: Counterfactual Thinking Creates Meaning," *Journal of Personality and Social Psychology* 98, no. 1 (January 2010).
18. Jean-François Bonnefon, Jiehai Zhang, and Ciping Deng, "L'Effet des justifications sur le regret est-il direct ou indirect?," *Revue internationale de psychologie sociale* 20, no. 2 (2007): 131–145.
19. Robert Folger and Russell Cropanzano, *Organizational Justice and Human Resource Management* (London: Sage, 1998).
20. G. L. Wells and I. Gavinski, "Mental Simulation and Causality," *Journal of Personality and Social Psychology* 56 (1989): 161–169.
21. Ruth M. J. Byrne, *The Rational Imagination: How People Create Alternatives to Reality* (Cambridge, MA: MIT Press, 2005), xi.
22. Christine Hooker, Neal J. Roese, and Sohee Park, "Impoverished Counterfactual Thinking Is Associated with Schizophrenia," *Psychiatry* 63 (2000): 326–335.
23. Neal J. Roese, Sohee Park, Rachel Smallman, and Crystal Gibson, "Schizophrenia Involves Impairment in the Activation of Intentions by Counterfactual Thinking," *Schizophrenia Research* 103 (2008): 343–344; S. Ursu and S. T. Carter, "Outcome Representations, Counterfactual Comparisons and the Human Orbitofrontal Cortex: Implications for Neuroimaging Studies of Decision-Making," *Cognitive Brain Research* 34 (2005): 51–60.
24. Robert N. Strassfeld, "If . . . : Counterfactuals in the Law," *George Washington Law Review,* January 1992.
25. Philippe Woodland, "Le Procédé de la fiction dans la pensée juridique" (PhD thesis, Université Paris II, 1981).
26. Olga Eveline Tellegen-Couperus, *A Short History of Roman Law* (London: Routledge, 1993).
27. Yan Thomas, "L'Extrême et l'ordinaire. Remarques sur le cas médiéval de la communauté disparue," in *Penser par cas,* eds. Jacques Revel and Jean-Claude Passeron (Paris: Éditions de l'EHESS, 2005), 45–73.
28. The role of this fiction is to encourage individuals to know and respect legislation and to prevent those who have broken the law from claiming ignorance.
29. Christina Accomando, "'The Regulations of Robbers': Legal Fiction of Slavery and Resistance," *Legacy* 20, nos. 1 and 2 (2003); Jen Camden and Kathryn E. Fort, " 'Channeling Thought': The Legacy of Legal Fictions from 1823," *American Indian Law Review* 33, no. 77 (2008/2009).
30. Gérard Cornu, ed., *Vocabulaire juridique,* Association Henri Capitant (Paris: Presses Universitaire de France, 1992).
31. Lon L. Fuller, *Legal Fictions* (Stanford, CA: Stanford University Press, 1967), 9. In the 1930s, Lon L. Fuller gave two possible definitions of juridical fictions: "Either a

statement propounded with a complete or partial consciousness of its falsity, or a false statement recognized as having utility."

32. Laurence Harang, "Les Fictions juridiques," conference, *Fiction, langage et référence,* Université de Provence, February 27–March 1, 2003.
33. Guillaume Wicker, *Les Fictions juridiques. Contribution à l'analyse de l'acte juridique* (Paris: LGDJ, 1997), 10.
34. Jean-Marie Schaeffer, *Pourquoi la fiction?* (Paris: Seuil, 1999)
35. Wicker, *Les Fictions juridiques.*
36. Hans Vaihinger, *La Philosophie du comme si* (Paris: Kimé, 2008).
37. Mikhail Xifaras, "Juridical Fictions," Seminar, Fiction, directed by Yasusuke Oura, University of Kyoto, February 25, 2008.
38. Barbara A. Spellman and Alexandra Kincannon, "The Relation between Counterfactual ("but for") and Causal Reasoning: Experimental Findings and Implications for Jurors' Decisions," *Law & Contemporary Problems* 241 (Autumn 2001).
39. Price Waterhouse v. Hopkins, 1989, https://www.law.cornell.edu/supremecourt/text/490/228.
40. "Without which it could not be."
41. Richard L. Wiener, M. Gaborit, C. C. Pritchard, and E. M. McDonough, "Counterfactual Thinking in Mock Jury Assessments of Negligence: A Preliminary Investigation," *Behavioral Sciences & The Law* 12, no. 1 (1994): 89–102.
42. "AF 447. Les pilotes mis en cause," *Le Journal du Dimanche* 29 (July 2011).
43. A symposium in the *Indiana Law Review* of April 1, 2011, was dedicated to counterfactual history in constitutional law: "What if? Counterfactuals in Constitutional History." A few years earlier, the work by Risa L. Goluboff revisited the history of civil rights in the United States through counterfactual analysis: Risa L. Goluboff, *The Lost Promise of Civil Rights* (Cambridge: Harvard University Press, 2007).
44. Marc Lange, "Who's Afraid of *Ceteris-Paribus* Laws? Or: How I Learned to Stop Worrying and Love Them," *Erkenntnis* 57, no. 3 (2002).
45. Jean Heffer, "Une histoire scientifique. La nouvelle histoire économique," *Annales ESC,* no. 4 (July–August 1977): 824–842.
46. John Williamson, *Late Nineteenth-Century American Development: A General Equilibrium History* (Cambridge: Cambridge University Press, 1974).
47. Jon Elster, *Logic and Society: Contradictions and Possible Worlds* (New York: Wiley, 1978), 206.
48. Douglass C. North, "Economic Performance through Time," *American Economic Review* 84 (1994): 359–368.
49. See http://cliometrics.org/. The association in 2013 consisted of some five hundred members chosen through a selection process. It holds an annual conference and has organized six meetings of the World Congress of Cliometrics (England, Spain, Germany, Canada, Italy, Scotland). It also publishes an online review, *The Newsletter of the Cliometric Society.*
50. For a critical discussion, see Isabelle Drouet, Stéphanie Dupouy, Laurent Jeanpierre, and Florian Nicodème, "Contrefactuels en histoire: du mot au mode d'emploi. Le

moment de la *new economic history,*" *Labyrinthe* 39 (2012): 81–112. Outside this association and university chairs, there are annual cliometrics conferences since 1960, along with the organization's own journals (*Explorations in Economic History, Cliometrica, Journal of Historical Economics and Econometric History*). An association was developed in France in 2001, L'Association française de cliométrie.

51. Avner Greif, "Cliometrics after 40 Years," *American Economic Review* 87, no. 2 (1997): 400–403; Claudia Goldin, "Exploring the 'Present through The Past': Career and Family across the Last Century," *American Economic Review* 87, no. 2 (1997): 396–399; John R. Meyer, "Notes on Cliometrics' Fortieth," *American Economic Review* 87, no. 2 (1997): 409–411; Douglass C. North, "Cliometrics 40 Years Later," *American Economic Review* 87, no. 2 (1997): 412–414; see also John S. Lyons, Louis P. Cain, and Samuel H. Williamson, eds., *Reflections on the Cliometrics Revolution: Conversations with Economic Historians* (London: Routledge, 2008).
52. Douglass C. North and Lance Davis, *Institutional Change and American Economic Growth* (Cambridge: Cambridge University Press, 1971).
53. Claude Diebolt and Jean-Luc Demeulemeester, "*Quo vadis?* Quel futur pour l'histoire économique en France. Réflexions et recommandations par deux économistes," Working Papers 10-02, Association française de cliométrie, 2010.
54. This is suggested by an exploration of the occurrences of the word "counterfactual" in articles in the *Journal of Economic History* from 2000 to 2013.
55. Pierre-Henri Bono, Russell Davidson, and Alain Trannoy, "Analyse contrefactuelle de l'article 55 de la loi SRU sur la production de logements sociaux," halshs-00796192, version posted on March 1, 2013.
56. Richard Ned Lebow, "What's So Different about a Counterfactual?," *World Politics* 52, no. 4 (July 2000): 550–585.
57. Imanuel Geiss, *July 1914: The Outbreak of the First World War* (New York: Charles Scribner's Sons, 1967).
58. Richard Ned Lebow, *Forbidden Fruit: Counterfactuals and International Relations* (Princeton, NJ: Princeton University Press, 2010).
59. This work has been developed by Yuen Foong Khong in his article "Confronting Hitler and Its Consequences," in *Counterfactual Thought Experiments in World Politics: Logical, Methodological, and Psychological Perspectives,* ed. Philip E. Tetlock and Aaron Belkin (Princeton, NJ: Princeton University Press, 1996).
60. Stuart J. Thorson and Donald A. Sylvan, "Counterfactuals and the Cuban Missile Crisis," *International Studies Quarterly* 26 (1982).
61. Philip E. Tetlock and Aaron Belkin, eds., *Counterfactual Thought Experiments in World Politics: Logical, Methodological, and Psychological Perspectives* (Princeton, NJ: Princeton University Press, 1996); Richard Ned Lebow, *Forbidden Fruit: Counterfactuals and International Relations* (Princeton, NJ: Princeton University Press, 2010).
62. Consider for example the following counterfactual: If Richard M. Nixon had been president of the United States during the Cuban Missile Crisis, would he have been more aggressive than Kennedy and ordered air strikes and an invasion of Cuba, thereby setting off a nuclear war? If one decides to examine Nixon's behavior during

the Cuban Missile Crisis, then one must imagine that he won the 1960 election instead of John F. Kennedy. These previous counterfactual calls into question the pertinence of the initial hypothesis. Indeed, if Nixon had been president, other hypotheses would have been proposed: he could have overthrown Fidel Castro, etc. In this case, the missile crisis would not have taken place. In sum, in the elaboration of the counterfactual proposal, it is a question of identifying the most important change, for example, the presidential election of 1960.

63. Lebow, "What's So Different about a Counterfactual?," 550–585. These "miracle-world counterfactuals" possess nonetheless the virtue of stimulating the imagination and attracting researchers' attention to questions that have been avoided and problems that have been forgotten.
64. See http://gking.harvard.edu/whatif/; Heather Stoll, Gary King, and Langche Zeng, "WhatIf: Software for Evaluating Counterfactuals," *Journal of Statistical Software* 15 (2005); Gary King and Langche Zeng, "When Can History Be Our Guide? The Pitfalls of Counterfactual Inference," *International Studies Quaterly* 51, no. 1 (March 2007).
65. Gary King and Langche Zeng, "Improving Forecasts of State Failure," *World Politics* 53, no. 4 (July 2002). This data concerns the opening of markets, infant mortality rates, degrees of democratization, the percentage of the population who become officers in the army, legislative efficiency, and density.
66. "Counterfactual Reasoning: A Basic Guide for Analysts, Strategists, and Decision Makers," *Proteus Monograph Series* 2, no. 5 (October 2008).
67. In the middle of the 1980s, the geographer William Norton insisted on the value of this approach: *Historical Analysis in Geography* (New York: Harlow, 1984).
68. David Gilbert and David Lambert, "Counterfactual Geographies: Worlds That Might Have Been," *Journal of Historical Geography* 36, no. 3 (July 2010): 245–252.
69. Colin G. Pooley, "Landscapes without the Car: A Counterfactual Historical Geography of Twentieth-Century Britain," *Journal of Historical Geography* 36 (2010): 266–275.
70. Luc Boltanski, "Le Pouvoir est de plus en plus savant," *La Vie des idées,* August 28, 2011, 11.
71. Thomas Aquinas, *Commentary on the Sentences,* bk. 1, and *Summa Contra Gentiles,* bk. 2; Duns Scotus, *Ordinatio,* pt. 1, 36; Jacob Schmütz, "Qui a inventé les mondes possibles?," in *Les Mondes possibles,* ed. J.-Ch. Bardout and V. Jullien, vol. 42 (Caen, France: Cahiers de l'université de Caen, 2006); Stéphane Chauvier, *Le Sens du possible* (Paris: Vrin, 2010).
72. Notably, "Semantical Considerations on Modal Logic," *Acta Philosophica Fennica* 16 (1963): 83–94. Also see Saul Kripke, *Naming and Necessity* (Cambridge, MA: Harvard University Press, 1980).
73. David Lewis, *Counterfactuals* (Oxford: Blackwell, 1973); David Lewis, *On the Plurality of Worlds* (Oxford: Blackwell, 1986). We thank Jean-Matthias Fleury for his insights into these different points.
74. See chapter 6.

75. Nicholas Rescher, *A Theory of Possibility: A Constructivistic and Conceptualistic Account of Possible Individuals and Possible Worlds* (Oxford: Blackwell, 1975); and in his recent version, Stéphane Chauvier, *Le Sens du possible*, for whom "possibilizing" is a cognitive faculty that allows one to reveal freedoms and hidden powers of the real that we don't otherwise see. It is particularly useful in philosophical knowledge.
76. Jacques Bouveresse, *L'Homme probable. Robert Musil, le hasard, la moyenne et l'escargot de l'Histoire* (Paris and Tel-Aviv: Éditions de l'Éclat, 1993); Jacques Bouveresse, "Robert Musil et le problème du déterminisme historique," in *La Voix de l'âme et les chemins de l'esprit* (Paris: Seuil, 2001).
77. Frédéric Nef and Pierre Livet, *Les Êtres sociaux, processus et virtualité* (Paris: Hermann, 2009); and Pierre Livet, "La Substituabilité comme propriété des êtres sociaux, les conditionnels et la prédication," *Igitur: Arguments philosophiques* 2, no. 2: 1–13.
78. Jean-Mattias Fleury, "Forces et dispositions, l'ontologie dynamiste de Leibniz à l'épreuve des débats contemporains" (PhD thesis, directed by Pascal Engel, Université Paris I, 2009); Pierre Fasula, "Musil, Wittgenstein: L'homme du possible" (PhD thesis directed by Christiane Chauviré, Université Paris I, 2013).
79. Thomas Pavel, *Univers de la fiction* (Paris: Seuil, 1988), 68.
80. "Univers de fiction: Un parcours personnel," in Françoise Lavocat, ed., *La Théorie littéraire des mondes possibles* (Paris: Éditions du CNRS, 2010), 309.
81. Marie-Laure Ryan, "Possible Worlds," *The Living Handbook of Narratology*, http://hup.sub.uni-hamburg.de/lhn/index.php/Possible_Worlds [accessed March 2012].
82. Lavocat, *La Théorie littéraire*, 31.
83. Marc Escola, "Théorie des textes possibles," *CRIN* 57 (2012). See also the research of the writer Pierre Bayard on the possible within literature and in particular the literary experiments that he drew from it.
84. The work on the distinction between the domain of fiction and nonfiction has been one of the paths that has been followed in order to clarify this problem. See the articles in "Fiction/non-fiction" on the Fabula website, http://www.fabula.org/atelier.
85. Lubomír Doležel, *Heterocosmica: Fiction and Possible Worlds* (Baltimore, MD: Johns Hopkins University Press, 1998).
86. Lubomír Doležel, *Possible Worlds of Fiction and History: The Postmodern Stage* (Baltimore, MD: Johns Hopkins University Press, 2010). See also "Récits contrefactuels du passé," in *La Théorie littéraire,* ed. Lavocat, 82–99. For further developments, see Françoise Lavocat, *Fait et fiction* (Paris: Seuil, "Poétique," 2016).
87. It is also necessary to mention the position of Nelson Goodman for whom it is less useful to imagine other possible worlds than to examine the way in which possible worlds are present in the real, and those we are constantly creating with art or science within such worlds. See Nelson Goodman, *Faits, fictions et prédictions* (1st ed. 1955; Paris: Minuit, 1985); and Nelson Goodman, *Manières de faire des mondes* (1st ed., 1978; Paris: Gallimard, 2007).
88. Jorge Luis Borges, "The Garden of Forking Paths," in *Collected Fictions,* trans. Andrew Hurley (New York: Viking, 1998).
89. James Gleick, *La Théorie du chaos* (Paris: Flammarion, 1988).

90. E. N. Lorenz, "Predictability: Does the Flap of a Butterfly's Wings in Brazil Set off a Tornado in Texas?," lecture given to the American Association for the Advancement of Science, 1979. Contrary to the interpretation that was later popularized, the meteorologist did not mean to argue that the flapping of a butterfly's wings could cause a tornado. If the flapping of wings, like all animal and human activities, could influence the formation of a tornado, it could not cause one.
91. Ilya Prigogine, *Is Future Given?* (Singapore: World Scientific Publishing, 2003), 39. In biology, the work of Stephen J. Gould merits special mention as does his attention to "historical contingency in order to discuss the theory of evolution and the species selection." See his *Wonderful Life: The Burgess Shale and the Nature of History* (New York: Norton, 1990). See also a discussion centered on the question of unpredictability in John Beatty, "Chance Variation and Evolutionary Contingency: Darwin, Simpson, *The Simpsons,* and Gould," in *Oxford Handbook of the Philosophy of Biology,* ed. Michael Ruse (Oxford: Oxford University Press, 2008).
92. His recourse to this method was limited: such analyses allow one at best to imagine plausible scenarios and not purely fantastical ones.
93. Ilya Prigogine, *Les Lois du chaos* (Paris: Flammarion, 1994), 97. For a partial English translation, see Ilya Prigogine, "The Laws of Chaos," *Review* (Fernard Braudel Center) 19, no. 1 (Winter 1996): 1–9.
94. Prigogine, *Les Lois du chaos,* 95.
95. Jaume Garriga and Alexander Vilenkin, "Many Worlds in One," *Physical Review D: Particles and Fields* 64, no. 4 (February 2001). See also on these questions: Aurélien Barrau, Patrick Gyger, and Max Kistler, *Multivers. Mondes possibles de l'astrophysique, de la philosophie, de l'imaginaire* (Paris: La Ville brûle, 2010).
96. According to the *New Scientist,* this is one of the "seven wonders of the quantum world" (May 2010), http://www.newscientist.com/special/seven-wonders-of-the-quantum-world.
97. Leonard Susskind, *The Cosmic Landscape: String Theory and the Illusion of Intelligent Design* (Boston: Little Brown, 2008).
98. Bernard Carr, *Universe or Multiverse?* (Cambridge: Cambridge University Press, 2007); Stephen Hawking, *The Grand Design* (New York: Bantam, 2010); Lee Smolin, *Rien ne va plus en physique! L'Échec de la théorie des cordes* (Paris: Seuil, "Points," 2010).

PART TWO. DECODING

1. Leopold von Ranke, *History of the Reformation in Germany,* bk. 4, Foreign Relations, Foundation of the National Church of Germany, 1521–1528, vol. 2, trans. Sarah Austin (London: Longman, 1845), 467–68.

CHAPTER 5. THE HISTORICAL IMAGINATION AND COUNTERFACTUAL APPROACHES

1. Maurice Godelier, *Lévi-Strauss* (Paris: Seuil, 2014), 496.
2. Carlos M. N. Eire, "Pilate Releases Jesus, Then What?," in *What If? 2,* ed. R. Cowley (New York: Berkeley Books, 2001), 61–63.
3. Krzysztof Pomian, *Sur l'histoire,* part 1: *Histoire et fiction* (Paris: Gallimard, 1999).

4. Jules Michelet, *Introduction to World History* (1831); Opening Address at the Faculty of Letters, January 9, 1834; Preface to *History of France,* trans. Edward Kaplan (1869; Cambridge, UK: Open Book Classics, 2013.)
5. Michelet, *Introduction to World History.*
6. Gabriel Monod, "Introduction. Du progrès des études historiques en France depuis le XVIe siècle," *Revue historique* 1, no. 1 (January–June 1876).
7. The relationship between Monod and the "specter" of Michelet is complex when one examines the archives. See Yann Potin, "Les Fantômes de Gabriel Monod. Papiers et paroles de Jules Michelet, érudit et prophète," *Revue historique* 664, no. 4 (2012): 803–836.
8. Charles-Victor Langlois and Charles Seignobos, *Introduction to the Study of History,* trans. G. G. Berry (1898; London: Duckworth, 1912).
9. Numa-Denis Fustel de Coulanges, *Histoire des institutions politiques de l'ancienne France, 3. La monarchie franque* (Paris: Hachette, 1888). See also François Hartog, *Le XIXe siècle et l'histoire. Le cas Fustel de Coulanges* (Paris: Seuil, 2001).
10. Lucien Febvre, *Vivre l'histoire* (Paris: Robert Laffont, 2009).
11. Lucien Febvre, *Combats pour l'histoire* (Paris: Armand Colin, 1995).
12. Lucien Febvre, *Le Problème de l'incroyance au XVIe siècle. La religion de Rabelais* (Paris: Albin Michel, 1968), 15.
13. Lucien Febvre, "La Sensibilité et l'histoire. Comment reconstituer la vie affective d'autrefois," in *Combats pour l'histoire* (Paris: Armand Colin, 1995), 221–239.
14. Ibid.
15. Ernest Labrousse, *La Crise de l'économie française à la fin de l'Ancien Régime et au début de la Révolution* (Paris: Presses universitaires de France, 1944).
16. Alain Corbin, *Historien du sensible. Entretiens avec Gilles Heuré* (Paris: Éditions la Découverte, 2000).
17. Paul Ricoeur, *La Mémoire, l'histoire, l'oubli* (Paris: Seuil, 2000), 359–368.
18. Blaise Pascal, *Pensées,* frag. 81 (Paris: Classiques Garnier, 2011), 20.
19. Febvre, *Le Problème de l'incroyance*, 20.
20. Ibid.
21. Jean-Pierre Vernant, *Myth and Thought Among the Greeks* (Brooklyn, NY: Zone Books, 2006), 17–18.
22. Georges Duby, *William Marshal* (New York: Knopf/Doubleday, 2011).
23. For example, *Le Mystère Ötzi,* documentary-fiction by Richard Dale and Andrew Bampfield, BBC One, 2005.
24. Philippe Vigier, *La Vie quotidienne à Paris et en Province pendant les journées de 1848* (Paris: Hachette, 1982).
25. Patrick Boucheron, *Léonard et Machiavel* (Paris: Verdier, 2008).
26. Alain Corbin, *Le Monde retrouvé de Louis-François Pinagot (1798–1876)* (Paris: Flammarion, 1998).
27. Ibid., 100.
28. See the debate proposed by the journal *Ruralia,* no. 3 (1998): "'Recherches pinagotiques.' À propos du Monde retrouvé de Louis-François Pinagot," and in particular the article by Corinne Boujot, "Ruptures et innovations dans le protocole de l'écriture scientifique."

29. Norbert Elias, *Engagement et distanciation. Contributions à une sociologie de la connaissance* (Paris: Fayard, 1993), 33. In Elias's work, engagement means emotional involvement, which is sometimes understood as subjectivity or irrationality. Distantiation, on the other hand, denotes a tension toward objectivity or rationality. But these are just two extreme poles of a continuum between which every individual in a society, and especially the researcher, is caught. Believing in the absolute distinction of the two domains is an error for Elias and prevents us from conducting a relevant sociological analysis (ibid., 9–11). On this point, see also Florence Delmotte, "Termes clés de la sociologie de Norbert Elias," in *Norbert Elias,* ed. Quentin Deluermoz (Paris: Tempus/Perrin, 2012), 67–70.
30. Charles W. Mills *L'Imagination sociologique* (Paris: François Maspero, 1967). One might also take into consideration the anthropology of Clifford Geertz, *The Interpretation of Cultures* (New York: Basic Books, 1973).
31. Howard S. Becker, *Tricks of the Trade: How to Think about Your Research While You're Doing It* (Chicago: University of Chicago Press, 1989).
32. One may define a social imaginary as a group of representations of a society, marked by the dual idea of coherence and creativity.
33. Paul Veyne, *Les Grecs ont-ils cru à leurs mythes? Essai sur l'imagination constituante* (Paris: Seuil, "Des travaux," 1983).
34. Henri-Irénée Marrou refers to this as the "sympathy" of the historian: *De la connaissance historique* (Paris: Seuil, 1954).
35. Hervé Mazurel, "Voir avec leurs yeux? La Hantise de l'anachronisme et la compréhension des hommes d'autrefois," in *Nuova Civiltà delle Macchine,* ed. Enzo Di Nuoscio, 25, no. 1 (2007): 115–128.
36. Michel de Certeau, *Histoire et psychanalyse entre science et fiction* (Paris: Gallimard, 1987); Roger Chartier, *On the Edge of the Cliff: History, Language, and Practices,* trans. Lydia G. Cochrane (Baltimore, MD: Johns Hopkins University Press, 1997).
37. A recent exploration of this perspective can be found in Ivan Jablonka, *L'Histoire est une littérature contemporaine* (Paris: Seuil, 2014).
38. See Jacques Revel, "Ressources narratives et connaissance historique," *Enquête* 1 (1995): 43–70.
39. Carlo Ginzburg, *The Cheese and the Worms: The Cosmos of a Sixteenth-Century Miller,* trans. John and Anne C. Tedeschi (Baltimore, MD: Johns Hopkins University Press, Press, 1980).
40. See "Les Savoirs de la littérature," *Annales HSS* 2 (2010), and in particular Étienne Anheim and Antoine Lilti's "Introduction," 253–260.
41. See Philip Tetlock and Aaron Belkin, "Counterfactual Thought Experiments in World Politics: Logical, Methodological, and Psychological Perspectives," in *Counterfactual Thought Experiments in World Politics,* ed. Philip Tetlock and Aaron Belkin (Princeton, NJ: Princeton University Press, 1996), 1–39.
42. According to the terms outlined by Carlo Ginzburg, *Wooden Eyes: Nine Reflections on Distance* (New York: Columbia University Press, 2001).
43. A good example of this danger can be found in Roger Chartier, "History, Time, and Space," *Republics of Letters: A Journal for the Study of Knowledge, Politics, and the Arts* 2, no. 2 (June 1, 2011).

44. We employ a wide and pragmatic definition of fiction here. See Jean-Marie Schaeffer, *Pourquoi la fiction?* (Paris: Seuil, 1999); and Jean-Marie Schaeffer, "Vérités de la fiction," *L'Homme,* 2005, 175–176. In this context, the diversity of objects likely to be considered fictional is very large (fiction, myths, scientific hypotheses, games, and mystifications, etc.). We understand here, for the moment, fiction in its literary dimension and its relationship to the problem of truth and falsehood. On the distinction to be made between fiction and literature, see Étienne Anheim and Antoine Lilti, "Introduction," *Annales HSS* 2.
45. Nikolay Koposov, *De l'imagination historique* (Paris: Éditions de l'EHESS, 2009).
46. Ginzburg, *Wooden Eyes.*
47. Carlo Ginzburg, *Threads and Traces: True False Fictive,* trans. Anne C. Tedeschi and John Tedeschi (Berkeley: University of California Press, 2012), 6.
48. Philip E. Tetlock, Richard New Lebow, and Geoffrey Parker, eds., *Unmaking the West: "What-If" Scenarios That Rewrite World History* (Ann Arbor: University of Michigan Press, 2006).
49. John Keegan, *What If? The World's Foremost Historians Imagine What Might Have Been* (London: Penguin, 2000).
50. Joachim Losehand, *Die letzten Tage des Pompeius* (Vienna: Phoibos Verlag, 2008), 235–374.
51. Jacques Dalarun, *Vers une résolution de la question franciscaine* (Paris: Fayard, 2007), 186–187.
52. Didier Méreuze, "La 'Vie' retrouvée de François d'Assise," *La Croix* 26 (January 2015).
53. The theme of anticipated wars has been studied in particular by Olivier Cosson, *Préparer la Grande Guerre. L'armée française et la guerre russo-japonaise (1899–1914)* (Paris: Les Indes savantes, 2013). The recent synthesis by André Loez on the Great War proposes, for example, a subsection with the suggestive title "La Guerre anticipée et imaginée" in *La Grande Guerre* (Paris: La Découverte, 2010).
54. CFP (Call for papers): *Future Wars, Imagined Wars: Towards a Cultural History of the Pre-1914 Period,* November 2011. See also Roxanne Panchasi, *Future Tense: The Culture of Anticipation in France Between the Wars* (Ithaca, NY: Cornell University Press, 2009).
55. See the research project: "Profutur: savoirs et techniques d'anticipation. Prévision et organisation du futur en Europe aux XVIIIe et XIXe siècles," http://crh.ehess.fr/index.php?2477 [accessed October 2020].
56. David Carr, "Place and Time: On the Interplay of Historical Points of View," *History and Theory* 40, no. 4: *Agency after Postmodernism* (December 2001): 153–167.
57. Eric Hobsbawm, *On History* (London: Abacus, 1998).
58. For example, on Boris Godounov, see Richard Taruskin, "*Boris Godounov,*" *New Grove Dictionary of Opera* (Oxford: Oxford University Press, 2007–2009). See also the more general analysis proposed by Pierre-Michel Menger, "Le Travail à l'œuvre, enquête sur l'autorité contingente du créateur dans l'art lyrique," *Annales HSS,* 2010.
59. Pierre Bourdieu, "Le Mort saisit le vif. Les relations entre l'histoire incorporée et l'histoire réifiée," *Actes de la recherche en sciences sociales* 32–33 (1980).

60. "As history progresses, these possibilities become more improbable, more difficult to achieve, because their passage into existence presupposes the destruction, the neutralization, or the reconversion of a greater or lesser part of the historical legacy—which is also capital—and more difficult even to think of the fact that the schemes of thought and perception are each time the product of the order of things. Any action to oppose the possible to the probable . . . must count on the weight of the reified and incorporated history, which, like in the aging process, tends to reduce the possible toward the probable." Ibid., 12–13.
61. Pierre Bourdieu, *On the State: Lectures at the Collège de France 1989–1992,* ed. Patrick Champagne, Remi Lenoir, Franck Poupeau, and Marie-Christine Rivière, trans. David Fernbach (Cambridge: Polity, 2014).
62. Christophe Charle, *La Crise des sociétés imperiales* (Paris: Seuil, 2001), 27.
63. On the function of distantiation in fiction, see Jean-Marie Schaeffer, *Pourquoi la fiction?* (Paris: Seuil, 1999).
64. Marc Bloch, *Apologie pour l'histoire ou métier d'histoire,* 2nd ed. (Paris: Armand Colin, 1952), 60.
65. François Dosse, *Renaissance de l'événement." Un défi pour l' historien: entre sphinx et phénix* (Paris: Presses Universitaires de France, 2010).
66. Mona Ozouf, *Varennes* (Paris: Gallimard, 2005), 112. This is also present in Timothy Tackett, *When the King Took Flight* (Cambridge, MA: Harvard University Press, 2004).
67. "Fonctions heuristiques et dérives constructivistes du raisonnement contrefactuel en sciences sociales," conference given in the context of the seminar organized by Quentin Deluermoz, Jean-Matthias Fleury, and Pierre Singaravélou, Collège de France, 2011, http://www.college-de-france.fr/site/jacques-bouveresse/usages-et-enjeux-du-raisonnement-contrefactuel-en-histoire-et-dans-les-sciences-sociales-seminaire-organise-par-quentin-delue__2.htm#|p =./jacques-bouveresse/ usages-et-enjeux-du-raisonnement-contrefactuel-en-histoire-et-dans-les-sciences-sociales-seminaire-organise-par-quentin-delue__2.html. See also Pierre-Michel Menger, "Kontrafakten," in A. Kwaschik, M. Wimmer, eds., *Von der Arbeit des Historikers: Ein Wörterbuch zu Theorie und Praxis der Geschichtswissenschaft* (Berlin: Transcript Verlag, 2010), 123–127.
68. For example, for the last three cases, see: Daniel Vickers, "Those Dammed Shad: Would the River Sheries of New England Have Survived in the Absence of Industrialization?," *William & Mary Quarterly,* 3d ser., 61 (2004): 685–712; Peter B. Bowler, *Darwin Deleted, Imagining a World without Darwin* (Chicago: University of Chicago Press, 2013); David Edgerton, *Quoi de neuf? Une histoire des techniques depuis 1900* (Paris: Seuil, 2013); J. Mokyr, "King Kong and Cold Fusion, Counterfactual Analysis and the History of Technology," in Tetlock, Lebow, and Parker, *Unmaking the West.*
69. Alain Corbin, "Préface," in *Le XIXe siècle, science politique et tradition,* by Isabelle Poutrin (Paris: Berger-Levrault, 1995), xii.
70. Benjamin Wurgaft, "Walter Benjamin and the Counterfactual Imagination," *History and Theory* 49 (October 2010): 361–383.
71. Chartier, *On the Edge of the Cliff.*

72. This distinction is borrowed from the economist and philosopher Pierre Livet. The "virtual" designates possibilities that have more factuality than mere possible representations. For him, "social and economic activities do not depend only on the actual factual, but on counterfactuals: facts that are no longer, facts that are not yet, states of things whose existence is avoided or that we have not succeeded in passing on to life." In fact, "we can even show that without these virtual beings, societies would not exist." Pierre Livet, "La Substituabilité comme propriété des êtres sociaux, les conditionnels et la prédication," *Igitur: Arguments philosophiques* 2, no. 2: 1–13.
73. Gérard Monnier, unpublished manuscript (cited with the permission of the author).
74. Guillaume Bridet, "Ce que les sciences humaines font aux études littéraires (et ce que la littérature fait aux sciences humaines)," *Fabula-LhT,* no. 8, "Le Partage des disciplines" (May 2011), http://www.fabula.org/lht/8/bridet.html; Pierre Bayard, *Peut-on appliquer la littérature à la psychanalyse?* (Paris: Minuit, "Paradoxe," 2004).

CHAPTER 6. CAUSAL INFERENCE AND COUNTERFACTUAL REASONING

1. Robert Musil, *The Man Without Qualities,* vol. 2 (London: Secker and Warburg, 1961), 970.
2. Antoine Augustin Cournot, *Essai sur les fondements de nos connaissances et sur les caractères de la critique philosophique* (1851; Paris: Vrin, 1975), 35.
3. Stephen Jay Gould, *Wonderful Life: The Burgess Shale and the Nature of History* (New York: Norton, 1990), 48 and 51.
4. See the perspectives offered by Antoine Prost, *Douze leçons sur l'histoire* (Paris: Seuil, 1996), 169–187.
5. Among those who have discussed this issue, for philosophy, see Cornelius Castoriadis, *The Imaginary Institution of Society,* trans. Kathleen Blamey (Cambridge, MA: MIT Press, 1987); for sociology, see William H. Sewell Jr., "Refiguring the Social in Social Science: An Interpretivist Manifesto," in *Logics of History: Social Theory and Social Transformation* (Chicago: University of Chicago Press, 2005), 318–373; for anthropology, see Maurice Godelier, *The Mental and the Material* (London: Verso, 2011).
6. *Post hoc, ergo propter hoc* ("after this, therefore because of this") and *cum hoc, ergo propter hoc* ("with this, therefore because of this" or "correlation does not imply causation"). Succession and contiguity of two phenomena in space and time do not necessarily imply a causal relationship.
7. This positivist conception is only determinist when the causal relationship is necessary and inevitable.
8. Raymond Aron, *Introduction to the Philosophy of History: An Essay on the Limits of Historical Objectivity* (Boston: Beacon Press, 1961).
9. Patrick Gardiner, *The Nature of Historical Explanation* (Oxford: Oxford University Press, 1952).
10. Polybius, *The Histories,* vol. 2, trans. W. R. Paton, Loeb Classical Library (Cambridge, MA: Harvard University Press, 1922–1927), 6.
11. At least since Polybius, it has been the determination of causality that gives a historical fact its true meaning.

12. In his *Physics* (bk. 2, ch. 3), Aristotle distinguishes between four types of causes: material causes, formal causes, efficient causes, and final causes.
13. As François Dosse suggests in *L'Histoire* (Paris: Armand Colin, 2000), Bodin's determinism prepares the terrain for Montesquieu's deterministic vision. Jean Bodin *Method for the Easy Comprehension of History,* trans. Beatrice Reynolds (London: Octagon Books, 1966); Montesquieu, *The Spirit of the Laws,* trans. Anne M. Cohler, Basia Carolyn Miller, Harold Samuel Stone (Cambridge: Cambridge University Press, 1989).
14. Philosophers of history have retained these elements as premises for an "epistemology of the probable." Thierry Martin, "La Philosophie de l'histoire de Cournot," *Revue d'histoire des sciences humaines* 1, no. 12 (2005).
15. Fernand Braudel, *The Mediterranean and the Mediterranean World in the Age of Philip II,* trans. Sian Reynolds (Berkeley: University of California Press, 1995); and Fernand Braudel, "Histoire et sciences sociales. La longue durée," *Annales ESC,* October–December 1958, 725–753.
16. Michel Foucault, *The Archaeology of Knowledge,* trans. Sheridan Smith (New York: Vintage, 2010).
17. Cornelius Castoriadis, *Thucydide, la force et le droit. Ce qui fait la Grèce 3. Séminaires 1984–1985. La création humaine IV* (Paris: Seuil, 2011), seminar of May 15, 1985, 313–317; and Cornelius Castoriadis, *Sujet et vérité dans le monde social-historique. La création humaine I* (Paris: Seuil, 2002), seminar of November 26, 1986 (for this use of Weber and other complementary elements), 31–34; seminar of June 3, 1987, 411–413.
18. "All history is counterfactual. The only way to identify causality is to transport oneself via imagination into the past and to ask if, through a hypothesis, the unfolding of events could have been the same if such and such a factor, considered in isolation, had been different," writes Antoine Prost in *Douze leçons.*
19. Max Weber, "Critical Studies in the Logic of the Cultural Sciences," in *Max Weber: Collected Methodological Writings,* ed. Hans Henrik Bruun and Sam Whimster (1906; New York: Routledge, 2012).
20. Eduard Meyer, *Zur Theorie und Methodik der Geschichte* (Halle, Germany: Niemeyer, 1902).
21. Weber, "Critical Studies," 169.
22. Ibid., 169–170.
23. Meyer, *Zur Theorie und Methodik,* 43.
24. Ibid., 170–171.
25. Johannes Von Kries, "Über den Begriff der objektiven Möglichkeit und einige Anwendungen desselben," in *Vierteljahresschrift für wissenschaftliche Philosophie* (Leipzig: Band 12, 1888).
26. Weber, "Critical Studies," 175.
27. Raymond Aron, *Introduction to the Philosophy of History,* trans. George J. Irwin (1938; London: Weidenfeld and Nicolson, 1961).
28. Paul Ricoeur, *Time and Narrative,* vol 1. trans. Kathleen McLaughlin and David Pellauer (Chicago: Chicago University Press, 1984), 127, 185.
29. Aron, *Introduction to the Philosophy of History,* 179.

30. Ibid.
31. David Lewis, *Counterfactuals* (Oxford: Blackwell, 1973).
32. David Lewis, "Causation," *Journal of Philosophy* 70, no. 17 (1973): 556–567.
33. David Lewis, *On the Plurality of Worlds* (Oxford: Blackwell, 1986).
34. See chapter 4.
35. There are numerous works of this type. For an attempt at translating a sociological approach directly into a mathematical and statistical model, see, for example, Stephen L. Morgan and Christopher Winship, *Counterfactuals and Causal Inference: Methods and Principles of Social Research* (Cambridge: Cambridge University Press, 2007). The difference with Lewis's proposals and the desire to furnish rigorous methodological tools is directly discussed in the introduction. For an idea on the variety of objects of analysis, see also the papers summarized on the page "Counterfactual Analysis" by Professor Christopher Winship in the Harvard Department of Sociology, https://scholar.harvard.edu/cwinship/links [accessed October 2020].
36. Gary King and Langche Zeng, "Improving Forecasts of State Failure," *World Politics* 53 (July 4, 2002): 623–658, http://gking.harvard.edu/ les/abs/civil-abs.shtml.
37. Gary King and Langche Zeng, "When Can History Be Our Guide? The Pitfalls of Counterfactual Inferences," *International Studies Quaterly* 51 (2007).
38. Michael W. Doyle and Nicholas Sambanis, "International Peacebuilding: A Theoretical and Quantitative Analysis," *American Political Science Review* 94, no. 4 (December 2000): 779–801.
39. A wide range of texts and actors have nourished this debate. Among recent works in French have been, for example, an account of the field that offers a qualitative and quantitative approach for historians: Claire Lemercier and Claire Zalc, *Méthodes quantitative pour l'historien* (Paris: La Découverte, 2008). For a sociological point of view that recalls the importance of the mathematical formalization of American sociology and the questions it raises, see Pierre-Michel Menger, "La Sociologie face à la mathématisation," *Enquête* 8 (1993): 51–78.
40. Hans-Ulrich Wehler, *Deutsche Gesellschaftsgeschichte,* vol. 3, 1849–1914 (Munich: Beck, 1995), 465.
41. Ibid., 1293–1294.
42. David Blackbourn and Geoff Eley, *The Peculiarities of German History: Bourgeois Society and Politics in Nineteenth-Century Germany* (1980; Oxford: Oxford University Press, 1984).
43. See the synthesis by Jürgen Kocka: "Assymetrical Historical Comparison: The Case of the German Sonderweg," *History and Theory* 28 (1999): 40–50.
44. Kenneth Pomeranz, "Without Coal? Colonies? Calculus? Counterfactuals and Industrialization in Europe and China," in *Unmaking the West: "What-If" Scenarios That Rewrite World History,* ed. Philip Tetlock, Ned Lebow, and Geoffrey Parker (Ann Arbor: University of Michigan Press, 2006), 241–276.
45. Kenneth Pomeranz, *The Great Divergence: China, Europe, and the Making of the Modern World Economy* (Princeton, NJ: Princeton University Press, 2000).
46. Paul Lacombe, *De l'histoire considérée comme science* (Paris: Hachette, 1894), 63–64.
47. Aron, *Introduction to the Philosophy of History,* 179.

48. Raymond Aron, *Dimensions de la conscience historique* (Paris: Plon, 1961), 186–187.
49. Aron, *Introduction to the Philosophy of History*, 178.
50. Ricoeur, *Time and Narrative,* 188.
51. Paul Veyne, *Comment on écrit l'histoire. Essai d'épistémologie* (Paris: Seuil, 1974), 194.
52. Ibid., 202–203.
53. Paul Veyne, *Le Quotidien et l'intéressant* (Paris: Les Belles Lettres, 1994).
54. "Un échange de lettres entre Raymond Aron et Norbert Elias (July 1939)," *Vingtième Siècle. Revue d'histoire* 2, no. 106 (2010): 97–102.
55. Norbert Elias, *Engagement et distanciation. Contributions à la sociologie de la connaissance* (Paris: Fayard, 1993).
56. Norbert Elias, "La Critique de l'État chez Thomas More," in *L'Utopie* (Paris: La Découverte, 2014), 31–103, trans. from "Thomas Morus' Staatskritik. Mit Überlegungen zur Bestimmung des Begriffs Utopie," in *Utopie-forschung, interdisziplinäre Studien zur neuzeitlichen Utopie,* ed. Wilhelm Voßkamp, vol. 2 (Stuttgart, Germany: Metzler, 1982), 101–151.
57. Norbert Elias, *The Society of Individuals,* ed. Michael Schröter, trans. Edmund Jephcott (New York: Continuum, 1991), 130.
58. Marc Bessin, Claire Bidart, and Michel Grossetti, ed., *Bifurcations. Les sciences sociales face aux ruptures et à l'événement* (Paris: La Découverte, 2010).
59. Everett C. Hughes, "Cycles, Turning Points and Careers," in *The Sociological Eye* (Chicago: Aldine, 1971), 124–131.
60. Robert J. Sampson and John H. Laub, *Crime in the Making: Pathways and Turning Points through Life* (Cambridge MA: Harvard University Press, 1993).
61. Michel Dobry, "Le Politique dans ses états critiques. Retour sur quelques aspects de l'hypothèse de continuité," in *Bifurcations. Les sciences sociales face aux ruptures et à l'événement,* ed. Marc Bessin, Claire Bidart, and Michel Grossetti (Paris: La Découverte, 2010).
62. William H. Sewell Jr., "Three Temporalities: Toward an Eventful Sociology," in *Logics of History: Social Theory and Social Transformation* (Chicago: University of Chicago Press, 2005), 81–123, 106.
63. It is necessary to include as well the explicit and careful use by Ivan Ermakoff. In *Ruling Oneself Out: A Theory of Collective Abdications* (Durham, NC: Duke University Press, 2008), he combines counterfactual arguments with causal claims in his analysis of the July 1940 vote in France and the March 1933 vote in Germany. In chapter 11 of his book ("The Event as Statement"), he explicitly elaborates a counterfactual rationale (pp. 328–333). A broader reflection is proposed in "The Structure of Contingency," *American Journal of Sociology* 121, no. 1 (July 2015): 1–61.
64. Andrew Abbott, "Transcending General Linear Reality," in *Time Matters: On Theory and Method* (Chicago: University of Chicago Press, 2001).
65. Andrew Abbott, "Temporality and Process in Social Life," in *Time Matters,* 219–239.
66. Andrew Abott, *Method of Discovery: Heuristics for the Social Sciences* (New York: Norton, 2004), 158–161.
67. Ibid., 234.

68. Andrew Abbott, “On the Concept of Turning Point,” *Comparative Social Research* 16 (1997).
69. The proximity with Norbert Elias’s position outlined above is obvious.
70. Claire Lemercier and Claire Zalc, “Quantification, réseaux et trajectoires,” in *Méthodes quantitatives pour l’historien* (Paris: La Découverte, “Repères,” 2008), 80–102. The authors also discuss the role of event history analysis for examining these sequences (pp. 95–102).
71. Nicolas Mariot and Claire Zalc, *Face à la persécution. 991 Juifs dans la guerre* (Paris: Odile Jacob, 2010).
72. Claire Zalc, “Trajectoires de persécution. Apports de la lecture d’Andrew Abbott à l’écriture historienne” in *Andrew Abbott et l’héritage de l’école de Chicago,* ed. Morgan Jouvenet and Didier Demazières (Paris: EHESS, 2016).
73. Charles C. Ragin and John Sonnett, “Between Complexity and Parsimony: Limited Diversity, Counterfactual Cases and Comparative Analysis,” in *Vergleichen in der Politikwissenschaft,* ed. Sabine Kropp and Michael Minkenberg (Wiesbaden, Germany: VS Verlag fur Sozialwissenschaften, 2005), 180–197.
74. See, for example, for two groups of Latin American countries having completed a political transition toward democracy at different periods, Davide Grassi, “La Survie des régimes démocratiques. Une AQQC des démocraties de la ‘troisième vague’ en Amérique du Sud,” *Revue internationale de politique comparée* 1 (2004): 17–33.
75. Hence, the use of counterfactualism is different in this case from that mobilized by statistical studies. Statistical studies use it to illustrate their results when the research in this case uses counterfactuals to estimate the model of analysis by studying the blanks in the configurations defined by the causal variables. For clarifications on this point, see James Mahoney and Gary Goertz, “Causal Models and Counterfactuals,” *Handbook of Sociology and Social Research,* 2013, 75–90). By allowing us to be more precise about the sets of conditions that potentially lead to the effect that one is searching for, counterfactuals contribute then to the expertise that the sociologist can offer to political decision-making: Charles C. Ragin and John Sonnett, “Between Complexity and Parsimony: Limited Diversity, Counterfactual Cases, and Comparative Analysis,” in *Vergleichen in der Politikwis-senschaft,* ed. Sabine Kropp and Michael Minkenberg (Wiesbaden, Germany: VS Verlag fur Sozialwissenchaften, 2005), p. 180-197.
76. David Byrne and Charles C. Ragin, eds., *The Sage Handbook of Case-Based Methods* (London: Sage, 2009), 71
77. Noël Bonneuil, “The Mathematics of Time in History,” *History and Theory* 49 (December 2010): 28–46.
78. We are developing here the analysis of Anne-Sophie Bruno, whom we thank for bringing this approach to our attention.
79. Noël Bonneuil, “Jeux, équilibres et régulation des populations sous contrainte de viabilité. Une lecture de l’œuvre de l’anthropologue Fredrik Barth,” *Population* 4 (1997): 947–976.
80. “The rate of predations c (t) is a command: it is flexible and can be chosen within a certain group [cmjn, cmax] where cmin represents the rate of minimal predation (the

limit of survival) and cmax represents the rate of maximal predation (abundance)" [Le taux de prédation c (t) est une commande: il est flexible et peut être choisi à l'intérieur d'un certain ensemble [cmjn, cmax], où cmin représente le taux de prédation minimale (la limite de la survie) et cmax le taux de prédation maximale (l'abondance)]. Ibid., 952.

81. Ibid., 967.
82. Noël Bonneuil, "Viability in Dynamic Social Networks," *Journal of Mathematical Sociology* 24, no. 3 (2000): 175–192 (based on the study of John F. Padgett and Christopher K. Ansell, "Robust Action and the Rise of the Medici, 1400–1434," *American Journal of Sociology* 6 (May 1993): 1259–1319; and the work of Fredrik Barth: Bonneiuil, "Jeux, équilibres et regulation"; on this subject, see also Noël Bonneuil and Patrick Saint-Pierre, "Domaine de victoire et stratégies viables dans le cas d'une correspondance non-convexe. application à l'anthropologie des pêcheurs selon Fredrik Barth," in *Mathématiques et sciences humaines* 142 (1998): 43–66.
83. Bonneuil, "The Mathematics of Time in History," 38.
84. Ibid., 45.
85. See, among others, Jean-Yves Grenier, Claude Grignon, and Pierre-Michel Menger eds., *Le Modèle et le récit* (Paris: Éditions de la Maison des sciences de l'homme, 2001).

INTERLUDE. THE DOMINION OF FACTS IN THE SOCIAL SCIENCES

1. Jean-Claude Passeron, *Le Raisonnement sociologique* (Paris: Albin Michel, 2006). One must also keep in mind here the cautions expressed by the author regarding literary temptations within sociology.
2. Karl Popper, *The Poverty of Historicism* (1957; London: Routledge, 2002; and Karl Popper, *The Logic of Scientific Discovery* (1935; New York: Routledge, 1992).
3. Carlo Ginzburg, "Aristote encore une fois," in *Rapports de force. Histoire, rhétorique, prevue* (Paris: Gallimard/Le Seuil, 2003), 43–53.
4. Siegfried Kracauer, *L'Histoire des avant-dernières choses* (1961; Paris: Stock, 2006), 157–158. On this question, see the introduction by Jacques Revel, "Siegfried Kracauer et le monde d'en bas," 7–42.
5. Ginzburg, "Aristote encore une fois," 52–53.
6. Pierre Livet, "La Substituabilité comme propriété des êtres sociaux, les conditionnels et la prédication," *Igitur: Arguments philosophiques* 2, no. 2: 1–13. See also the analyses of Henri Lefebvre in his *Critique of Everyday Life,* vols. 1 and 2, trans. John Moore (London: Verso, 2002), who writes, "Specialists have every right, except the right to condemn critical thought to silence in the name of a conception of the real which they rarely explain and which is not relevant to anything. The 'positivity' of this realness derives from critical thought, which begins by establishing that the negative and the possible are just as 'real' as the positive real." (vol. 2, p. 25).

CHAPTER 7. THE PAST FUTURES OF OTHERS

1. Jorge Luis Borges, *The Garden of the Forking Paths* in *Collected Fictions,* trans. Andrew Hurley (New York: Viking, 1998).

2. Jean-Claude Schmitt, "L'appropriation du futur," *Le Corps, les rites, les rêves, le temps* (Paris, Gallimard, 2001), 417.
3. On historicity and the relationship to time, see Reinhart Koselleck, *Futures Past: On the Semantics of Historical Time,* trans. Keith Tribe (New York: Columbia University Press, 2004); François Hartog, *Régimes d'historicité. Présentisme et expériences du temps* (Paris: Seuil, 2003); Christian Delacroix, François Dosse, and Patrick Garcia, eds., *Historicités* (Paris: La Découverte, 2009); as well as the discussion led by Gérard Lenclud, "Traversées dans le temps," *Annales HSS* 5 (September–October 2006). See also Ludivine Bantigny and Quentin Deluermoz, eds., "Historicités du XXe siècle. Coexistence et concurrence des temps," *Vingtième Siècle. Revue d'histoire* 117 (January–March 2013), notably Ludivine Bantigny, "Quelques jalons sur une notion," 3–27.
4. Georges Duby, *Le Dimanche de Bouvines. 27 juillet 1214* (Paris: Gallimard, 1973).
5. Marcel Granet, *La Pensée chinoise* (Paris: Albin Michel, 1934; 1988).
6. Ibid., "Le Temps et l'espace," 77–99.
7. Or "position," "power," or "energy."
8. E. E. Evans-Pritchard, *The Nuer: A Description of the Modes of Livelihood and Political Institutions of a Nilotic People* (Oxford: Oxford University Press, 1940).
9. Ibid., "Time and Space," 94–138.
10. Jamake Highwater, *The Primal Mind: Vision and Reality in Indian America* (Harper & Row, 1981).
11. Ibid., "Time," 89–118.
12. Johannes Fabian, *Time and the Other: How Anthropology Makes Its Object* (1983; New York: Columbia University Press, 2014).
13. The debate around Johannes Fabian's critique is thoroughly presented in Philippe Simay, "Le temps des traditions. Anthropologie et temps historique," in *Historicité,* ed. Christian Delacroix, François Dosse, and Patrick Garcia (Paris: La Découverte, 2009).
14. Prasenjit Duara, "Histoire et concurrence des temps. Le cas de l'Asie orientale," in special issue "Historicités du XXe siècle. Coexistence et concurrence des temps," ed. Ludivine Bantigny and Quentin Deluermoz, *Vingtième Siècle. Revue d'histoire* 117 (January–March 2013): 27–42.
15. Michael Puett, *The Ambivalence of Creation: Debates Concerning Innovation and Artifice in Early China* (Stanford, CA: Stanford University Press, 2001).
16. François Jullien, *Du "temps." Éléments d'une philosophie du vivre* (Paris: Grasset, 2001); François Jullien, *La Pensée chinoise dans le miroir de la philosophie* (Paris: Opus, 2007).
17. François Jullien, *Les Transformations silencieuses* (Paris: Grasset, 2009).
18. Ibid., 127.
19. Marcel Griaule, *Masques dogons* (Paris: Institut d'ethnologie, 1938). We have focused here on the reading of Georges Balandier in *Anthropo-logiques* (Paris: Presses Universitaires de France, 1974), 211–213.
20. Jean-Pierre Boutinet, *Anthropologie du projet* (Paris: Presses Universitaires de France, 2012).
21. Nathalie Camille, Giorgio Coricelli, Jérôme Sallet, Pascale Pradat-Diehl, Jean-René Duhamel, and Angela Sirigu, "The Involvement of the Orbitofrontal Cortex in the Experience of Regret," *Science* 304, no. 5674 (May 21, 2004): 1167–1170.

22. Time may also play a role in this conception. But it would stretch across the millennia required for evolutionary change.
23. See the synthesis by Michael L. Platt and Ben Hayden, "Learning: Not Just the Facts, Ma'am, but the Counterfactual As Well," *PLOS Biology* 9, no. 6 (2011). See also Aron K. Barbey, Frank Krueger, and Jordan Grafman, "Architecture of Counterfactual Thought in the Prefrontal Cortex," in *Predictions in the Brain,* ed. Moshe Bar (Oxford: Oxford University Press, 2011).
24. Jean-Pierre Changeux and Paul Ricoeur, *Ce qui nous fait penser. La nature et la règle* (Paris: Odile Jacob, 1998).
25. Antonio Damasio takes these considerations into account in *Self Comes to Mind: Constructing the Conscious Brain* (New York: Vintage: 2012). See also Andy Clark, *Being There: Putting Brain, Body, and World Together Again* (Cambridge, MA: MIT Press, 1997). For a more general synthesis on "social cognition," see the article by the linguist Marie-Anne Paveau, "Réalité et discursivité. D'autres dimensions pour la théorie du discours," *Semen. Revue de sémio-linguistique des textes et discours* 34 (November 2012): 95–116.
26. George Steiner, "Le futur du verbe," *Revue de métaphysique et de morale* 2 (2007): 147. Criticism on the temporality of verbs has also been developed recently by the anthropologist Gérard Lenclud, *L'Universalisme ou le pari de la Raison* (Paris: Seuil/EHESS, 2013).
27. Balandier, *Anthropo-logiques,* 243–263.
28. Philippe Simay, "Le temps des traditions. Anthropologie et historicité," in Delacroix, Dosser, and Garcia, *Historicités*; Michel Naepels, ed., "L'anthropologie face au temps," *Annales HSS* 65, no. 4 (2010).
29. Chris Ballard, "La fabrique de l'histoire. Événement, mémoire et récit dans les Hautes Terres de Nouvelle-Guinée," in *Les Rivages du temps. Histoire et anthropologie du Pacifique,* ed. Isabelle Merle and Michel Naepels (Paris: L'Harmattan, 2003), 111–133.
30. Ibid., 113–114.
31. Claude Lévi-Strauss, "Histoire et ethnologie," *Annales. Économies, sociétés, civilisations* 38, no. 6 (1983): 1229.
32. Alain Testart, *Avant l'histoire, l'évolution des sociétés, de Lascaux à Carnac* (Paris: Gallimard, 2012), 79, 107, 285. See also the remarks by Philippe Descola in "Histoires de structures," in *Par-delà nature et culture* (Paris: Gallimard, 2005), 496–532.
33. Ross Hassig, "Counterfactuals and Revisionism in Historical Explanation," *Anthropological Theory* 1 (2001): 57–72.
34. Ibid., 69.
35. Koselleck, *Futures Past.*
36. Marshall Sahlins, "Captain James Cook; or The Dying God," in *Islands of History* (Chicago: University of Chicago Press, 1985).
37. Or, in his terms, "a set of historical relationships that at once reproduce the traditional cultural categories and give them new values out of the pragmatic context." Ibid., 125.
38. Ibid., 109.
39. Ibid., 108.

40. Ibid., 126.
41. Marshall Sahlins, *How "Natives" Think: About Captain Cook, for Example* (Chicago: Chicago University Press, 1995), in response to Gananath Obeyesekere, *The Apotheosis of Captain Cook: European Mythmaking in the Pacific* (Princeton, NJ: Princeton University Press, 1992).
42. See Marshall Sahlins, "Structure and History," in *Islands of History* (Chicago: University of Chicago Press, 1985).
43. There has been a tradition of questioning the idea of societies without history. Claude Lévi-Strauss and Claude Lefort presented important arguments on this point. See Claude Lefort, "Société 'sans histoire' et historicité" (1952), in *Les Formes de l'histoire. Essais d'anthropologie politique* (1978; Paris: Gallimard, 2000). See also Marc Abélès *Anthropologie de la globalisation* (Paris: Payot et Rivages, 2008); and Michel Naepels "L'anthropologie face au temps," *Annales HSS* 65, no. 4 (2010): 873–884.
44. See Philippe Lacour, "Figures temporelles," EspacesTemps.net, https://www.espacestemps.net/articles/figures-temporelles/ [accessed October 2020].

CHAPTER 8. POLITICAL USES OF COUNTERFACTUAL HISTORY

1. Walter Benjamin, *On the Concept of History,* thesis VII (Frankfurt am Main: Gesammelten Schriften I:2. Suhrkamp Verlag, 1974), https://www.marxists.org/reference/archive/benjamin/1940/history.htm [accessed October 2020].
2. Winston Churchill, "If Lee Had Not Won the Battle of Gettysburg," in *If It Had Happened Otherwise,* ed. John C. Squire (London: Longmans, 1931).
3. While they are similar, the two positions, conservative and neoconservative, must be kept apart. The neoconservatives joined the Republicans during the Reagan presidency, adopting the essential ideas of this administration (critique of big government, tougher crime policies, etc.) Their specificity resided in the imperialist and nationalist dimensions of their doctrine, founded on American exceptionalism and their support for foreign military intervention. See Justin Vaïsse, *Histoire du néoconservatisme aux États-Unis* (Paris: Odile Jacob, 2008).
4. Niall Ferguson, ed., *Virtual History: Alternatives and Counterfactuals* (New York: Basic Books, 1997); Andrew Roberts, ed., *What Might Have Been* (London: Weidenfeld and Nicolson, 2004).
5. Roberts, *What Might Have Been*, 3.
6. Newt Gingrich and William Forstchen, *Gettysburg* (New York: Thomas Dunne Books, 2003); Gingrich and Forstchen, *Grant Comes East* (New York: Thomas Dunne Books, 2004); Gingrich and Forstchen, *Never Call Retreat: Lee and Grant: The Final Victory* (New York: Thomas Dunne Books, 2005).
7. Richard Evans, conference given at Queen's University Belfast in October 2002; Richard Evans, "Telling It Like It Wasn't," *Historically Speaking* 5, no. 4 (March 2004): 11–15.
8. Tristram Hunt, "Pasting Over the Past," *The Guardian,* April 7, 2004.
9. Georges Lefebvre, "Compte rendu du livre de Pierre Vendryès, *De la probabilité en histoire,*" *Annales historiques* 135 (April–June 1954).

10. Ibid., 186–187.
11. Auguste Blanqui, *Eternity by the Stars* (1872), The Blanqui Archive, https://blanqui.kingston.ac.uk/texts/eternity-by-the-stars-1872/.
12. "In the end, it is in the Fort du Taureau, in the solitude of prison surrounded by water that he was not even allowed to see that Blanqui wrote *Eternity by the Stars* in 1871," explains Jacques Rancière in his preface to Louis Auguste Blanqui, *L'Éternité par les astres* (Paris: Les Impressions nouvelles, 2012), 7.
13. Karl Marx, *Capital,* vol. 1, trans. Samuel Moore and Edward Aveling (Moscow: Progress Publishers, 1887).
14. Stefano Perri, "The Counterfactual Method of Marx's Theory of Surplus," *Review of Political Economy* 15, no. 1 (2003).
15. Karl Marx, *The Eighteenth Brumaire of Louis Bonaparte,* in *Selected Writings,* ed. Lawrence H. Simon (Indianapolis, IN: Hacket, 1994), 197.
16. See Michel Vadée, *Marx, penseur du possible* (Paris: Klincksieck, 1992).
17. Ibid., 234.
18. Daniel Bensaïd, *Marx l'intempestif. Grandeurs et misères d'une aventure critique (XIX*[e]*–XX*[e] *siècles)* (Paris: Fayard, 1995), 12.
19. Slavoj Žižek, "Lenin Shot at Finland Station," *London Review of Books* 27, no. 16 (August 18, 2005): 23.
20. Paul Ricoeur, *Time and Narrative,* vol. 1, trans. Kathleen McLaughlin and David Pellauer (Chicago: University of Chicago Press, 1984), 188.
21. Slavoj Žižek, *The Sublime Object of Ideology* (1989; London: Verso, 2008), 158.
22. He then defends an original idea: the alliance of objective neoconservatism and postmodernism. This alliance, he argues without blinking, brings together Andrew Roberts and Simon Heffer with "Michel Foucault and Jacques Derrida," who all agree on the importance of the role of "great men." Hunt is clearly mistaken in this portrayal.
23. Francis Fukuyama, *The End of History and the Last Man* (New York: Free Press, 1992).
24. Jeremy Black, *What If? Counterfactualism and the Problem of History* (London: Social Affairs Unit, 2008), 37.
25. François Hartog, *Regimes of Historicity: Presentism and Experiences of Time,* trans. Saskia Brown (New York: Columbia University Press, 2016).
26. Gavriel D. Rosenfeld, *The World Hitler Never Made: Alternate History and the Memory of Nazism* (Cambridge: Cambridge University Press, 2006).
27. Antoine Garapon, *Peut-on réparer l'histoire? Colonisation, esclavage, Shoah* (Paris: Odile Jacob, 2008).
28. This phenomenon has been identified for some time by historians: Henry Rousso, *La Hantise du passé* (Paris: Textuel, 1998); François Hartog and Jacques Revel, eds., *Les Usages politiques du passé* (Paris: Éditions de l'EHESS, 2001).
29. Elazar Barkan, *The Guilt of Nations: Restitution and Negotiating Historical Injustices* (London: W. W. Norton, 2000); Janna Thompson, *Taking Responsibility for the Past: Reparation and Historical Injustice* (Cambridge, UK: Polity Press, 2002); Mark Gibney et al., *The Age of Apology: Facing Up to the Past* (Philadelphia: University of Pennsylvania Press, 2008).

30. *U.S. and Allied Efforts to Recover and Restore Gold and Other Assets Stolen or Hidden by Germany During World War II,* report of the Department of State, coordinated by Stuart Eizenstat, May 7, 1997, Introduction, see http://fcit.usf.edu/holocaust/resource/gold/GoldF2.htm.
31. Ibid.
32. Krister Wahlbäck, professor from the University of Umea in Sweden declared, "Mr. Eizenstat's suggestion of a Swedish boycott of trade with Germany in 1943 reflects, I think, a changed awareness in recent years. Today, as we have come to realize fully how much of the Holocaust, as well as other suffering and destruction actually took place in the final stage of the war, it is natural that we look for alternative developments that might have shortened the war. We engaged in the might-have-beens of history, or what historians call "counterfactual" history." (*The Eizenstat Report and Related Issues Concerning United States and Allied Effort to Restore Gold and their Assets Looted by Nazis During World War II,* June 25, 1997, House of Representatives, Committee on Banking and Financial Services, Washington, DC, p. 70), https://digitalcommons.wcl.american.edu/cgi/viewcontent.cgi?referer=https://www.google.com/&httpsredir=1&article=1301&context=auilr [accessed October 2020].
33. "Did the Swiss Prolong the War?" *Final Report of the Independent Commission of Experts Switzerland—Second World* War (Zurich: Pendo, 2002), 518.
34. Agence France Press, "Swiss Bank Holocaust Fund Paid Out $1.24 Billion for Survivors and Relatives, *Huffington Post,* July 15, 2013, https://www.huffpost.com/entry/swiss-bank-holocaust-fund_n_3597359 [accessed October 2020].
35. Ariel Colonomos, "L'entreprise morale globale," *Vacarme* 34 (Winter 2006).
36. Ibid.
37. David Cortright and George Lopez, "Are Sanctions Just? The Problematic Case of Iraq," *Journal of International Affairs* 52, no. 2 (1999): 735–756; Ariel Colonomos, "Raison et justification morale dans les relations internationales," *Revue internationale des sciences sociales* 1, no. 191 (2007).
38. Robert Nozick, *Anarchy, State, and Utopia* (New York: Basic Books, 1974).
39. Here we are drawing in particular on the work of the geographer David Lambert, who carefully analyzed the role of counterfactual argumentation in claims for compensation. See "Black-Atlantic Counterfactualism: Speculating about Slavery and Its Aftermath," *Journal of Historical Geography* 36, no. 3 (July 2010).
40. Pierre Jallee is the author of *Pillage du tiers-monde,* one of the classic works of Third-Worldism published in Paris 1965 by Éditions Maspero.
41. Ronald W. Walters, "African Reparations: Dealing with a Unique and Unprecedented Moral Debt," in *Africa in the 21st Century: Toward a New Future,* ed. Ama Mazama (New York & London: Routledge,2007), 268, cited by Lambert in "Black-Atlantic Counterfactualism," 286.
42. Elazar Barkan, *The Guilt of Nations: Restitution and Negotiating Historical Injustices* (New York: Norton, 2000), 289.
43. Similar proposals have been made in England. Robert Beckford, who teaches theology and black culture at the University of Birmingham, made a different calculation in the context of the show entitled *The Empire Pays Back,* aired on August 15, 2005 on

British television. With the help of a historian, an actuary, and a lawyer, he estimated the reparations at £7.5 trillion, £4 trillion of which were the unpaid salaries of slaves from the British West Indies. The procedure of reparations was designed to draw from all the institutions that played a role in slavery and forced labor, like the Bank of England, HSBC, Barclays, the Crown, and the Church of England.

44. George Schedler, *Racist Symbols & Reparations: Philosophical Reflections on Vestiges of the American Civil War* (Lanham, MD: Rowman & Littlefield Publishers, 1998).
45. George Schedler, "Responsibility for and Estimation of the Damages of American Slavery," *University of Memphis Law Review* 33, no. 2 (Winter 2003): 307–335.
46. David Swinton has offered a synthesis through an evaluation of the cost of slavery by measuring the value of nonremunerated work and the suffering that was endured, as well as the opportunities and the freedom that slaves were denied. David H. Swinton, "Racial Inequality and Reparations," in *The Wealth of Races: The Present Value of Benefits from Past Injustices,* ed. Richard F. America (Westport: Greenwood Press, 1990).
47. Daniel Tetteh Osabu-Kle, "The African Reparation Cry: Rationale, Estimate, Prospects, and Strategies," *Journal of Black Studies* 30, no. 3 (January 2000): 344.
48. Ibid., 340.
49. Walter Rodney, *How Europe Underdeveloped Africa* (Dar es Salaam, Tanzania: Bogle-L'Ouverture Publications, 1973), 101.
50. Ibid.
51. Lambert, "Black-Atlantic Counterfactualism.
52. Rodney C. Roberts, "The Counterfactual Conception of Compensation," *Metaphilosophy* 37, nos. 3–4 (2006).
53. Lewis v. US State, US District Court for Northern California, 1994 (lexis 7868); Lloyd v. US State (Lexis 7869); Jackson v. US State (Lexis 7872)—all cited in Elazar Barkan, *The Guilt of Nations: Restitution and Negotiating Historical Injustices* (New York: Norton, 2000).
54. On the moral dimension of such reasoning (with the usage of the category of evil) and the impasses to which they have led in historical analysis, see Alexander Demandt, "Ein historisches gedankenspiel," in *Es hätte auch anders kommen können* (Berlin: Propyläen Verlag, 2010), 14–16.
55. Howard Eiland and Michael W. Jennings, eds., "On the Concept of History," in *Walter Benjamin: Selected Writings,* vol. 4, 1938–1940, trans. Edmund Jephcott et al. (Cambridge, MA: Belknap/Harvard University Press, 2003), 392. Stéphane Mosès, *L'Ange de l'histoire. Rosenzweig, Scholem, Benjamin* (Paris: Seuil, 1992); Michael Löwy, *Walter Benjamin: avertissement d'incendie. Une lecture des theses "Sur le concept d'histoire"* (Paris: Presses Uuniversitaires de France, 2001).
56. Walter Benjamin, "On the Concept of History," in "On the Concept of History," ed. Howard Eiland and Michael W. Jennings, in *Walter Benjamin: Selected Writings,* vol. 4, 1938–1940, trans. Edmund Jephcott et al. (Cambridge, MA: Belknap/Harvard University Press, 2003), 397.
57. Mosès, *L'Ange de l'histoire*, 23.
58. Michèle Riot-Sarcey, interview with Jean-Paul Monferran, "Écrire le souterrain de l'histoire," *L'Humanité,* March 8, 2001.
59. Michèle Riot-Sarcey, *Le Réel de l'utopie* (Paris: Albin Michel, 1998).

60. Michèle Riot-Sarcey, "Le livre des passages, un XIXe siècle à découvrir. Un siècle de révolutions sans révolution," in *Walter Benjamin,* ed. Philippe Simay (Paris: L'Herne, "Cahiers d'anthropologie sociale," 2008), 74.
61. Ludivine Bantigny, "Le Temps politisé. Quelques enjeux politiques de la conscience historique en mai-juin 1968," *Vingtième Siècle. Revue d'histoire* 117 (January–March 2013): 215–229.
62. Patrick Boucheron, *Faire profession d'historien* (Paris: Publications de la Sorbonne, 2010).
63. Patrick Boucheron, *L'Entretemps* (Paris: Verdier, 2012).
64. Patrick Boucheron, "Sauver le passé," preface to Walter Benjamin, *Sur le concept d'histoire* (Paris: Payot, 2013).
65. Bronislaw Baczko, "La responsabilité morale de l'historien," *Diogène* 67 (July–October 1969).
66. François Bédarida, "Praxis historienne et responsabilité," *Diogène* 168 (1994): 3–8.
67. Christophe Charle, "Être historien en France. Une nouvelle profession?," in *L'Histoire et le métier d'historien en France 1945–1995,* ed. François Bédarida (Paris: Éditions de la Maison des Sciences de l'Homme, 1995); Henry Rousso, *La Hantise du passé,* interview with Philippe Petit (Paris: Textuel, 1998), 81–84; Hartog and Revel, *Les Usages politiques du passé*; Maryline Crivello, Patrick Garcia, and Nicolas Offenstadt, *Concurrences des passés. Usages politiques du passé dans la France contemporaine* (Aix-Marseille, France: Publications de l'université de Provence, 2006).
68. See chapter 5.
69. James Scott, *Domination and the Arts of Resistance* (New Haven, CT: Yale University Press, 1992).
70. Giovanni Levi, "Le passé lointain. Sur l'usage politique de l'histoire," in Hartog and Revel, *Les Usages politiques du passé.*
71. Or, in another register, certain conceptions of historical sociology, notably the proposals of William Sewell Jr. in "The Temporalities of Capitalism," *Socio-Economic Review* 6 (2008): 517–537.
72. Ricoeur, *Time and Narrative*, 188.
73. Ricoeur, "Identité narrative et communauté historique," *Cahier de politique autrement,* October 1994.
74. Vincent Lemire, *Jérusalem 1900, une ville à l'âge des possibles* (Paris: Armand Colin, 2013), 19–21.
75. Jérôme Baschet, *Adieux au capitalisme* (Paris: La Découverte, 2014), 10–11.
76. Jacques Revel, "Ressources narratives et connaissance historique," *Enquête* 1 (1995) *Les Terrains de l'enquête*, 2007.
77. Elisabeth S. Clemens, "Afterword: Logics of History? Agency, Multiplicity, and Incoherence in the Explanation of Change," in *Remaking Modernity: Politics, History, and Sociology,* ed. Julia Adams, Elisabeth Clemens, and Ann Shola Orloff (Durham, NC: Duke University Press, 2005).
78. Ibid., 507.
79. Yannick Barthe, Damien de Blic, Jean-Philippe Heurtin, Éric Lagneau, Cyril Lemieux, Dominique Linhardt, Cédric Moreau de Bellaing, Catherine Rémy, and Dany Trom, "Sociologie pragmatique: Mode d'emploi," *Politix* 103, no. 3 (2013).

80. Frédéric Audren, Sandrine Kott, Antoine Lilti, Nicolas Offenstadt, and Stéphane Van Damme, "Temps, histoire et historicité: Un point de vue historien," in *Historicités de l'action publique,* ed. Pascale Laborier and Dany Trom (Paris: Presses Uuniversitaires de France, 2003), 517.
81. While this is common practice, it may be less banal than it appears. In a recent postface to Natalie Zemon Davis's famous *Return of Martin Guerre,* Carlo Ginzburg returns to this point based on a quotation by the author ("I had my own historical laboratory, generating not proofs, but historical possibilities."), on the question of the relationship between imagination, narrative, proof, and history. Considering the new perspectives on the division between history and fiction, it is now necessary to distinguish between "truth"/"invented" and "proof"/"possibilities." These allow one to bring facts back to their context as a site of historically determined possibilities. Only "inventions" may be entirely rejected. When they are well done, these counterfactuals appear to be among the possible explorations. Carlo Ginzburg, *Threads and Traces: True False Fictive,* trans. Anne C. Tedeschi and John Tedeschi (Berkeley: University of California Press, 2012).
82. See Noël Bonneuil, "The Mathematic of Time in History," *History and Theory* 49 (December 2010): 28–46; Michel Dobry, "Le Politique dans ses états critiques: Retour sur quelques aspects de l'hypothèse de continuité," in *Bifurcations. Les sciences sociales face aux ruptures et à l'évènement,* ed. Marc Bessin, Claire Bidart, and Michel Grossetti (Paris: La Découverte, 2010).

PART THREE. EXPERIMENTS

1. Howard S. Becker, *Telling About Society* (Chicago: University of Chicago Press, 2007), 275.

CHAPTER 9. TESTING EMPIRE

1. Fernand Braudel, *The Mediterranean and the Mediterranean World in the Age of Philip II,* vol. 2, trans. Sian Reynolds (Berkeley: University of California Press, 1995), 679.
2. David Fieldhouse, book review of *Colonialism and Development: Britain and Its Tropical Colonies, 1850–1960,* by Michael Havinden and David Meredith, *Journal of Historical Geography* 21, no. 1 (January 1995): 98.
3. Aimé Césaire, *Discourse on Colonialism* (New York: Monthly Review Press, 2000), 6.
4. Letter from Harry Johnston to Cecil Rhodes, October 13, 1890, Rhodes Papers, Rhodes House, Oxford, cited in Jean Stengers, "*The Partition of Africa.* L'impérialisme colonial de la fin du XIXe siècle. Mythe ou réalité?," *Journal of African History* 3 (1962): 490.
5. A rectangular piece of cotton tied around the waist.
6. Parashuram, *Selected Stories* (1929; London: Penguin Books, 2006).
7. Daniel Headrick, *The Tools of Empire: Technology and European Imperialism in the Nineteenth Century* (Oxford: Oxford University Press, 1981), 9.
8. Since the 1970s, this characteristic of colonial historiography has drawn the attention of the Norwegian Africanist Jarle Simensen, who was inspired by his compatriot, the

philosopher Jon Elster, and wrote a pioneering article in which he demonstrated how the principal historians of the scramble for Africa mobilized different types of counterfactuals in order to defend their competing theories. We have drawn heavily on this stimulating work. Jarle Simensen, "Counterfactual Arguments in Historical Analysis: From the Debate on the Partition of Africa and the Effect of Colonial Rule," *History in Africa* 5 (1978): 169–186.

9. Headrick, *The Tools of Empire,* 11.
10. M. K. Gandhi, "The Condition of India (continued): Railways," chap. ix of *Hind Swaraj or Indian Home Rule,* Gujarat columns of *Indian Opinion,* December 11 and 18, 1910.
11. Vladimir I. Lenin, *Imperialism, the Highest Stage of Capitalism: A Popular Outline* (New York: Penguin, 2010).
12. Ronald Robinson and John Gallagher, *Africa and the Victorians* (London: Macmillan, 1961), 163.
13. Ibid., 465.
14. Stengers, "*The Partition of Africa,*" 490.
15. Ibid.
16. Ibid., 472.
17. Ibid., 491.
18. C. W. Newbury and A. S. Kanya-Forstner, "French Policy and the Origins of the Scramble for West Africa," *Journal of African History* 10 (1969): 253–276.
19. Antony G. Hopkins, "The Victorians and Africa: A Reconsideration of the Occupation of Egypt, 1882," *Journal of African History* 27 (1986): 390.
20. Pierre Renouvin, "Introduction," *Les Politiques d'expansion impérialiste* (Paris: Presses Universitaires de France, 1949), 1.
21. Harry Johnston to Cecil Rhodes, October, 13 1890, letter in Rhodes Papers, Rhodes House, Oxford, cited in Stengers, "*The Partition of Africa,*" 490.
22. Juhani Koponen, "The Partition of Africa: A Scramble for a Mirage?" *Nordic Journal of African Studies* 2, no. 1 (1993): 134.
23. Ibid.
24. Ibid., 135.
25. Ibid.
26. Simensen, "Counterfactual Arguments in Historical Analysis," 174.
27. Henri Brunschwig, *L'Avènement de l'Afrique noire du XIXe siècle à nos jours* (Paris: Armand Colin, 1963), 212.
28. John Darwin, *The Empire Project: The Rise and Fall of the British World-System, 1830–1970* (Cambridge: Cambridge University Press, 2011); Pierre Singaravélou, "Situations coloniales et formations impériales," in *Les Empires coloniaux,* ed. Pierre Singaravélou (Paris: Seuil, 2013).
29. Fieldhouse, review of *Colonialism and Development,* 98–99.
30. Frantz Fanon, *The Wretched of the Earth,* trans. Richard Philcox (1st French ed. 1963; New York: Grove Press, 2004), 58.
31. Eric Williams, *Capitalism and Slavery* (Richmond: University of North Carolina Press, 1944).

32. Patrick K. O'Brien, "European Economic Development: The Contribution of the Periphery," *Economic History Review* 85 (1982): 1–18.
33. Jacques Marseille, *Empire colonial et capitalisme français: Histoire d' un divorce* (Paris: Albin Michel, 1984).
34. Bouda Etemad, "Un bilan économique de la colonisation. Approches, débats, résultats," in Singaravélou, *Les Empires coloniaux*, 302. See also Bouda Etemad, *De l'utilité des empires. Colonisation et prospérité de l'Europe* (Paris: Armand Colin, 2005).
35. David K. Fieldhouse, "The Metropolitan Economics of Empire," in *Oxford History of The British Empire,* ed. Judith Brown and W. M. Roger Louis, vol. 4 (Oxford: Oxford University Press, 1999): "It must be said at the start that it is impossible to draw up a reliable calculation of the benefits and disadvantages of empire to an imperial state such as Britain without setting up a counter-factual: How might the British economy have performed had Britain possessed no colonies? It might be possible to explore such an investigation, but it is beyond the scope of this study. The questions to be considered here are concrete rather than hypothetical."
36. Bernard Porter, *The Absent-Minded Imperialists: Empire, Society, and Culture in Britain* (Oxford: Oxford University Press, 2004), 254.
37. Jacques Frémeaux, *Les Empires coloniaux dans le processus de mondialisation* (Paris: Maisonneuve et Larose, 2002), 363.
38. John H. Elliott, *Empires of the Atlantic World: Britain and America, 1492–1830* (New Haven, CT: Yale University Press, 2006), 411.
39. Fernando Cervantes, "Too near Madrid," *Times Literary Supplement,* August 4, 2006.
40. Bouda Etemad, *De l'utilité des empires. Colonisation et prospérité de l'Europe, XVIe–XXe siècles* (Paris: Armand Colin, 2005).
41. Ibid.
42. Elise Huillery, "Histoire coloniale, développement et inégalités dans l'ancienne Afrique-Occidentale française" (PhD thesis in economic science, EHESS, 2008), 13.
43. Niall Ferguson, "Introduction," in *Empire: How Britain Made the Modern World* (London: Penguin Press, 2004), xxii.
44. Ibid., xxv.
45. Ibid., xxiii.
46. Niall Ferguson, "A World without Power," *Foreign Policy* 143 (July–August 2004): 32–39.
47. Sunny John Kaniyathu, "The Balance Sheet of Colonialism: Economic Development in the Colonial Period" (PhD, Department of Politics, New York University, 2007), ii.
48. Lewis Gann and Peter Duignan, *Burden of Empire* (New York: F. A. Praeger, 1967), 376.
49. Huillery, "Histoire coloniale, développement," 13.
50. Jennifer Pitts, *A Turn to Empire: The Rise of Imperial Liberalism in Britain and France* (Princeton, NJ: Princeton University Press, 2006), 32.
51. Roy Bin Wong, *China Transformed: Historical Change and the Limits of European Experience* (Ithaca, NY: Cornell University Press, 1997); Andre Gunder Frank,

ReOrient: Global Economy and the Asian Age (Berkeley: University of California Press, 1998).

52. Kaniyathu, "The Balance Sheet of Colonialism," 20.
53. Aimé Césaire, *Discourse on Colonialism,* trans. Joan Pinkham (New York: Monthly Review Press, 1972).
54. Kenneth Pomeranz, *The Great Divergence: China, Europe, and the Making of the Modern World Economy* (Princeton, NJ: Princeton University Press, 2000).
55. Richard Ned Lebow, "Counterfactual Thought Experiments: A Necessary Teaching Tool," *The History Teacher* 40, no. 2 (February 2007): 155.
56. Kenneth Pomeranz, "Without Coal? Colonies? Calculus? Europe, China, and the Industrial Revolution," in *Unmaking the West: "What-If" Scenarios That Rewrite World History,* ed. Philip Tetlock, Ned Lebow, and Geoffrey Parker (Ann Arbor: University of Michigan Press, 2006), 241–276.
57. Eric Williams, *Capitalism and Slavery* (Chapel Hill: The University of North Carolina Press, 1944).
58. Max Weber, *The City,* ed. Don Martindale and Gertrud Neuwirth (1st ed. 1921; Glencoe, IL: Free Press, 1958), 81.
59. Christopher A. Bayly, *The Birth of the Modern World, 1780–1914* (Oxford: Blackwell, 2004), 8.
60. Patrick Manning, *Navigating World History: Historians Create a Global Past* (New York: Palgrave Macmillan, 2003), 300.
61. Immanuel Wallerstein, "Does India Exist?" in *The Essential Wallerstein* (New York: New Press, 2000), 310. This goes back to the three temporalities of Saint Augustine: the present time of things past, the present time of things present, and the present time of future things (*Confessions,* bk. 11, chap. 20).
62. Manning, *Navigating World History*, 300.
63. Daniel S. Milo, "Pour une histoire expérimentale, ou la gaie histoire," *Annales. Économies, sociétés, civilisations* 45, no. 3 (1990): 717–734.
64. Ian Morris, *Why the West Rules—for Now: The Patterns of History and What They Reveal about the Future* (New York: Farrar, Straus and Giroux, 2010), 566–567.
65. Ibid., 567: "If we could return to the past like an experiment, leaving everything else the same but substituting bungling idiots for great men (and vice versa), things would have turned out much the same, even if they might have moved at a slightly different pace. Great men (and women) clearly like thinking that by force of will alone they are changing the world, but they are mistaken."
66. Fernand Braudel, "Expansion européenne et capitalisme (1450–1650)," in *Les Ambitions de l'Histoire*, by Fernand Braudel (Paris: Éditions de Fallois, 1997), 383.
67. Ibid.
68. Ibid., 384.
69. Fernand Braudel, "The Expansion of Europe and the 'Longue Durée,'" in *Expansion and Reaction: Essays on European Expansion and Reaction in Asia and Africa,* ed. Henk L. Wesseling (Leiden: Leiden University Press, 1975), 18–27.
70. Ian Morris, *Why the West Rules,* 11.
71. Tetlock, Lebow, and Parker, *Unmaking the West.*

72. Jared Diamond, *Guns, Germs and Steel: A Short History of Everybody for the Last 13,000 Years* (London: Vintage, 1998), 355.
73. David Gilbert and David Lambert, eds., "Counterfactual Historical Geographies," special issue, *Journal of Historical Geography* 36 (2010): 243–366.
74. Paul Kennedy, *The Rise and Fall of the Great Powers* (London: Random House, 1987).
75. Fernand Braudel, "Expansion européenne et capitalisme (1450–1650)," in *Les Ambitions de l'Histoire* (Paris: Éditions de Fallois, 1997), 384.
76. Pierre Chaunu, *L'Expansion européenne du XIII*[e] *au XV*[e] *siècle* (Paris: Presses Universitaires de France, 1995), 259n.
77. Ibid.
78. Joseph Needham, *Science and Civilization in China,* vol. 4 (Cambridge: Cambridge University Press, 1971), 487.
79. Janet Abu-Lughod, *Before European Hegemony: The World System A.D. 1250–1350* (New York: Oxford University Press, 1989), 321.
80. William McNeill, "World History and the Rise and Fall of the West," *Journal of World History* 9 (1998): 229.
81. Robert Finlay, "Portuguese and Chinese Maritime Imperialism: Camões's *Lusiads* and Luo Maodeng's *Voyage of the San Bao Eunuch,*" *Comparative Studies in Society and History* 34, no. 2 (1992): 227.
82. Ibid., 228.
83. Address by the President of the People's Republic of China before the Australian Parliament, October 24, 2003, http://www.aph.gov.au/About_Parliament/Parliamentary_Departments/Parliamentary_Library/.
84. Gavin Menzies, *1421: The Year China Discovered the World* (London: Random House, 2002).
85. Geoff Wade, "The Zheng He Voyages: A Reassessment," Asia Research Institute Working Paper Series no. 31, October 2004; Edward L. Dreyer, *Zheng He: China and the Oceans in the Early Ming Dynasty, 1405–1433* (London: Pearson, 2007).
86. A number of works have called this commonplace into question over recent years including Odd Arne Westad, *Restless Empire: China and the World Since 1750* (New York: Basic Books, 2012).
87. Gang Deng, *Maritime Sector, Institutions, and Sea Power of Premodern China* (Westport: Greenwood Publishing Group, 1999), 218.
88. Patrick Boucheron, ed., *Histoire du monde au XV*[e] *siècle* (Paris: Fayard, 2009), 28.
89. Bayly, *The Birth of the Modern World.*
90. Richard Drayton, for example, organized a workshop entitled "Lost Futures in the History of Modern European Empires," King's College London, May 24–25, 2012.
91. Romain Bertrand has therefore used equally and in the same way Western sources and Asian sources, and attempted to show that "Java was not the passive recipient of 'European modernity,' but rather contained the possibilities of another History." Romain Bertrand, *L'Histoire à parts égales* (Paris: Seuil, 2011), 22.
92. Frederick Cooper, *Colonialism in Question: Theory, Knowledge, History* (Berkeley: University of California Press, 2005), 18.
93. Ibid., 231.

94. Frederick Cooper, *Citizenship between Empire and Nation: Remaking France and French Africa, 1945–1960* (Princeton, NJ: Princeton University Press, 2014), 10.
95. Sanjay Subrahmanyam, "'Un grand dérangement': Dreaming an Indo-Persian Empire in South Asia, 1740–1800," *Journal of Early Modern History* 4 (2001).
96. Jean-Jacques Matignon, *L'Orient lointain. Chine, Corée, Mongolie, impressions et souvenirs de séjour et de tourisme* (Paris: A. Storck, 1903), 160–162.
97. Jean de Ruf de Pontevès, *Souvenirs de la colonne Seymour: Les marins en Chine* (Paris: Plon-Nourrit, 1903), 300–301.
98. Anonymous, "L'Europe et la Chine," *La Revue de Paris,* September–October 1900, 15.
99. Georges Weulersse, *Chine ancienne et moderne* (Paris: Armand Colin, 1902), 344–345.
100. Pierre Loti, *The Last Days of Pekin,* trans. Myrta L. Jones (Boston: Little, Brown, 1902), 268–269.
101. "Les Affaires de Chine," *Questions diplomatiques et coloniales* 11 (January–June 1901): 112.
102. Henri Frey, *Français et Alliés au Pé-Tchi-Li* (Paris: Hachette, 1904), 114.
103. Stanley Spector, *Li Hung Chang and the Huai Army: A Study in Nineteenth-Century Chinese Regionalism* (Seattle: University of Washington Press, 1974), 163.
104. Arnold Savage-Landor, *China and the Allies* (New York: Scribner, 1901), 188.
105. Hans van de Ven, *Warfare in Chinese History* (Leiden: Brill, 2000), 22.
106. Cäcilie von Rodt, *Voyage d'une Suissesse autour du monde* (Neuchâtel, Switzerland: F. Zahn, 1904), 200.
107. De Pontevès, *Souvenirs de la colonne Seymour*, 288 and 301.
108. Alexis Daoulas, *Le Siège de Tien-Tsin (15 juin–15 juillet 1900)* (Paris: Berger-Levrault, 1903), 279.
109. "Journal du siège de Tientsin," *La Revue de Paris,* January 15, 1902, 244.
110. Daoulas, *Le Siège de Tien-Tsin*, 106.
111. Comment by Robert Hart in the *Fortnightly Review,* cited by General H. Frey, *Français et Alliés au Pé-Tchi-Li* (Paris: Hachette, 1904), 115.
112. Indeed, in the Confucian political tradition, the recourse to force is a sign of failure: "For the emperor to resort to violence was an admission that he had failed in his own conduct as a sage pursuing the art of government. The resort to warfare (*wu*) was an admission of bankruptcy in the pursuit of *wen.* Consequently, it should be a last resort, and it required justification both at the time and in the record." John K. Fairbank and F. A. Kierman, eds., *Chinese Ways in Warfare* (Cambridge: Cambridge University Press, 1974), 7.
113. Ibid., 11.
114. Jane Elliott, *Some Did It for Civilization, Some Did It for Their Country* (Hong Kong: Chinese University Press, 2002), 387.
115. Letter from the consul Henri Leduc to the minister of foreign affairs, Archives diplomatiques de Nantes, 691 PO/1, Consulate of Tientsin, 291.
116. T. O. Matzmura, "History of the Development of the Japanese Concession, Tientsin," *North China Star,* Anniversary Magazine, August 12, 1920, 10.

117. Mads Mordhorst, "From Counterfactual History to Counter-Narrative History," *Management & Organizational History,* November 7, 2012.
118. Excerpts from "Boxer posters" cited in "Les Affaires de Chine," *L'Ouest-Éclair* (Rennes), no. 432 (October 15, 1900): 2.
119. François Thierry, "Fausses dates et vraies monnaies. Rites, information, propagande et histoire dans la numismatique chinoise," *Extrême-Orient, Extrême-Occident* 32 (2010): 55–56; Emmanuel Poisson, "Faux, falsification, pouvoir et société," *Extrême-Orient, Extrême-Occident* 32 (2010): 9.
120. Weulersse, *Chine ancienne et modern,* 336–337.
121. Ja Ian Chong, "Breaking Up Is Hard to Do: Foreign Intervention and the Limiting of Fragmentation in the Late Qing and Early Republic, 1893–1922," *Twentieth-Century China* 35, no. 1 (November 2009): 75–98.
122. Charles Tenney, "Li Hung Chang," in *The Papers of Charles Tenney,* Dartmouth College Library, 1919–1925, 4–5.
123. Julia Lovell, *The Opium War: Drugs, Dreams and the Making of China* (Basingstoke/Oxford: Picador, 2011).
124. Wolfgang Knöbl, "Civilizational Analysis and the Problem Of Contingency" (working paper no. 82, Centre on Migration, Citizenship and Development, Bielefeld, Germany, 2010).

CHAPTER 10. "TODAY, ONLY THE LANGUAGE OF DREAMS CAN TRANSLATE HISTORY"

1. Maxime Du Camp, *Souvenirs de l'année 1848* (Paris: Hachette, 1876), 9.
2. Maurice Agulhon, *1848 ou l'apprentissage de la République 1848–1852* (Paris: Seuil 1992), 398. Maurice Agulhon, *The Republican Experiment, 1848–1852,* trans. Janet Lloyd (Cambridge: Cambridge University Press, 1983). (This quotation translated by S. Sawyer.)
3. Placard signed Auguste Siberd, brigadier, 82, rue de la Tixéranderie, cited by Jean-Claude Caron, *Les Feux de la discorde. Conflit et incendie dans la France du XIXe siècle* (Paris: Hachette-Littérature, 2006), 73.
4. Alban Bensa and Éric Fassin, "Les Sciences sociales face à l'événement," *Terrain* 38 (2002).
5. Pierre Nora, "Le Retour de l'événement," in *Faire de l' histoire,* ed. Jacques Le Goff and Pierre Nora, vol. 1: *Nouveaux Problèmes* (Paris: Gallimard, 1974), 210–229; Andrew Abbott, "From Causes to Events: Notes on Narrative Positivism," *Sociological Methods & Research* 20, no. 4 (May 1992): 428–455; Bensa and Fassin, "Les Sciences sociales face à l'événement"; Marc Bessin, Claire Bidart, and Michel Grossetti, eds., *Bifurcations. Les sciences sociales face aux ruptures et à l'évènement* (Paris: La Découverte, 2010); François Dosse, *Renaissance de l'évènement. Un défi pour l'historien: entre sphinx et phénix* (Paris: Presses Universitaires de France, 2010); Jacques Revel, "Retour sur l'évènement: Un itinéraire historiographique," in *Le Goût de l'enquête. Pour Jean-Claude Passeron,* ed. Jean-Louis Fabiani (Paris: L'Harmattan, 2001), 95–118; William H. Sewell Jr., "Historical Events as Transformations of Structures," *Theory and Society* 2 (1996): 841–881.

6. The expression is from Rémi Gossez, *Les Ouvriers de Paris. L'organisation, 1848–1851* (Paris: Société d'histoire de la révolution de 1848, 1967).
7. "Les Événements de la journée," *Le Siècle,* February 24, 1848, 2.
8. Alphonse de Lamartine, *Histoire de la Révolution de 1848* (Paris: Perrotin, 1849); Daniel Stern, *Histoire de la Révolution de 1848* (Paris: Charpentier, 1862); Alexis de Tocqueville, *Souvenirs* (1850; Paris: Gallimard, 1964–1978); Maxime Du Camp, *Souvenirs de l'année 1848* (Paris: Hachette, 1876); Henri de La Rochejaquelein, *À mon pays. Défense de ma proposition sur l'appel à la nation (pour opter entre république ou monarchie)* (Paris: Garnier, 1850); Louis Ménard, *Prologue d'une révolution. Février–juin 1848, Au bureau du people* (1849; Paris: La Fabrique, 2007). We have also consulted numerous newspapers and petitions for this study, including *Le Siècle* and *Le Journal des débats* (one week of each month from February to June), the entirety of the *Tocsin des travailleurs,* which appeared from June 1 to 23, and the excerpts from *L'Ami du peuple* and the *Journal des travailleurs.* We also consulted the *Procès-verbaux du Comité du travail à l'Assemblée constituante de 1848,* 3 vols., vol. 3 (Paris: Bibliothèque de la Révolution de 1848, 1908) and thirty-some petitions focused on the Provisional Government and the Constituent Assembly conserved in the National Archives (C 2226–2227) and the Bibliothèque nationale de France.
9. Agulhon, *The Republican Experiment.* On the context more generally, see also Bertrand Goujon, *Monarchies postrévolutionnaires, 1814–1848* (Paris: Seuil, 2012).
10. Suffrage was based on a poll tax. One needed to pay a certain amount of tax in order to be able to vote.
11. Du Camp, *Souvenirs de l'année 1848.*
12. Ernest Labrousse, "1848–1830–1789. Comment naissent les révolutions," *Actes du congrès historique du centenaire de la Révolution de 1848* (Paris: Presses Universitaires de France, 1948), 1–20. Regular revisions have followed. In one of the most recent focusing on 1848, we see that it followed a very winding path. Vincent Robert, "Comment naît une révolution?" in *Le Temps des banquets* (Paris: Publications de la Sorbonne, 2010), 382–384.
13. See the approaches of Maurizio Gribaudi and Michèle Riot-Sarcey in *1848, La Révolution oubliée* (Paris: La Découverte, 2009), 31–32.
14. Alexis de Tocqueville, *The Recollections of Alexis de Tocqueville,* ed. Comte de Tocqueville, trans. Alexander Teixeira de Mattos (New York: Macmillan, 1896), 80–81.
15. See Boris Gobille, "De l'étiologie à l'historicité des crises. Sociologie des crises politiques et sociohistoire du temps court," in *La Logique du désordre, relire Michel Dobry,* ed. Myriam Aït-Aoudia and Antoine Roger (Paris: Presses de Sciences-Po, 2015), 153–176.
16. Alain Garrigou, *Histoire sociale du suffrage universel en France, 1848–2000* (Paris: Seuil, 2002).
17. François Jarrige, "Dire le refus des machines: Les pétitions ouvrières et les représentations de l'ordre économique (France, 1848)," *Annales des Mines,* Série réalités industrielles, 2009, 99–118.

18. Here we are drawing on the reflections that were proposed in the workshop: "References to the Past" co-organized by Claude Moatti and Michel Riot-Sarcey. For 1830, see also Sylvie Aprile, Jean-Claude Caron, and Emmanuel Fureix, "Introduction," in *La liberté guidant les peuples* (Paris: Champ Vallon, 2013).
19. G. Desjardins, *De l'organisation de la fraternité ou d'une constitution sociale à donner au people* (Paris: Perrotin/Furne, 1848), 3.
20. Jean-Pierre Gross, *Fair Shares for All: Jacobin Egalitarianism in Practice* (Cambridge: Cambridge University Press, 1997); Bernard Gainot, "La République comme association de citoyens solidaires. Pour retrouver l'économie politique républicaine (1792–1799)," in *Pourquoi faire la revolution,* by Jean-Luc Chappey, Bernard Gainod, Guillaume Mazeau, Frédéric Régent, and Pierre Serna (Marseille: Agone, 2012), 149–180.
21. *Le Journal des travailleurs,* June 11, 1848 (newspaper founded by the worker delegates at the Luxembourg Commission).
22. Cited in Yves Deloye, *Les Voix de Dieu. Pour une autre histoire du suffrage électoral: le clergé catholique français et le vote. XIXe–XXe siècles* (Paris: Fayard, 2006), 72.
23. Société des droits de l'homme et du citoyen, "Liberté, égalité, fraternité unité," Placard, Sedan, France, imprimerie de Laroche-Jacob, April 11, 1848 (Bibliothèque nationale de France, FOL-LB53–1084).
24. Aby Warburg, *Essais florentins* (Paris: Klincksieck, 1990). On the invisible but constant anachronisms and heterogeneous discourses that rip open the normal course of things and leave the door open behind them, see, for example, Georges Didi-Huberman, *Devant le temps. Histoire de l'art et anachronisme des images* (Paris: Minuit, 2000). The banquets were part of this, as was the theater. For a precise example of the shift in meaning, see Vincent Robert, "Théâtre et révolution à la veille de 1848. Le Chevalier de Maison-Rouge," *Actes de la recherche en sciences sociales* 186–187 (March 2011): 30.
25. Emmanuel Fureix, "L'Iconoclasme politique: Une violence fondatrice? (1814–1848)," in *Entre violence et conciliation. La résolution des conflits sociopolitiques en Europe au XIXe siècle,* ed. Jean-Claude Caron, Frédéric Chauvaud, and Emmanuel Fureix (Rennes, France: Presses Universitaires de Rennes, 2008), 231–241; and Emmanuel Fureix, ed., *Iconoclasme et révolutions, de 1789 à nos jours* (Seyssel, France: Champ Vallon, 2014).
26. Alphonse Dupront, "Temporel et éternel, anthropologie religieuse et histoire," in *Du Sacré* (Paris: Gallimard, 1996), 467–537.
27. The declarations of the candidacies in April 1848 and the innumerable posters produced after February 24 are other such sources.
28. Benoît Agnès, "L'Appel au pouvoir. Essai sur le pétitionnement auprès des chambres législatives et électives en France et au Royaume-Uni entre 1814 et 1848" (PhD thesis directed by Christophe Charle, Université Paris 1, 2009); François Jarrige, "Une 'barricade de papiers': Le pétitionnement contre la restriction du suffrage universel masculin en mai 1850," *Revue d'histoire du XIXe siècle* 29 (2004): 53–70.
29. Archives nationales, C 2428–2430. (The National Assembly received 3,097 petitions between 1849 and 1851.)

30. The Constituent Assembly replaced the Provisional Government on May 10, 1848.
31. Pierre Rosanvallon, *Le Sacre du citoyen* (Paris: Gallimard, 1992), 372–387.
32. "Pétition du comité de colonisation de la France orientale à l'Assemblée nationale," Paris, imprimerie de Schneider, June 1, 1848. This committee consisted of an ex-missionary, a lawyer at the Paris Court of Appeal, and a student of medicine (Bibliothèque nationale de France, 4-LK11–83).
33. Ferdinand Jammes, "Pétition à l'Assemblée nationale en faveur des employés de bureau," Batignolles, France, imprimerie de Hennuyer, 1848 (Bibliothèque nationale de France, 8-LB54–1320).
34. Among other petitions recorded in the registers of the Labor Committee in the Constituent Assembly one finds: "The establishment in the countryside, with the support of the state, of small industries such as silkworm manufactures, extraction of potato starch, beet sugar, by a delegation of mechanics for agricultural instruments, rue Paradis-Poissonière." May 11, in *Procès-verbaux du Comité du travail à l'Assemblée constituante de 1848,* vol. 3 (Paris: Bibliothèque de la Révolution de 1848, 1908).
35. This was a crucial problem in the nineteenth century: Jean-Claude Caron, *Les Feux de la discorde. Conflit et incendie dans la France du XIXe siècle* (Paris: Hachette-Littérature, 2006); François Jarrige and Bénédicte Reynaud, "Les Usines en feu. L'industrialisation au risque des incendies dans le textile (France, 1830–1870)," *Le Mouvement social* 249, no. 4 (2014).
36. "Pétition contre le monopole des assurances par l'État," Paris, imprimerie de Delanchy, 1848 (Bibliothèque nationale de France, 4-LB54–525).
37. The expression "dreams of police" comes from Vincent Denis, Paris Police Prefecture Archives, DB 31, 1829–1852.
38. *Journal des débats,* March 6, 1848.
39. Eugénie Niboyet, *La Voix des femmes,* March 21, 1848.
40. George Sand, "Lettre aux membres du comité central," April 1848, in *Correspondance,* vol. 8 (Paris: Classiques Garnier, 1971), 400–408.
41. Michèle Riot-Sarcey, *La Démocratie à l'épreuve des femmes. Trois figures critiques du pouvoir, 1830–1848* (Paris: Albin Michel, 1994).
42. The expression refers to "a set of psychic operations by which certain categories of identity are made to elide historical differences and create apparent continuities." Joan W. Scott, "Fantasy Echo: History and the Construction of Identity," *Critical Inquiry* 27, no. 2 (2001): 284–304.
43. L. L. T. V. "La République des pères de famille devant l'Assemblée nationale, ou pétition motivée en faveur de leur imprescriptible et inaliénable souveraineté," Saint-Brieuc, France, imprimerie de L. Prud'homme, 1848 (Bibliothèque nationale de France, 8-LB54–969). "If you accept the task of formulating into law the fundamental principles which have nonetheless withstood the test of time and consistently saved societies at risk, and which alone, inscribed in a European charter, would gradually lead all peoples toward a future that was indefinitely and wisely progressive."
44. Anne Verjus, *Le Bon mari. Une histoire politique des hommes et des femmes à l'époque révolutionnaire* (Paris: Fayard, 2010).

45. Émile Durkheim, *Les Formes élémentaires de la vie religieuse* (Paris: Presses universitaires de France, 1912).
46. On desire, see Sigmund Freud, *L'Interprétation du rêve* (1900; Paris: Presses universitaires de France, 2012); on the creative dimension, see Gilles Deleuze and Félix Guattari, *L'Anti-Œdipe* (Paris: Minuit, 1972), 32–35.
47. It is also necessary to add that in spite of new social opportunities, a majority of the parliamentary and executive bodies were composed of the wealthiest sectors of society.
48. For a general sense of the context, see Gérard Noiriel, *Les Ouvriers dans la société française* (Paris: Seuil, 1986); on 1848, see Roger Price, *Revolution and Reaction: 1848 and the Second Republic* (London: New York, 1975); John M. Merriman, *The Agony of the Republic: The Repression of the Left in Revolutionary France, 1848–1851* (New Haven, CT: Yale University Press, 1978); on the world of Parisian workers in 1848, see Rémi Gossez, *Les Ouvriers de Paris. L'organisation, 1848–1851* (La Roche-sur-Yon, France: Imprimerie de l'Ouest, 1968).
49. Alain Dewerpe, *Le Monde du travail en France* (Paris: Armand Colin, 1989).
50. *Procès-verbaux du Comité du travail à l'Assemblée constituante de 1848* (Paris: Ed. Cornély, 1908).
51. Citoyen Martin (from Mâcon), "Pétition à l'Assemblée constituante pour la création d'une banque nationale ouvrière," Paris, imprimerie de Vinchon, 1848 (Bibliothèuqe Nationale de France, 8-LB54–413).
52. "Manifesto of the Delegates of the Guilds of Luxembourg," *Journal des travailleurs,* June 8, 1848.
53. Philippe Vigier, "Lyon, 25 février 1848," in *La Vie quotidienne en Province et à Paris pendant les journées de 1848* (Paris: Hachette, 1982), 81–109.
54. François Jarrige, "Artisanat et industrie," in *Le Peuple de Paris au XIXe siècle* (Paris: Musée Carnavalet, 2012), 67. For a more detailed perspective, see Barrie M. Ratcliffe and Christine Piette, *Vivre la ville. Les classes populaires à Paris (1re moitié du XIXe siècle)* (Paris: La Boutique de l'histoire, 2007).
55. Jacques Rougerie, "Par-delà le coup d'État, la continuité de l'action et de l'organisation ouvrière," in *Comment meurt une République? Autour du 2 décembre,* ed. Sylvie Aprile, Nathalie Bayon, Laurent Clavier, Louis Hincker, and Jean-Luc Mayaud, *Actes du colloque de Lyon, December 2001, Société d'histoire de la révolution de 1848 et des révolutions du XIXe siècle* (Paris: Créaphis, 2004), 267–284; Jacques Rougerie, "Le mouvement associatif populaire comme facteur d'acculturation politique à Paris de la Révolution aux années 1840. Continuité, discontinuités," *Annales historiques de la Révolution française* 297 (1994): 493–516.
56. Laurent Clavier, "'Quartier' et expériences politiques dans les faubourgs du nord-est parisien en 1848," *Revue d'histoire du XIXe siècle* 33 (2006): 121–142.
57. Gossez, *Les Ouvriers de Paris,* vol. 1.
58. On this question, see Ivan Ermakoff, "Contingence historique et contiguïté des possibles," *Tracés* 24 (2013): 23–45.
59. Vigier, *La Vie quotidienne en Province et à Paris pendant les journées de 1848* (Paris: Hachette, 1982).

60. Unless one adopted a perspective closer to that of Walter Benjamin, which would consist of expressing the presentism of these forms of action in our present. The choice is then more strictly historical and political, and adapted to contemporary transformation. On the changing presentism of 1848 between 1975 and 1991, see Maurice Agulhon, *Les Quarante-Huitards* (Paris: Gallimard-Julliard, "Archives," 1976).
61. For example, Gribaudi and Riot-Sarcey, *1848, La Révolution oubliée*; Louis Hincker, *Citoyen-Combattant à Paris, 1848–1851* (Villeneuve-d'Ascq, France: Presses universitaires du Septentrion, 2008); François Jarrige, *Au temps des "tueuses de bras." Les bris de machines à l'aube de l'ère industrielle (1780–1860)* (Rennes, France: Presses universitaires de Rennes, 2009); Maurizio Gribaudi, *Paris, ville ouvrière, une histoire occultée (1789–1848)* (Paris: La Découverte, 2014).
62. George Sand, "Aux riches," March 16, 1848, cited in Gribaudi and Riot-Sarcey, *1848, La Révolution oubliée*, 113.
63. During the creation of a union of fraternal associations, Gossez, *Les Ouvriers de Paris*.
64. Tocqueville, *Souvenirs*.
65. *Karl Marx, Friedrich Engels: Collected Works*, vol. 7: *1848* (New York: International Publishers, 1976).
66. Rémi Gossez, "Diversité des antagonismes sociaux vers le milieu du XIXe siècle," *Revue économique*. 7, no. 3 (1956): 439–458.
67. Mark Traugott, *Armies of the Poor: Determinants of Working-Class Participation in the Parisian Insurrection of June 1848* (Princeton, NJ: Princeton University Press, 1985).
68. Laurent Clavier, Louis Hincker, and Jacques Rougerie, "Juin 1848, L'insurrection," in *1848. Actes du colloque international du cent cinquantenaire*, ed. Jean-Louis Mayaud (Paris: Creaphis, 2002).
69. Here we are following the argument of William Sewell based on his reading of Mark Traugott. See William H. Sewell Jr., "Three Temporalities: Toward and Eventful Sociology," in *Logics of History: Social Theory and Social Transformation* (Chicago: University of Chicago Press, 2005), 81–123.
70. Yves Deloye, *Sociologie historique du politique* (Paris: La Découverte, 2007).
71. Thomas Bouchet, *Un jeudi à l'Assemblée. Politiques du discours et droit au travail dans la France de 1848* (Québec: Nota Bene, 2007).
72. Agulhon, *The Republican Experiment*, 61.
73. Bernard Ménager, *Les Napoléon du peuple* (Paris: Aubier, 1988).
74. Auguste Romieu, *Le Spectre rouge de l'année 1852* (Paris: Ledoyen, 1851).
75. Maurice Agulhon writes, "And yet, Merriman, like ourselves, does not think that democracy was necessarily destined to come to an end at the beginning of 1849. Far from drawing out a long terminal illness, it was a victim of strikes against it in a battle with exciting or minor episodes, provincial or Parisian, folkoloric or legislative, all of which formed the essential content of the three years of our story. This reevaluation of 1849, 1850 and 1851 in the chronological development is therefore bound to a reevaluation of political voluntarism in the explanatory mechanism." Maurice Agulhon, book review of *The Agony of the Republic*, by John Merriman, in *Annales, ESC* 35,

no. 6 (1980): 1306–1307. On the fear of 1852, see also Guillaume Cuchet and Sylvain Milbach, "The Great Fear of 1852," *French History* 26 (2012–2013): 297–324.

76. Morny still regrets in March 1851 in a letter to his father, his "loyal resignation," in Éric Anceau, *Napoléon III. Un Saint-Simon à cheval* (Paris: Taillandier, 2008), 174–179.
77. Ménager, *Les Napoléon du people.*
78. From this perspective, the approach explored here is quite similar to the analyses proposed by Maurizio Gribaudi and Michèle Riot-Sarcey on the discontinuities used for the period from February to June 1848. See their *1848. La Révolution oubliée*; Michèle Riot-Sarcey, "Temps et histoire en débat," *Revue d'histoire du XIXe siècle* 25 (2002), http://rh19.revues.org/index414.html.
79. Bensa and Fassin, "Les Sciences sociales face à l'événement," 5–20.
80. We are borrowing the expression from Lynn Hunt, "The French Revolution: Time's Degree Zero" (unpublished). We thank the author for sharing this text with us. See also "The World We Have Gained: The Future of the French Revolution," *American Historical Review* 108, no. 1 (2003): 1–19. These works allow one to consider the impression of living "time's degree zero," where time accelerates, where the past, present, and future are confused and imbued with sacredness. The value of 1848 is that if the French Revolution is lived as an authentic "time zero" without a past, 1848 appears to be a "time zero" with a past, that is, the French Revolution.
81. Michel Dobry, "Ce dont sont faites les logiques de situation," in *L'Atelier du politiste* (Paris: La Découverte, 2007); Luc Boltanski and Laurent Thévenot, *De la justification. Les économies de la grandeur* (Paris: Gallimard, 1991); Laurent Thévenot, *L'Action au pluriel. Sociologie des régimes d'engagement* (Paris: La Découverte, 2006).
82. Louis Hincker, *Citoyen-Combattant à Paris, 1848–1851* (Villeneuve-d'Ascq, France: Presses universitaires du Septentrion, 2008); Michel Dobry, "Les voies incertaines de la transitologie: Choix stratégiques, séquences historiques, bifurcations et processus de *path dependence*," *Revue française de science politique* 50, nos. 4–5 (2000).
83. Christophe Charle, "Géopolitique révolutionnaire," in *Discordance des temps. Une brève histoire de la modernité* (Paris: Armand Colin, 2011), 105–109; Robert J. W. Evans and Hartmut Pogge von Strandmann, eds., *The Revolutions in Europe 1848–1849: From Reform to Reaction* (Oxford and New York: Oxford University Press, 2000).
84. Mark Traugott, *The Insurgent Barricade* (Oakland: University of California Press, 2010).
85. This hierarchy evolved over the course of time. Berlin and Vienna became more important as the French Republic was reduced.
86. But also within an imperial and global framework. See Miles Taylor, "The 1848 Revolutions and the British Empire," *Past and Present* 166, no. 1 (2000): 146–180.
87. Helge Berger and Mark Spoerer, "Economic Crisis and the European Revolution of 1848," *Journal of Economic History* 61, no. 2 (June 2001): 293–326.
88. Agulhon, *1848 ou l'apprentissage de la République*, 112.
89. Christophe Charle, *Histoire sociale de la France au XIXe siècle* (Paris: Seuil, 1991), 198.
90. Vigier, *La Vie quotidienne en Province et à Paris.*

91. On the question of the impact of the 1848 on the development of the French state, see Stephen W. Sawyer, *Demos Assembled: Democracy and the International Origins of the Modern State, 1840–1880* (Chicago: University of Chicago Press, 2018). For the question of the development of socialism, one could ask: What would have come of the thoughts and socialist reforms without 1848? Did the failure of 1848 not contribute to the return of emancipatory thinking like the utopists at the very moment when they began to gain strength and legitimacy in the public sphere? Would Marxism have become so central without the Revolution of 1848, which seemed to corroborate his ideas in *The Communist Manifesto* published in 1848, when he referred to them as mere utopists? Loïc Rignol, Anne-Sophie Chambost, Ludovic Frobert, and Edward Castleton, "1848 as a Turning Point in Political Thought," workshop at King's College, Cambridge, April 11–12, 2012.
92. Eric Hobsbawm, *Nations and Nationalism since 1780* (Cambridge: Cambridge University Press, 1992); Anne-Marie Thiesse, *La Création des identités nationales. Europe XVIIIe–XXe siècle* (Paris: Seuil, 1999).
93. Christophe Charle, *Discordance des temps. Une brève histoire de la modernité* (Paris: Armand Colin, 2011).
94. Du Camp, *Souvenirs de l'année 1848.*
95. Alphonse de Lamartine, *Histoire de la Révolution de 1848* (Paris: Perrotin, 1849).
96. Reinhart Koselleck, *Futures Past: On the Semantics of Historical Time,* trans. Keith Tribe (New York: Columbia University Press, 2004); François Hartog, *Regimes of Historicity: Presentism and Experiences of Time,* trans. Saskia Brown (New York: Columbia University Press, 2015).
97. Alain Plessis, *De la fête impériale au mur des fédérés, 1852–1871* (Paris: Seuil, 1973); Charle, *Histoire sociale de la France*; Anceau, *Napoléon III*; Price, *Revolution and Reaction*; Philip Nord, The *Republican Moment: Struggles for Democracy in Nineteenth-Century France* (Cambridge, MA: Harvard University Press, 1995). (This is a selected list.)
98. See Jacques Rougerie, *La Commune de 1871* (Paris: Presses Universitaire de France, 2009), notably "La Semaine de l'incertitude," 51–63.
99. Jacques Rougerie and Robert Tombs, "La Commune de Paris," in *Histoire des mouvements sociaux en France,* ed. Michel Pigenet and Danièle Tartakosvky (Paris: La Découverte, 2011), 141–151.
100. Jeanne Gaillard, *Communes de province, Commune de Paris* (Paris: Flammarion, 1971); Marc César, *Mars 1871: La Commune révolutionnaire de Narbonne* (Sète, France: Éditions Singulières, 2008).
101. On the echoes, see Éric Fournier, *La Commune n'est pas morte* (Paris: Libertalia, 2013); Hongsheng Jiang, *La Commune de Shanghai et la Commune de Paris* (Paris: La Fabrique, 2014).
102. Martin Malia, *Histoire des Révolutions* (Paris: Tallandier, 2008).
103. Guillaume Mazeau, "La ronde des révolutions," *La Vie des idées,* April 16, 2013.

CHAPTER 11. THE CONSOLE AND THE CHALKBOARD

1. Introduction to the video game *Wolfenstein: The New Order* (Bethesda Softworks, Machine Studios, 2014).

2. Alternate History, Forum, "WWI Video Games More Popular," May 2013, https://www.alternatehistory.com/forum/threads/ahc-wwi-video-games-more-popular.279922/ [accessed October 2020].
3. Jean-Marie Schaeffer, *Pourquoi la fiction?* (Paris: Seuil, 1999), 57.
4. For the nineteenth century, see Stéphane Gerson, *The Pride of Place: Local Memories and Political Culture in Nineteenth-Century France* (Ithaca, NY: Cornell University Press, 2003).
5. Jean-Clément Martin and Charles Suaud, *Le Puy du Fou en Vendée. Histoire d'une mise en scène* (Paris: L'Harmattan, 1996).
6. See http://www.reconstitution-historique.com [accessed October 2020]; http://https://livinghistoryworldwide.com/ [accessed October 2020].
7. In July 2013, thirty thousand people participated in the reconstruction of the Battle of Gettysburg in Pennsylvania for the 150th anniversary of the event.
8. Eli Lehrer and Mark Hemingway, "Living History," *American Enterprise,* March 2003.
9. See Maryline Crivello, "Du passé, faisons un spectacle," *Société et représentations,* 2001; Jean-Luc Bonniol and Maryline Crivello, eds., *Façonner le passé* (Aix-en-Provence, France: Publications de l'université de Provence, 2004); Gilles Heuré, "Fou d'histoire," *Télérama,* July 2004.
10. See the article "Lauris, deux mille visiteurs plongés dans l'histoire et l'imaginaire du village," *La Provence,* September 14, 2010.
11. Hence, the distinction between "living history," which is designed to reproduce past experiences, and "reenactment," which consists of replicating the sequence of events exactly.
12. Michael Kilian, "Ironclads Do Battle Once Again: As in 1862, This Clash Yields No Clear Victor," *Chicago Tribune,* March 11, 1996. There is also a new tourism sector dedicated to these sites and events of alternate history. See Chris Ryan, ed., *Battlefield Tourism: History, Place and Interpretation* (London: Routledge, 2007), 23.
13. See, for example, Olivier Caïra, *Définir la fiction* (Paris: EHESS, 2012).
14. Presentation of the game *Khaos 1795,* Les XII Singes, 2008.
15. Such worlds can also be created by more immediately external events. In *Lux Labis,* the players participate in an alternative Russia of the seventeenth century, thrown into a "long night" after the fall of Lux Labis, a comet that touches Earth in 1204 in Southeast Asia.
16. "Uchronia 1890: Aventures, Complots et Machines Infernales," http://uchronia.free.fr/ [accessed October 2020].
17. "Uchronia 1890: Aventures, Complots et Machines Infernales," http://uchronia.free.fr/Introduction.htm [accessed October 2020].
18. See http://jeux.dombres.free.fr/spip.php?article88; http://saint-epondyle.net/blog/2011/12/20/luchronie-et-le-jeu-de-roles/ [accessed spring 2014].
19. Ibid. See, for the United States, RPG (role-playing game), the GURPS series, for example, Kenneth Hite, Craig Neumeier, and Michael S. Schiffer, *GURPS Alternate Earths,* ed. Sean Punch, Steve Jackson Games, 1996.
20. Source: AFJV (Association française pour le jeu vidéo) and Ministère de la Culture et de la Communication, http://www.culturecommunication.gouv.fr/ Disciplines-secteurs/Industries-culturelles/Dossiers-thematiques/Le-jeu-video.

21. Similarly, the historical backgrounds can sometimes be modified for the necessities of the game and the pleasure of the viewer. See Guillaume Delalande, Mehdi El Kana, and Nicolas Courcier, "*Assassin' s Creed*": *Entre voyages, vérités et complots* (Paris: Prix n'love, 2013). This version of *Assassin's Creed* generated debate in France, to which the historical advisors responded (the names were discovered after the game appeared). See Laurent Turcot and Jean-Clément Martin, *Au cœur de la Révolution. Les leçons d'histoire d'un jeu video* (Paris: Vendémiaire, "Chroniques," 2015).
22. *Castle Wolfenstein* (Muse Software, 1981).
23. *Command and Conquer*: *Red Alert* (Virgin Interactive, 1996) and *Resistance*: *Fall of Man* (Sony Computer Entertainment, 2006).
24. There was also *Homefront* (Kaos Studios, 2011), in which Kim-Jong Un invades South Korea in 2012. Then, weakened by diminished oil reserves after a war in Saudi Arabia, Iran and the United States are attacked in 2025 by the "Great Korean Republic."
25. *Europa Universalis* (Strategy First, 2000); *Total War* (Electronic Arts, 2000); *Hearts of Iron* (Strategy First, 2002); *Civilization* (Hartland and MicroProse, 1991).
26. See https://www.civilization.com/us/news/.
27. Heather Chaplin, "Is That Just Some Game? No, It's a Cultural Artifact," *New York Times,* December 3, 2007.
28. Review of Civilization V, https://www.commonsensemedia.org/game-reviews/sid-meiers-civilization-v [accessed October 2020]; Aaron Whelchel, "Using Civilization Simulation Video Games in the World History Classroom," *World History Connected* 4, no. 2 (2007), http://worldhistory-connected.press.illinois.edu/4.2/whelchel.html; Kurt Squire, "Replaying History: Learning World History Through Playing "Civilization III" (unpublished diss., Indiana University, 2004); Scott Carlson, "Can Grand Theft Auto Inspire Professors?," *Chronicle of Higher Education* 49 (August 15, 2003): 31–33.
29. See also the profile of Niall Ferguson by Robert S. Boynton, "Thinking the Unthinkable," *New Yorker,* April 12, 1999.
30. Niall Ferguson, "How to Win a War," *New York Magazine,* October 23, 2006. This reference and reflection has drawn from the well-informed blog *Jeux vidéo et épistémologie de l'histoire* (edited under the pseudonym ElDesdichado), https://forum.reseau-js.com/blogs/blog/15-jeux-vid%C3%A90-et-epist%C3%A9mologie-de-lhistoire/ [accessed October 2020].
31. "Niall Ferguson Aims to Shake Up History Curriculum with TV and War Games," *The Guardian,* July 9, 2010. In May of this same year, he spoke of his desire to include a condensed and more simple version of his manual on Western civilization with the game, http:// www.wargamer.com/article/2866/making-history-ii-interview-with-niall-ferguson.
32. Niall Ferguson, "Villain of the Piece," *Financial Times,* September 7, 2007.
33. Ibid.
34. "Niall Ferguson Aims to Shake Up History Curriculum."
35. Niall Ferguson, "Villain of the Piece"
36. Gonzalo Frasca, "Simulation versus Narrative: Introduction to Ludology," in *The Video Game Theory Reader,* ed. Mark Wolff and Bernard Perron (London: Routledge,

2003), 221–235. It is also worth noting the interesting case of docu-fictions and other "documentaries." See Harold Deluermoz, *L'Ironie dans le documentaire. Partie 1: Le documenteur, allusion et faux-semblants,* master's thesis defended at the EHESS, 2012.

37. In this game, Chernobyl suffered a second explosion in 2006. Strange phenomena and then creatures born from radiation take place in the region around it, known as the "Zone." The players are stalkers, adventurers who go into this Zone in search of artefacts that they may sell for a fortune.
38. For example, *Urgent Evoke* created by the World Bank and some universities in Africa, which is designed to find solutions to great world threats: social innovation, food security, the energy crises, water crises, money and financial development, empowering women, urban resilience, indigenous knowledge, and crisis networking, http://www.urgentevoke.com/. There is also *Food Force,* designed to make players aware of food problems across the world, and *Stop Disasters!* created by ONU/ISDR, http://www. stopdisastersgame.org/fr/playgame.html.
39. On ARG, see Jenkins Henry, *Convergence Culture: Where Old and New Media Collide* (New York: NYU Press, 2006); Dave Szulborski, *This Is Not a Game: A Guide to Alternate Reality Gaming* (Seattle: Incunabula, 2005).
40. Laurent Checola, "'World without Oil,' plus de pétrole mais un gisement d'idées," *Le Monde,* May 10, 2007.
41. Timothy Compeau and Robert MacDougall, "'Tecumseh Lies Here': Goals and Challenges for a Pervasive History Game in Progress," in *Pastplay: Teaching and Learning History with Technology,* ed. Kevin Kee (Ann Arbor: University of Michigan Press, 2014), 87–108.
42. At the time of publication of the French text, the game was located at http://www. tecumsehlieshere.org/. On the game, see http://activehistory.ca/2012/05/tecumseh-lies-here/ [accessed October 2020].
43. Indeed, the tendency toward a "true" past and the effort involved in achieving it would give the game a particular power, contemporary relevance, and social utility.
44. For France, besides the other blog already mentioned, see *Jeux vidéo et épistémologie de l'histoire*; the working group Aggiornamento Hist-Géo has also proposed discussions on these questions, http://aggiornamento.hypotheses.org/.
45. Information and Communications Technology.
46. Gaglio Connie Marie, "The Role of Mental Simulations and Counterfactual Thinking in the Opportunity Identification Process," *Entrepreneurship Theory and Practice* 28, no. 6 (December 2004): 533–552; Ruth M. J. Byrne, *The Rational Imagination: How People Create Alternatives to Reality* (Boston: MIT Press, 2007).
47. Michael L. Platt and Ben Hayden, "Learning: Not Just the Facts, Ma'am, but the Counterfactuals as Well," *PLOS Biology* 9 (June 6, 2011).
48. Robert D. Kavanaugh and Paul L. Harris, "Pretense and Counterfactual Thought in Young Children," in *Child Psychology: A Handbook of Contemporary Issues,* ed. Lawrence Balter and Catherine Tamis-LeMonda (Philadelphia: Psychology Press, 1999), 158–176.
49. Schaeffer, *Pourquoi la fiction*?

50. For example, Magne Angvik and Bodo von Borries, eds., *Youth and History: A Comparative European Survey on Historical Consciousness and Political Attitudes among Adolescents* (Hamburg: Körber-Stiftung, 1998); Roy Rosenzweig and Thelen David, *The Presence of the Past: Popular Uses of History in American Life* (New York: Columbia University Press, 1998). In 2011, a vast study was done with 5,245 adults from Western countries (Canada, United States, Great Britain, France) on their relationship to national history. The results (insistence on wars, ignorance, regularly mobilized historical narratives, etc.) were analyzed in Gani Raphael, "'Comment résumeriez-vous l' histoire de votre pays?' Enquête auprès de Canadiens, Américains, Britanniques, et Français" (2011), master's thesis, Université de Laval, 2014.
51. Susan McLester, "Game Plan," *Technology and Learning* 3 (2005): 18–26; Kurt Squire, *Replaying History*, 153.
52. Garfield Gini-Newman, "Counterfactual History: Bad History, Good Teaching?," *Journal of the Ontario History and Social Sciences Teacher's Association,* Winter 2004.
53. Bernard Eric Jensen, "Counterfactual History and Its Educational Potential," in *History in Education: Proceedings from the Conference History in Education,* ed. Peter Kemp, held at the Danish University of Education March 24–25, 2004 (Copenhagen: Danmarks Pædagogiske Universitets Forlag, 2005).
54. Muzzy Lane has specialized in creating games that integrate teaching, the pursuit of concrete objectives and fun, http://muzzylane.com/company. See also *Historia,* a simulation game designed for teaching, created by Rick Brennan and Jason Darnell, social science teachers in Houston. See https://edgamer.net/?p=24899 [accessed October 2020].
55. See *World History Connected,* https://worldhistoryconnected.press.uillinois.edu/ [accessed October 2020].
56. Kurt Squire, *Video Games and Learning: Teaching and Participatory Culture in the Digital Age* (New York: Teachers College Press, 2011).
57. For Germany, see Alexandra Oeser, *Enseigner Hitler. Les adolescents face au passé nazi en Allemagne* (Paris: Éditions de la Maison des Sciences de l'Homme, 2010). In France, see the experiment pursued at the Junior High School of Bretteville/Laize (Calvados), in March 2000, recounted on the blog at http://histgeo.discip.ac-caen.fr/ludus/jeuhist.htm.
58. See *Reacting to the Past,* https://wwnorton.com/reacting-to-the-past [accessed October 2020].
59. "Counterfactual History and Individual Agency," *Pedagogical Introduction,* p. 2, http://reacting.barnard.edu/sites/default/ les/inline/reacting_pedagogical_ introduction-9–20–2010.pdf.
60. See *Reacting to the Past,* https://reacting.barnard.edu/about [accessed October 2020].
61. *Chronicle of Higher Education,* November 2001, September 2011, and July 2012; *New York Times,* June 23, 2004; *USA Today,* November 29, 2011.
62. As well as beyond the American continent, according to the report that was released. See John Burney, Richard Gid Powers, and Mark Carnes, "Reacting to the Past: A New Approach to Student Engagement and to Enhancing General Education," white

paper report submitted to the Teagle Foundation, 2010, http://reacting.barnard.edu/headlines/ white-paper-report-now-available-teagle-funded-fresh-thinking-education-initiative.

63. Elizabeth Bonsignore et al., "Game Design for Promoting Counterfactual Thinking," *Proceedings of the SIGCHI Conference on Human Factors in Computing Systems* (New York: ACM, 2012), 2079–2082. Also see the website http://www.arcanegalleryofgadgetry.org/.
64. Ibid., 2080.
65. This is outside of the more thorny question of using games created by private profit-driven companies designed to entertain in the context of the classroom.
66. Jensen, "Counterfactual History and Its Educational Potential."
67. The Prime Minister in Canadian Life and Politics (for teachers), http://collections-canada.gc.ca/primeministers/kids/index-e.html.
68. Rodney P. Carlisle and J. Geoffrey Goslon, *America in Revolt during the 1960s and 1970s, Turning Points: Actual and Alternate Histories* (Santa Barbara, CA: ABC Clio, 2008).
69. David MacKenzie, *Apis, the Congenial Conspirator* (New York: East European Monographs/Columbia University Press, 1989). This has since been thoroughly explored by Christopher Clark, *The Sleepwalkers: How Europe Went to War in 1914* (New York: Harper Collins, 2013).
70. Olivier Cosson, *Préparer la Grande Guerre. L'armée française et la guerre russo-japonaise (1899–1914)* (Paris: Les Indes savantes, 2013).
71. Nicole Lautier and Nicole Allieu-Mary, "La didactique de l'histoire, note de synthèse," *Revue française de pédagogie* 162 (2008): 95–131.
72. Nicole Tutiaux-Guillon, "L'Enseignement et la compréhension de l'histoire sociale au collège et au lycée: L'exemple de la société d'Ancien Régime et de la société du XIXe siècle" (PhD thesis, Université de Paris 7, under the direction of Henri Moniot, 1998) (Villeneuve-d'Ascq, France: Septentrion, 2001).
73. "Image de la discipline et pratiques d'enseignement en histoire-géographie et éducation civique, juridique et sociale au lycée professionnel," *Les Dossiers évaluations et statistiques DEPP* (Direction de l'évaluation, de la prospective et de la performance, ministère de l'Éducation nationale, de l'Enseignement supérieur et de la Recherche), no. 188, September 2007.
74. Michel Deleplace and Daniel Niclot, *Les Apprentissages conceptuels des élèves en histoire et en géographie* (Reims, France: CRDP, 2005).

CHAPTER 12. WRITING HISTORY TOGETHER

1. Luigi Pirandello, *Six Characters in Search of an Author* (London: Penguin, 1995), 14.
2. Friedrich Nietzsche, *The Gay Science,* trans. Thomas Common (Mineola, NY: Dover Publications, 2006), 198.
3. See the website for *Refaire Société,* http://www.refairesociete.fr/ [accessed October 2020].
4. LKP, *Liyannaj Kont Pwotasyon,* is a group of trade unions and social movements in Gaudeloupe.

5. Pierre Jalée is the author of *Pillage du tiers-monde* (Paris: Maspero, 1965), one of the key texts of Third-Worldism.
6. Ronald Walters, "African Reparations. Dealing with a Unique and Unprecedented Moral Debt," in *Africa in the 21st Century: Toward a New Future,* ed. Ama Mazama (New York and London: Routledge, 2007), 268; cited by David Lambert, "Black-Atlantic Counterfactualism: Speculating about Slavery and Its Aftermath," *Journal of Historical Geography* 36, no. 3 (July 2010): 286–296.
7. Gerald L. Early, *This Is Where I Came In: Black America in the 1960s* (Lincoln: University of Nebraska Press, 2003).
8. Ira Berlin, *Many Thousands Gone: The First Two Centuries of Slavery in North America* (Cambridge: Harvard University Press, 1998).

CONCLUSION. BECOMINGS IN THE WORLD

1. Joachim du Bellay, *"Les regrets" with "The Antiquitiies of Rome,"* a bilingual edition, ed. and trans. Richard Helgerson (Philadelphia: University of Pennsylvania Press, 2006), 83.
2. Michel Foucault, *Courage of Truth: The Government of Self and Others II: Lectures at the Collège de France, 1983–1984,* ed. Arnold Davidson, Frédéric Gros, François Ewald, and Alessandro Fontana, trans. Graham Burchell (New York: Palgrave, 2008), 340.
3. Michel de Certeau, *Histoire et psychanalyse entre science et fiction* (Paris: Gallimard, 1987), 70–87.
4. We would like to thank Hervé Mazurel for our discussions on these issues.

Index